Political Economy of Human Rights

The plethora of literature produced over the past decade in response to the perceived failure of the human rights project to deliver results for billions of people living in "adverse" environments has usually focused on international legal standards and mechanisms, with little regard for the root structural realities that constrain their implementation. Hence, a text that primarily focuses on the major challenge of realisation of human rights in the context of diverse realities is urgently needed. This book, then, provides an analytical as well as inspirational text on human rights from a contextual perspective; it offers a reconceptualisation of human rights as not merely legal resources, but political tools as well.

After an introduction that familiarises the reader with some of the key concepts used throughout, the book is divided into six chapters. The first two combine a critique of the overly legal use of human *rights* with a reconceptualisation of their potential as powerful tools outside of the legal context. The next two chapters examine the nature of the structural challenges that face realisation, both on the global and on the local level. The last two chapters analyse two major areas of the global human rights deficit: the structural non-implementation of the rights of the poor and the failing protection of non-dominant collectivities. The author concludes his pioneering quest for effective strategies with a reassessment of the human rights world's commitment, its tactics and its tools.

The book combines rigorous juridical study with a focus on political-economic analysis of rights in context. Hence, it aims at an interdisciplinary treatment of human rights as opposed to current texts that have a tendency to be monodisciplinary. The book should be of interest to students of human rights, political economy, law and conflict studies, as well as those who work or research in these areas.

Bas de Gaay Fortman is the Emeritus Chair in Political Economy of the International Institute of Social Studies of Erasmus University Rotterdam, and Professor of Political Economy of Human Rights at the Utrecht University Law School, the Netherlands.

Routledge frontiers of political economy

1 **Equilibrium Versus Understanding**
Towards the rehumanization of economics within social theory
Mark Addleson

2 **Evolution, Order and Complexity**
Edited by Elias L. Khalil and Kenneth E. Boulding

3 **Interactions in Political Economy**
Malvern after ten years
Edited by Steven Pressman

4 **The End of Economics**
Michael Perelman

5 **Probability in Economics**
Omar F. Hamouda and Robin Rowley

6 **Capital Controversy, Post Keynesian Economics and the History of Economics**
Essays in honour of Geoff Harcourt, volume one
Edited by Philip Arestis, Gabriel Palma and Malcolm Sawyer

7 **Markets, Unemployment and Economic Policy**
Essays in honour of Geoff Harcourt, volume two
Edited by Philip Arestis, Gabriel Palma and Malcolm Sawyer

8 **Social Economy**
The logic of capitalist development
Clark Everling

9 **New Keynesian Economics/ Post Keynesian Alternatives**
Edited by Roy J. Rotheim

10 **The Representative Agent in Macroeconomics**
James E. Hartley

11 **Borderlands of Economics**
Essays in honour of Daniel R. Fusfeld
Edited by Nahid Aslanbeigui and Young Back Choi

12 **Value, Distribution and Capital**
Essays in honour of Pierangelo Garegnani
Edited by Gary Mongiovi and Fabio Petri

13 **The Economics of Science**
Methodology and epistemology as if economics really mattered
James R. Wible

14 **Competitiveness, Localised Learning and Regional Development**
Specialisation and prosperity in small open economies
Peter Maskell, Heikki Eskelinen, Ingjaldur Hannibalsson, Anders Malmberg and Eirik Vatne

15 **Labour Market Theory**
A constructive reassessment
Ben J. Fine

16 **Women and European Employment**
Jill Rubery, Mark Smith, Colette Fagan and Damian Grimshaw

17 **Explorations in Economic Methodology**
From Lakatos to empirical philosophy of science
Roger Backhouse

18 **Subjectivity in Political Economy**
Essays on wanting and choosing
David P. Levine

19 **The Political Economy of Middle East Peace**
The impact of competing trade agendas
Edited by J.W. Wright, Jnr

20 **The Active Consumer**
Novelty and surprise in consumer choice
Edited by Marina Bianchi

21 **Subjectivism and Economic Analysis**
Essays in memory of Ludwig Lachmann
Edited by Roger Koppl and Gary Mongiovi

22 **Themes in Post-Keynesian Economics**
Essays in honour of Geoff Harcourt, volume three
Edited by Claudio Sardoni and Peter Kriesler

23 **The Dynamics of Technological Knowledge**
Cristiano Antonelli

24 **The Political Economy of Diet, Health and Food Policy**
Ben J. Fine

25 **The End of Finance**
Capital market inflation, financial derivatives and pension fund capitalism
Jan Toporowski

26 **Political Economy and the New Capitalism**
Edited by Jan Toporowski

27 **Growth Theory**
A philosophical perspective
Patricia Northover

28 **The Political Economy of the Small Firm**
Edited by Charlie Dannreuther

29 **Hahn and Economic Methodology**
Edited by Thomas Boylan and Paschal F. O'Gorman

30 **Gender, Growth and Trade**
The miracle economies of the postwar years
David Kucera

31 **Normative Political Economy**
Subjective freedom, the market and the state
David Levine

32 **Economist with a Public Purpose**
Essays in honour of John Kenneth Galbraith
Edited by Michael Keaney

33 **Involuntary Unemployment**
The elusive quest for a theory
Michel De Vroey

34 **The Fundamental Institutions of Capitalism**
Ernesto Screpanti

35 **Transcending Transaction**
The search for self-generating markets
Alan Shipman

36 **Power in Business and the State**
An historical analysis of its concentration
Frank Bealey

37 **Editing Economics**
Essays in honour of Mark Perlman
Edited by Hank Lim, Ungsuh K. Park and Geoff Harcourt

38 **Money, Macroeconomics and Keynes**
Essays in honour of Victoria Chick, volume one
Edited by Philip Arestis, Meghnad Desai and Sheila Dow

39 **Methodology, Microeconomics and Keynes**
Essays in honour of Victoria Chick, volume two
Edited by Philip Arestis, Meghnad Desai and Sheila Dow

40 **Market Drive and Governance**
Reexamining the rules for economic and commercial contest
Ralf Boscheck

41 **The Value of Marx**
Political economy for contemporary capitalism
Alfredo Saad-Filho

42 **Issues in Positive Political Economy**
S. Mansoob Murshed

43 **The Enigma of Globalisation**
A journey to a new stage of capitalism
Robert Went

44 **The Market**
Equilibrium, stability, mythology
S.N. Afriat

45 **The Political Economy of Rule Evasion and Policy Reform**
Jim Leitzel

46 **Unpaid Work and the Economy**
Edited by Antonella Picchio

47 **Distributional Justice**
Theory and measurement
Hilde Bojer

48 **Cognitive Developments in Economics**
Edited by Salvatore Rizzello

49 **Social Foundations of Markets, Money and Credit**
Costas Lapavitsas

50 **Rethinking Capitalist Development**
Essays on the economics of Josef Steindl
Edited by Tracy Mott and Nina Shapiro

51 **An Evolutionary Approach to Social Welfare**
Christian Sartorius

52 **Kalecki's Economics Today**
Edited by Zdzislaw L. Sadowski and Adam Szeworski

53 **Fiscal Policy from Reagan to Blair**
The left veers right
Ravi K. Roy and Arthur T. Denzau

54 **The Cognitive Mechanics of Economic Development and Institutional Change**
Bertin Martens

55 **Individualism and the Social Order**
The social element in liberal thought
Charles R. McCann Jnr

56 **Affirmative Action in the United States and India**
A comparative perspective
Thomas E. Weisskopf

57 **Global Political Economy and the Wealth of Nations**
Performance, institutions, problems and policies
Edited by Phillip Anthony O'Hara

58 **Structural Economics**
Thijs ten Raa

59 **Macroeconomic Theory and Economic Policy**
Essays in honour of Jean-Paul Fitoussi
Edited by K. Vela Velupillai

60 **The Struggle over Work**
The "end of work" and employment alternatives in post-industrial societies
Shaun Wilson

61 **The Political Economy of Global Sporting Organisations**
John Forster and Nigel Pope

62 **The Flawed Foundations of General Equilibrium Theory**
Critical essays on economic theory
Frank Ackerman and Alejandro Nadal

63 **Uncertainty in Economic Theory**
Essays in honor of David Schmeidler's 65th birthday
Edited by Itzhak Gilboa

64 **The New Institutional Economics of Corruption**
Edited by Johann Graf Lambsdorff, Markus Taube and Matthias Schramm

65 **The Price Index and its Extension**
A chapter in economic measurement
S.N. Afriat

66 **Reduction, Rationality and Game Theory in Marxian Economics**
Bruce Philp

67 **Culture and Politics in Economic Development**
Volker Bornschier

68 **Modern Applications of Austrian Thought**
Edited by Jürgen G. Backhaus

69 **Ordinary Choices**
Individuals, incommensurability, and democracy
Robert Urquhart

70 **Labour Theory of Value**
Peter C. Dooley

71 **Capitalism**
Victor D. Lippit

72 **Macroeconomic Foundations of Macroeconomics**
Alvaro Cencini

73 **Marx for the 21st Century**
Edited by Hiroshi Uchida

74 **Growth and Development in the Global Political Economy**
Social structures of accumulation and modes of regulation
Phillip Anthony O'Hara

75 **The New Economy and Macroeconomic Stability**
A neo-modern perspective drawing on the complexity approach and Keynesian economics
Teodoro Dario Togati

76 **The Future of Social Security Policy**
Women, work and a citizens' basic income
Ailsa McKay

77 **Clinton and Blair**
The political economy of the third way
Flavio Romano

78 **Marxian Reproduction Schema**
Money and aggregate demand in a capitalist economy
A.B. Trigg

79 **The Core Theory in Economics**
Problems and solutions
Lester G. Telser

80 **Economics, Ethics and the Market**
Introduction and applications
Johan J. Graafland

81 **Social Costs and Public Action in Modern Capitalism**
Essays inspired by Karl William Kapp's theory of social costs
Edited by Wolfram Elsner, Pietro Frigato and Paolo Ramazzotti

82 **Globalization and the Myths of Free Trade**
History, theory and empirical evidence
Edited by Anwar Shaikh

83 **Equilibrium in Economics**
Scope and limits
Edited by Valeria Mosini

84 **Globalization**
State of the art and perspectives
Edited by Stefan A. Schirm

85 **Neoliberalism**
National and regional experiments with global ideas
Edited by Ravi K. Roy, Arthur T. Denzau and Thomas D. Willett

86 **Post-Keynesian Macroeconomics**
Essays in honour of Ingrid Rima
Edited by Mathew Forstater, Gary Mongiovi and Steven Pressman

87 **Consumer Capitalism**
Anastasios S. Korkotsides

88 **Remapping Gender in the New Global Order**
Edited by Marjorie Griffin Cohen and Janine Brodie

89 **Hayek and Natural Law**
Eric Angner

90 **Race and Economic Opportunity in the Twenty-First Century**
Edited by Marlene Kim

91 **Renaissance in Behavioural Economics**
Harvey Leibenstein's impact on contemporary economic analysis
Edited by Roger Frantz

92 **Human Ecology Economics**
A new framework for global sustainability
Edited by Roy E. Allen

93 **Imagining Economics Otherwise**
Encounters with identity/difference
Nitasha Kaul

94 **Reigniting the Labor Movement**
Restoring means to ends in a democratic labor movement
Gerald Friedman

95 **The Spatial Model of Politics**
Norman Schofield

96 **The Economics of American Judaism**
Carmel Ullman Chiswick

97 **Critical Political Economy**
Christian Arnsperger

98 **Culture and Economic Explanation**
Economics in the US and Japan
Donald W. Katzner

99 **Feminism, Economics and Utopia**
Time travelling through paradigms
Karin Schönpflug

100 **Risk in International Finance**
Vikash Yadav

101 **Economic Policy and Performance in Industrial Democracies**
Party governments, central banks and the fiscal–monetary policy mix
Takayuki Sakamoto

102 **Advances on Income Inequality and Concentration Measures**
Edited by Gianni Betti and Achille Lemmi

103 **Economic Representations**
Academic and everyday
Edited by David F. Ruccio

104 **Mathematical Economics and the Dynamics of Capitalism**
Goodwin's legacy continued
Edited by Peter Flaschel and Michael Landesmann

105 **The Keynesian Multiplier**
Edited by Claude Gnos and Louis-Philippe Rochon

106 **Money, Enterprise and Income Distribution**
Towards a macroeconomic theory of capitalism
John Smithin

107 **Fiscal Decentralization and Local Public Finance in Japan**
Nobuki Mochida

108 **The 'Uncertain' Foundations of Post-Keynesian Economics**
Essays in exploration
Stephen P. Dunn

109 **Karl Marx's *Grundrisse***
Foundations of the critique of political economy 150 years later
Edited by Marcello Musto

110 **Economics and the Price Index**
S.N. Afriat and Carlo Milana

111 **Sublime Economy**
On the intersection of art and economics
Edited by Jack Amariglio, Joseph W. Childers and Stephen E. Cullenberg

112 **Popper, Hayek and the Open Society**
Calvin Hayes

113 **The Political Economy of Work**
David Spencer

114 **Institutional Economics**
Bernard Chavance

115 **Religion, Economics and Demography**
The effects of religion on education, work, and the family
Evelyn L. Lehrer

116 **Economics, Rational Choice and Normative Philosophy**
Edited by Thomas A. Boylan and Ruvin Gekker

117 **Economics Versus Human Rights**
Manuel Couret Branco

118 **Hayek Versus Marx and Today's Challenges**
Eric Aarons

119 **Work Time Regulation as Sustainable Full Employment Policy**
Robert LaJeunesse

120 **Equilibrium, Welfare and Uncertainty**
Mukul Majumdar

121 **Capitalism, Institutions and Economic Development**
Michael Heller

122 **Economic Pluralism**
Robert Garnett, Erik Olsen and Martha Starr

123 **Dialectics of Class Struggle in the Global Economy**
Clark Everling

124 **Political Economy and Globalization**
Richard Westra

125 **Full-Spectrum Economics**
Toward an inclusive and emancipatory social science
Christian Arnsperger

126 **Computable, Constructive and Behavioural Economic Dynamics**
Essays in honour of Kumaraswamy (Vela) Velupillai
Stefano Zambelli

127 **Monetary Macrodynamics**
Toichiro Asada, Carl Chiarella, Peter Flaschel and Reiner Franke

128 **Rationality and Explanation in Economics**
Maurice Lagueux

129 **The Market, Happiness, and Solidarity**
A Christian perspective
Johan J. Graafland

130 **Economic Complexity and Equilibrium Illusion**
Essays on market instability and macro vitality
Ping Chen

131 **Economic Theory and Social Change**
Problems and revisions
Hasse Ekstedt and Angelo Fusari

132 **The Practices of Happiness**
Political economy, religion and wellbeing
Edited by John Atherton, Elaine Graham and Ian Steedman

133 **The Measurement of Individual Well-Being and Group Inequalities**
Essays in memory of Z.M. Berrebi
Edited by Joseph Deutsch and Jacques Silber

134 **Wage Policy, Income Distribution, and Democratic Theory**
Oren M. Levin-Waldman

135 **The Political Economy of Bureaucracy**
Steven O. Richardson

136 **The Moral Rhetoric of Political Economy**
Justice and modern economic thought
Paul Turpin

137 **Macroeconomic Regimes in Western Industrial Countries**
Hansjörg Herr and Milka Kazandziska

138 **The Political Economy of the Environment**
Edited by Simon Dietz, Jonathan Michie and Christine Oughton

139 **Business Ethics and the Austrian Tradition in Economics**
Hardy Bouillon

140 **Inequality and Power**
The economics of class
Eric A. Schutz

141 **Capital as a Social Kind**
Definitions and transformations in the critique of political economy
Howard Engelskirchen

142 **Happiness, Ethics and Economics**
Johannes Hirata

143 **Capital, Exploitation and Economic Crisis**
John Weeks

144 **The Global Economic Crisis**
New perspectives on the critique of economic theory and policy
Edited by Emiliano Brancaccio and Giuseppe Fontana

145 **Economics and Diversity**
Carlo D'Ippoliti

146 **Political Economy of Human Rights**
Rights, realities and realization
Bas de Gaay Fortman

Political Economy of Human Rights

Rights, realities and realization

Bas de Gaay Fortman

Routledge
Taylor & Francis Group
LONDON AND NEW YORK

First published 2011
by Routledge
2 Park Square, Milton Park, Abingdon, Oxon OX14 4RN

Simultaneously published in the USA and Canada
by Routledge
711 Third Avenue, New York, NY 10017

Routledge is an imprint of the Taylor & Francis Group, an informa business

British Library Cataloguing in Publication Data
A catalogue record for this book is available from the British Library

Library of Congress Cataloging in Publication Data
Gaay Fortman, Bastiaan de.
A political economy of human rights : rights, realities, and realization / by Bas de Gaay Fortman.
p. cm.
Includes bibliographical references and index.
1. Human rights. I. Title.
JC571.G225 2010
323–dc22
2010050826

ISBN: 978-0-415-58120-2 (hbk)
ISBN: 978-0-203-81373-7 (ebk)

Typeset in Times
by Wearset Ltd, Boldon, Tyne and Wear

MIX
Paper from responsible sources
FSC® C004839

Printed and bound in Great Britain by
TJI Digital, Padstow, Cornwall

To my students, from all over the world (1960–2010)

Contents

Figures and tables

Figures

Tables

Preface

By some way of providence I read both law and economics. It drew me towards their interface: the interdisciplinary field of political economy of law and jurisprudence. For some time my focus was on economic policy, a field of practice and study typified by the confrontation of economic, political and legal principles (De Gaay Fortman 1966). During my years with the University of Zambia, I was personally confronted with politico-economic environments characterised by both structural material hardship and the quest for true "development". Back in the Netherlands it was through my students at the Institute of Social Studies that I was pulled towards human rights in a political economy perspective. For 20 years I co-organised a postgraduate programme, titled Development, Law and Social Justice. It was meant for academically trained leaders of civil society organisations from all over the globe, many of whom lived and worked in "disabling" environments. From them I "learned" human rights.

In 2000 Utrecht University appointed me as Chair in Political Economy of Human Rights, a new field of study in which there is no other Chair in our world today. In the new Masters in Conflict Studies and Human Rights I was requested to teach this subject. It confronted me with the plethora of literature produced on human rights over the past decade, mostly in the form of textbooks explaining international human rights law and political-philosophical studies on the meaning of human dignity and rights in a world of power politics. However, there appeared to be little regard for the root structural realities that constrain the realisation of rights. Hence, with my students I felt the need for a text which primarily focuses on the major challenges of *realising* human rights in the context of diverse, and particularly adverse, realities.

This book, then, offers a reconceptualisation of human rights as not merely legal resources, but political tools as well. It provides an analytical as well as engaging text on human rights from a contextual perspective. The methodology behind contextual human rights presented in this volume has been gradually developed during the last 30 years, resulting in many publications in articles and chapters in books. It now receives systematic disclosure through a monograph focusing on the role of human rights not only in enabling, but also in disabling (adverse) political, economic and socio-cultural environments.

My endeavour in this volume has been to combine rigorous juridical scholarship with political-economic analysis of rights in context. Hence, it aims at an interdisciplinary treatment of human rights as opposed to texts written from distinct monodisciplinary perspectives. Thus, the economy–polity–society triangle, in which *economy* includes issues of distribution, *polity* includes law and jurisprudence, and *society* includes culture and religion, constitutes the book's core perspective. Both opportunities and obstacles in the use of human rights instruments are reviewed through contextual analysis, looking at resources and constraints not merely from a legal point of view, but also from socio-cultural, political and economic angles. The book thus is directed not only at colleagues and students in academic and public policy circles, but also at those practitioners whose work confronts them particularly with human rights deficits. This applies, amongst others, to those involved in collective conflict.

Acknowledgements

For the past seven years I have benefited from an annual short internship of *Juris Doctor* students from the University of Cincinnati (Ohio). For their help in various realms of human rights research my thanks go to Michelle Berry, Elizabeth Tull, Dave Owens, Katherine Klaeren, Laura Hils, Julie Restifo, Maxwell Smith, and their professor Bert Lockwood. With Julie I prepared a successful book proposal. Above all, I wish to mention now the invaluable support of Maxwell Smith. This *Political Economy of Human Rights* could not have been produced without his professional editorial assistance. Decisively, during the summer of 2010 he became my sparring partner and remained so thereafter, creatively criticising, co-thinking and rethinking the main theme and subthemes of this book.

I am grateful to my colleagues at the Utrecht Law School and the Netherlands Institute of Human Rights. This study also reflects the interaction with my students and the continuing exchanges with our alumni; quite a few can find their names in the Bibliography. Patrick Crossman, who followed my lectures at the University of Peace in Costa Rica, assisted professionally with the figures and tables. In both the Institute of Social Studies and Utrecht University I worked closely with Nikhil Dhanrajgir. Together we wrote a long article on American security concerns in the current world order (Dhanrajgir and De Gaay Fortman 2005); I thank him particularly for his consent to ground part of Chapter 3 in that analysis. With Emma Sydenham, former LLM student in Utrecht, I co-founded EqualinRights, an international NGO to support rights-based strategies against poverty. Her comments on the draft manuscript for this book were most helpful. At the stage of proofreading invaluable assistance was offered by Michela Marcatelli. Naturally, full responsibility for any remaining errors in this volume is just mine.

Finally, for a student of political economy and jurisprudence it is an honour to publish with an international house that produced their own edition of Adam Smith's *Wealth of Nations* as early as the nineteenth century. In addition, to work with the twenty-first century Routledge staff and their associates has been a real pleasure.

Abbreviations

ACLU	American Civil Liberties Union
AIV	Advisory Council for International Affairs
CAT	Convention Against Torture
CEDAW	Committee on the Elimination of Discrimination against Women
CERD	Convention on the Elimination of Racial Discrimination
CMW	Convention on Migrant Workers
CNG	compressed natural gas
DAC	Development Assistance Committee
DTA	Detainee Treatment Act
ECOSOC	Economic and Social Council
ECRML	European Charter for Regional or Minority Languages
ECtHR	European Court of Human Rights
FBI	Federal Bureau of Investigation
FDI	foreign direct investment
FDR	Franklin Delano Roosevelt
FGM	female genital mutilation
GA	General Assistance
GDP	Gross Domestic Product
HDI	Human Development Index
HFI	Human Freedom Index
HIPC	Highly Indebted Poor Countries
HR	The Netherlands Supreme Court
HRC	Human Rights Committee
ICC	International Criminal Court
ICCPR	International Covenant on Civil and Political Rights
ICESCR	International Covenant on Economic Social and Cultural Rights
ICJ	International Court of Justice
IFI	international financial institutions
ILO	International Labour Organisation
IMF	International Monetary Fund
LIC	low-income countries
MDG	Millennium Development Goals
MIC	middle-income countries

MNC	multinational corporation
MOSOP	Movement for the Survival of the Ogoni People
MP	Member of Parliament
NATO	North Atlantic Treaty Organization
NBER	National Bureau of Economic Research
NEM	New Economic Model
NEP	New Economic Policy
NGO	nongovernmental organisation
NIZA	Netherlands Institute for Southern Africa
ODA	Official Development Assistance
OECD	Organisation for Economic Co-orporation and Development
OHCHR	Office of the High Commissioner for Human Rights
PIL	public interest litigation
PPA	Participatory Poverty Assessment
PPG	pro-poor growth
"PPP"	purchasing power of the poor
PPP	purchasing power parity
PRSP	Poverty Reduction Strategy Papers
R2P	Responsibility to Protect
RWF	Rwanda Patriotic Front
UDHR	Universal Declaration of Human Rights
UN	United Nations
UNCESR	United Nations Convention on Economic Social and Cultural Rights
UNDP	United Nations Development Program
UNESCO	United Nations Educational, Scientific and Cultural Organization
UPR	Universal Periodic Review
WDR	World Development Report
WTO	World Trade Organisation

Introduction

Rights, realities and realisation

> There is a place now for the modern equivalent of the old Political Economist, namely the worker who … specializes in generalisation.
>
> James Meade (1965: 8)

Rights unrealised

On the afternoon of 23 August 1997, Dr Kenneth Kaunda, for 27 years the President of Zambia, attempted to participate in a political rally in Kabwe organised by the Alliance of opposition parties chaired by Dr Rodger Chongwe, former Minister of Justice in the cabinet of Kaunda's successor and then President, Frederick Chiluba.[1] When he arrived the town was already full of paramilitary police. Apparently, the permit had been cancelled without notice and Alliance supporters had been beaten up (Chongwe and Jägers 2011). After cancelling the event, the two leaders left the ground together in one vehicle. On the way out both men were shot and wounded by the Zambian paramilitary police. While Kaunda's injuries were minor, Chongwe, who had been hit in the neck, was treated in Kabwe General Hospital. The medical report stated: "Local examination revealed puncture wound on the right cheek communicating with a bleeding wound on the upper aspect of the neck". Fearing for his life, Chongwe fled to Australia where he submitted a complaint to the Human Rights Committee (HRC), which is the United Nations' Committee established under the International Covenant on Civil and Political Rights. Zambia had ratified that treaty, including the Optional Protocol on individual complaints.

In its meeting of 25 October 2000 the HRC first admitted the complaint, considering that the required exhaustion of domestic remedies did not apply as Chongwe was a refugee and had no access to domestic tribunals, a position the Zambian state had failed to contest (Human Rights Committee 2000). The Committee concluded on substance that there had been violations of Article 6.1 of the Covenant on the right to life and Article 9.1 on the right to security of the person. Zambia was requested to submit information within 90 days about the measures it had taken to give effect to the Committee's views.

The Chiluba administration ignored all correspondence from the HRC. In his first communication on the matter half a year after the Concluding Observations on Chongwe's complaint, the Zambian Attorney General requested the HRC to review its decision even though the Committee's rules of procedure make no provision for an appeal. The government of Chiluba's successor, Mwanawasa, refused to acknowledge responsibility for acts committed on behalf of the state under a previous administration. Under Mwanawasa's successor, Banda, a settlement was reached in late 2009, which was subsequently withdrawn, falling back on the old odd "argument" that responsibility was with the previous (Chiluba) government, as if legal personality could lie with a government rather than with the state. Consequently, the (quasi-)judicial decision of the United Nations Human Rights Committee of October 2000 is still hanging in the air as this book goes to press.

The Chongwe case exposes the impunity of state-related perpetrators of serious violations, which is part of what may be called "the human rights deficit" (De Gaay Fortman 2001: 3).[2] It is, indeed, illustrative of the lack of effective remedies in international human rights law combined with failing national enforcement. Lamentably, such cases of rights without remedies are all too common. Here, two primary problems manifest themselves. First, while there is general agreement that the state ought to have a crucial role in the protection of the basic dignity of each and every human being on its territory, it is precisely that same institution which has the highest record of gross and systematic human rights violations. The catch-22 is of course that for effective protection against abuse of power one needs power, and power is often abused. Second, effective legal incorporation of human rights into national legislation requires a well-functioning state based on the rule of law, which is all too often lacking. Indeed, a June 2008 UN report estimated that four billion people live without the protection of the rule of law (Haugen and Boutros 2010: 52), and hence, implicitly, in an adverse environment for human rights realisation. Thus, even where people's internationally proclaimed rights have been nationally declared, too, a justice gap persists, reflecting the failure of international human rights to live up to their promise.

Generally, however, in the halls of power as well as in academic studies, human rights are discussed in the context of international legal standards and mechanisms with little regard to the root structures and issues behind their non-implementation, both globally and locally. The analysis in this volume concentrates specifically on the environments that underlie these structural failures and particularly emphasises their impact on the realisation of human rights. Thus, the triangle economy–polity–society (including culture and religion) constitutes the book's core empirical perspective. Both opportunities and obstacles in the use of human rights instruments are reviewed in the setting of contextual analysis, looking at resources and constraints not merely from a legal but also from a socio-cultural, political and economic perspective. Indeed, human rights become more meaningful to people when they are linked to the contents of their world-views, beliefs and religious practices and related to specific contexts, including serious constraints to their realisation.

A crisis in human rights

The 1 March 2010 cover of *Newsweek* magazine screams "The Death of Human Rights". The article by Joshua Kulantzick, which confines its title to this mission's *Downfall*, shows a primary concern with the declining importance of human rights on the agendas of major state actors, international civil society and the public at large.[3] That lack of interest is not related to controversy over which rights ought to be enjoyed by all, but rather the obvious structural failure of the mechanisms that were meant to bring about the realisation of those rights. In many instances, even where the rights have been successfully incorporated into national legal instruments, they remain rights only on paper because of inadequate public enforcement and implementation systems in both the international and national contexts (Hagen and Boutros 2010).

The "crisis in human rights" has invited a bulk of academic literature proposing various solutions to compensate for the failure of the human rights project to deliver results for billions of the world's most vulnerable people. These proposals tend to focus on the development and refinement of international legal standards and mechanisms or the definition and legitimisation of human rights from a theoretical perspective, defining their intellectual and spiritual foundations. One example of the latter is Upendra Baxi's book, *Human Rights in a Posthuman World* (2007), which is emblematic of the kind of academic, poststructuralist fretting about the human rights project and its theoretical underpinnings that is so abstract as to be irrelevant to its subject: the victims of human rights abuses. James Griffin, to mention another theoretician, seems unconvinced that we can go forward with human rights without a more solid ethical ground upon which to base those rights (Griffin 2008). While the philosophical search for such a ground is intellectually stimulating, it rather misses the point.[4] A solid moral-political basis for human rights already exists in the Preamble to the UN Charter of 1945, in which the "Peoples of the United Nations … *reaffirm faith* in fundamental rights, in the dignity and worth of the human person, in the equal rights of men and women and of nations large and small" (emphasis added). The Universal Declaration of Human Rights (UDHR or "the Declaration") of 1948 similarly affirms its "recognition of the inherent dignity and of the equal and inalienable rights of all members of the human family" as the "foundation of freedom, justice and peace in the world". This reaffirmation of *global faith in human dignity*, then, however philosophically, politically and socio-culturally supported in diverse national settings – an important and ongoing project – is the starting point of the human rights mission as a serious global endeavour.

The perceived difficulties in the interpretations of human rights that Griffin refers to (2008: 16) are addressed by the basic principle that human rights are founded on the protection of human dignity against abuse of power. Actions that violate human dignity, as related to people's fundamental freedoms and entitlements, violate human rights. Certainly the definition of more and more specific human rights within the context of the UN covenants and conventions is not meant to be an exhaustive list, but it is a substantial and more than adequate basis for moving the whole mission closer to reality. While a more specific, ethically based definition of what constitutes human rights is no doubt of intellectual interest, it is certainly not necessary for action – based on the already-declared rights – to move forward.

Others are closer to the mark. Paulina Tambakaki's critique of the limitations of human rights as legal instruments (2010: 7) is largely accurate. However, her dismissal of human rights in favour of citizenship rights as an alternative approach to human dignity protection fails to perceive the potential of the human rights discourse in that mission. Citizenship rights as such are fine for countries in which the state is functioning effectively and the rule of law recognised. But for billions of the world's people who live without the protection of the law, citizenship rights – which imply the legal recognition of not only negative freedoms but also certain entitlements – mean little where human security and a socio-economic perspective are lacking. The question posed in this volume is what human rights can still mean for people living in such adverse environments.

In his essay "Whose Universal Values? The Crisis in Human Rights" (1999), Michael Ignatieff discerns three sources at the basis of the crisis in human rights:

1 a political crisis, manifesting itself particularly in regard to state sovereignty, humanitarian intervention and the double standards that tend to persist in the use of internationally mobilised power;
2 a cultural crisis, displayed in the discourses of fundamentalism and post-modernism; and
3 a spiritual crisis apparent in a lack of human rights-sustaining convictions and a surrender to relativism.

Yet he concludes that "[h]uman rights is the only globally available moral vernacular which validates" the claims of the oppressed (1999: 37). This is undoubtedly true, but the challenge remains to enhance their relevance in the lives of people. That had already been seriously put in doubt at the end of last century by An-Na'im:

> The international human rights movement is facing growing problems of irrelevance to people's daily concerns, marginalization in local and global politics, and cooptation by ruling elites, privileged classes and global economic forces in local as well as global politics. In order to resolve these problems, the movement needs to critically re-examine some of its assumptions and policies in order to recapture its original mandate, revise its concepts and methods.
>
> (1998: 3)

Critical re-examination in order to enhance the relevance of human rights in our world today: that is precisely the aim of this study.

Political economy of human rights

When the *Review of Political Economy* started, its mission statement defined the approach as follows:

> Political economy is best defined as an approach to economics, which puts first priority on practical, and policy issues, and tailors theoretical and empirical work accordingly. The economy is regarded as being located in historical time, interacting with a political, social and natural environment. Within the system the agents change and interact in a manner, which cannot be described adequately by the assumptions of neoclassical theory.
>
> (quoted by Dow 1990: 351)

It is particularly in adverse conditions, such as those pertaining to situations of extreme pressure on scarce resources, that such an analysis may be enlightening. It implies a meta-juridical approach that looks beyond disciplinary boundaries. Empirically, the triangle economy–polity–law is of central importance. The analysis of economic, political and legal aspects of problems and policies at their interface and in their interaction is crucial.

Political economy of human rights, then, is a way of looking behind systemic violations and structural non-implementation. Naturally, its primary contribution lies in the field of socio-economic rights. Here the core focus is acquirement: why and how people succeed or fail in acquiring what they need for sustainable livelihoods. Yet, its significance is not restricted to economic, social and cultural rights. Lack of implementation of civil, political and cultural rights also has to be assessed in a politico-economic context. Often non-implementation of human rights is structural, related to what might be called a "justice gap" (Lederach 1999).

Two genealogies of human rights

Human rights reflect a determined effort to protect the dignity of each and every human being against abuse of power through fundamental rights. The spiritual source of this endeavour lies in the crucial belief that the protection of universal human dignity is a responsibility of society at all its different layers and levels. This principle should generally limit and govern any use of power over human beings. Its starting point is the acknowledgement of every person's right to exist. People count and in principle no individual counts more, or less, than any other. No one, in other words, is to be excluded from the typical human rights term *everyone*.

Notably, in the global political idea of human rights that emerged after the Second World War, two genealogies converged:

1 the fight for universal recognition and equal protection of the dignity of each and every human being; and

2 the struggle for fundamental rights as a way to protect citizens against abuse of power, in particular by their own sovereign (the state).

Strikingly, while the emergence of the basic rights idea as legal protection against abuse of power, particularly by one's own sovereign, may indeed be called a "Western" history,[5] the narrative of universal recognition and protection of human dignity could just as well be termed "anti-Western" history in the sense that equal dignity had to be vindicated in contravention of Western ideas and powers. For instance, the idea of legal principles was already part of Roman law (*generalia iuris principia*). One of these referred to freedom as something of inestimable value (*libertas inaestimabilis res est*);[6] yet the application of this principle excluded subjugated peoples in general and slaves in particular. In fact, the whole story of the realisation of universal human dignity must be understood as an ongoing political struggle.[7] Indeed, the struggles against colonisation and conquest, and the historical efforts to fight racial and ethnic hierarchy, have shaped the idea of truly universal human rights (Gilroy 2009). Note, for example, the following insight gained by Angelina Grimké, daughter of a slaveholder who became an active abolitionist:

> The investigation of the rights of the slave has led me to a better understanding of my own. I have found the Anti-slavery clause to be the high school of morals in our land – the school in which morals are more fully investigated and better understood and taught, than in any other. Here a great fundamental principle is uplifted and illuminated, and from this central light rays innumerable stream all around. Human beings have *rights*, because they are moral beings: the rights of all men grown out of their moral nature; they have essentially the same rights.
>
> (Grimké 1838: 10)

This perception is plainly echoed in Article 1 of the UDHR: "born free and equal in dignity and rights, and endowed with reason and a *conscience*" (emphasis added).

Grimké's deeply felt apprehension was that a country, which at the time of Independence had already declared as "self-evident" truths that "all men are created equal, that they are endowed by their Creator with certain unalienable Rights, and that among these are Life, Liberty and the Pursuit of Happiness", yet tolerated slavery:

> man is never vested with … dominion *over his fellow man*; he was never told that any of the human species were put *under his feet*; it was only *all things*, and man, who was created in the image of his Maker, *never* can properly be termed a *thing*, though the laws of Slave States do call him "a chattel personal;" *Man* then, I assert was *never* put *under the feet of man*, by that first charter of human rights which was given by God, to the Fathers of the Antediluvian and Postdiluvian worlds, therefore this doctrine of equality is based on the Bible.
>
> (Grimké 1838: 9–10)

Apparently, for this activist the belief in universal human rights was founded in the Bible. Obviously, however, to sustain this conviction there is no common Faith (with a capital F). To be sure, the world religions are not as universal as the belief in human dignity; thus that global faith (with a small f) has to be upheld by a plurality of worldviews. Indeed, the preamble of the United Nations Charter uses the term faith (with a small f) in the sense of a universally shared moral conviction. Thus, "[w]e the peoples" express our determination "to reaffirm faith in fundamental human rights, in the dignity and worth of the human person, in the equal rights of men and women and of nations large and small". The two historical lines reflected in this language – faith in the dignity of the human being and in fundamental rights – are reiterated in the preamble of the UDHR: "Whereas recognition of the inherent dignity and of the equal and inalienable rights of all members of the human family is the foundation of freedom, justice and peace in the world". The two genealogies then unite in Article 1 of the UDHR: "All human beings are born free and equal in dignity and rights. They are endowed with reason and conscience and should act towards one another in a spirit of brotherhood."[8] This global political confession (in legal terminology *ius divinum*) reflects the two grand principles that underlie these paired but distinct genealogies, one of a substantive and the other of a procedural nature: *universal human dignity* and *inalienable fundamental rights*.

The first of those two overarching principles, human dignity, refers to the inherent worth of each and every human being, simply as an innate consequence of human existence whether or not an individual person is herself convinced of that (De Blois 1998).[9] Inherent is, indeed, the adjective used in the Preamble of the Universal Declaration of Human Rights, meaning that human dignity is a matter of being rather than having, and hence implying that it cannot be taken away. In fact, as argued by United States Supreme Court Justice, William Brennan (1974 quoted in Wermiel 1998: 232), "even the vilest criminal remains a human being possessed of common human dignity".[10] Yet, although inalienable, human dignity can be violated, by the individual himself – the drunkard, for example – as well as by others. In the vilest criminal's case both occur at the same time; a rapist, for instance, violates the dignity of both his victim and himself.

It should be clear from the above discussion that the discourse of human dignity and human rights long predates the UDHR of 1948 as well as the famous eighteenth-century documents such as the French Declaration of the Rights of Man, and is much broader in its application than mere legal protection of interests. It is a discourse of incredible moral and political force. Nevertheless, while protection of the inherent dignity and worth of the human being is indeed crucial to the whole human rights venture, the implied public-political challenges involve more than just equal and inalienable rights on the basis of good governance and the rule of law. Hence, this study looks at human dignity from an innovative and integrated perspective.

Two "golden" triangles of human dignity

Human dignity, then, is to be seen as not so much an element of human rights but its core. This may be represented by two distinct triangles, one on its manifestation and the other on its realisation. The qualification "golden" in this respect refers to the nature of the triangle as an ideal type.

Human dignity manifestation

The global faith expressed in Article 1 of the UDHR sees human dignity as the core value sustaining human rights, to which three basic principles relate: liberty, equality and solidarity ("brotherhood").[11] This may be represented as in Figure I.1.

First, human dignity qualifies the three major human rights principles – liberty, equality and solidarity – with the adjective *all*. Second, it connects the three principles behind distinct human rights. Hence, it would be a mistake to see one specific right – freedom of expression, for example, as formulated in Article 19 of the UDHR – as just linked to one principle, such as liberty in this case. Equality requires in this respect that the environment in which press freedom is being exercised should be conducive to free speech for everyone, while solidarity means that such freedom is not absolute in the sense of a right disconnected from the community in which it is being enjoyed. Human dignity, in any case, is the core value to which the exercise of any human right must be tested.

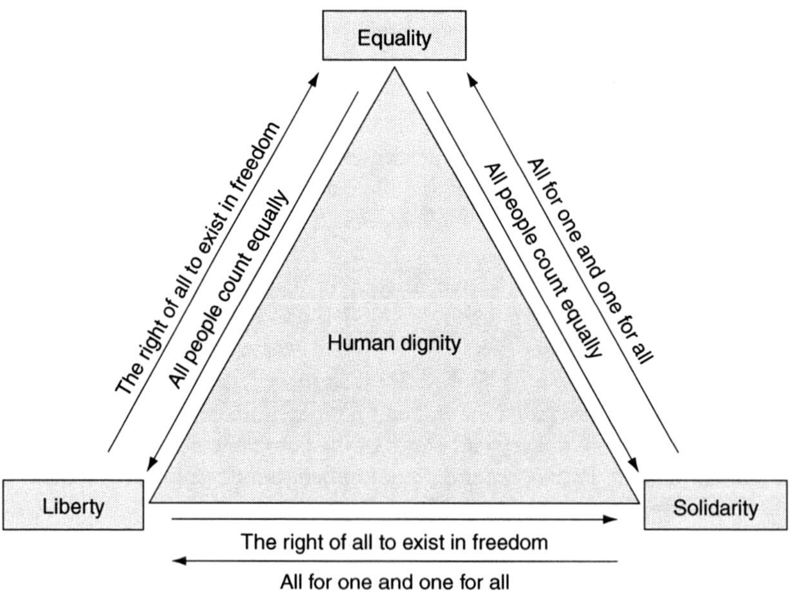

Figure I.1 The golden triangle of human dignity manifestation.

Human dignity realisation

In practice, however, the recognition and realisation of human dignity remain an ongoing struggle of emancipation from the bounds of abusive power. Strikingly, hundreds of millions of humans are still being denied the enjoyment of human rights because of their group identity, whether that is imposed from without or elected from within, and through other means of exclusion.

The starting point in the endeavour to overcome such constraints is the conviction, first, that human beings qua persons are distinctive in having the capacity to value their own existence while making their own judgments and taking their own decisions. Realisation in this sense implies an uplifting of human self-reliance, in other words, empowerment. Born free in dignity and with reason as well as a conscience, people ought to be respected and protected in their individual capacities. Second, human dignity implies global responsibility for the elimination of structural constraints on the realisation of human rights that encumber people's everyday living conditions.

From an operational perspective, then, the public-political implications of human dignity as the core of a global "faith" in human civilisation encompass more than good governance and the rule of law as exemplified by human rights. Notably, the idea of a Universal Declaration of Human Rights was based to a considerable extent on the thinking of the American wartime president Franklin Delano Roosevelt (FDR). His "four freedoms" comprised freedom of speech, freedom of worship, freedom from want and freedom from fear. These are naturally interrelated, not only within the global human rights mission, but also in close connection with the two major ventures that form the other points of what might be called the "Golden Triangle of Human Dignity Realisation": human security, as based on FDR's freedom from fear, and human development, as tuned towards his freedom from want.

Human development, from this perspective, means that life becomes more than a mere struggle to sustain daily livelihoods; it implies, in other words, that people acquire certain options in their lives: a socio-economic perspective. Human security, then, entails protection against violence in people's lives and with that freedom from daily fears. Human rights, finally, means defence of fundamental freedoms and basic entitlements by state law, implying, indeed, a functioning state, the rule of law, and good governance.

Human development might be further interpreted in the sense of global responsibilities towards an uplifting of people's material well-being through human empowerment and the elimination of structural constraints to sustainable livelihoods. Naturally, that venture has to do with self-esteem, culture and religion, politics and other aspects of life, too. The "product" of human development, as mentioned already, is that it provides a socio-economic perspective in people's lives.

The lack of a socio-economic perspective, as a result of poverty and exclusion, may be seen as a major factor contributing to intra-state violence. Indeed, the following observation from Adam Smith's *Wealth of Nations*, published in 1776, is still valid:

> [c]ommerce and manufactures gradually introduced order and good government, and with them the liberty and security of individuals, among the inhabitants of the country, who had before lived almost in a continual state of war with their neighbours, and of servile dependency upon their superiors.
>
> (Smith 1900 [1776]: 313)

Conversely, a well-functioning economy requires protection against violence. In a broad sense, security entails safety. Safety implies protection against disaster. Security adds a dimension of prevention: a minimisation of threats to human (co) existence. Thus, it means freedom from disaster, anxiety, attack and violent disruption of what is considered a "normal" life.

The three angles of human dignity are substantially interlinked. Yet, in the international venture that took off with the founding of the United Nations in 1945, these missions were compartmentalised into three distinct projects: international security through the Security Council; international justice through distinct Charter and Treaty Bodies charged with setting and supervising human rights standards; and international development through the international financial institutions and the UN Development Agencies. Not surprisingly, however, in the countries at the bottom of the Human Development Index (HDI) ranking, as annually published in the United Nations Development Program's *Human Development Report* (HDR), significant weaknesses in human security and human rights are correlated. The challenge today is twofold: to integrate these three separated endeavours, and to renovate each of them in conformity with their human (dignity) dimension. It is, indeed, the intrinsic connection between those three manifestations of human dignity in a public political context – human security, human development and human rights – that constitutes the core of global universal responsibilities.

Figure I.2 illustrates the aforementioned linkages: in order to achieve human security, a socio-economic perspective (and hence a functioning economy) is required as well as good governance and the rule of law (and hence a functioning state); for the realisation of human rights, it is also important that people enjoy a socio-economic perspective in their lives while living in peace in a context of political stability; this last aspect is important for human development, too, as well as good governance based on the rule of law.

The idea of human dignity protection as a universal mission with interconnected implications has a great and diverse cultural backing. However, human dignity as a fundamental standard of judgment easily gets twisted into a norm applying "to us but not to all those others", implying that the fundamental ideas of human dignity and equality are considered inapplicable to the latter. Hence, crucial qualifications of human rights such as "inalienable" and "universal" tend to meet with a great deal of practical resistance.

Even more problematic than the support for protection of everyone's human dignity as such is the way in which such protection is to be secured. With the formation of nation-states, law became the primary instrument in efforts to protect people's basic dignity. It still plays a vital role today, but the limits of its

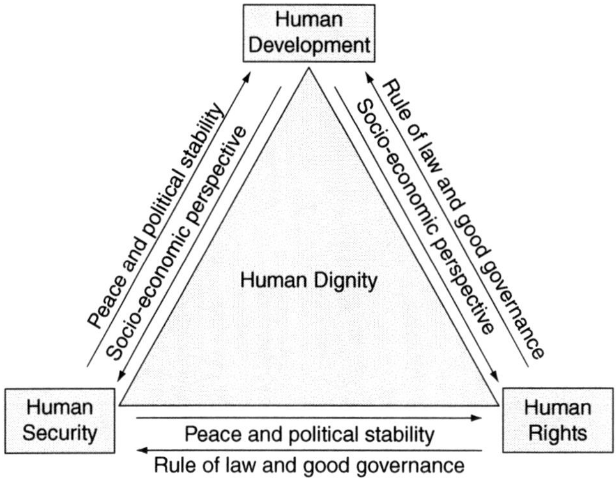

Figure I.2 The golden triangle of human dignity realisation.

effectiveness in advancing and protecting human dignity are becoming more and more obvious, as *Chongwe* (the case discussed at the beginning of this chapter) illustrates.

It seems useful to start therefore, with a view on human rights strategies that connects downstream approaches, which are utilised within the field of international human rights law, with upstream strategies that arise from people's own convictions concerning concrete freedoms and entitlements relating to their human dignity.

An orchestration of upstream and downstream efforts

Human rights, recall, constitute an attempt to protect basic human dignity by law (De Gaay Fortman 2001). As an international endeavour, this effort is of relatively recent origin. It is a venture of a highly juridical nature, grounded in three stages: setting standards and norms, monitoring the observance of those norms, and enforcement.

The concentric circles presented in Figure I.3 below schematically exemplify human rights as a downstream effort: from standards set internationally coupled with mechanisms for supervision downward towards people's daily lives. However, this whole downstream venture is faced with three critical limitations.[12] Briefly, these may be summarised as follows:

1 Protection of human dignity by law assumes "law and order" in the sense that law functions as a way of guaranteeing security of people in their persons, in their possessions and in their deals (implying enforcement of the rule that *pacta sunt servanda*), and settling disputes based upon conflicting interests in a peaceful manner. Yet, in many a politico-juridical setting the role of universalist state law is rather constrained.

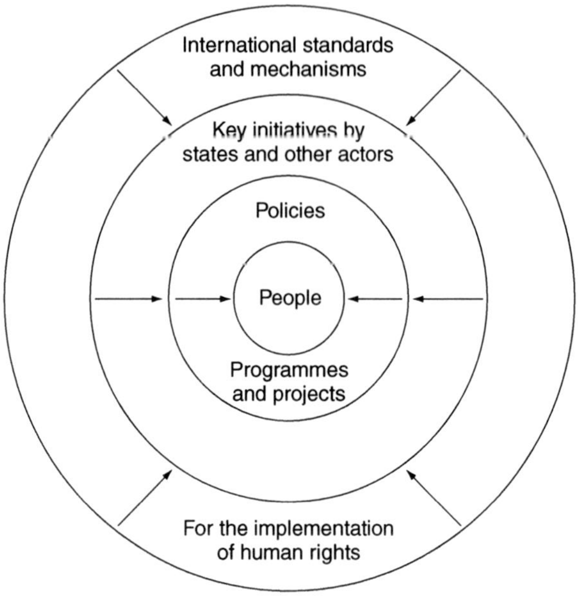

Figure I.3 Human rights in a downstream perspective.

2 The values behind human rights norms have to be "received" in the sense of a cultural reception of the law (De Gaay Fortman 1995). In reality there tend to be serious cultural constraints to reception, although these may well differ from context to context, depending upon the concrete socio-cultural environment.
3 Human rights norms do not reflect all core aspects of justice in the same way. Their meaning is particularly limited regarding the principle that equality signifies more than mere formal equality of all before the law. The reason is that inalienable subjective rights tend to be formulated in a rather absolute manner: "everyone has the right to…", whereas the struggle for social justice is directed against substantive inequality (Sen 2009: *passim*). As a result, human rights do not appear to function as a fully effective instrument in the fight against growing socio-economic inequality.

There is an ancient legal principle, developed already in Roman law, that may provide a drive to overcome these constraints: *Quod omnes tangit debet ab omnibus approbari* ("What touches all should be approved by all"). Indeed, a determined endeavour to involve those whose dignity is at stake as principal actors may serve as a driving force in efforts to overcome institutional obstacles through more participatory governance. It may also function as an inspiration to embark upon the whole human rights venture *upstream*, i.e. from the perspective of *omnes* in the first part of that old *regula iuris*. To understand what that means, let us now look at human rights as an upstream venture (see Figure I.4).

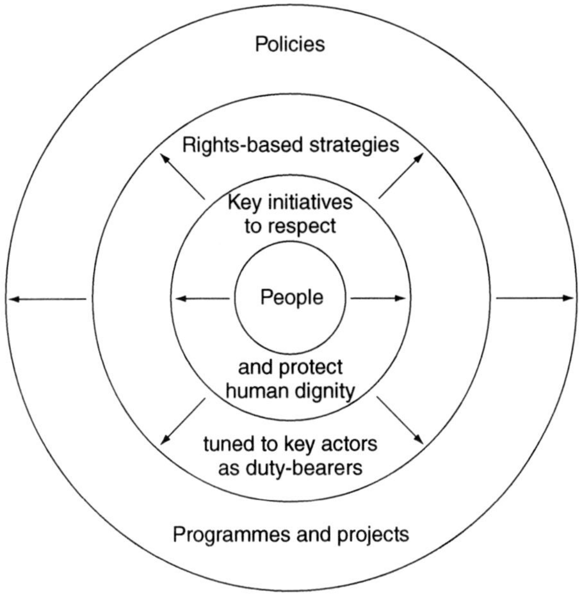

Figure I.4 Human rights in an upstream perspective.

Here the whole course of action begins with people in processes of self-identification as right-holders. The challenge they face in their daily lives is to find protection against all abuses of power and to acquire the fundamental freedoms and basic entitlements that follow from respect for everyone's basic human dignity. Those at the grassroots are themselves the ones who know best what they are due within their own socio-political-economic context. The result, then, should be collective efforts to identify duty-bearers responsible for the often structural constraints that the right-holders face in their struggles for a decent life.

Downstream and upstream perspectives on human rights can be distinguished only theoretically; in reality they constitute two sides of what is basically one process: realisation of the fundamental freedoms and basic entitlements that follow directly from the need to respect and protect the dignity of each and every person.

Practical realisation of the freedoms, entitlements and connected claims that flow from human dignity, then, is the primary perspective from which this book examines the crisis in human rights. A constant background to the analysis is a focus on structural non-implementation in societies and communities that, from a human rights realisation perspective, may be seen as disabling (adverse) rather than enabling.

A new approach

A comprehensive response to the current crisis in human rights encompasses three facets that will be argued in the following chapters. First, we must conceptualise human rights above all as "declared" rights, meant to be realised but still confronted with that huge deficit that is all too often submerged in the general euphoria of human rights declarations, conferences, committee meetings and workshops (see above, p. 2). The fundamental weakness in the current conceptualisation of human rights as mere legal instruments is revealed by this basic and very factual failure: real rights as public-politically proclaimed protection by law, do not routinely constitute conclusive rights, in the sense of effective legal protection of freedoms and entitlements that have gained legitimacy in the eyes of the societies in which they exist. Such rights can have impact only if strategies for their implementation look beyond judicial remedies to social transformation: conceiving of human rights as not just legal resources but also political instruments. Chapters 1 and 2 focus on such a reconceptualisation of human rights.

Second, the realisation of human rights must be approached contextually, taking account of the socio-economic and international and national political landscape in which the rights-holders live: the "lifeworld" in Jürgen Habermas' terminology (1997 [1973]). Chapters 3 and 4 examine these realities from first a global and then a local perspective.

Finally, this reconceptualisation and contextualisation of human rights will be analysed with a view towards realisation. Chapters 5 and 6 discuss two major themes in rights-enforcement that face serious structural constraints: the rights of the poor and the rights of collectivities. In both cases it will be shown how human rights may move beyond the mere legal recognition and judicial enforcement of rights and how, by integrating human development and human security in equal measure as indispensible parts of the same effort, the basic dignity of each and every human being may be protected. Our quest for effective strategies will be concluded with a reassessment of the human rights world's commitment, its tactics and its tools.

1 Rights

The dialectics of power and protection

> Law is not self-executing. It may open up possibilities, it may even facilitate changes and trends, but it is an instrument strongly susceptible to manipulation and neutralisation by other forces. To consider that the mere passage of a law has achieved its objectives is seriously to misunderstand the nature of law.
>
> Yash Ghai (1978: 123)

Power and its limits

Power is habitually defined as the capacity to enforce one's will against the will and the resistance of others.[1] Notably, however, there exists no pure power, in the sense of an ability to completely isolate one's own will and objectives from the community within which power is exercised. A striking illustration of this principle is offered by Anouil's *Antigone* (2001 [1944]). King Creon, Antigone's uncle, had ordered that the corpses of his slain enemies should be left rotting outside the walls of the city. Yet, she collects the body of her brother Polynices in order to give him a decent burial. In their dialogue Creon stresses his power to kill her. Yes, Antigone admits, but that means actually doing something he does not really want to do:

ANTIGONE: "Me, I am not obliged to do what I do not want to do. You did not want that either, did you, to refuse a tomb to my brother? Hence tell me, you had not wanted this."

CREON: "I told you already." [He had tried to explain to her earlier that such brutal orders were unfortunately necessary because, otherwise, the brutes he had to rule would never understand that they should not rebel against his orders.]

ANTIGONE: "And you have done it all the same. And now you are going to kill me without wanting it. So that is what it means to be king!"

CREON: "Yes, that is what it is!"

ANTIGONE: "Poor Creon! With my nails broken and full of dirt and all the bruises on my arms caused by your guards, with all my fear that turns my stomach, I am Queen."

(ll. 26–36)

In what follows, Antigone shows no interest whatsoever in King Creon's theory of power. In her own words:

> I didn't say yes. I can say no to anything I think vile, and I don't have to count the cost. But because you said yes to your lust for power, all that you can do, for all of your crown, your trappings, and your guards – all that you can do is have me killed.
>
> (I. 18)

Power, as this passage painfully illustrates, is not identical to freedom. The core of power is the capacity to enforce, not the ability to act according to one's own will.

Power and freedom

Another observation subsequent to Antigone's dialogue with King Creon is that the *structure of power* is often more important than the individual power-holder's will. Indeed, power may also be conceived as "the potential ability of an actor or actors to select, to change and to attain the goals of *a social system*" (Terry N. Clark in Stalpers 1975: 30 [emphasis added]). Although Creon had created the system himself, it still undermined his own freedom to act as he really wanted. Hence, to understand the true nature of power, we have to investigate such systems. But let us now go a little deeper into the issue of power and freedom.

Between power and freedom lies a fundamental normativity that is intrinsically connected with the reality in which we live. Naturally, Creon did not want to kill Antigone. "You are too sensitive to make a good tyrant", she tells him (Anouil 2001: l. 20). This remark could well apply, hopefully, to most people. Hence one might conclude, turning sideways to economics as a social science, that a value-free realisation of pure self-interest is just hypothetical. In real life, to avoid confrontation with values transferred from generation to generation over the ages appears to be impossible. We are, indeed, moral beings, as stipulated in Article 1 UDHR.

Based on the Biblical Thora, Calvin called this fundamental normativity between power and freedom *civilis* (or *politicus*) *usus legis*, the civil or political meaning of the Law, with a capital L: a public–political morality that has been written in the hearts of all human beings and accordingly constitutes the backbone of human community (Rothuizen 1962). In a secular shape such fundamental values have found reflection in universal human rights.

Thus, the normativity expressed in these rights encompasses many aspects of human life, including the need for an effective allocation of scarce resources so as to optimally satisfy human wants. Economic effectiveness is, indeed, a principle – the economic principle as Van der Kooy has suggested (1954) – that cannot be separated from other norms such as public justice, which is the primary juridical principle.

While in neo-classical economics a school of thought may be typified by a certain model, in political economy, that "broad approach to the study of economy and society" (O'Hara 1999: 868), the dominating characteristic is a vision (Schumpeter 1954). The vision lying at the basis of the present study may be summarised in the term "simultaneous realisation" (Van der Kooy 1954). Indeed, for the student of political economy of human rights, the challenge is to understand the close relationship between effectiveness in the allocation of scarce resources, and justice in the sense of ends and means rooted in the right public-political principles, decision-making that follows rules of due process, and an outcome based on fair balancing of the different interests at stake. For example, a law regulating entrepreneurial behaviour is not fair to the unwilling entrepreneur, if it is not effective for all; and it is not effective for all if it is unfair to the unwilling entrepreneur (Gerbrandy 1935: 19).

Yet power, as we know, will not automatically be exercised in accordance with norms and values tuned to the well-being of the community within which it functions. History has taught that perceived self-interest is a driving force of formidable dimensions, which is not necessarily in line with public justice. Hence, those affected by the use of power need protection, and there are distinct methods of securing this. A first way is to strictly delimit positions of power, both quantitatively and by tying these to certain clear functions. Thus, functional power becomes authority or "office". Where power has been made subservient to the attainment of certain objectives, we can, indeed, speak of its use and abuse. Naturally, this is not enough. "Power", John Acton wrote, "tends to corrupt, and absolute power corrupts absolutely.... There is no worse heresy than that the office sanctifies the holder of it" (Acton 1887). Hence there is an obvious need to control the exercise of power while those affected by its use need protection. To this end, an effort may be made to direct the use of power by prescriptions and prohibitions and to monitor observance. The point is that there be regulated enforcement, or, law. Indeed, throughout the history of human civilisation protection has come from an effective rule of law, itself developed through conscientisation and participation of those who were being ruled, and supported by an equally participative monitoring.

A limited state – as opposed to a totalitarian one – and a state subject to law have become essential elements of what is now written with capitals as "Rule of Law". In its broader sense this includes treating people as human beings with rights, including the right to determine how and by whom they wish to be governed. In other words, "Hobbesian" democracy: a social contract[2] coupled with the substitutability of those in power.

A more indirect method of seeking protection against harmful use of power is through positive and negative incentives: the carrot and the stick. Yet another way is to avoid its concentration while ensuring a proper spread of capacities to enforce: creating checks and balances, in other words. Deconcentration, decentralisation and separation of powers – "Montesquieuean" democracy in other words. And finally, attempts may be made to correct unacceptable outcomes of the use of power. One may think here of policies for redistribution of wealth and income.[3]

What all these ways and means of protecting people against use of power harmful to their interests have in common, is that they demand regulation and hence law. Law is meant to ensure an orderly protection of interests and an orderly settlement of disputes arising out of conflicting interests. Thus, it regulates and delimits power. At the same time, law naturally reflects existing power relations. Consequently, every community and society manifests an inescapable dialectic of law and power (De Gaay Fortman 1990). The position of a certain country on a hypothetical scale from 100 per cent pure power and 0 per cent pure law, to its opposite of 100 per cent pure law with 0 per cent pure power, depends on factors such as the democratic character of its institutions and historically grown cultures of personal leadership.[4] Naturally, in the real world law and power cannot be simply separated, nor indeed can they be fully identified in the way Karl Marx has suggested.[5]

Law, power and morality: who wins?

Should Thucydides be read in the light of the Sophists or is he better understood as a predecessor of Aristotle? Although his account of the Peloponnesian War was written almost two and a half millennia ago, the question still bothers the minds of students of International Relations. The usual interpretation of this Greek author, founder of the Realist School, bases itself particularly on the Melian Dialogue (Thucydides 1972).[6] Crucial in that exchange of views between the militarily strong Athenians and the weak inhabitants of the island of Melos is an admonition by the former to the latter:

> not to imagine that you will influence us by saying … that you have never done us any harm … since you know as well as we do that, when these matters are discussed by practical people, the standard of justice depends on the equality of power to compel and that *in fact the strong do what they have the power to do and the weak accept what they have to accept.*
>
> ("δυνατα δε οι προυχοντες πρασσουσι και οι ασθενεις ξυγχωρουσιν")[7]

The Melians, however, did *not* accept; instead, they trusted in the justice of their cause and hoped for the help of their gods and the Spartans. Subsequently, the whole story ends with the conquest of Melos by the Athenians, the killing of all male inhabitants of military age and the selling of all women and children into slavery. Justice, the message seems to be, is not for international politics. What counts is "the law of the stronger".

In a comment on this memorable history, Nancy Kokaz (2001) argues that Thucydides criticised Sophistic dichotomies of power and justice, human nature and convention, domestic and international politics.[8] Her point is that throughout the Melian dialogue "there is never a doubt that the Athenian action violates rules of 'fair play and just dealing' " (Kokaz 2001: 34). The Melians used the wrong arguments, when they referred to their own self-constraint in regard to the Athenians and to Athenian self-interest – if you conquer and destroy us, the Spartans will come and do the same unto you – while at the same time hoping for outside help. They did not, however, appeal to justice. In fact, according to Thucydides, the Athenians had a normative view on power: "to stand up to one's equals, to behave with deference towards one's superiors, and to treat one's inferiors with moderation" (quoted in Kokaz 2001: 42). According to Kokaz, this maxim is to be called "safe rule" rather than "just rule" because in the Athenian mind there could be no conflict between genuine considerations of safety and justice. The condition of humanity[9] is not that power automatically amounts to domination: it "offers both constructive and destructive possibilities depending on its use" (Kokaz 2001: 41). The Athenians only maintained that the standard of justice varies with the power of those concerned. What Thucydides hated, like Aristotle after him, is mere "cleverness" as expressed in the Melian arguments. Practical wisdom goes deeper; it requires moderation and justice. Thucydides, Kokaz (2001: 49) argues, "offers us an invitation to move beyond the Sophists and rediscover our human potential for political excellence".

Here we are, in the beginning of the third millennium, and still discussing Thucydidean perspectives on moderating power. But should that surprise us? Has humankind in the ages since Thucydides found conclusive answers in the triangle of law, power and morality? Should *human rights* be seen as a way out of these dialectics, indeed some sort of synthesis in the form of a decisive instrument to moderate power by binding its use to internationally accepted legal standards? Is this humankind's definitive response to the moral history of inhumanity as exemplified by the killing of the Melian men and all those terrible violations of human dignity through the ages?[10] No, this book sets out to argue, it is a beginning, marked by strong ideals and convictions, but also by constraints and setbacks: a constant struggle with realities.

The dialectics of law and power

The tendency to abuse power is as old as human history; hence the incessant efforts to tie the use of power to certain norms. Where such norms express legal protection of the fundamental freedoms and basic entitlements of each and every human being, we speak of "human rights". Since here human dignity itself is at stake, claims based on these rights should normally trump other types of claims, both private and public.

The way in which this human rights mission has been conceptualised in legal instruments and mechanisms has placed great emphasis on the second foundational principle of human rights: the quest for fundamental rights (cf. above, pp. 5–7). The major flaws that affect implementation can be traced to this overreliance on legal, judicially enforceable rights as such. International mechanisms for the realisation of human rights were set up as if the emancipatory struggles preceding adoption of the legal model had already been definitively concluded with the victory of the allied forces in the Second World War. That model is based on three stages: standard-setting, supervision through monitoring of compliance and enforcement. Its capacity to enforce international human rights law, however, is terribly weak, as we shall see in Chapter 2. Indeed, the responsibility for implementing all those internationally declared rights still rests basically at the national and local level.

A major complication in this regard is that more than half of the global population lives in socio-cultural environments in which the notion of a "right" is of fairly recent origin (in the Bantu languages, for example) or etymologically close to power per se (China, for instance, Perry 2008). As rights are interests protected by law, let us now take a closer look at law and the ways it may provide a normative setting in contemporary society.

Law's domain

Legality means no more or less than that the law is applied for all: "equally in equal cases". Its foundation lies in a simple division of responsibilities: the legislature determines legality in the abstract, the executive decides on policies and concrete execution on that basis, and the judiciary determines the consequences of legality in individual cases.

The essence of law is that it binds power to certain norms, implying at the least normative processes of settling disputes. This is a mission of a highly noble character as exemplified in the inscription shown in the reading room of the Harvard Law School's library: OF LAW NO LESSE CAN BE ACKNOWLEDGED THAN THAT HER SEAT IS THE BOSOM OF GOD. In a Biblical perspective this implies an allegiance to justice. Legal norms then are meant not only to regulate in the sense of securing order but also to reflect what is generally seen as "right" and hence ought to be enforced. Law, in other words, binds power to a morality that is seen as essential to the integrity of the community as such.[11]

This rather idealistic view depicts law as it is meant to be: justice incognito. At the other extreme we find "anti-law": the use of legal instruments to institutionalise injustice. One may think here, for example, of the Neurenberger race laws and the South African apartheid legislation.[12] Karl Marx (2009 [1875]: 21) saw law as rooted in class relations. Socio-economic power, in that view, completely dominates law. Or, in the words of a sixteenth-century English song: "Law grinds the poor and rich men make the law."[13]

Reality, as we saw, tends to lie somewhere between: on the one hand, the binding of power to norms rooted in morality and, on the other hand, the reflection of existing power relations in the setting and execution of such standards. These dialectics of law and power are appealingly echoed in the way in which the notorious villain Bull Super – a comic figure in Marten Toonder's "Adventures of Tommy Cat" – expresses his view on law: "right is something crooked that has been bent".

The issue then, is law's moral foundations and connections. Obviously, human rights are rooted in justice, first and foremost. Yet, the global venture for the protection of human dignity is shaped in modern state law by bureaucratic mechanisms of standard-setting, monitoring and procedures to secure compliance. Consequently, the whole project has certain traits of a functional system, and it is precisely in its fundamental link to morality that the human rights system needs constant renurturing from a lifeworld perspective.

The terminology used here is based on Jürgen Habermas' distinction between "system" and "lifeworld".[14] For Habermas (1988, 1997), the impersonal relationships that typify an exchange economy as well as a modern polity, imply that both tend to function as systems, separated from the "lifeworld" of culture, social interaction and personality. A topical illustration of what this refers to is the organisation of agriculture in the European Union and its alienation from the lifeworld of animals and people. Law, then, secures the independence of economy and state from lifeworld structures. It regulates exchange relations through property and contract, and institutionalises the political system by defining bureaucratic positions based on administrative law. Modern law is not grounded in normative rightness but is: positive in the sense of the outcome of established processes of law-making; legalistic, implying an orientation towards rules; and formal, meaning that cases are judged under what has been regulated with a view to "equal" treatment of "equal" cases.

Yet, it is indeed in the lifeworld that morality (and immorality for that matter) finds its roots.[15] Thus, modern law is functional coercion and is in need of normative justification. As such, we are confronted with the crucial notion of legitimacy. While Max Weber (1976 [1922]: 941ff.) saw law's claim to legitimacy as based purely on political domination, Habermas (1992) argued that enacted law cannot secure the basis of its legitimacy simply through legality. Indeed, with its many manifestations of illegitimate rule, the twentieth century has generally confronted humankind with the complexity of legitimacy as a concept transcending formal-procedural legality. Grounded in people's conviction that the way power is exercised over them and the way in which they are being ruled are *right*, legitimacy transforms power into authority. In this light legitimacy becomes not so much a fact but a process. The right procedures (due process) are only one aspect of this; other elements concern the right principles and institutions and an outcome acceptable to those affected by the exercise of power (Klein Goldewijk and De Gaay Fortman 1999). In other words, the continuous challenge with regard to legitimacy is to locate law in its "lifeworld" connection to justice.[16] It is in this light that we may now return to the meaning of rights as envisaged in the human rights mission.

From rights to realised claims

Rights protect freedoms and entitlements through legal acknowledgement of claims based on these. They enable us, among other things, to participate in processes of production, distribution and consumption of goods and services. Economic rights represent "the abstract acknowledgement of the legitimacy of claims to income and to participation in resource allocation" (Samuels 1974: 118).

But the problem with rights is their relativity. One individual's rights are limited by another person's rights. Ownership, for example, is not to be regarded today as an absolute right "to use and abuse" property but rather as a general presumption of entitlement on the part of the owner. Whether the owner's claims will, indeed, be realised, depends also on other people's interests and the possible protection of these interests through rights.

Behind different rights there are different interests. Rights legitimise claims only in so far as there are corresponding obligations on the part of others to respect these rights. This depends on the relative strengths of the respective rights. In a society that tries to settle conflict through law, the conflicting interests are weighed against one another by some institution or person not part of the conflict (a "judge"), on the basis of norms (rules) as well as the values behind these.

Because of the general uncertainty as to the acceptance of a person's claims, Samuels has argued that rights cannot be regarded as pre-existing: "The economic reality is that rights which are protected are rights only because they are protected; they are not protected because they are pre-existing" (Samuels 1974: 118–119). Here he confuses rights and effectuated claims, as becomes further apparent in the sentence: "Each present right is only one successful claim or expectation among others which did not materialise" (119). If, however, a claim does not materialise it does not mean that the person (A) had no (pre-existing) right. There was just something lacking in the conditions necessary for the materialisation of his claim. The problem may have been the existence of a conflicting claim by another individual (B) whose right had to take precedence. To say "that for Alpha to have a right is for Beta to have a nonright, when both are in the same field of action" (Samuels and Kelsey 1991: 134) is a misunderstanding following from American legal positivism.[17]

Actually, law is a process of continuous change in the way in which human behaviour is ordered through making and applying rules and settling disputes. Inevitably, legal rules are imprecise, requiring a non-mechanical application. This makes it impossible to determine in a normative and fully predictable manner which types of loss or injury to private persons should be compensated. The compensation problem, in other words, is theoretically insoluble (Samuels 1974, Samuels and Mercuro 1977, 1980).

Yet, legal anthropologists have taken great trouble in trying to describe real types of legal order in terms of different distributions of rights and duties among individuals and groups. Such attempts are, however, bound to be frustrated by the radical indeterminacy of any type of legal order. The actuality of pre-existing rights does not imply a pre-existing legality since, as was pointed out above, one person's rights may collide with another person's rights or with public interests. Hence, Sally Falk Moore has proposed a conceptual framework that takes indeterminacy as the theoretical basis of social, cultural and legal relationships, an indeterminacy which individuals either try to exploit through "processes of situational adjustment" or try to combat through "processes of regularisation" (Falk Moore 1983: Ch. 7).

Certainly, to have a title – i.e. "to be entitled" – by no means implies having one's rights actually realised. Rights are just images of power; to realise a concrete claim, certain action must be taken. Subjective rights, in other words, are generally action-oriented. This applies even more to rights of a subsidiary nature. Thus, examples abound of people in adverse conditions who do not succeed in acquiring the benefits intended for their welfare. Indeed, the problem of non-take-up of benefits is well known in the literature on social welfare.[18] It is, indeed, in such dialectics of law and power that people's entitlements get actually determined. Here some insight may be gained by looking at the institutional settings in which concrete entitlements find structural protection.

Entitlement systems

The methodology put forward in this volume is inspired by Amartya Sen's notion of "entitlement failure", as advanced in his *Poverty and Famines* (1981). Indeed, behind failing claims to essential goods and services are deficient entitlement positions, and behind entitlement failure are malfunctioning entitlement systems.

Amartya Sen, Nobel Prize winner in economics (1998), first drew attention to what he calls "the acquirement problem". The expression has been coined by Sen, probably because the more current term "acquisition" has obtained a different usage. Acquirement is to be understood here as the practice of getting access to the necessary resources and acquiring the goods and services needed. Sen speaks of "legal channels of acquirement" (Sen 1987: 8). "The acquirement problem", he argues, "is often neglected not only by non-economists, but also by many economists, including some great ones" (Sen 1986: 5).

Sen had already suggested approaching the acquirement problem as based on individual entitlement with a focus on ownership:

> In an economy with private ownership and exchange in the form of trade (exchange with others) and production (exchange with nature), E_i [the entitlement set of person i in a given society, in a given situation] can be characterised as depending on two parameters, viz. the endowment of the person (the ownership bundle) and the exchange entitlement mapping (the function that specifies the set of alternative commodity bundles that the person can command respectively for each endowment bundle). For example, a peasant has his land, labour power, and a few other resources, which together make up his endowment. Starting from that endowment he can produce a bundle of food that will be his. Or, by selling his labour power, he can get a wage and with that buy commodities, including food. Or he can grow some cash crops and sell them to buy food and other commodities. There are many possibilities.
>
> (Sen 1981: 45–46)

What Sen describes here is the whole field of socio-economic relations governed by private state law (principally property and contract). He disregarded, however, the extent to which the socio-legal order in society is based on interaction in and among organisations (Falk Moore 1983: 23). Indeed, the acquirement problem cannot be studied satisfactorily without a corporate focus. Individuals are members of various corporate groups. A corporate analysis is necessary to escape

> from the conventional Western juristic categories, which though very useful for some purposes, are more often than not narrowly addressed to a particular kind of property, a particular category of transaction, or a particular category of relationship, rather than to a social milieu in the round.
>
> (Falk Moore 1983: 25)

A focus on the whole social environment reveals, moreover, that people have not only rights but obligations as well, not only freedom but responsibility.

In Chapter 5, poverty as entitlement failure will be our specific focus. In this methodological chapter just a brief explanation of the essence of entitlements analysis may suffice. First, a basic distinction must be made between rights, entitlements and claims. A right implies neither more nor less than an abstract acknowledgement of claims. Entitlement comes in between rights and claims: it signifies structural protection of making legitimate claims. Legitimacy is distinct from legality as it is a function of both power – actual command – and law in the sense of formal protection.

Entitlement implies possession of an effective title, legal or extra-legal. In a political economy perspective it signifies legitimate access to resources and/or command over a good or service in a specified use (De Gaay Fortman 1999). Thus, entitlements provide structural protection of acquiring what people need. A claim is an actual *act* of acquirement. Let us take a concrete example here: the owner of a house is generally presumed to be free to use her property on the basis of that property right. This includes the presumption of an entitlement to live there. Hence she may well claim actual occupancy of those premises. But it is quite possible that another person is already entitled to occupy that house based on a more specific right: a tenant, for example. If both claim occupancy at the same time the relevant judicial institution will have to look behind the conflicting claims and weigh the relative strengths of the respective rights as well as the different interests of the parties, namely, their entitlements. If in the light of the rules and the facts the case seems to be unclear, general legal principles may well provide the clarity that is needed to find the law in this specific dispute. In regard to this type of case, for example, an old legal rule says "Nemo de domo sua extrahi debet" ("No one is to be removed from his own house"); a modern principle is "Sale can break no rent".

As there can be rights without entitlements, the opposite may also obtain. Thus, a peasant may have lawful access to a plot simply because a relevant authority – e.g. the chief of his tribe – granted this for as long as he works that piece of land. Indeed, institutional relations may serve as entitlement (sub) systems. Highly relevant is the relationship between citizens and their state, too.

Generally, state power may function as a source of many concrete entitlements. However, the state may also interfere negatively in people's entitlements, through expropriation for example. Consequently, for the purpose of human rights implementation, government policies and actions have to be closely monitored in their effects upon the entitlement positions of those living in daily hardship. "Budgeting rights" is the modern term for that exercise (e.g. German Institute of Human Rights 2009).

In the same way in which the relation between abstract rights and concrete entitlements is not mechanical, neither is there an automatic link between entitlements and honoured claims (actual acquirement). Usually, in order to claim what one wants certain activities are required within processes of production, distribution and consumption of goods and services: land has to be worked, commodities have to be manufactured and sold, services have to be delivered, consumer goods have to be bought in shops, a door has to be opened with a key, etc. Entitlements provide neither more nor less than acknowledged access to such processes; actual acquirement (implying honoured claims) also requires activities and action. Hence, it is in functioning entitlement systems that realisation of people's wants is rooted.

The centre of Figure 1.1 depicts the environment in which people attempt to acquire sustainable livelihoods. In situations of structural acquirement failure, these are likely to be highly adverse in terms of a malfunctioning economy, bad government, and serious socio-cultural constraints. Actual acquirement is a matter both of activities and honoured claims; in order to work the land, for example, one needs access. While a person's activities are rooted in her capacities, claims find their basis in entitlements, i.e. legitimate access to resources and legitimate command over goods and services.

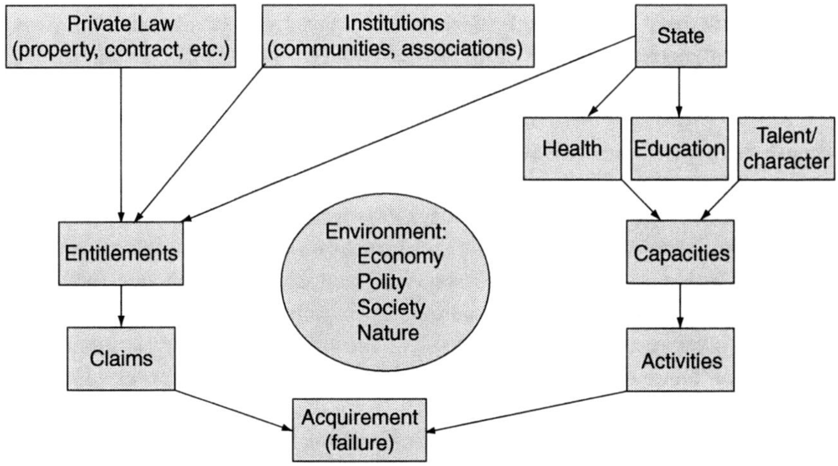

Figure 1.1 Acquirement to sustain daily livelihoods, as rooted in entitlement systems.

The figure represents three distinct entitlement systems:

1 direct access to resources;
2 affiliation to institutions;
3 arrangements by the state.

Direct resource-connected entitlement

The keyword in entitlement positions that are based on direct access to resources is the adjective *own*: his own land, her own labour, his own shop, her own knowledge, etc. Such ownership enables people to engage in transactions with others on the basis of rights and obligations. Indeed, property and contract constitute the juridical basis of such entitlement positions.

Here it is private law, as guaranteed by the state, that is to provide security in the sense of "the predictive states of mind, the expectations, that result from assurances given by the law of property and contracts" (Karst and Rosenn 1975: 637). Thus, a person who owns a piece of land may expect to be able to use its produce because society protects property, and a person who sells something under contract may expect payment because organised society has provided a regularised means of enforcing contracts. It is the law that enables individuals to make legitimate claims.

Unlike institutions with a "real" existence, i.e. forming part of reality whatever their legal status may be, property and contract are not real things but legal constructions, conceptions created by law. As Jeremy Bentham has put it: "Property and law are born together and die together. Before laws were made there was no property; take away laws and property ceases" (Bentham 1975 [1690]: 69; De Gaay Fortman 1982b: 79).

Private law is based on individual freedom coupled with individual responsibility. It has developed mechanisms for weighing different interests against one another on the basis of universal rules which ought to be applied equally in equal cases. Thus it constructed a law of torts. Where other people's interests are harmed, even an owner may act unlawfully and hence be condemned to restoration or at least compensation. Yet there remain many cases of damages without compensation because the action concerned was not considered to be unlawful (*damnum absque injuria*). A judgment in this respect can be made only post factum, as already discussed when we touched upon the compensation problem (p. 22).

Direct resource-connected entitlement typically relates to a market economy based on freedom of enterprise and consumption and free exchange through a system of prices and markets. In such an institutional setting there tends to be continuous change of which individual A, through the use of his rights, may benefit more than individual B. Thus, some people may see their wealth growing while others sink into a state of poverty. It is not the primary function of private law to correct this. Beside freedom, though, it does accept equality as a legal principle. This takes, first of all, a formal character (both partners in a contract are "equal" before the law).

Through concepts like "abuse of law" and "undue influence" there has also been a growing attention for material inequality in the sense of inequality following from an unequal distribution of power. Principally, however, private law is not particularly well equipped to prevent substantial socio-economic inequality from arising, nor to tackle the relative poverty resulting from such conditions (Langemeijer 1970: 41). The law, in its majestic quality, forbids the rich as well as the poor to sleep under bridges, to beg in the streets, and to steal bread, as Anatole France has cynically observed (France 1894: VII).

The debate in the British parliament in the early nineteenth century on the abolition of slavery presents an interesting view on the dichotomy between private law and public justice. While some members maintained that the masters must be compensated for the loss of their slaves Benjamin Pearson argued that "he had thought it was the slaves who should have been compensated". Samuels, who discusses this example in the framework of his analysis of the compensation principle, sees it as an indication "of the need, in advocating public policy, of an ethical system, of a concept of justice" (Samuels 1974: 126 note 29). Although to some extent a "socialisation" of private law may well take place (De Gaay Fortman 1982a: 477–478), this type of law remains rather unrelated to social justice. Its essence lies in the old Justinian precept *suum cuique tribuere* (giving everyone her due) in the sense of respecting existing rights rather than guaranteeing to people the entitlement that morally should be theirs. Modern systems of private law are of a "universalist" rather than "particularistic" nature. It is the market, with its impersonal relationships, which calls for rules formulated in such a manner that they can be applied to everybody in a more or less predictable way. In case of dispute the idea is primarily to apply the rules pertaining to the case rather than restoring harmony. It is not so much the two individuals A and B (plaintiff and defendant respectively) but society as a whole that should be able to live with the decision in the case between A and B. Essential is a certain degree of legal security in the sense of predictability of legal decisions. For this purpose disputes are brought to a judiciary whose independence, impartiality and professional competence are considered to be essential. It is one of the tasks of lawyers to assist their clients in such a way that economic relations are embedded in a proper juridical setting. Thus, an adequate functioning of direct resource-connected entitlement in society requires much more than just a set of laws with jurisprudence.

It should be realised in this regard that substantive law is only part of the legal system; other elements include procedural law, decision rules, personnel organisation and resources. Law-declaring, law-enforcing and dispute settlement constitute, furthermore, only part of the regularisation of society. Other types of activities may result in the reconstruction or even unmaking of law.

Law is, indeed, not a product, in the sense of a given set of rules and given procedures for their enforcement and for dispute settlement, but rather a process (Falk Moore 1978). Law is not a noun but a verb. It cannot be abstracted from its social context. The decisions people make are not only influenced by law but also by rivalry, social, religious or economic coercion, various types of inducement and collaboration. This is the perceptual background in which distinct entitlement systems that have to sustain claims upon which actual acquirement is based, have to be examined.

Institutional entitlement

As protective sources of entitlement positions, institutions may be seen as "semi-autonomous social fields". An institution is autonomous in the sense that it possesses its own rule-making capacities, and the means to induce or coerce compliance. It is only *semi*-autonomous as it is part of a larger social matrix which may invade its autonomy (Falk Moore 1983: 55–56).

An obvious example of such a 'semi-autonomous social field' is the tribe which allocates access to the land together with entitlement to the fruits of its exploitation – usually under the chief's authority – at the same time expecting the fulfilment of various obligations. The (extended) family, too, is an important institution that regulates entitlement. But modern society is full of such institutions as well, taking the form of associations rather than more traditional communities.

Other institutions in which entitlement may be rooted are political parties, trade unions, schools, universities, sports clubs, churches and other religious organisations. Business organisations, too, tend to function as entitlement subsystems. Indeed, a job usually means much more than just a transaction in which labour is hired for a certain price (*locatio/conductio operum*). Within enterprises people are likely to acquire substantial and complicated entitlement positions. Socio-economic security – the feeling of being protected against economic threats and risks – is derived from the relationship to such institutions.

While attempts may be made to rule modern institutions as Weberian bureaucracies, dispute settlement within such organisations tends to be of a more particularistic nature, i.e. it considers an individual's place in the system not so much on the basis of general rules, but according to her own relative authority within the association and the particular nature of the relationships in which she finds herself.

For different categories of people, peasants for example, in a certain area, or workers in a certain industry or people in a certain neighbourhood or town, analyses may be made of their entitlement basis. This is, to a large extent, a matter of organisations, their relative power and their external and internal arrangements. In her book on *Law and Social Change: the Semi-autonomous Social Field as an Appropriate Subject of Study*, Falk Moore presents such an analysis of the production of expensive readymade women's dresses in New York:

> The key figures in this part of the dress industry are the allocators of scarce resources, whether these resources are capital, labor, or the opportunity to make money. To all of those in a position to allocate the resources there is a flow of prestations, favors, and contacts, producing secondary gains for individuals in key positions. A whole series of binding customary rules surrounds the giving and exchange of these favors. The industry can be analysed as a

> densely interconnected social nexus having many interdependent relationships and exchanges, governed by rules, some of them legal rules, and others not. The essential difference between the legal rules and the others is not in their effectiveness. Both sets are effective. The difference lies in the agency through which ultimate sanctions might be applied. Both the legal and the non-legal rules have similar immediately effective sanctions for violation attached. Business failures can be brought about without the interventions of legal institutions. Clearly, neither effective sanctions nor the capacity to generate binding rules are the monopoly of the state.
>
> (1983: 79)

Thus, an analysis of institutions as bases of entitlement and commitment should focus not so much on rules per se but rather on the sources of the rules and the sources of effective inducement, coercion and claiming. This appears to be largely a matter of networks and people's positions within these. In this respect, marginalisation may be regarded as a process of outplacing people in the sense of disconnecting them from effective networks.

One institution that does get increasing attention among economists concerned with income inequality is the family. The standard of living of individuals often does not depend so much on the income they themselves earn as on the total income of the household to which they belong and how the household organises the use of its income. In the light of intra-household gender relations, the term "organises" might be seen as a euphemism here. It is, indeed, through gender analysis that at least in economic studies the public/private divide is gradually being broken.

The crucial role of the state

Before specifically examining state-arranged entitlement, it may be helpful to recall Adam Smith's view on the role of government in a free market economy in general. "The sovereign", Smith stated in his *Inquiry into the Nature and Causes of the Wealth of Nations*, is completely discharged from "the duty of superintending the industry of private people, and of directing it towards the employments most suitable to the interest of the society" (Smith 1900 [1776]: 540). Yet, there remain three duties of great importance:

> I. the duty of protecting the society from the violence and invasion of other independent societies;
>
> II. the duty of protecting, as far as possible, every member of the society from the injustice or oppression of every other member of it, or the duty of establishing *an exact administration of justice*; and
>
> III. the duty of erecting and maintaining certain public works and certain public institutions, which it can never be to the interest of any individual, or group of individuals, to erect and maintain.
>
> (Smith 1990 [1776]: 540, emphasis added)

After the great depression of the 1930s, it was generally realised in the "capitalist" world that government operations have their effect on the whole economy. Hence, the duties of the state had to be supplemented with "the responsibility of government to gear its total program to the achievement of full production and full employment" (President Truman in his State of the Union Message of January 1946). Following processes of emancipation through collective action from below, a fifth major duty of the state was found in establishing and guaranteeing social welfare for everyone, including the most vulnerable, or, in political terminology, "systems of enduring solidarity". Limited though these five tasks may be in comparison to the role of centralised socialist government, they still provide major challenges, particularly in economically less advanced environments.

Legal infrastructures are necessary to order all markets. Law enforcement aims at keeping criminal behaviour at the margins of society so that those who plant can expect to harvest, too. When crime gets to the centre, including the realm of the state, the economy loses its orientation towards productive efforts while becoming the scene of theft and robbery. In the civil and commercial sphere, too, an accessible and operational legal system of a universalist nature[19] is imperative.

Where increasing returns to scale result in natural monopolies – in the case of public utilities, for example – some degree of public (administrative) regulation becomes inevitable. The same is true for situations in which the price mechanism cannot function satisfactorily, in unstable markets for example (De Gaay Fortman and Tinbergen 1990). "Externalities", i.e. effects of economic activities whose costs are not attributed to those who take the decisions, also require special regulatory measures. The need for sustainability in respect of the natural environment has strongly put this to the fore.

While the state, then, exerts a huge influence on processes of acquirement in general, state-arranged entitlement in a narrow sense relates to access to healthcare, education, police protection and other collective goods largely regulated by the state. State law produced for this purpose tends to be of an instrumental character in the sense that it is supposed to support and promote policies for collective action. Processes of socio-economic collectivisation are based on interdependence within modern economies (De Swaan 1988: 13).

Notably, the state not only gives, it also takes, through various forms of taxation. Thus, it rearranges entitlement. Policies for this purpose are, however, not always easily accepted. People may try to circumvent laws by changing the situation on which their treatment by the state was supposed to be based. In reaction to increased taxation, for example, they may attempt lifting up the level of their deductible costs. One might call this *fiscalisation* of behaviour. It results in side law (*ius obliquum*) in the sense that not the intended effects of instrumental law but rather *unintended effects* predominate. A similar situation may arise in cases of subsidisation. People may try to fall into the category that would entitle them to a subsidy although clearly this subsidy was not intended for the likes of them. As an example we may mention subsidised housing of which persons in higher income categories manage to benefit. The opposite occurs when people in the lower income categories do not succeed in acquiring subsidies intended for their benefit (cf. note 18).

Indeed the modern state does not restrict itself to provision of collective goods; it also tries to implement policies on income distribution. To this end citizens are classified into different categories entitled to receive support, such as "minimum incomes" or "people living below the poverty line". For administrative purposes such classifications have to be translated into legal categories. For reasons of distributive justice the definition of one social category leads to definitions of other categories that would otherwise get into an unfair position. Thus, in the Netherlands in the 1980s 13 different categories of "social minima" had been defined. Schaffer speaks in this regard of "the irony of equity" (Schaffer and Lamb 1981). A bureaucratic measure aimed at achieving equity itself results in new inequity that is corrected with a new bureaucratic measure. Apart from financial problems – a high degree of taxation requires strong government and even then there will be increasing attempts at circumvention, if not evasion – bureaucratisation constitutes a major constraint to state-arranged entitlement. There appear to be clear limits to the effectiveness of central administration.

Instrumentalist policies tend to be faced with not just side-effects and attempts to "circumvent" intended entitlement reductions, but also with a simple reluctance to obey the law. Thus, apart from a formal (official) sector and an informal ("circumventing") sector, an evading sector (black market) comes into existence. As a result it becomes rather difficult to analyse, let alone direct, processes of entitlement.

A general problem with state-arranged entitlement is its *subsidiary* nature. Subsidiary entitlement is not to be interpreted as charity, as it remains rights-based. Yet, in practice there are no "acquired rights" in the sense of a permanent and standing guarantee of entitlement by the state. Notions such as "deregulation" and "privatisation" have resulted in new policies with direct effects on the entitlement situation of certain categories of people. Indeed, state-arranged entitlement makes people dependent on those who are in a position to use (or manipulate) state power. This becomes particularly problematic in situations of a corruptive nature in the sense that the whole process of declaring and enforcing state law and settling disputes is misused for purposes other than their public-political aims. Where the distribution and organisation of power is of a highly personal nature – networks of patron–client relationships – the introduction of new authority for public officials might merely promote corruption. Corruption, in a general way, may be defined as the misuse of office. In terms of legal sociology it may be regarded as the combination of universalism in theory with particularism in practice. This way of putting things makes clear that some degree of corruption is bound to exist everywhere.

Obviously, state power may be used not merely to establish separate state-arranged entitlement systems but also to intervene in entitlement positions in general. To prevent undue intervention in private and corporate entitlement relations – corruption or, worse, tyranny – state power has to be depersonalised. The binding of all power, including that of the state, to law – "not might but right" – is, indeed, a first principle of the Rule of Law. Other such principles are accountability, accessibility and substitutability of those executing state power, and a judiciary independent from the executive.

The Rule of Law requires administrative law in three distinct functions: law legitimising the execution of state power, instrumental law aiming at certain policy effects and law guaranteeing the rights of citizens in processes of collective action. Often these three different aspects can be found in the same statute. As an example we may mention the field of environmental protection. The state should have power in this field, that power ought to be used for certain specified purposes and where it is used there should be guarantees for residents whose entitlement in terms of rights to health and well-being would be affected. Generally, in such an area of public policy, entitlement is arranged through a specification of duties including certain obligations on the part of the state. In a state ruled by law, citizens may demand that these be maintained.

Obviously, then, as an effort to guarantee essential freedoms and entitlements, the human rights venture as envisaged in the international endeavour requires dynamic law that is based on functioning legal systems, internationally as well as in domestic settings.

Human rights as a *laborious* element in legal systems

Human rights, then, may be seen from a legal-philosophical perspective as connecting general principles of justice with the conception of human beings as individuals with subjective rights. Each distinct human right has a *core* that relates to human dignity. Behind that core is a general principle, which is connected with public justice in the sense of a communal conviction of what is right and so crucial for the integrity of the public-political community that it ought to be enforced. Examples of such principles of justice as reflected in the "International Bill of Human Rights"[20] are liberty, equality and solidarity as proclaimed in Article 1 of the Universal Declaration of Human Rights (see above p. 8, Figure I.1), due process (with sub-principles such as *habeas corpus* and objectivity and impartiality in judicial decision-making), humanity (the value of human life per se), the integrity of the body, privacy, stability of possessions,[21] participation,[22] etc. The next step, in terms of standard-setting, is to elaborate these principles in legal texts aimed at incorporation in different types of domestic law. The relative success of such attempts to further incorporate human rights into positive law depends first on the question whether, in the country in question, legal systems do function; second on their judicial and political openness to the crucial issue of legitimacy as a notion transcending pure formal legality; and third on socio-cultural factors.[23]

While the international community lacks the means to enforce the fundamental freedoms that have been declared as universal rights, basic entitlements for each and every human being apparently have not even acquired a universal human rights profile by simple declaration. Thus, the world of human rights is a world of unfulfilled expectations. While, inevitably, human rights have to be incorporated in the legal systems of our time, a serious concern today is that they have become a typical system of their own: intergovernmental and nongovernmental centres, compliance and complaints procedures with commissions, committees and courts of law, training programs and academic teaching courses, often quite far removed from lifeworld perspectives. The term "secular religion" is used in this connection, which is meant particularly in an institutional sense. Yet, the proclamation of rights entailing basic entitlements in respect of education, health-care, food, clothing, housing and employment as "rights" has raised expectations and "rights-based approaches" further increase these aspirations. Indeed, there is a huge "development deficit" too, that is not commonly associated with human rights.

Is it advisable, then, to capitulate and abandon that whole venture for the protection of human dignity through rights? The answer is no, because in the global struggle to bind all use of power to essential standards, our world has nothing that could better suit the requirements of protecting people's human dignity in a modern setting. Rhetoric, it is true, but a strong and morally compelling rhetoric for that matter. Rights do, indeed, fulfil the important function of providing legal protection to subjective claims based on recognised interests, and hence incorporation of human rights in functioning legal systems must be seen as essential. However, even where this is not yet the case they can still be seen as *statements of what is right*, an objective moral code, in other words.

For the purposes of the current study, the word "moral" refers to the grounding of these rights in morality and does not imply that human rights should be considered as "moral rights" as opposed to "legal rights". It is particularly in political science circles in North America that we find that juxtaposition. The term "moral rights" stands for rights that cannot be enforced or, in other words, rights without remedies.[24] Well, one might ask, isn't that the essence of the human rights deficit: rights without remedies? But the point is that remedies are never automatic; for one thing right-holders always have to claim what they are due. So the term "conclusive rights" should not be misinterpreted to mean rights with automatic remedies. Rights are "performative" (Austin 2000) and one of the things that make human rights distinct is that, perhaps more than other rights, they are particularly performative. The point made earlier is that in many respects the struggle for their implementation is still in its early stages, and hence these rights often cannot offer immediately effective remedies.

From a human rights perspective, the development deficit in our world today manifests itself as structural non-implementation of economic, social and cultural rights.[25] The term "structural non-implementation" entails that a response cannot generally be found in case-by-case litigation. This does not mean, however, that these rights would not have a legal content, as Amartya Sen (2004) implied in a speech to the Interaction Forum in Washington, DC:

> Since the concept of rights has a legal origin, it's useful to begin by recognizing that many of the cases in which the idea of rights is used, and often to

> great effect, are not matters of legal right at all, but what can broadly be called moral or ethical rights.... This applies particularly to rights that relate to development, such as the right to food or to medicine, or to some basic income.

Sen does acknowledge, however, that these rights have a meaning, not as "children of law" but as "parents of law" (he credits this distinction to Tom Paine). This corresponds precisely to the differentiation between conclusive rights and declared rights. Indeed, human rights do not merely function as legal resources, but also as political instruments in the sense of rhetorically powerful tools in processes of emancipation and transformation. Yet, it unnecessarily weakens declared rights to depict them as "moral" as opposed to legal rights. Rights, as Grotius (1625) already pointed out, give those who hold them a contention to insist on their due as a matter of law, and indeed, that distinguishes them from wider ethical notions about honour or moral desert (Rabkin 2003). But that is exactly why the term "moral rights" is not accurate. Rights signify a public-political responsibility towards enforcement, and no matter whether they have been incorporated in national legislation or not, this is always a matter of action by right-holders first, addressing duty-bearers next, and then looking for ways and means to secure their implementation. Rights are generally action-oriented, human rights even more so, and economic, social and cultural rights most of all. The simple fact, however, that they have been defined as "rights" implies an essential connection with the public interest.

The interests that are protected by international human rights law are of a fundamental character in the sense of being directly linked to basic human dignity. Human rights, then, function as abstract acknowledgements of fundamental freedoms and titles that support people's claims to live in freedom while sustaining their daily livelihoods. The category of rights that protect fundamental freedoms – originally called "the first generation of human rights" – has been termed "civil and political rights" while the cluster that protects basic entitlements has become known as "economic, social and cultural rights" (the so-called "second generation"). Obviously, the two are intertwined. It makes not much sense, for example, to tell a starving person that she has fundamental freedoms, including free speech. Nor would a "right to food" be meaningful when people are not free to say that they are hungry. (The latter has actually happened in practice, for instance in cases of famine in Ethiopia and the Sudan.) Notably, implementation of civil and political rights would be meaningless without a simultaneous realisation of "survival rights" while for a realisation of economic, social and cultural rights, civil and political rights function as empowerment rights as we saw already, enabling collective action addressing the structures behind non-implementation. This indivisibility and interdependence of distinct categories of human rights received formal recognition in the final declaration of the United Nations Human Rights Summit in Vienna in 1993. It includes the incorporation of a third "generation" in the system: the rights of collectivities. By and large, the ordering in first, second and third reflects diminishing degrees of international attention to the rights in question. Indeed, the protection of non-dominant collectivities appears to be one of the most problematic elements in the international endeavour for the realisation of human rights. In this study that problematique is explored in Chapter 6.

Generally, the problem with declared rights is that the freedoms and entitlements that they are supposed to guarantee by law have not yet been obtained. Many people, for example, have an internationally declared right to health but no daily access to clean water and sanitary services. Hence, the implementation of such rights becomes a struggle, confronting the status quo of existing power relations (Klein Goldewijk and De Gaay Fortman 1999). Further on in his Washington speech, Sen (2004) used more appropriate terminology when he spoke of unrealised rights that are acknowledged rights, not yet fulfilled, and "not completely fulfillable without some social changes". The social struggles required here correspond directly to human development as a global responsibility.

The word "right", then, holds a legal significance, implying that what is confirmed in such terminology is morally right and ought to be protected by law through the exercise of public-political power so as to guarantee realisation. Like law itself, rights find their meaning in order and justice. As human rights are rooted in justice, their realisation is not just a matter of enforcing positive law but also a moral issue.

Human rights strategies

Let us now return to the strategic model on which the global human rights venture is based: international standard-setting and monitoring of compliance primarily coupled with local struggles for enforcement and implementation. In this endeavour, international agencies for development cooperation, such as the United Nations Development Program (UNDP), have chosen to concentrate their efforts on "enabling environments" in the sense of enhancing the right type of conditions under which people can exercise their human rights. It is abundantly clear, however, that many people live in environments which, far from being conducive to local implementation, must be regarded as hostile to any efforts for the protection of basic human dignity. In such "disabling conditions" human rights tend to function not so much as legal resources but as political instruments to mobilise dissent, protest, opposition and collective action aimed at social and economic reform.

Yet, the implication of such critical constraints in the operational impact of universal human rights is not that these rights lose all meaning in processes of development and the attack on poverty. While in Western history individual human rights received a place in the statute books at the end of processes of societal transformation, in most of the developing world these internationally accepted standards stand at the beginning of emancipation and social change. Their function, in other words, is not so much protection via their role as legal resources (what ought to be legally protected would still have to be politically obtained), but rather transformation through their function as political

Table 1.1 Human rights in a functional as well as an instrumental setting

Functional / Instrumental	Protective	Transformational
Legal resources	Judicial action (case by case)	Legal literacy programmes aiming at awareness-building
Political instruments	Dissent and protest against policies and actions violating human dignity	Collective action addressing power relations embodying structural injustice

instruments, in the sense of internationally enacted standards of legitimacy that are meant to govern any use of power.

Actually, a judicial case-by-case approach to concrete violations of human rights is just one facet, effective so far as it goes, in efforts to realise human rights. Legal literacy programmes are a way of raising awareness on people's rights in general. A political case-by-case approach uses protest and other forms of dissent as ways of protecting fundamental interests against policies and action that violate people's human dignity. Even in the lives of those already facing daily hardships, such resistance appears to be often necessary. But the most pressing challenges lie in persistent structural non-implementation of human rights. It is the economic, political and social structures behind situations where rights are not realised that need to be addressed. Here, collective action would be called for, aiming at structural reforms.

Thus, four distinct types of human rights strategies may be illustrated by a simple matrix (see Table 1.1) showing the focus of human rights with regard to two major functions, protection and transformation, as well as two categories of means towards implementation: legal resources and political instruments.

Human rights as a creative approach to law, power and morality

Notably, the possibility of taking human rights abuse to court tends to be underestimated, particularly in regard to economic, social and cultural rights. Although, as has been pointed out, a homeless individual cannot habitually sue the state for provision of a house, forced evictions or cutting off essential services can be contested in courts of law. There is a difference, in other words, between a state of non-implementation and a concrete act of violation. Now, if human rights were no more than subjective rights, albeit of a special type, the four major areas of impunity characterising the human rights deficit (impunity of state-related violators of basic human dignity, of perpetrators of crimes within the four walls of the home, of oppressors of minorities, and of those responsible for socio-economic deprivation) would have a paralysing effect on the whole venture. In that case the issue would be confined to *justiciability*. However, the main point made in this study is that precisely in situations in which reliance on legal resources becomes problematic, the function of human rights as "standards of legitimacy" is activated: confrontation of abuse of power with norms based on protection of human dignity. Government housing policies, to come back to our example, must be based on the right of everyone to live in a decent house, and government budgets should reflect the priority given to the satisfaction of people's housing needs.

Human rights, then, must be seen not merely as subjective rights – to be enforced through claims based on entitlements derived from these rights – but also as general principles of justice. In the latter meaning they may also play their part in adjudication, not as a direct basis for the acceptance of certain claims but to throw light upon a case, a generally neglected effect of human rights that will be further explored in Chapter 2 (see pp. 61–67).[26]

Thus far, the emphasis has been on law in a modern universalistic sense, i.e. enforcement of rules through regularised mechanisms. If, however, the realisation of fundamental norms binding the use of power were purely dependent on formal legal processes, in many places deficits in the enforcement of crucial standards would be much worse. Fortunately, however, law can also work through informal mechanisms or, in another terminology, as "living law".[27]

While "law" manifests itself as regulation of power, living law has the nature of "anti-power". An illustration may be taken from the social history of slavery in Barbados. Records of slave births and sales show that from the end of the eighteenth century onwards infants were no longer sold apart from their mothers and the nuclear family became a common phenomenon among slaves, implying among other things that husbands and wives were not sold separately either (Beckles 1989: 105, 107). Apparently female slaves regarded motherhood as "a customary right"; yet there was no justiciability whatsoever since slaves were regarded as chattel and certainly not recognised as legal subjects. Thus what emerges is noticeable self-enforcement of human rights by informal means.[28]

Moreover, as has already been extensively explained, human rights function not only as legal resources, but also as political instruments: standards of legitimacy, applicable to any exercise of power, whether by the state or by non-state actors. The processes through which this is effectuated may have a formal as well as an informal character. Besides living law, in other words, we also touch upon "living politics" as a way of confronting power with human rights standards. To illustrate the meaning of living politics it may be helpful to juxtapose two distinct situations: a parliament without a free press means dead politics, a free press without a parliament would lead to living politics. In the case of the fishermen threatened by "development" (p. 71), those in power might feel aware of a potential resistance that is still submerged but would be likely to get activated when the local population see their fishing grounds destroyed. Such a hidden potential, based as it is on strong feelings of justice and injustice, might discourage big trawlers from fishing in shallow waters. It is, indeed, in a case such as this hypothetical situation, that living politics may become increasingly relevant in confrontations with non-state actors.[29]

Notably, globalisation today has altered interpretations of legitimacy: principles in regard to the use of power become more and more general in the sense of being shared in the whole *ius gentium*. In regard to human rights, this opens the way to more *inductive* approaches. To clarify: a deductive approach derives concrete rights from international treaties and other formal sources; an inductive approach – "upstream" in the terminology introduced above (p. 13, Figure I.4) – starts from what people themselves see as the fundamental freedoms and entitlements that everyone should enjoy. Such a growing focus on lifeworld contexts also applies to processes of legitimisation.

In short, then, institutional decisions that affect the lives of people are more and more confronted with universal standards of legitimacy, including the old *regulae iuris* and modern human rights. While the international venture for the protection of human rights has been set up with particular emphasis on the role of the state, today there is a growing attention to human rights observance by non-state actors (*Drittwirkung*).[30] Since the applicability of rules of justice has never historically been confined to the state, such a development should not surprise us. Moreover, in facing the major challenge of bridging the gap between functional systems and lifeworld morality, states and non-state actors need each other.

In concluding this review of human rights in struggles for protection of human dignity against abuse of power, let us note the pedigree of the problematique. Our concern has been with human rights as a global response to the dialectics of power and justice as discussed almost two and a half millennia ago by Thucydides. The project of protecting the basic human dignity of each and every human being by declaring universal rights has proven to be intricate. Declared rights are rights, and a rights-based organisation of society requires functioning legal systems. Declaring rights further implies that much more is necessary than just protecting already obtained bundles of entitlements. Human rights law is thus laborious law. In many a politico-economic context, the transformation of these declared rights into conclusive rights with guaranteed freedoms and entitlements for everyone calls for the courage to face long and enduring struggles. As for civil and political rights, it is the political order that must be confronted. In the case of economic, social and cultural rights it is the entitlement (sub) systems that lie behind structural non-implementation which must be changed, which means a confrontation with the economic powers that be.

Yet, it must be acknowledged that the whole human rights venture faces three major threats from within. The first is a simplification of the idea of human rights, with universality seen as just a matter of international law – and, as such, an already settled issue. Although apparent in a legal sense, in political and cultural terms universality remains a major challenge, requiring continuous mobilisation of support from every possible quarter in the struggle to protect the dignity of all. Indeed, the global human rights venture necessitates so much more than just the involvement of international lawyers, however important their role may be.

The second danger lies in a conceptualisation of human rights as pure system, far removed from lifeworld realities. It is the charm of legal instrumentalism –

law as an instrument of social change – that constitutes the obstacle here. In fact, the assessment "rights with remedies" is as simplistic as "rights without remedies". The real challenges we are facing today are no longer primarily in standard-setting but in the tribulations of realisation.

The third risk is in capitulation: the feeling that human rights law is of such a laborious nature that one had better abandon the whole venture. What contextual analysis shows today is, first, that laborious law is not impossible law so long as one refrains from positivist dogmatism, while being prepared to look creatively for new ways of using human rights as legal resources. It must be recognised that human rights were conceptualised as not just subjective rights in the conventional sense, but as general principles of justice which may play their part in adjudication in a way similar to that of the old *regulae iuris*. In regard to economic, social and cultural rights, as well as collective rights, this opens up new possibilities in litigation. In that connection, human rights play their part as general standards of legitimacy. As such, they may function in alternative approaches to the dialectics of power and morality such as living law, and also as instruments in the politics of protecting human dignity.

The human rights mission, then, is to be seen as a laborious, but not impossible, venture and from a civilisational perspective a crucial challenge in our world today.

2 Rights

The dialectics of international norms and national practice

> It is only if the judiciary is sensitive to the misery and suffering of the people and responsive to their hopes and aspirations that basic human rights can become meaningful to the large masses of people in the country.
>
> Justice Bhagwati of the Indian Supreme Court (1990: 104)

A contextual view on "transitional justice"

More than 30 years after the Cambodian Killing Fields, the United Nations had organised the trial of Kaing Guek Eav, known as Comrade Duch, the Khmer Rouge commander of the notorious Tuol Sleng prison. Marshall Kim (2009), a refugee from that genocide and now owner of an American hair salon, read the testimony of people who, like himself, had been victims and witnesses of torture and murder while losing almost all their loved ones. And he finds himself asking:

> What sort of justice is possible now? After ignoring our suffering when action might have saved our country, what does the United Nations expect to do for Cambodia now? Placing elderly Khmer Rouge leaders on trial will not bring back those who lost their lives in the Killing Fields, or bring peace to the survivors. It will only stir more anger and misery and hate. Pol Pot, the chief criminal, is long dead. So are many of the others who killed and tortured at his command.
>
> For Cambodians, this should be a time of cooperation, peace and prosperity. Around 70 percent of Cambodia's population is under 30 years old. They didn't experience the Killing Fields, and they face enough challenges in their daily struggle to make ends meet. We who were lucky enough to survive once looked forward to trials, but it has been 30 years – too much time has gone by for us to want to waste our energy seeking revenge.
>
> I don't mean to say we should forget. We can't. Let the horrors be documented in books and films and let the truth be recorded for the entire world to learn. But by pursuing this trial instead of working to improve the lives of young Cambodians, the United Nations demonstrates it still has not learned the lesson of the Killing Fields: Act before it's too late.
>
> (Kim 2009: A27)[1]

"What sort of justice is possible now?" is Kim's pertinent question in relation to post-genocide Cambodia. *Transitional justice* this is called, meaning justice adapted to societies transforming themselves after a period of gross and systematic human rights abuse. It includes criminal prosecutions, truth commissions, reparations programmes, gender justice, security system reform and efforts to commemorate the past. International finance and expertise are available to support such processes in countries in transition. Yet, it is the first of these – the criminal law response – that has become overwhelmingly predominating.

The costly tribunal reaction to intra-state terror is, indeed, illustrative of the international answer to systemic human rights violations, narrowly aimed at special cases, rather than the general prevention of injustice. Meanwhile, the UN moved from a period of organising special tribunals towards an International Criminal Court (ICC). After a long period of preparation that began in 1995, the Rome Statute on the ICC entered into force on 1 July 2002. During the following eight years, the Court commenced only three trials in which it had the accused in custody, of which the first case – against the Congolese warlord Lubanga – is not anywhere near its conclusion.[2] Nonetheless, the Court works on an annual budget of well over €100 million (ICC 2009a). In 2010 the number of people working in the ICC office, including interns, approached 1,000.

Naturally, the struggle against impunity is an obvious priority in the international venture for the realisation of human rights. Yet, although victims' reparations constitute a recognised part of that endeavour, the available funding is primarily spent on case-by-case prosecutions and the related overhead costs and variable lawyers' fees and expenses. Hence, one may wonder whether these huge amounts of resources could not be spent more effectively on inclusive programmes of support for less formal modes of criminal justice – such as the "Justice without Lawyers" model in Rwanda (Clark 2010) – victims' redress and fostering environments embodying a functioning rule of law – justice that is done and seen to be done – as well as human security and human development. These are, indeed, legitimate questions, which get only rarely discussed within the setting of transitional justice and international human rights.[3]

In our attempt to grasp the dialectics of international law and national justice, let us start now by looking more closely at the international human rights mission as envisaged by the United Nations in 1945 and elaborated in the decades thereafter.

The international venture for the realisation of human rights

With the founding of the United Nations the incorporation of human rights into international law received a crucial impetus. After a frightful period in which an ideology of dehumanisation of whole peoples had led to a world war with subsequent mass destruction and genocide, a general feeling of "never again" had emerged. As a result, in October of 1945, a new institution, called the United Nations, was founded on a three-pronged mission: international peace and security, international development and international justice. Each prong was connected to specific new institutions and procedures. The UN's security mission was set up as, above all, a political venture with the Security Council as its major body. The development mission was seen as principally an economic challenge with the international financial institutions and the subsequently created Development Agencies as main organisations. The global justice endeavour was seen as primarily a matter of international law, under a Commission on Human Rights. This implied an extension of the law of states (*ius intra gentes*) to global provisions applying to individual human beings as well (a new *ius gentium*).

Charter-based provisions

In this post-war re-engineering of the "international community", then, the emphasis was on international security with supplementary roles for international development and international justice. In respect of the latter, the Charter stipulated "promoting and encouraging respect for human rights" as one of the purposes of the UN, while connecting this to global peace and stability. Certain institutional arrangements were laid down to establish a Charter-based framework for "respect, encouragement and promotion of human rights". The UN General Assembly was charged with the initiation of studies and the making of recommendations to assist in the realisation of human rights, referring to further institutional arrangements such as the establishment of a Commission. The Commission on Human Rights (the Commission) was established in 1946. Under the guidance of its Chair, Eleanor Roosevelt, it submitted the draft of a Universal Declaration of Human Rights as a basis for a new "International Bill of Human Rights". (This Bill also encompasses two major covenants adopted in 1966; see below, as well as pp. 44–45.) After slightly amending the draft text, the UN General Assembly accepted the Declaration on 10 December 1948, whose gist and significance we already came across in the previous chapters.

While the Charter had remained wholly vague on the substance of human rights, the Declaration specifies the implications of universal protection of human dignity and equal inalienable rights more concretely. A first category, termed "civil and political rights" encompasses protection against discrimination, life, liberty and security of person, no torture, effective legal remedy and due process, equality before the law, protection of privacy and of family life, citizenship and participation in political decision-making, seeking asylum in case of persecution, freedom of conscience and religion as well as expression of one's thoughts, property, equal access to public services, and freedom of peaceful assembly and association. A second category, entitled "economic, social and cultural rights", includes the right to a decent standard of living with adequate food, clothing and shelter, access to public health and education, work, and cultural participation. The two major covenants that followed the adoption of the Declaration both begin with a "collective right": self-determination of peoples. Such rights are conceived as being of a third category. However, all human rights are envisaged as being "universal, indivisible and interdependent, and interrelated".[4]

The Commission that was set up as an international political institution to supervise the implementation of the Charter's directives on human rights, consisted of 53 representatives of member states, elected by the UN Economic and Social Council (ECOSOC). Not surprisingly then its decisions reflected global and regional political divisions. Thus, its procedures comprised two major exceptions to the legal model envisaged:

1 Contrary to the legal rule *Nemo iudex in sua propria causa*,[5] the members acted as judges in their own case. For instance, when Bhutan expelled a great number of its Nepali-speaking countrymen, resulting in a conflict with neighbouring Nepal where these people had sought refuge, both countries made sure that they were at once elected in the Commission.
2 As it never referred cases concerning gross and systematic human rights abuse to the Security Council, the Commission played no part in enforcement whatsoever.

Meanwhile, the political theatre habitually enacted in the Commission came more and more under critique in human rights circles. While from a legal perspective states, regardless of their political basis, are under a general obligation to respect and promote human rights – particularly in regard to certain core rights whose implementation is regarded as *obligationes erga omnes*[6] – procedures to enforce their realisation by unwilling governments are of a political rather than judicial nature. "Composed of Member States, the Commission on Human Rights has become a House of Impunity", Zoller concluded his review of the Commission's session in 2002 (1). A few years later former High Commissioner for Human Rights Mary Robinson summarised the critique as follows: "It was therefore deeply frustrating to see its work increasingly undermined by block voting and procedural manoeuvres that prevented some of the world's worst human rights violators from being held to account for their abuses" (Robinson 2006).

The proposed reform of the Charter-based UN human rights body resulted in replacement of the Commission by a Human Rights Council (the Council) as an intergovernmental body within the UN system, again made up of member-states, (47 now), responsible for strengthening the "promotion and protection of human rights" around the globe. Assisted by the Office of the High Commissioner for Human Rights (OHCHR) it still acts as the UN's principal intergovernmental human rights body, charged with responsibilities to ensure human rights "promotion and protection" by:

- addressing violations of human rights;
- contributing to prevention of human rights violations;
- responding promptly to human rights emergencies;
- recommending new standards (e.g. by drafting new treaties and new (optional) protocols to existing treaties);
- promoting and monitoring implementation of human rights;

- providing advisory and technical services;
- Universal Periodic Review (UPR) of all UN member states;
- proposing new programmes and policies related to human rights.

Although the composition of the Council was supposed to better reflect positive national human rights records, actual membership still includes countries notorious for gross and systematic human rights violation such as Angola, Cameroon, China, Cuba, Libya, Russia and Saudi Arabia. In 2009, more than ten countries with questionable human rights records were all re-elected.[7] Yet, contrary to the period of the Commission in which any discussion on the human rights record of a country could immediately be blocked by a 'no action' motion, there is now a requirement to periodically review all states instead of a selected few. The information that is submitted includes reports of special rapporteurs and Treaty-based committees.

This assessment of all 192 UN member-states through a kind of peers' review with a "troika" of three countries preparing a first list of questions is seen as the major institutional step forward as compared to the Commission. Yet, this type of assessment is hampered by conventional UN procedures based as these are on the doctrine of equality of states. For instance, for plenary session discussion there are three hours whether China or San Marino faces review. Moreover, the Human Rights Council remains a gathering of peers and, indeed, a number of these have feeble human rights records.

The substance of the recommendations that the countries having come up for review by their "peers" have received is rather revealing. Indeed, the whole process, as it is conducted, deserves the title that UN Watch gave its recent evaluation of the process: "Mutual Praise Society" (2009). Notably, out of 55 countries taking part in the UPRs of 32 actual performance as based on human rights standards and issues was rated as either detrimental, very detrimental or even destructive (UN Watch 2009: 3). In Chapter 6 we shall discuss the role of UPR particularly with regard to the protection of collectivities.

Perhaps the most effective role of the Council lies in the appointment of special rapporteurs and working groups with a special mandate. In this way concrete research is being done into actual violations and their causes. It is particularly through the co-operation of international and national nongovernmental organisations (NGOs) that this contributes towards public exposure of human rights abuse.

Treaty-based provisions

In the period directly following the adoption of the Declaration, the international human rights project was principally interpreted as a challenge to define new standards and to create juridical provisions for monitoring of compliance, interpretation and judgment of individual and state complaints. Thus, the Charter-based arrangements were followed by the creation of Treaty-based mechanisms, beginning with the two principal covenants complementing the Declaration in what is usually called "the International Bill of Human Rights": the International Covenant on Civil and Political Rights (United Nations 1966a) and the International Covenant on Economic, Social and Cultural Rights (United Nations 1966b). Later, seven major international human rights treaties followed, each with its own supervisory committee.[8] The committees issue general comments on the interpretation of the treaty in question and concluding observations on country reports as well as cases involving individual complaints. This last function pertains to most of the covenants and conventions. Some committees have an autonomous right of inquiry, too.

The committees supervise the implementation of the international legal obligations of state parties in respect of the specific rights enacted in the respective treaties. Indeed, the core focus of their investigations is on state duties to respect, protect and fulfil obligations following from international human rights law. They deal with country reports while some committees hear individual complaints as well.[9] Other procedures include early warning and urgent action; interpretation of the Treaty in question through General Comments; inter-state complaints; and the submission of information for an inquiry. By means of civil society involvement their actual influence in the national context of a state party can be much enhanced. Through parallel reports or shadow reports civil society can use the committees for concrete human human rights advocacy and action.

The various treaty-committees meet two to three times per annum. They are composed of "independent experts"; in practice, however, appointment requires lobbying state representatives with the full support of one's own government. Clearly, such procedure qualifies the meaning of both the independence and the expertise of elected candidates.

Human rights in the context of international relations

Sixty-five years after the founding of the United Nations, human rights looks like an insular world unto itself: a system with its own standards, institutions and mechanisms, a world of experts still far from being intrinsically connected to people's daily lifeworlds. Insofar as the mass media pay attention to human rights questions and issues, their focus is primarily on international relations and foreign policy. This would not give any reason for concern if the emphasis were just on human rights as an end to be achieved; what permeates international relations is, however, human rights as an instrument to uplift a state's own credibility while undermining that of other states. In that respect two distinctive ways of twisting human rights may be discerned: "offensive" and "defensive" human rights.

"Offensive human rights" implies a focus on violations by other states. Illustrative in this respect is the usual practice in the relations between Cuba and the United States: in whatever forum possible, motions are put forward to censure the rival state. The term "defensive human rights", on the other hand, refers to the practice of signing and ratifying whatever treaty possible (not uncommonly with preannounced reservations) as well as incorporating human rights standards in the country's national constitution, not as a first step towards implementation but simply as a point of positive reference whenever questions are asked as to the country's human rights record. To be sure, the ensuing state obligations are internationally enforceable only if systematic non-compliance were first reported to the UN Security Council and next resulted in action in the form of sanctions. This could happen only very rarely as international governance is extremely weak in practice. Consequently, state sovereignty – also a UN foundational principle (UN Charter Article 2) – has remained a crucial obstacle to international human rights law. Thus, in practice, the states participating in Treaty-based mechanisms can refrain from submitting country reports as well as ignoring concluding observations that require a clear follow-up,[10] and in the Charter-based bodies they can disregard motions and resolutions requesting essential changes in their human rights policies and practices, while even denying access to mandated UN representatives seeking entry into the country under scrutiny.

The point is that while the international standards and mechanisms have been created as a legal venture, implementation has always been dominated by international relations. Thus, there is no world court of human rights comparable to the European Court of Human Rights in Strasbourg, whose judgments are executed as standard practice. As mentioned, membership of the Charter-based bodies is through state representation, implying that states are involved in judging their own cases.

A critical appraisal

In the context of globalisation and the end of the Cold War one would have expected a revival of human rights as a genuine global venture capable of engaging and mobilising mass constituencies. That such support has not been forthcoming must be seen as a disappointment (Normand and Zaidi 2008: xxviii). In this respect some observations may serve to clarify certain flaws in the global human rights venture.

Defects in international human rights

The UN project as envisaged in the Charter was never meant to be legally enforceable by *international* means.[11] The terminology was remarkably weak from the start, with the core expression of "protection and promotion of human rights" as testimony to its "soft law" character.[12] The phrase "soft law" is used in respect of a quasi-legal model based on standard-setting without supervision through monitoring of compliance (let alone any efforts to enforce). While the term refers particularly to UN General Assembly resolutions, it pervades the operation of treaty law, too. Generally, then, the system manifests the following defects:

1 Even when country assessments and cases of human rights violations are treated as a very serious matter, there is remarkably little attention to the follow-up of cases in which evident violations of human rights were

established. This is one explanation why the global human rights deficit mentioned above strongly persists.[13]

2 The juridical nature of the international human rights venture went together with an emphasis on case-by-case approaches. Yet, national non-implementation is often of a structural nature, requiring primarily international political action. Insofar as such action has been forthcoming, it has suffered from the almost inherent double standards in the world of states. Effective action requires decision-making by the UN Security Council and that implies consent on the part of its permanent members, including China, Russia and the United States. Thus, gross and systematic violations of human rights cannot be effectively addressed in territories such as Chechnya and Tibet.

3 Effective protection of collectivities requires close co-operation between the UN's political set-up, which deals with international peace and security, and its juridical branch, which is tuned to the "promotion and protection" of human rights. Likewise, the realisation of economic, social and cultural rights needs the full commitment of relevant development-oriented agencies, including the international financial institutions (IFIs). Yet, "mainstreaming" human rights as envisaged in the whole UN system of governance has, above all, resulted in documents that reflect policy briefs, reports and policy guidelines rather than the genuine operationalisation of human rights at all levels and layers (Normand and Zaidi 2008).

4 There has not been much interest in global human rights as a *common* mission of the "United Nations", as envisaged in the Declaration. Instead, member-states appear to believe in setting up their own human rights mechanisms – not as complementary to the international framework but as an alternative – rather than committing themselves to truly supranational supervision and enforcement. Strikingly, even in academic circles the grounds of human rights, as expressed in the first article of the Declaration, are rarely discussed (except for philosophical reflections on human dignity).[14] The downside of that obvious endeavour to avoid discussions that might touch upon the axiom of global universality is that concrete human rights tend to get detached from the fundamental values that lie at the core of each distinct human right. Let us take freedom of opinion and expression as an example here. Its ground – liberty – is often interpreted in such a way that the first part of Article 1 of the Declaration is dissociated from the second: the conception of freedom becomes unhinged from an accompanying conception of people as moral human beings, implying personal responsibility. Consequently, through the above interpretation the grand principle of human dignity loses its significance. Indeed, certain interpretations, which utilise Article 19 of the Declaration as a licence to use offending language and to disseminate dignity-offending material, such as pornography, tend to alienate huge portions of the necessary constituency for the human rights mission, while also contributing towards a political constituency for relativist positions such as "Asian" or "Islamic" human rights.[15]

5 International human rights are not yet sufficiently focused on the economic, political, social and cultural aspects of the distinct environments in which these rights have to be realised. As the whole international venture for the protection of human dignity against abuse of power is based on well functioning legal systems that connect enforceable national law to international law, efforts to realise these rights primarily require the creation of good government based on the rule of law. In order to overcome the obstacles connected to failing and dictatorially ruled states, well functioning economies and policies to overcome cultural prejudice are essential. That would entail a shift of resources from purely juridical action towards policies supporting political transformation.

6 Devoid of global governance, economic globalisation has increased socio-economic inequality while creating an adverse environment for the realisation of economic, social and cultural rights. Simultaneously, non-state agencies became more relevant actors in the whole international endeavour for structural protection of human dignity. An effective check on human rights-affecting actions by multinational corporations (MNCs) is primarily the duty of states under whose responsibility these companies operate. While at the level of states an increased focus on MNC violations of human rights is clearly noticeable, international regulation will have to follow if violations reach a globally intolerable level (Ruggie 2008). Notably, even international governmental organisations such as the World Trade Organisation distance themselves from responsibilities for human rights implementation.

7 In the aftermath of 11 September 2001 (9/11) the world has seen a strong revival of "exceptionalism" in respect to international law. Exceptionalism is a term generally used to describe the ways and means by which states exempt themselves from the international legal and political order. The United States is the most obvious example of state-based exceptionalism.[16] Within the setting of the problematique that concerns us here, the phrase "exceptionalism" may be used to describe any attempt to exempt citizens and institutions from democratic public-political authority and its laws, policies and actual decisions, based on assumed incompatibility with national principles. In the wake of the "Global War on Terror" as the Pentagon termed the US response to 9/11, even rights very close to the core of human dignity such as due process and the prohibition of torture have been grossly and systematically violated. Highly problematic from a human rights perspective is the exceptionalist spillover to the rest of the world, including countries like Israel and Iran, too. This crucial issue will be further explored in Chapter 3.

Positive perspectives

Notwithstanding these serious flaws in the operation of the international human rights system, there are certain hopeful signs:

1 The global "faith" in universal dignity and inalienable rights that was mentioned in the preamble of both the UN Charter and the UDHR is implicit in the strong moral-political rhetoric of the Declaration as exemplified in the articles specifying the various rights beginning with "all", "everyone" or "no one". Indeed, everybody counts and no one is to be submitted to treatment violating her basic human dignity. In what way the declaration may have been finally drafted – "written in two days in a hotel room in San Francisco by Eleanor Roosevelt and two assistants" (Korzec 1993) – it is a simple fact that these words have a universal appeal. While this may not be the case in regard to all those who rule, it certainly applies to the ruled. In fact, just like Holy Scriptures such as the Bible, the Qur'an and the Bhagavad Gita, the UDHR appeals to a much wider circle of people than the cultural context in which it originated. Those who have ever carried copies of the Universal Declaration to countries with tyrannical regimes know that, in a cultural context entirely different from "the West", there can be an overwhelming demand for this document.

2 Notably, the whole venture is of a programmatic rather than an immediately conclusive nature. In fact, it all started with a Universal *Declaration* of Human Rights. This does not mean, however, that the term "rights" as used here is meant in the sense of a moral category as if these "moral rights" could be distinguished from "legal rights". Rights signify interests protected by law, meaning a public-political responsibility towards their protection, and in this sense human rights are not distinct from other rights. It should be noted that rights are never simply self-executing. Indeed, to realise one's rights under the law always requires action and this applies to declared rights in particular. Hence, although the "downstream" basis of the international human rights standards is rather weak, "upstream" action may well serve to actually secure the fundamental freedoms and entitlements that are meant to be protected.[17]

3 Although UN General Assembly Declarations do not routinely qualify as international law, through periods of customary state practice and guided by a strong *opinio iuris* (established legal opinion) these may well result in customary international law, in certain instances even regarded as *ius cogens* (non-derogable provisions of international law). This applies, for example, to the right to life, liberty and bodily integrity (prohibition of torture) and due process.[18] Yet, even to get *ius cogens* enforced through effective judicial remedies remains a huge challenge. Hence, the downstream venture will always need linkages to upstream action on the part of those whose rights are at stake and the agencies that support them.

4 The international human rights project was never intended as a separate venture, aside from regional and national mechanisms. Europe has created a very strong regional system through the European Convention on Human Rights and the adjoining European Court of Human Rights in Strasbourg. The regional mechanisms in Africa and in the Americas are gradually being reinforced. Even more importantly, national human rights institutions –

supervisory commissions and institutes – play an increasing role. Moreover, as will be illustrated below, national legislators and particularly national judiciaries often manifest an activist attitude when it comes to human rights implementation.

5 Despite its flaws from the legality perspective, international human rights law has created a strong notion of global legitimacy, based on common standards of justice and injustice. This implies that no use of power is considered legitimate if it violates international human rights standards. It is particularly in the absence of a reliable global instrument for human rights enforcement that the international standards behind human rights play an important part in the new civilising mission.

6 Particularly through the support of international civil society, linked to national NGOs in distinct contexts, international mechanisms for supervision of human rights compliance serve to bring concrete violations out into the open. *Quidquid latet apparebit* (whatever is hidden is to be revealed) as Thomas of Celano put it in his peroration on the final judgment *Dies Irae, Dies Illa.*

7 Although the original language of most documents originating in the international human rights venture is juridical and protective, in actual practice the project is at least as political and transformational. Indeed, while the history of civil and political rights is tuned in particular to the *protection* of citizens against sovereigns who want to rob them of their possessions, in a "Third World context" the declaration functions as a basis for the *emancipation* of the have-nots. This strategic observation has already been elaborated in Chapter 1 (see Table 1.1).

Thus, in the struggle for public justice, international human rights provide not just legal resources as based on positive law, but also political means anchored in public legitimacy. Additionally, human rights function not merely to protect people with regard to the freedoms and entitlements they have already acquired, but in their emancipatory struggles for socio-political transformation as well. Hence, the whole picture offers a multifaceted perspective based on a civilisational commitment of utmost importance. In the absence of reliable global mechanisms for the enforcement of human rights, international human rights laws and principles have to be connected, first and foremost, to national institutions and mechanisms with the power to enforce these standards. Indeed, while from an international legal perspective state sovereignty may well be seen as an obstacle, in a national context it might well constitute a basis for effective implementation. This does, however, require a functioning rule of law.

State sovereignty and the separation of powers

In the context of international relations, sovereignty is no more or less than the legal identity of a state based upon exclusive jurisdiction within the limits of its national territory combined with the right to autonomously interpret its own national interests and the discretionary authority to act accordingly. Like other legal principles governing jurisdiction, it is not absolute (Flinterman 2000). Indeed, universality and human dignity – those two grand principles that are the foundation of human rights – constrain the meaning of state sovereignty in theory as well as in actual practice (De Gaay Fortman 2006a). Naturally, to actually realise protection of individuals and collectivities against their own state requires a good deal of judicial activism.

The state is a historical reality that cannot be understood "apart from its realisation in the development of human society" (Dooyeweerd 1957: 411). Its core feature is to present itself as "an institution of the public interest, in which political authority is considered a public office, not a private property" (Dooyeweerd 1957: 412). The link with public justice implies duty rather than mere discretionary power. A real step forward in this connection is the current emphasis on the other side of the sovereignty coin: the "responsibility to protect" (International Development Research Centre 2001). In other words, sovereignty, in the sense of the execution of national authority, implies responsibility in addition to discretion, although the emphasis has been on the latter for too long. (Incidentally, that notion is far from new, as illustrated in the notion of *Carence de Souveraineté*.[19]) In Chapter 6 its implications in regard to "minorities' protection" will be further explored.

Originally, sovereignty as a combined right and duty to execute public-political authority lay with the Sovereign, i.e. the executive. As such, the role of the legislature was to act as a mere consultative assembly for monarchs (Loewenberg 2007). Yet, it is precisely in this branch of public office that the notion of limits to the powers of the state originates. Although they are the bearers of the responsibility to protect, legislatures are nevertheless restrained by their plural nature to being arenas for mere debate rather than effective decision-making bodies (Loewenburg 2007). This is clearly not the case regarding the third branch of state power: the judiciary. In order to protect citizens against any abuse of power that violates their basic rights, members of this institution have to be appointed to an independent position and they must preserve the autonomy of that position in day-to-day judicial decision-making. Indeed, the importance of creating and maintaining an independent, impartial, competent, legitimate and effective judiciary cannot be overestimated (Bakker 1998).

Indeed, sovereignty as "responsibility to protect" confronts us with the complex relationships between the three branches of state power: the legislature, the executive and the judiciary. In each of these, people charged with the execution of state authority – the "government" – are not free to use their powers in a fully discretionary manner, but are bound to principles, rules and values incorporated in laws. Foremost among these is the constitution, which creates a "regime" governing the realisation of public order and justice. In this regard, the relevant notions from a human rights perspective are democracy and the rule of law. In the narrow sense of the legality principle, the rule of law implies that everyone, including the state itself and its functionaries, is subject to the law in the sense of clear and unambiguous rules and standards that generally have no retroactive effect. It is rather questionable whether that would be possible without the fundamental characteristics of a democracy, namely, functioning mechanisms for the substitutability of individuals in power; a judiciary that is impartial, independent and accessible; and general arrangements for the participation of those affected by public-political decision-making. While Singapore, Hong Kong, Oman, Kuwait, Bahrain and the United Arab Emirates are often mentioned as undemocratic instances of an effectively functioning rule of law (Peerenboom 2005; Janse 2008),[20] in actual judicial practice protection of basic freedoms in these countries appears to be rather constrained. The acid test of democracy, as Geoffrey Robertson (1998) once put it, "is a justice system where there is at least a chance, a possibility of beating the state at its own game". A key concern underlying the effort to incorporate international human rights standards into sovereign political arrangements, in other words, lies in the relations between the three distinct branches of state power. Here, international standards and mechanisms on the limits of national discretion may well play their part.

A concept that illuminates the juxtaposition of international standards and national authority is the so-called "margin of appreciation", which the European Court of Human Rights developed in order to delimit the discretionary power of national authorities in interpreting the requirements of the European Convention of Human Rights.[21] The two principles underlying this interpretative jurisprudential principle are subsidiarity and the protection of democracy. Subsidiarity acknowledges the primacy of the national state in the realisation of the convention. This allows for certain local peculiarities insofar as the national authorities appreciate these as necessary in view of local needs and circumstances. The protection of democracy allows for a certain degree of diversity in the actual implementation of the convention insofar as that results from distinct national democratic decision-making processes.

After this rather abstract overture we shall now explore the dynamics of sovereignty and human rights in the context of concrete struggles for internal jurisdiction between the three branches of state power. Each of the three cases to be reviewed is illustrative and indicative in respect of the internal intricacies of human rights and the separation of powers. The first one, drawn from the jurisdiction of the United States, illustrates the role of politics with regard to changing positions of the judiciary and the legislature in efforts to uphold human rights against assertions of executive prerogative. The second case, taken from Dutch jurisprudence, refers to the importance of judicial prerogative in the interpretation of international human rights standards. Finally, a Zambian case will be discussed, which illustrates the growing significance of the judiciary in guaranteeing subjective rights in administrative decision-making in relatively new jurisdictions. All three cases deal with matters of national security, namely, the most sensitive area of asserted executive prerogative.

Clashing state powers in the United States

With the public declaration of a "war on terror", following the 9/11 attacks on the two towers of the World Trade Center in New York (2001), the Bush administration clearly intended to establish pure executive prerogative as against a possible role for the judiciary in issues of war and peace. In *Hamdi* v. *Rumsfeld* (2004: 536) the US government maintained that US citizens detained as "enemy combatants" had no right to a hearing. The Supreme Court insisted, however, that

> whatever power the United States Constitution envisions for the Executive in its exchanges with other nations or with enemy organizations in times of conflict, *it most assuredly envisions a role for all three branches when individual liberties are at stake* [emphasis added].

Two years later, in *Hamdan* v. *Rumsfeld* (2006), the judiciary continued to assert its role as a protector of individual liberties by halting a further reduction of the realm of legal protection. The essential query concerned the extent and scope of the executive's prerogative to wage a "war on terror" unconstrained by "a strategy of the weak using international fora, judicial processes and terror", as stated in the Pentagon's 2005 National Defence Strategy (quoted in Cole 2006: 43). The nature of the US separation of powers doctrine came into question, with the Court having to decide whether the President exceeded his authority in the manner in which detainees at Guantánamo Bay were being denied certain due process rights guaranteed under the US constitution.[22]

Notably, Salim Ahmed Hamdan (Osama Bin Laden's former driver) was one out of only 14 Guantánamo detainees who had been selected for trial; the others – numbering over 400 – had never been charged at all (Cole 2006). Hamdan himself had already been imprisoned at Guantánamo Bay for more than four years[23] and had filed his appeals, based on writs of *mandamus* and *habeas corpus* injunctions, prior to the enactment of the Detainee Treatment Act of 2005 (DTA), which effectively stripped all US courts of their jurisdiction to hear requests from detainees relating to such petitions. Consequently, his case was able to serve as a basis for the constitutional test of such legislation. The question presented was whether the only offence that he had been charged with (conspiracy to commit war crimes, to be tried by a special military commission) was to be regarded as enough to deprive him of due process rights such as the ability to have legal counsel and access to evidence against him.

At issue, then, was whether the DTA, which, the Court's majority conceded, does eliminate jurisdiction for future claims, also strips jurisdiction for writs already pending. If Justice Scalia had prevailed on this issue, the Court would have had to announce that it did not have standing to hear the case (*stare decisis*). However, the majority found that the ambiguous language of the DTA allowed them to maintain the power of judicial review for pending detainee cases, thus providing them the authority to disapprove of the executive's methods for dealing with detainee litigation:

> The Government's more general suggestion that Congress can have had no good reason for preserving habeas jurisdiction over cases that had been

> brought by detainees prior to enactment of the DTA not only is belied by the legislative history ... but is otherwise without merit. There is nothing absurd about a scheme under which pending habeas actions—particularly those, like this one, that challenge the very legitimacy of the tribunals whose judgments Congress would like to have reviewed—are preserved, and more routine challenges to final decisions rendered by those tribunals are carefully channelled to a particular court and through a particular lens of review.
> (*Hamdan* 2006: 583–584)

It is such reasoning that renders *Hamdan* a shining example of an active judiciary, using all jurisprudential tools at its disposal in an attempt to clarify the importance of rights and procedures in maintaining legal protection of individuals against the state. After consulting international law, the majority opinion, written by Justice Stevens, held that the arguments presented by the executive are untenable and hence Hamdan should not be subject to the military commissions as created by the Bush administration. Furthermore, the Court (*Hamdan* 2006: 635) concluded that the commissions themselves were invalid as they violated the US military Code of Justice as well as the Geneva Convention:

> We have assumed, as we must, that the allegations made in the Government's charge against Hamdan are true. We have assumed, moreover, the truth of the message implicit in that charge—viz., that Hamdan is a dangerous individual whose beliefs, if acted upon, would cause great harm and even death to innocent civilians, and who would act upon those beliefs if given the opportunity. It bears emphasizing that Hamdan does not challenge, and we do not today address, the Government's power to detain him for the duration of active hostilities in order to prevent such harm. But in undertaking to try Hamdan and subject him to criminal punishment, *the Executive is bound to comply with the Rule of Law that prevails in this jurisdiction* [emphasis added].

Behind the phrasing put in italics, one senses an immense reluctance on the part of the Court to abandon norms for legal protection that are the established result of a legal civilisational process, and hence its unwillingness to embrace the executive's employment of us–them distinctions as implied by the phrase "enemy combatants". Summing up *Hamdan*, Cole (2006: 42) concludes:

> The fact that the Court decided the case at all in the face of Congress's efforts to strip the Court of jurisdiction is remarkable in itself. That it then broke away from its history of judicial deference to security claims in wartime to rule against the President, not even pausing at the argument that the decisions of the commander in chief are "binding on the courts", suggests just how troubled the Court's majority was by the President's assertion of unilateral executive power. That the Court relied so centrally on international law in its reasoning, however, is what makes the decision truly momentous.

The substance underlying the Court's reasoning is even more striking than its mere references to "international law", "individual liberties" and "the rule of law". Without explicitly mentioning international human rights standards, the majority clearly valued the notions behind those standards such as "universality", "inalienability" and "everyone". One is indeed reminded of Judge Learned Hand's (1944 as quoted in Gunther 1998: 548) well known expression of faith in people's hearts and minds. "Liberty", he said, "lies in the hearts of men and women. When it dies there, no constitution, no law, no court can save it. While it lies there, it needs no constitution, no law, no court to save it". Obviously, crucial values of a moral-political nature ought to lie in the hearts of judges, too.

Furthermore, major changes have taken place in both the legislative and the judicial branches of state power since the Court's rulings in *Hamdi* and *Hamdan.* In the Supreme Court, new appointments by President George W. Bush shifted the balance away from the presumed tendency towards "judicial activism" and, in 2007, Congress received Democratic majorities in both Senate and the House of Representatives. As a result, it was once again the legislature that began to manifest an "activist" attitude towards the defence of individual liberties. This was directly connected to the apparent resilience of the Supreme Court when faced with the "State Secrets Privilege". The latter is a common law doctrine that allows ostensibly sensitive information to be excluded from courtroom proceedings in the interest of national security. The privilege originated in England but was later exported to the United States, where it probably "has its initial roots in Aaron Burr's trial for treason" (*United States* v. *Burr* 1807 as quoted by Lyons 2007: 102), a case in which the government opposed the disclosure of a letter to President Thomas Jefferson from one of his top generals on the grounds that the correspondence might reflect state secrets that, if revealed, could jeopardise national security. The court accepted the government's argument, declaring "if the letter did contain information which would be imprudent to disclose, and the Executive did not wish the information to be disclosed, the information could be suppressed" (ibid).

Whereas the US government had called upon the state secrets privilege in only four cases between 1953 and 1976, the Bush administration invoked it in 23 cases following the 9/11 attacks (Lyons 2007). Significantly, in the case of Khalid El-Masri, an illegally abducted and detained citizen of German nationality,[24] against the US government, a federal district court judge dismissed all charges on the grounds that a trial would "present a grave risk of injury to national security" (*El-Masri* v. *Tenet* 2006: 537). The American Civil Liberties Union (ACLU), which represented El-Masri in the case, appealed the decision on his behalf, but an appeals court upheld the prior ruling. The ACLU then appealed to the Supreme Court, which denied certiorari. Remarkably, it did so without comment (Greenhouse 2007).

Regarding this particular post-9/11 issue, then, it was the US legislature that stood up for human rights in the face of an executive that apparently did not consider them universal. The cases involving El-Masri and others, in which the state secrets privilege had been recently invoked, led to increased criticism of this controversial doctrine – not by the judicial branch, which has generally deferred to state secret claims – but by commentators and members of Congress. In January 2008, Democratic Senators Edward Kennedy and Patrick Leahy, together with their Republican colleague Arlen Specter,[25] co-sponsored the "State Secrets Protection Act", seeking to regulate the privilege in civil cases for the first time through legislative means. The Bill (United States Senate 2005: Sec. 4051) defines a "state secret" as "any information that, if disclosed publicly, would be reasonably likely to cause *significant* harm to the national defence or foreign relations of the United States" (emphasis added). Excluded from this definition is information that would cause less than significant harm (though determinations in this regard would remain at least partially subjective), and information that is already in the public domain (such as information concerning El-Masri's detention and torture, which two courts asserted would undermine US national security). It also requires the Attorney General to regularly inform lawmakers about the privilege's invocation. Adoption of the Act by Congress will therefore provide much needed clarity to and oversight of this doctrine, and it will also confer additional rights on litigants seeking restitution in civil cases. In February 2009 the Bill was reintroduced in the new US Congress that had been elected together with President Obama in November 2008.

A 2008 decision from the Supreme Court, however, demonstrated that it still retains an active stance when it comes to the protection of individual liberties explicitly guaranteed by the constitution. In *Boumediene* v. *Bush*, a 5–4 decision from 12 June 2008, the majority of the Court held that Guantánamo Bay detainees are entitled to the constitutional privilege of *habeas corpus* and can challenge their detention in a federal court. Writing the Court's opinion, Justice Kennedy (*Boumediene* v. *Bush* 2008: 2277) then confirmed *habeas corpus* as a "right of first importance", putting the issue in unequivocal terms:

> Our opinion does not undermine the Executive's powers as Commander in Chief. On the contrary, the exercise of those powers is vindicated, not eroded, when confirmed by the Judicial Branch. Within the Constitution's separation-of-powers structure, few exercises of judicial power are as legitimate or as necessary as the responsibility to hear challenges to the authority of the Executive to imprison a person. Some of these petitioners have been in custody for six years with no definitive judicial determination as to the legality of their detention. Their access to the writ is a necessity to determine the lawfulness of their status, even if, in the end, they do not obtain the relief they seek…
>
> The political branches, consistent with their independent obligations to interpret and uphold the Constitution, can engage in a genuine debate about how best to preserve constitutional values while protecting the Nation from terrorism. Cf. *Hamdan*, 548 U.S., at 636 (Breyer, J., concurring) ("[J]udicial insistence upon that consultation does not weaken our Nation's ability to deal with danger. To the contrary, that insistence strengthens the Nation's ability to determine – through democratic means – how best to do so").

> It bears repeating that our opinion does not address the content of the law that governs petitioners' detention. That is a matter yet to be determined. We hold that petitioners may invoke the fundamental procedural protections of habeas corpus. The laws and Constitution are designed to survive, and remain in force, in extraordinary times. Liberty and security can be reconciled; and in our system they are reconciled within the framework of the law. The Framers decided that habeas corpus, a right of first importance, must be a part of that framework, a part of that law.

Notably, then, while after 9/11 the US executive demonstrated little trustworthiness in the defence of fundamental rights, it was the two other branches of government that took up the protection of human dignity in the context of shifting balances of power. With the inauguration of Barack Obama – former lecturer in international human rights law – as President in January 2009, it was the executive again of which a fair amount of rule of law-based activism could be expected.

Constraining legislative prerogative in the Netherlands

The role of national courts in relation to legislation that contradicts already established international and national human rights standards is a topic of pressing importance. In a common law context such authority is usually blocked in keeping with the principle of "parliamentary supremacy". In the United Kingdom it is, indeed, a controversial issue, particularly with regard to European Convention rights entrenched in the Human Rights Act that was adopted in 1998 (A. Young 2008). However, in the Netherlands, the power of the judiciary to overturn legislation contradicting international treaty obligations is a constitutional prerogative. But what if new law takes the form of a ratified treaty rather than just an Act of Parliament?

The clash between the branches of government on national jurisdiction in cases involving international legal protection is, indeed, well-illustrated in the Dutch *Cruise Missiles* case (*Cruisemissiles* [1989] Supreme Court of the Netherlands: HR 10 November 1989, 13698, NJ 1991, 248). In this lawsuit an effective appeal was made to preserve the legitimacy of international sources of law for judicial protection of *Dutch* citizens even after parliament had already ratified a new treaty allegedly contrary to international human rights law. Even though the substance of the matter had been resolved by other means by the time the case reached the "Hoge Raad" (the Netherlands Supreme Court), it was nonetheless decided on final appeal.[26] Indeed, from a legal point of view the issue remained crucial: whether the Dutch courts are free to adjudicate possible incompatibilities between new treaties – in this case a bilateral treaty between the Netherlands and the United States to place US cruise missiles on Dutch territory – and already established norms under international treaties previously ratified. The Court of Appeal had interpreted Article 94 of the Dutch constitution, which declares statutory regulations inapplicable if they are in conflict with "provisions of treaties that are binding on all persons" in conjunction with Article 120, which prohibits judicial review of the constitutionality of Acts of Parliament and ratified treaties. Thus, the Court held that it was parliament (the States-General) that had the final say as to the constitutionality of both statutory law and treaties; in the Court's opinion the question of whether or not a new treaty were incompatible with previous treaty obligations should also be seen as a matter for the exclusive jurisdiction of parliament.

However convincing this analogical argumentation by the Court of Appeal might have appeared, the Supreme Court disagreed, arguing that, since the judiciary is constitutionally obliged to consider ratified treaties as the primary source of law, it also has to assess whether Acts of Parliament meet the test of established treaty law. Would that judicial protection not apply when the executive opted for a formal treaty to be submitted to the legislature for ratification? The legal consequence of such an interpretation would be that citizens might be deprived of rights entrenched in international legal norms due to the simple fact of a state action being subsumed under a Treaty rather than just an Act of Parliament. The court found this outcome unacceptable. As to the practical effects of this jurisprudential stance, however, the Supreme Court emphasised that it did not necessarily imply that already established international law would automatically prevail: in a case of conflicting treaty norms, the relevant court would have to come to a reasoned decision. Given its conviction that in the case under review a conflicting norm of international law was not at issue, the Supreme Court further held that deliberations on how such incompatibilities would have to be resolved could now be skipped.

Nevertheless, this decision is of enormous jurisdictional significance. If, for example, the Supreme Court had felt that the *lex posterior*[27] rule simply applied, this would have implied that established norms of international law, including those containing human rights guarantees, could at all times be overruled by new bilateral treaty rules. Subsequent to the ruling in *Cruise Missiles*, however, whenever doubts arise as to the compatibility of a new treaty with already existing treaty law, the Dutch parliament has to consider the likely possibility of judicial review. Doubtless, the principle of the inalienability of fundamental protections for everyone, which underlies the drive towards human rights, played a significant part in this bold judgment.

Judicial review in Zambia

If there is one set of cases in which the power of the judiciary to uphold human rights norms as against the executive is at stake, it is judicial review of administrative decisions. A remarkable case in this respect is *Attorney General* v. *Roy Clarke* (2008) in the Republic of Zambia. It touches upon specific human rights such as freedom of the press and protection of the family, executive discretion in matters of national security and, above all, the power of the judiciary to correct executive orders taken to preserve peace and good order in the country.

In January 2004, Roy Clarke, a British citizen living in permanent residence in Zambia for more than 30 years, was served a deportation order by the Home Affairs Minister after he had written a column in *The Post* in which he had depicted the Zambian leadership as animals in a game park (Chan 2007). In an obvious parallel to George Orwell's *Animal Farm*, the leader in the piece was depicted as an elephant with a name referring to foolishness. The character was clearly meant to be identified as Levy Mwanawasa, the country's President, who had just visited a game park. Listening to their leader's Christmas message, familiar ministers emerged as long-fingered baboons, a red-lipped snake (in charge of legal reform), a knock-kneed giraffe (in charge of agriculture) and a hungry crocodile (in charge of child welfare). According to Home Affairs Minister Shikapwasha, the column could not be seen as a mere joke; rather, it represented an insult to the President and the whole nation. Based on his discretionary powers under the Immigration and Deportation Act, he issued a 24-hour deportation notice to Clarke, whose children and grandchildren were all living in the country as Zambian nationals. With his client in hiding, a lawyer secured an immediate stay against the order, pending an appeal. Although Minister Shikapwasha defended the government's verdict to revoke Clarke's residency status, the Lusaka High Court upheld Clarke's residency status. Three months later High Court Judge Phillip Musonda revoked the deportation order on the grounds that it had been illegal and unreasonable. The latter is particularly noteworthy because, in the jurisprudential consideration on which it is based, Lord Diplock (*Council of Civil Service Unions* v. *Minister for the Civil Service* 1985: 410–411) refers to "a decision which is so outrageous in its defiance of logic or accepted moral standards that no sensible person who had applied his mind to the question to be decided could have arrived at it".

The point here is that what in the common law is usually referred to as "Wednesbury unreasonableness" (*Associated Provincial Picture Houses* v. *Wednesbury Corporation* 1948) rests on the assumption that it is up to the subordinate body to which parliament has delegated certain discretionary powers to exercise that authority and not to the courts. Yet, what the judiciary should control is whether that other body has faithfully observed the parameters of the powers delegated to it. It is in this context that unreasonableness becomes a ground for review, as further specified in Lord Diplock's formula (quoted above). In respect of Minister Shikapwasha's decision to deport Roy Clarke, the question was whether any public officer in his right mind could consider a column intended to be satirical as a threat to the country's peace and good order. An earlier observation by Chief Justice Matthew Ngulube, in which he referred to the argument that illiterate people can easily misinterpret a cartoon as they cannot read the captions, is noteworthy in this connection:

> Illiteracy as we all know is a misfortune and not a privilege, and the standard to be applied in a case arising out of the written word is that of a reasonable reader, that is a literate reasonable person who can read the captions and relate pictures to their context. Any meanings assigned by an out-of-context illiterate imagination would not qualify as the reasonable understanding of

> the judicially acceptable reasonable average person who ordinarily reads newspapers.
>
> (*Sata* v. *Post Newspapers Limited and Another* 1992)

Almost four years after Judge Musonda's ruling, the Supreme Court in the final instance judged that unreasonableness did not apply as Zambia's cultural values and norms were based on respect for leaders, which did not allow for the kind of satire employed by Mr Clarke. The minister's decision was not upheld, however, as in the light of Clarke's family circumstances and the threat he represented to peace and good order in Zambia, it had to be regarded as a disproportional measure (*Attorney General* v. *Roy Clarke* 2008).

Thus, notwithstanding the self-restraint the common law requires of the judiciary, in deference to the decision of parliament to entrust the executive authority with its specific decision-making power, judicial review does imply some real remedies to challenge executive discretion. *Roy Clarke* shows how in a young nation-state like Zambia a balance of state powers is emerging into a local dynamics of the rule of law in which human rights obtain national incorporation.

The "internal" intricacies of state sovereignty

While the principal rule holds simply that for the execution of national sovereignty states maintain full authority, our review of cases emerging from the separation of state power into three branches of government illustrates the need for close observation of the often complicated interface of national sovereignty and international standards for the realisation of human rights.

In effect, human rights implementation always implies a power struggle that requires strategies combining international *downstream* efforts tuned to the relevance of universal standards and mechanisms in (unique) national settings (Figure I.3) with *upstream* action focusing on mobilisation of local agents of change (Figure I.4). Such strategies have to start from concrete "power and change" analyses in which national and international constraints and resources are plainly identified. Our review of the diversity of local dynamics in regard to sovereignty and the separation of powers has pointed to a distinct need to take account of the internal aspects of state sovereignty. Thus, in the jurisdiction of the United States we looked at shifting roles of both the judiciary and the legislature in the defence of individual liberties when faced with assertions of executive prerogative in respect of national security. Since 9/11 this struggle has been particularly concentrated on due process rights. While the basis for these internal dynamics of sovereignty is rooted in the rule of law, the relative significance of the distinct branches of state power emerges as closely linked to the operation of democracy as a set of arrangements for representative, accountable and participatory government.

If, however, in their exercise of sovereignty the executive and the legislature together overrule *erga omnes* obligations rooted in international human rights law, the national state nevertheless remains subject to international judicial review

(*Barcelona Traction, Light and Power Company, Limited (Belgium* v. *Spain)* 1964). Whereas this is commonly accepted today, enforcement of judgments pronounced in such cases continues to be generally weak. Indeed, even where international enforcement is strong, as in Europe's regional mechanism, "margin of appreciation" practices still limit the realisation of human rights protection by supranational means. Hence, a national dynamics of the rule of law that is linked to democratic checks and balances remains of utmost importance. It is in that setting that we shall now focus on the role of human rights principles in the quest for national remedies against violation of international human rights standards.

Judicial law development

"I'm a romantic optimist about the law", Lord Scarman (1986) said when his long period of service as a British law lord had come to an end. "I believe it can always be reformed to make it better". While such an outlook on law may be accepted from academic jurists as a rather harmless pastime, this tends to change when it is judges themselves who start "developing" the law into something "better". "Judicial activism" it is called, often pejoratively.

Actually, there are two distinct ways of understanding "judicial activism". First, the term may refer to deliberate attempts to influence judicial decision-making from a political angle. A primary observation in this respect is that this is not a prerogative of the left. In the United States, for example, there appears to be continuous political pressure from the right to get judges appointed who would judge from a partisan rightist perspective on issues such as abortion, capital punishment, and the role of international law in US national jurisdiction.[28] Political pressure on judicial decision-making is, however, not this book's focus, neither from left nor right. In contrast, the second way of understanding judicial activism is premised on judicial impartiality proceeding from a serious striving for judicial neutrality and objectivity. Accordingly, the "activist" judgments discussed here are of a different nature: an active attempt to ground judicial decisions in strong as well as sustainable notions of what is right. The challenging endeavour is to move law forward through a kind of global civilising process: a "universal legal advancement".[29]

Notably, in judicial practice judges are usually confronted with the need for substantive as above merely procedural legitimisation. Indeed, strict and complete legalism as a way of confronting judicial activism (in the first sense described above) has developed into a rather rare attitude, prevailing particularly in the United States, with Supreme Court Justices Scalia and Thomas as its major exponents. (Their "textualism" is based on a continuous attempt to trace the original "ordinary" meaning of statutory texts.) Yet, as recently concluded in a standard textbook (Thomas 2005: 3), the "belief that judges do not make law is hopelessly out of date. As Lord Reid famously said as long ago as 1972: 'We do not believe in fairy-tales anymore' ". Indeed, J.H.A. Lokin (1994) put it rather bluntly, the text of the law is no more than an empty covering, which is to receive its substance from the judge.

It was the eminent Dutch jurist Paul Scholten (1931) who introduced the term *law finding*, to be understood as the creative activity performed to unveil the hidden treasures of the law, hidden in texts and principles, through the art of interpretation. Lokin (1994) criticises that term precisely from an anti-legalist perspective: law is being created rather than merely found. Against Scholten (1931: 26–27), who had stated that every law *could* require interpretation, he quotes Ulpianus: *Quamvis sit manifestissimum edictum praetoris, attamen non est negligenda interpretatio eius*, implying that all laws *do* require interpretation, including those whose phrasing is unequivocal.[30]

A famous case in the Netherlands, illustrative of such law creation by the judiciary, is *Lindebaum* v. *Cohen* (1919). The legal question at issue in this case concerned the interpretation of unlawful conduct (*iniuria*) as a basis for extra-contractual damage compensation. In this early twentieth-century judgment, the Netherlands Supreme Court extended its interpretation of a tort beyond what had already been legally defined as unlawful, to "general standards of due care". Thus, the law of "torts", within which each distinct tort had been legally defined, became a law of tort that could in principle be invoked by anyone affected by unfairly inflicted damage: an evident example of judge-created law. Indeed, the case clearly illustrates how the range of legal protection was extended by recognising legitimate interests that had hitherto gone judicially unprotected. This, as will be further argued below, is the juridical core of the human rights idea: extending legal protection to all whose interests merit protection from a universal human dignity perspective.

In the art of law creation – as distinct from law-making, a term pertaining above all to legislators and their staff – it is in particular the British judge Lord Denning whose decisions received the qualification "activist".[31] His focus was on "the just result" while asserting "that he would search the case books, high and low, until he found the precedent or the principle that would achieve justice" (Kirby 1999a: 1). Notably, finding justice in a concrete case involves more than just equity in respect of the parties: the public-political community must be able to live with it as well. Judicial decisions, in other words, must not merely be legal in the sense that they are based on the law,[32] but also legitimate. Legitimacy, we recall, is a normative concept referring to decisions based on the right institutions and principles, due process and a socio-politically acceptable outcome (see above, p. 21) Accordingly, the term activist is used here as an affirmative label. It applies to judgments transcending "the law" as hitherto understood (*ius positivum*), from a civilisational perspective. The latter phrase is seen here as being linked to structural progress in the implementation of human rights.

The role of legal principles in judicial decision-making

In cases requiring substantive legitimisation, those well-established principles of law finding (the *regulae iuris*) have always played their part. It has been Ronald Dworkin (2006), in particular, who called the attention of his fellow jurists time and again to the inevitability of judicial law creation and, hence, the necessity for judges to be grounded not only in their understanding of legal systems, but also in "very abstract principles of political morality". In *Justice in Robes* Dworkin (2006: 56) states:

> My claim, to repeat, is that legal reasoning presupposes a vast domain of justification, including very abstract principles of political morality, that we tend to take that structure as much for granted as the engineer takes most of what she knows for granted, but that we might be forced to re-examine some part of the structure from time to time, though we can never be sure, in advance, when and how.

Notably, that need to transcend purely formal legality is nothing new. Through the ages substantial legitimisation has been enhanced by applying the old principles of law-finding: the *regulae iuris*. Those principles throw light upon concrete cases in which legal rules first have to be determined as applicable and then applied in line with a correct interpretation. As *maximae propositiones* these rules in interpretation rest on everyday common sense; as concise declarations of the demands of justice (*generalia iuris principia*) they are rooted in morality.[33] Often the *regulae* combine elements of both logic and fairness, illustrated, for example, by the rule that who carries the burden should also be entitled to the benefits.[34] Generally, their form tends to be short and succinct while their authority rests on past experience in law-finding. In the difficult task of attaching legal weight to the different interests involved, the *regulae* assist those charged with law-making as well as those responsible for law-finding in concrete cases.

These principles, then, exert an immediate appeal to both the heart and the mind. Hence, Baldus argued that a party in a court case who can invoke a *regula iuris* may be considered as being prima facie in the right (Stein 1966). While this could apparently already be said in the fourteenth century, the *regulae* have maintained their validity throughout history. For example, the stipulation that policies cannot be changed to another person's unfair detriment has acquired a modern translation in the principle of good government, which demands that expectations that have been justifiably raised cannot be ignored.[35] Scholten (1931) has typified such general principles of law as the desk light that may shine so unmistakably upon the case that what the ceiling light of statute book and precedent could not reveal suddenly becomes clearly visible.

Some *regulae* are quite precise, particularly those that pertain to due process. For example, the well known rule that not just one party, but both parties should be heard (*audi et alteram partem*), and the rule that people cannot be judges in their own case (*nemo iudex in sua propria causa*). Also, a rule of an obvious moral-political nature, which is common to many legal questions beyond contract law, is the requirement of good faith (*bona fides*). Other *regulae* are of a highly general character: e.g. the statement that where law prevails there is a remedy (*ubi ius ibi remedium*).[36] New principles follow particularly from the global human rights project. One could think here of the value of life per se, but also of norms underlying rights of a collective nature such as the right to self-determination, the right to development and the right to a healthy environment. In actual litigation, as we shall see, these "rights" often function as modern principles of law.

While most principles originate in Roman law, many have been incorporated in the *Corpus Iuris Canonici* as well. Yet, legal incorporation in recognised law books such as Dinus' treatise on the Rules of the Sext is not the essence of their legitimacy. What is important is not the formal source of a general rule of law, but its immediate appeal to the legal mind and the moral heart. Above all, the role of the principles lies in the need for legitimacy rather than pure legality. It is that evident "moral-political" (Dworkin 1993) connection to formal and substantive justice which can play such a significant part in judicial and administrative decision-making. As "the general principles of law recognised by civilised nations", the *regulae iuris* have been acknowledged as a source of law-finding for the International Court of Justice (United Nations 1946, ICJ Statute: Article 38[1] [c]). Apart from this formalised role, however, they tend to serve as guidelines in adjudication in general as well as in law-making and administration. In a Habermasean framework they may be seen as a mode of resistance by the life-world to rules-driven systems of jurisprudence. It is in this connection that the modern notion of the human being as *an individual with rights* may play its part.

Human rights as fundamental principles of law

At the root of human rights, we recall, lie two grand principles, one of a procedural and the other of a substantive nature: universal rights (and with that their inalienability) and universal human dignity. These two elements do not only play their part through incorporation in positive law or just vis-à-vis the state. Indeed, while the primary focus of the international project for the realisation of human rights used to be on ways of limiting and governing political power, today other institutions have come within its range of attention, including the corporate world. For instance, a "human rights approach" to poverty has now gained a place on the development agenda (see below, pp. 153–167). It is precisely in this context that, besides their original protective function as safeguards of individually obtained freedoms and entitlements against the state, human rights have come to play the transformative role already discussed above (see Table 1.1), namely, as catalysts for incorporation of hitherto unprotected interests in current public-political systems of protection, including the judicial system. The driving force in this respect is not so much positive human rights law – feebly grounded as this tends to be – but the human rights idea as expressed in principles, values and what may perhaps be regarded as an emerging "culture of rights".[37]

The spiritual source, so to speak, of such a culture lies in the fundamental belief, already set out in Chapter 1, that the protection of human dignity and equality is a responsibility of society at all its different layers and levels. This culture should theoretically limit and govern any use of power over human beings. However, assertions of crucial aspects of human rights such as their "inalienable" and "universal" features tend to meet with a great deal of practical resistance. Consequently, human rights implementation requires huge efforts. It is in such struggles that the judiciary has to play an obvious part by offering direct protection as well as fulfilling an exemplary (awareness-building) role.

In the comparative exploration of "activist" judgments that will be embarked on, our focus will be on the political morality of human rights as a driving force in judicial activism. It is assumed, in other words, that where the judiciary is "active" human rights may play their part as general principles of law, as distinct from rules already incorporated in positive law. Indeed, wherever power is executed and disputes arise, human rights may influence processes of judicial decision-making as well as their outcomes. "The language of human rights", Justice Bhagwati of the Indian Supreme Court (1989: 1) once observed, "carries great rhetorical force.... At the level of rhetoric, human rights have an image which is both morally compelling and attractively uncompromising". It is, particularly, the judiciary that may play an important part in translating this rhetoric into normative decisions affecting the lives of individual right-holders. Judges tend to reason in an evaluative manner, not so much oriented towards goals, but rather towards norms (Graver 1988). They judge facts in the light of set norms ("standards") while simultaneously weighing and balancing various interests and the values behind these against one another.

It is, indeed, against the background of judicial activism that the potential of human rights as a moral-political force is best illustrated. The perspective, however, is not the *creation* of law by the courts per se, but rather the ways and means in which the human rights idea has encouraged judges to make decisions that imply an overturning or advancement of "settled" law, thus providing real remedies against human rights violation. Notably, attention will be focused on the way in which human rights affect positive law in a manner different from the "normal" processes of international, regional and national standard-setting connected with the establishment of new supervisory institutions and mechanisms. Therefore, we shall not concentrate on characteristic international human rights cases, nor examine the case-law of typical human rights courts such as the European Court of Human Rights in Strasbourg. Instead, the focus is on major decisions by national courts on issues that were not generally regarded as human rights cases. In this endeavour, the exploration aims to be no more than an initial comparative overview, intended to illustrate a function of human rights that is not normally highlighted: namely, its role as an inspirational force towards "activist" judgments. Yet, the judicial potential illustrated here is of great significance, as it already reveals its capacity to induce law development founded squarely upon the two principal pillars underpinning the international quest for the realisation of human rights: universality and human dignity. The cases examined are intended to substantiate the hypothesis, namely, that notions underlying human rights protection such as universality and human dignity may play a significant part as modern *regulae iuris*.

In actual practice, judicial law development inspired by human rights principles is quite conspicuous, as will be demonstrated below. Yet, a caveat is appropriate: the cases reviewed are not intended to be read as harbingers of a worldwide trend, as that is not our point. What we intend to show is the great *potential* that universality and human dignity display as *regulae iuris* in the judicial development of national law. Accordingly, the cases serve to substantiate and illustrate our premise that even within the legal realm itself an analysis of the impact of human rights cannot be confined to positive human rights law and its application. The human rights idea, as a moral-political force based on the principal pillars of universality and human dignity, exerts a major influence on the processes inherent in judging. The "adventurous" judgments examined serve to illustrate that capability.

Adventurous judgments

In the following examination of cases, a distinction may be made between procedure and substance. First we shall look at cases in which the realm of protection is extended in such a way that *universally* adopted norms and standards, which were conventionally supposed to be inapplicable, are henceforth considered relevant. The second category of cases constitutes a manifestation of judicial legal development in the actual application of universal norms and principles in terms of judicially activated freedoms and entitlements. Here the core principle is inclusive *human dignity*.

Universal rights-based protection: upholding and incorporating international sources

Suppose settled law includes nothing to grant a remedy in a particular situation. This does not necessarily mean that the remedy is unavailable, but just that it has not succeeded in the past. Therefore, it will be necessary for the judge to embrace a morality of some sort to fill the gap (Dworkin 2006). The question, then, is where to look for sources.

Fairchild

The *Fairchild* case (*Fairchild* v. *Glenhaven Services Ltd and Others* 2002) in the United Kingdom is particularly remarkable as to the means by which the law lords struggled to find justice in a situation in which positive law impeded a remedy that would compensate victims of wrongful conduct. This was due to the element of causation that is required to be proven in torts cases. The injustice that they wished to avoid had to do with workers who had contracted mesothelioma after being wrongfully exposed to significant quantities of asbestos dust at different times by more than one employer or occupier of premises. Consequently, the person claiming compensation on behalf of a worker who had contracted the disease could not establish "on the balance of probabilities when it was he inhaled the asbestos fibre, or fibres, which caused a mesothelial cell in his pleura to become malignant", as the Court of Appeal had noted. The House of Lords overturned that decision, ruling that the worker or his relatives could sue any of those whose duty it had been to protect him, notwithstanding that he could not prove which exposure had caused the disease. Considerations on the part of the law lords included terms such as "recognising and righting wrongful conduct", and "a broader view of causation". "Any other outcome", Lord Nicholls observed, "would be deeply offensive to instinctive notions of what justice requires and fairness demands". Yet, despite a fairly clear moral imperative, the right outcome had to be argued in terms of established principles and procedures.

Significant as *Fairchild* may be regarding the right to health and responsibility for occupational disease, as well as in its discussion of causation, it is particularly remarkable regarding its law-finding methodology. Embracing a truly universal perspective, the law lords reviewed not only common law sources, but also case law from Austria, Germany, Greece, Italy, France, the Netherlands, Spain and Switzerland, noting that:

> The problem of attributing legal responsibility where a victim has suffered a legal wrong but cannot show which of several possible candidates (all in breach of duty) is the culprit who has caused him harm is one that has vexed jurists in many parts of the world for many years ... The texts show that, in a certain form, problems with unidentifiable wrongdoers had begun to exercise the minds of Roman jurists not later than the first century BC ... Julian considers whether someone "kills" a slave for these purposes if he mortally wounds him and later someone else attacks the slave who dies more quickly as a result. Julian takes the view, which was probably not shared by all the jurists, that both persons who attacked the slave should be liable for "killing" him.
>
> (*Fairchild* v. *Glenhaven Funeral Services Ltd and Others* 2002)[38]

Even among jurists, this type of openness to universality in law-finding is not generally accepted, closely connected as it is to judicial activism. For example, when the US Supreme Court engaged in a certain amount of comparative law-finding in *Lawrence* v. *Texas* (2003) in order to overturn its previous holding in *Bowers* v. *Hardwick* (1986) (upholding a law prohibiting sodomy in Georgia), Justice Scalia, in his dissent, depicted "these foreign views" as "meaningless dicta". Yet, as globalisation affects the practice and meaning of the law no less than myriad other cultural institutions (Auby 2003), the comparative method is unquestionably gaining ground.

Another issue with respect to the sources of judicial protection for individuals whose legal position appears to be weak is the extension of local sources of law to incorporate international law. We shall now look at a case where international law had not yet been locally incorporated through the traditional practice(s) of law-making, and yet played its jurisprudential part.

Basu (India)

The Supreme Court of India has already been known for a long time for its judicial activism, which has led it to truly "becom[e] the Supreme Court for Indians" (Baxi quoted in Bhagwati 1990: 111). It is evident that human rights function as a motivational force on the Court, as Justice Bhagwati, for one, has frequently underlined. Notably, in a speech at a human rights seminar in the Caribbean in 1989, he had already cited several cases in which human rights had been positivised by the Indian judiciary: for example, by establishing free legal aid for criminal defendants through an interpretation of the Indian constitution in conjunction with Article 2 (3)(a) taken together with Article 14 (3)(d) of the United Nations (1966a) Covenant on Civil and Political Rights (Bhagwati 1989). The case we shall now review, *Shri D.K. Basu* v. *State of West Bengal* (1996), stemmed from the acknowledged abuse of power structures in the Indian criminal law system in general and the mistreatment or torture of detainees while in police custody in particular. The question explicitly asked of the Court concerned the remedy for such abuses: what could be "just" compensation when one has been tortured or, even more horrid, died at the hands of the police? No more was requested of the judiciary than simply interpreting the term "compensation". However, the Court chose also to address the underlying issue of a person's rights when arrested. While other jurisdictions might have narrowly construed the task and decided only on the issue of compensation that had been submitted to their jurisdiction,[39] the Court here admirably chose to tackle the underlying issues, and ultimately issued reforms for the whole of the nation with the explicit purpose of realising the protetion of rights, which ultimately ensures the legitimacy of the entire endeavour.

The justification for that extensive ruling was to be found in the commonality of the problem across the states of India, as well as in the fundamental importance of protecting basic human dignity. The Court acknowledged the role of the Universal Declaration of Human Rights (UDHR) as well as India's own constitution in its reasoning, persuasively stating:

> Fundamental rights occupy a place of pride in the Indian Constitution. Article 21 provides "no person shall be deprived of his life or personal liberty except according to procedure established by law". Personal liberty thus, is a sacred and cherished right under the Constitution. The expression "life or personal liberty" has been held to include the right to live with human dignity and thus, it would also include within itself a guarantee, against torture and assault by the State or its functionaries.
>
> (Paragraph 17)

> The increasing incidence of torture and death in custody has assumed such alarming proportions that it is affecting the creditability of the Rule of Law and the administration of the criminal justice system. The community rightly feels perturbed. Society's cry for justice becomes louder.
>
> (Paragraph 18)

Before simply concluding that because human rights have been affirmatively adopted in the Indian constitution this judgment merely reflects conventional judicial interpretation, we have to pay attention to the compelling counter-argument of the state that through its police functionaries it is faced with the need to obtain useful information during interrogation after arrest; this, indeed, could prevent future criminal activity. Put differently, a balance was to be struck between, on the one hand, the personal rights and liberties of an arrested person, and, on the other hand, the interest of society as a whole in the maintenance of law and order. The Court responded as follows:

> Any form of torture or cruel, inhuman or degrading treatment would fall within the inhibition of Article 21 of the Constitution whether it occurs during investigation, interrogation or otherwise. If the functionaries of the Government become lawbreakers, it is bound to breed contempt for law and would encourage lawlessness and every man would have the tendency to become law unto himself thereby leading to anarchism. No civilised national can permit that to happen. Does a citizen shed off his fundamental right to life, the moment a policeman arrests him? Can the right to life of a citizen be put in abeyance on his arrest? These questions touch the spinal cord of human rights jurisprudence. The answer, indeed, has to be an emphatic "No". The precious right guaranteed by Article 21 of the Constitution of India cannot be denied to convicts, under trials, detainees and other prisoners in custody except according to the procedure established by law by placing such reasonable restrictions as are permitted by law.
>
> (Paragraph 22)

Therefore, although the question presented to the judiciary had merely been what financial remedies might exist for victims of police mistreatment, the Court chose to address the underlying problem and did so by formulating an awe-inspiring list of new requirements. No less than 11 procedural changes were handed down as obligations for every police department in the nation. These range from obliging arresting officers to wear clear insignia of identification to requiring all information from an arrest to be prominently displayed within 12 hours of the arrest. The changes were presented as requirements, with punitive measures attached in case of non-compliance. Even more astounding was that the scope of application of the Court's ruling extended beyond the police department, applying these new procedures to all governmental agencies with power to arrest or detain. This was indeed a clear example of judicial law creation inspired by the view that the principles of human rights should trump any *lex particularis*, thus enabling the Court to remedy the underlying problems which gave rise to the specific instance brought before it.

Obviously, judicial activism in the incorporation of human rights in positive law is possible only where the judiciary is independent, creative and committed to human rights. But even then, these rights will not lead to truly functioning freedoms and entitlements if the law does not reign supreme. It proved to be difficult, for example, to implement the Indian Supreme Court's condemnations of bondage in outlying areas in which feudal landlords, rather than the law, were in control. Thus, the dialectics of law and power are likely to pose even more serious challenges than just the dialectics of human rights and "settled" law (De Gaay Fortman 2001).

Inclusive human dignity: concrete recognition of freedoms and entitlements hitherto unacknowledged

While rights are a manifestation of the legal protection of interests, human rights, as we saw, are intended to protect fundamental human interests, namely, those that are directly connected to basic human dignity. It is crucial to acknowledge, in the context of judicial law development, that human dignity presupposes certain freedoms and entitlements. Fundamental freedoms, we recall, are presumed to be protected by civil and political rights, whereas basic entitlements relate to the protection of claims essential to the sustenance of daily livelihood. Both categories of rights face the problem that they are declared rather than conclusive in nature. Yet, in the struggle to realise affirmative rights, the judiciary has a primary part to play. In this respect, the Indian case discussed above serves as a good example. The cases reviewed below give some indication of the concrete consequences of the general recognition of inclusive human dignity as a grand principle of law.

Hussain (India)

An example of an Indian judgment with substantial implications in respect of people's entitlement positions is *F.K. Hussain* v. *Union of India* (1990). The case was brought in response to a writ petition to stop the mechanical pumping of potent ground water from the coral islands of Lakshadweep as this would upset the fresh water equilibrium leading to salinity in the available water resources. The findings of the Judge, Chettur Sankaran Nair, of the High Court of Kerala, indicated a strong disposition to preserve ground water as a natural resource, protected by the human right to life. The writ was brought under Article 21 of the Indian constitution, already quoted above: "no person shall be deprived of his life or personal liberty except according to procedure established by law."

The judge first established that this was a new type of conflict, with two competing principles: the need for development and the necessity of preserving limited resources. Scientific research seemed to maintain deferential power, and the competing claims both relied on findings. The Court appeared to favour the research indicating the need to preserve ground water as a seriously limited natural resource:

> The Executive Government has onerous responsibilities in the matter of providing civic amenities. The Technocrat too has his role to play, in view of

> the impact the matter has on environmental and hydrogeological concerns. There must be an effective and wholesome interdisciplinary interaction. At once, the administrative agency cannot be permitted to function in such a manner as to make inroads into the fundamental right under Article 21. The right to life is much more than the right to animal existence and its attributes are manifold, a life itself. A prioritisation of human needs as a new value system has been recognised in these areas. The right to sweet water, and the right to free air, are attributes of the right to life, for these are the basic elements that sustain life itself.

The language shows a strong preference to maintain a right to sweet and hence potable water, here interpreted as a collective human right.[40] Since development and the pressure on resources it inherently creates are also compelling interests, one could indeed speak of significant development of the law by the judiciary when they held that the interest of citizens in having access to potable water outweighed the interest in development. Human rights, as in this case, must not only be regarded as purely subjective rights – to be enforced through claims based on entitlements deriving from them – but also as general principles of justice. Even in this latter role they may play a part in adjudication, not as a direct basis for the acceptance of certain claims, but to shed light upon a case, in the same way in which the old *regulae iuris* perform that function.

To further illustrate the significance of the role of human rights as general principles in judicial interpretation, let us take, for example, the damages suffered by small fishermen when, in the name of development, big trawlers are introduced that go into the shallow waters, destroying the breeding grounds for the fish that form the basis of their livelihoods. It is true that in contentious action these people may fail to get recognition of claims based on a subjective "right to development" as declared by the UN General Assembly (1986), but in concrete litigation procedures that right to development may well be invoked in order to determine responsibility for a tort.[41]

Boehm (USA)

Remarkably, while the United States has not ratified the United Nations Convention on Economic, Social and Cultural Rights (UNCESCR), let alone incorporated the relevant rights into its national legal system,[42] in the American jurisdiction the concept of social rights appears to play its part too. In the Californian case of *Boehm* v. *Superior Court* (1986), for example,[43] the question was what aspects of human welfare and dignity a county administration had to take into account in determining the level of welfare benefits due to those in need of assistance. The county first attempted to reduce the benefits without any justification at all, an action which the courts enjoined as arbitrary and capricious. The County Administration responded by reducing the General Assistance welfare payments (GA) based on two studies that merely assessed the payments' sufficiency in light of subsistence needs for food and shelter. On a second appeal, the reduction in benefits was found to be arbitrary and capricious because the studies failed to address basic needs beyond food and shelter, such as clothing, transportation and access to medical treatment. The Court's opinion, written by Judge Hamlin, mandates that the GA code should be liberally construed to ensure the protection of basic human dignity: "The evolution of public welfare has been from public 'charity' toward social justice. Courts should facilitate such development by an enlightened and liberal interpretation of all welfare laws" (*Boehm* v. *Superior Court* 1986: 500–501).

> Indeed, it defies common sense and all notions of human dignity to exclude from minimum subsistence allowances for clothing, transportation and medical care. Such allowances are essential and necessary to "encourage [self-respect and] self-reliance" ... in a "humane" manner consistent with modern standards. Without a clothing allowance, recipients must wear tattered clothing and worn out shoes. The lack of adequate and decent clothing and essential transportation is damaging both to recipients' self-respect and their ability to obtain employment. Finally, to leave recipients without minimum medical assistance is inhumane and shocking to the conscience.
>
> (*Boehm* v. *Superior Court* 1986: 502)

This forceful reprimand to the county and the lower court is preceded by a reference to Article 25 of the UDHR (right to a decent living standard), even though in the United States the legal stature of the UDHR tends to be generally in doubt, while the articles on economic and social rights are definitely not considered to be *ius cogens*.

The opinion acknowledges the ever-present dilemma of limited government resources versus the need to provide for the deprived. Judge Hamlin disposes of this contention in favour of the state's responsibility in providing for the poor by liberally construing the laws established for their relief: "budgetary constraints cannot justify excluding from minimum subsistence grants to the indigent allowance for each of the basic necessities of life: food, housing (including utilities), clothing, transportation, and medical care" (*Boehm* v. *Superior Court* 1986: 503).

The case resulted in a preliminary injunction and retroactive pay for the petitioners as well as a remand commanding the lower court to instruct the county to complete a study on indigent relief incorporating the extended list of necessary benefits. The lower court was also instructed to determine whether the case should become a *class action suit*, to ensure justice for all those affected by the GA reduction. Notably, after this case the relevant legislature changed the law to reflect the previously omitted necessities of life.

Treatment Action Campaign (South Africa)

An exemplary South African case, in which the Constitutional Court goes extraordinarily far in the type of injunctions it issues, is *Treatment Action Campaign and Others* v. *Minister of Health and Others* (2002). It concerned

Nevirapine, an anti-retroviral drug that helps to reduce the risk of HIV/AIDS being spread at birth from mothers to newborn children. The government had limited its use to two research and training sites per province, denying distribution of the drug at public health sector hospitals. The most needy rural populations felt the greatest impact of this restriction. The High Court ruled that this action was unreasonable under the relevant provisions of the Bill of Rights. Specifically, section 27(1)(a) guarantees a right to adequate health-care for all, and section 28(1)(c) guarantees the same, especially for children. The government appealed the High Court's decision to the Constitutional Court. In fact, the argument was reducible to a judgment on the applicability of section 27(2) of the Bill of Rights – limiting the action constitutionally required of the government via language such as "reasonable" and "within available resources" – to the basic right to health-care services enshrined in section 27(1)(a).

Once again, the debate can be viewed through the lens of the separation of powers. Should the judiciary defer to the other branches that their efforts are reasonable, or should independent criteria and judgment be applied? The Court, issuing the decision *en banc*, forcefully maintained that it possessed the authority to be "active":

> This Court has made it clear on more than one occasion that although there are no bright lines that separate the roles of the legislature, the executive and the courts from one another, there are certain matters that are pre-eminently within the domain of one or other of the arms of government and not the others. All arms of government should be sensitive to and respect this separation. This does not mean, however, that courts cannot or should not make orders that have an impact on policy.
>
> (*Treatment Action Campaign and Others* v. *Minister of Health and Others* 2002: Paragraph 98)

> A dispute concerning socio-economic rights is thus likely to require a court to evaluate state policy and to give judgment on whether or not it is consistent with the Constitution … Section 38 of the Constitution contemplates that where it is established that a right in the Bill of Rights has been infringed a court will grant "appropriate relief." It has wide powers to do so and in addition to the declaration that it is obliged to make in terms of section 172(1)(a) a court may also "make any order that is just and equitable."
>
> (*Treatment Action Campaign and Others* v. *Minister of Health and Others* 2002: Paragraph 101)

With this justification, the Court proceeded to order the removal of the restrictions on the distribution of Nevirapine. Furthermore, the Court used this rationale to further address the underlying system, and in so doing ordered the government to devise and implement a programme "to realise progressively the rights of pregnant women and their newborn children to have access to health services to combat mother-to-child transmission of HIV" (*Treatment Action*

Campaign and Others v. *Minister of Health and Others* 2002: Paragraph 135). Here, the underlying concept of human dignity through human rights manifests itself in the decision of the Court.[44]

Delhi Pollution (India)

In India, the Supreme Court's firm stand on the use of green fuel ended a dispute between environmentalists and bus owners, who had the backing of corporate and political lobbies. In a decision taken in 1998, subsequent to public interest litigation (PIL),[45] the Court had issued a mandatory order for public transport to switch to compressed natural gas (CNG) "to improve the air quality in this choking city of 15 million" (Khan 2002). Time and again, both the administration and the private owners of buses used for public transport had pressed for extensions of the period in which they had to switch to "clean fuel", which does not cause pollution or otherwise injure health. In early 2001, the Court appeared to be fed up with vested interests and the way they argued their case:

> We are conscious of the fact that due to lack of effective action taken by the private bus operators and also by the governmental authorities with effect from 1.4.2001 inconvenience is likely to be caused to the commuting public, including the school children who use the city buses, but, this "urban chaos", (to use the expression used by the Administration) which may arise as a result of not extending the deadline fixed by this Court is a creation of the private operators and the administration and they have only themselves to thank for it. They are accountable to the commuting public for creating this situation. The administration does not admit its "lapses" but the learned Additional Solicitor General has time and again submitted for their lapses "let the commuting public not suffer". It appears to be an argument of despair.
>
> (Supreme Court of India 2001)

Consequently, no extension was granted beyond 1 April 2001, albeit with some relaxations for those who had already started a process of conversion. The transport department had to see to it that these concessions were not abused. As 2002 came to a close, all diesel buses had been converted to CNG and air pollution levels were considerably lower. In 2003 Delhi won the US Department of Energy's first "Clean Cities International Partner of the Year Award" for its "bold efforts to curb air pollution and support alternative fuel initiatives". Indeed, the entire city had suffered, listed as it used to be among the ten most polluted cities of the world, with vehicles accounting for more than 70 per cent of the polluting emissions.

Activism abounds! The way in which the judiciary confronted the administration with a mandatory order that left hardly any room for executive discretion in determining and executing policy is striking by itself. Still more interesting, within the context of the present inquiry, is the subject matter proper: a question concerning "the right to a healthy environment". Legally weak as this collective right might be,[46] in India since the Bhopal tragedy and its disgraceful legal aftermath it has acquired concrete significance in efforts to protect whole communities against pollution and other types of environmental damage. This is done in the judicial context through a rather broad interpretation of Article 21 of the Indian constitution on the right to life, while through public international law, cases can easily be presented for adjudication at the highest level. In this connection the collective right to a healthy environment may, indeed, be regarded as a modern *regula iuris*, throwing light on the meaning of Article 21 in concrete situations of environmental damage.

While praising such judgments from a human rights perspective, one should be careful, however, not to embrace an illusionary instrumentalism in the sense of a belief in law as an instrument of social change. Where the law is changed and rigorously applied, legal subjects may also change albeit in a different direction than had been intended. This might be called side law: regulation with unintended side-effects. Thus, whereas buses in New Delhi run on CNG today, private cars can still run on highly polluting fuel. Indeed, a disproportional shift to private transport, still running on petrol and gasoline, was evidently noticeable. Notably, in respect of sustainability pricing policies may function as an easier instrument than public interest litigation.

An emerging human rights culture?

In countries such as India and South Africa, human rights have been strongly incorporated into the national legal system, including the constitution, while an active judiciary demonstrates the great potential of judicial sensitivity to interests protected by internationally accepted human rights standards, even though not yet part of the country's *ius positivum*. Moreover, albeit perhaps in less spectacular ways, other judiciaries have also shown that they have been inspired by the worldwide need to extend the realm of interests to which judicial protection is given to include all interests that closely relate to basic human dignity. As *Boehm* demonstrated, even judicial decision-making in the United States, where the legal status of international human rights norms is in question, can reflect substantial recognition of basic entitlements based on inclusive dignity as a grand principle of law. Another way in which a judicial human rights culture is actually becoming discernible is through an evident reluctance to declare petitioners unqualified in cases involving evident injustices even when pure legal reasoning could easily substantiate such a formal decision. In the United States, *Hamdi* and *Hamdan* are cases in point. Also worth noting is the evident extension of legal sources in processes of judicial law creation in which the justice issue is unequivocal. *Fairchild* in the United Kingdom illustrates contemporary globalisation in law-creating methodologies.

Paradoxically, it is precisely vague and undefined notions and formulations that would seem to influence judicial decision-making as principles of law, comparable to the old *regulae iuris* in the sense of *generalia iuris principia*. Values behind terms such as "universal" and "inalienable" actually – and of course to a much larger extent potentially – influence judicial decision-making particularly when the judiciary faces executive attempts to restrict its role in the protection of inclusive human dignity. Indeed, when it comes to the global plague of us–them divides, it is the judiciary in particular whose armoury calls for the human rights weapon of "everyone", related as that is to the grand principle of "human dignity".

Some caution is appropriate, lest one become carried away with jurisprudential idealism. Although rights are abstract acknowledgements of claims in the sense of a general commitment to offer judicial protection for their realisation, the world remains full of denials of claims founded upon universal freedoms and basic entitlements. Indeed, while the whole idea of rights is based upon the expectation that evident violations would lead to contentious action resulting in redress, in failed, failing and dictatorially-ruled states human rights often remain without effective remedies. Hence, the primary struggle remains for the rule of law to be established as a public-political underpinning at the global, regional, national and local levels of execution of power. Indeed, it would be an illusion to think that major judicial progress in the implementation of human rights could be made while realities as experienced by people at the grassroots level reflect views closely approaching the old *Rex est Lex*. As D.L. Sheth (1990: 73), for one, has observed concerning the law in India, a country that knows the blessing of a legal superstructure and which can be considered "progressive" both in letter and spirit, "it is the law operating at the grassroots that regularly undermines the rights of the citizens". Obviously, then, a judiciary committed to the human rights venture and convinced of its basic ideas is not to be regarded as a substitute for a human rights culture at all levels of decision-making. Upstream struggles for the actual realisation of people's fundamental freedoms and basic entitlements thus remain essential. In countries in which there is no adequate basis for judicial action such struggles will take a primarily political character.

Finally, the role of collective rights in judicial legal development appears, remarkably, to be on the rise. Although scarcely translated into hard, positive law, they may nevertheless acquire concrete meaning in judicial interpretation. Thus the right to a healthy environment, which has not been incorporated in firm legal texts, still appears to function as a general principle in judicial decision-making. Indeed, the human rights idea is more duty-oriented than is often realised, giving these rights a substantial role in upstream processes of acquiring concrete freedoms and entitlements, even against adverse forces that manifest themselves on the part of both the state and the corporate world. Cases reviewed in this chapter have illustrated how an active judiciary may support those involved in uphill struggles to acquire freedoms and entitlements formally protected by human rights, but not yet realised. What is needed, to quote Bhagwati once more, is a judicial awareness that "the violation of the human rights of the poor is caused mostly by unjust social and economic structures" (Bhagwati 1990: 106). Apart from knowing the law, in other words, an active judiciary must have a capacity for discerning injustice. The Supreme Court of India is itself living testimony to that contention. Yet, its judgments are far from self-executing. Hence, next to an active judiciary a strong society, pressing for the execution of human rights-based judgments, is another evident necessity.

3 Global realities

Conflict and confrontation

Justice and peace embrace each other.

Psalm 85: 10

The United States and the United Nations

In respect of global politics and international affairs, the first decade of the twenty-first century has been a time of serious controversy and polarisation. It began with the election of George W. Bush to the United States presidency at the end of the year 2000. Soon thereafter, Al Qaeda-trained terrorists attacked the World Trade Center in New York, spurring an American invasion into Afghanistan to deprive Al Qaeda of its home base. This mission found ample international approval. Yet, when the Bush administration threatened to invade Iraq[1] as the next phase in its "war on terror", the UN Security Council did not come forward with an unequivocal endorsement. During those deliberations in early 2003, Richard Perle, who chaired the US Defense Policy Board at the time, crystallised the American position by exclaiming "the United Nations is dead".

Such a pronouncement on the United Nations is not new. For eager supporters of an aggressive and militarised policy of international peace enforcement – peace by international use of force wherever required – the organisation had already fallen short in 1956 when it failed to put an end to the Soviet occupation of Hungary. Serious disappointments would follow: Tibet, Czechoslovakia, Poland, Afghanistan, East Timor, Rwanda, Darfur, to mention just a few. The United Nation's principal mission has always been international security in its prime meaning of avoiding war, while all that refers to "positive peace" in the sense of peace with justice has been seen as subservient to that strategic thrust. It was only after the end of the Cold War that some new optimism could arise as to a corrective role of the UN itself in cases of major aggression and grossly oppressive regimes. But then followed the disappointing 1990s: a period of missed opportunities.

The UN debate preceding the US invasion of Iraq was striking in that the United States – usually "realist" in its resistance to using international force to enforce "positive" peace – now ironically employed the "idealistic" peace enforcement discourse to declare the UN to be dead, again. It is true, of course, that Saddam Hussein constituted "a major dilemma to the international community", as the British Prime Minister Tony Blair put it to the House of Commons. However, in such dilemmas between human rights, democracy and disarmament on the one hand, and international security on the other, it had always been the latter that tipped the balance towards military action. This was probably in line with the intentions of the 51 states that had signed the Charter of the United Nations on 24 October 1945: a Security Council with much more power than the "softie" Council of the League of Nations, but with the big five countries also given veto rights as a guarantee against the use of such powers in a way that could endanger world peace. The predominant desire to militarily enforce only "negative peace", in other words, is grounded in that primary emotion of 1945: "Never Again!"[2]

Yet, the Iraq invasion cannot simply be interpreted as a victory of American peace idealists as against the realism of a Security Council in line with the UN's founders. One might rather speak of a new kind of realism, belligerently based on unilateral economic interests – oil supply to the North – but, above all, originating from a unipolar view on the exercise of power. In the Project for the New American Century's statement of principles (1997), men like Dick Cheney, Donald Rumsfeld and Paul Wolfowitz had already explicitly endorsed this new American realism. For example, the statement of principles issued an appeal "to accept responsibility for America's unique role in preserving and extending an international order friendly to our security, our prosperity, and our principles" (Project for the New American Century 1997). In line with this declaration, George W. Bush (2002) announced in his State of the Union message that his presidential doctrine was based on the following three principles: active global American leadership, regime change in case of "rogue" states, and global promotion of neo-liberal democracy. During his entire presidency, the actions of the United States conformed to those principles; showing time and again that – admittedly not unlike other member-states – the US government was with the UN only when it believed that its best interests were being served. Consider, for example, the negative stance of the United States with regard to the Kyoto Protocol on climate change and the International Criminal Court. Bypassing the Security Council in a "pre-emptive war" with a "rogue" state in the Middle East also fits into that picture. Above all, however, in its forceful opposition to the already heavily weakened Iraqi state, Bush *et al.* enjoyed an excellent opportunity to demonstrate American supremacy as the unipolar foundation of a new international political order.

In international circles reference is sometimes made to a *Pax Americana*, inspiring comparisons with the Pax Romana at the start of the first millennium and the Pax Britannica in the nineteenth century. Notably, these empires ruled with much brutality, including low-scale war across most of the known world, thus achieving a kind of "negative half-peace", ironically called *pax*. The obsession of the New American Century thinkers with "axes of evil" and regime change, however, principally implied full-fledged war: a series of *Bella*

Americana. Indeed, since 2001 the United States has considered itself as being in a perpetual state of war.[3]

The attitude of America's British ally in this endeavour was: "If you can't beat them, join them!" While this was not Prime Minister Tony Blair's official political line – which shifted from the dangers of weapons of mass destruction deployable within 45 minutes to justified war against regimes that cause their own subjects intolerable suffering – it would at least be a strategy one could follow. In the twenty-first century US military supremacy is indeed a fact of life and the only way to contain its consequences with regard to the international political order would be by staying together in one (Atlantic) alliance. Unfortunately, however, it was not the coalition that dictated policy on Iraq, but the mission itself: "the mission must determine the coalition, the coalition must not determine the mission" said Defense Secretary Donald Rumsfeld in 2002 (quoted in Van Ham 2003). This was merely an oblique way of saying that the United States called the shots. Illustratively, when Blair faced trouble in his British parliament, Rumsfeld rushed to point to the possibility of "going it alone". In such instances, even NATO was seen by the Bush administration as a possible impediment to the necessary flexibility. As for the US attitude towards the European Union, a senior State Department official (2003; quoted in Garton Ash 2003) declared that "disaggregation" (breaking European unity) was proclaimed to be the core of US foreign policy.

In this respect, it is worth pointing out that the international community as such is an abstraction. In other words, there is no legal entity or person by that name. For certain purposes, there is little doubt that the United Nations, which consists of almost all the states in the world, reflects the views of or acts done in the name of its member states, and to that extent represents a formal international community. But whether it does so substantially depends upon the actual power relations. There have been notable cases where the United Nations has failed to act when confronted with situations, which on any view are of general concern, while in some instances these constitute an affront to "the conscience of humankind".[4] It is, indeed, difficult to accept that the states and peoples of the world are now in a position where their legitimate collective concerns as to particular conduct on the part of other states are to be channelled exclusively through the United Nations.

In giving extensive powers and functions to the United Nations, and a limited monopoly on the use of force, the states and the peoples invoked in the Charter did not entirely give up their individual capacity to act. "World peace through world law" (Clark and Sohn 1958) is, indeed, not yet and most probably never will be a fully available option. Formation and execution of power for the sake of security without a solid legal base remains inevitable, especially in a global context. Yet, the point is that whenever that takes place, its objectives and focus have to be questioned continuously – within and without the United Nations – while a genuine effort has to be made to tie the use of not only political, but also military and economic power, to international legal norms. As formation and execution of global power cannot yet be based on principles of representative democracy, power sharing constitutes the next best alternative. Essential in this respect is the incorporation in decision-making of not primarily "the willing", but precisely those constituent parts of international opinion-making that hold different views. The consideration and incorporation of alternative viewpoints is precisely at the centre of global legitimisation that is, ultimately, the UN's central role. Military power may, indeed, provide security, but it can also attract danger and lead to new threats (De Gaay Fortman, W.F. 1966: 151), as illustrated rather horrendously indeed in post-war Iraq.

The contest for international legitimacy

The price extracted from other countries for the "join them" formula was an official endorsement of the Bush administration's drive to war. We are touching upon a complicated notion here, and one that in international debate is often overlooked. Even when power is "a fact of life", it is still confronted with the need for reception by those affected by its execution. The ruled, in other words, have to accept the rule of the rulers. George W. Bush *et al.* recognised this; hence the search for a "coalition of the willing"; the "embedding" of journalists in the US war machine; the fabrication of weapons of mass destruction. Legitimacy is, indeed, the inescapable condition for power without repression of the ruler's own people; and in our modern world that requires constant efforts at persuasion.

The legitimisation effort of the Bush administration appeared to be focused on a combination of ideological persuasion – the good guys versus the bad guys, the "clash of civilisations" – and an emphasis on the right outcome: "all's well that ends well". Legitimacy, recall, is a matter of three requisites: the right principles and institutions, the right processes, and the right outcomes.[5] Leaving process and outcome to the side now and focusing on principles, after 9/11 the US leadership no longer appeared to recognise the United Nations' Charter as the International Constitution. Here, from a human rights realisation perspective, a battle on principles is inescapable. International law, as incorporated in the Charter of the United Nations and further developed through decades of UN practice, is based on the primary principle of non-intervention by states (UN Charter, Article 2 [4]). Notwithstanding the international character of human rights obligations as *obligationes erga omnes* (ICJ 1964), in the international legal order humanitarian intervention cannot be based on unilateralist action.[6] It is, notably, the principles of the rule of law, so vigorously advocated in the United States internally, that have to be extended to global forms of governance: limited government, government by law, independent judging and respect for rights, both of individuals and of groups.

This political-philosophical confrontation between the United Nations and the "New American Century" position to which the Bush administration related rather closely, based as that used to be on the *wrong* (self-framed) principles, became part of the daily political debate within the United States itself. "America in the eyes of the rest of the world" figured prominently in Barack Obama's election platform. Europe, the birthplace of international law, also joined in, refuting the attempts at its "disaggregation". International civil society played its part, too.

In respect of the principles, it might further be said that today they are no less important to the international corporate world than to the international political world. International business used to understand genuine universality as associated with market related rights and values rather than being rooted in the fundamental freedoms and entitlements that follow from the Universal Declaration of Human Rights. This *People* deficit in the new triple value approach of the global corporate world – People, Planet, Profit – is now part of the agenda not just of the NGO community at the World Social Forum, but also at the international business-oriented World Economic Forum. An increasing focus on "corporate responsibility" is, indeed, gaining ground, particularly after the global financial crisis of 2008 broke out. (The complete absence of structural connections between these two principal global fora is, by the way, remarkable.)

American exceptionalism

The term "exceptionalism" may be used to describe any attempt to exempt citizens and institutions from democratic public-political authority and its laws, policies and actual decisions, based on assumed incompatibility with divine principles. While it is widespread in our world today, the United States is the familiar example of state-based exceptionalism.

The constant in US foreign policy

US exceptionalism, in respect of the international legal order and its effect on US foreign policy, is based on a combination of three elements: hegemony (and with that the idea of expansion), unilateralism ("going it alone") and pre-emptive strike (see above, Chapter 2, p. 48 and note 16). While it may well be argued that George W. Bush has distorted the notion of pre-emption (responding with a military attack to an immediate threat that could in no other way be dealt with) into aggressive prevention (responding militarily to future threats before these have manifested themselves as imminent), neither unilateralism nor hegemony are themselves exclusive to the Republican Party but reflect, rather, a general mindset in the US decision-making process. If there is one constant in US foreign policy, it is found in affirmations of this tripartite form of exceptionalism, especially in the aftermath of 9/11. Despite campaign rhetoric and debate over the "war on terror", the theme itself and its implied dissociation from international law remain relatively undisputed.

To illuminate this basic fact it is worth reviewing some basic US history. Throughout the nineteenth century, the main foreign policy controversy in US politics was actually an economic matter, namely the rate of tariffs on imports. The fundamental question of protectionism and the role of foreign capital were major concerns dividing the Democratic and Republican parties. It is also important to recall that the United States constitution, with its division of powers between the judicial, legislative and executive branches of the federal government, establishes that the executive branch set the foreign policy agenda. As "Commander in Chief" the President's main job is to provide for national security. While this may seem obvious, it plays a major part in how the Congress defers to the executive in matters of homeland security and the response to the terrorist threat following the events of 9/11. Americans expect their President to lead the country when it comes to issues of war and peace and the safety of the nation. When Americans evaluate presidential candidates, a very important qualification is strong leadership.

The constitution, however, also reserves an essential foreign policy role for the US Senate. Criticising former President George W. Bush for not signing the Kyoto Protocol, for example, it should be kept in mind that during the term of his predecessor, President Clinton, the Senate passed a resolution against the climate treaty by a vote of 95–0. Since the Senate must approve treaties by a two-thirds majority, it is clear that the impact of treaties on the domestic economy (and on Senators' re-election prospects) can outweigh foreign policy considerations.

Notably, the most dramatic example of the Senate's role in US foreign policy came during the period after the First World War. President Wilson, who had campaigned in 1916 on the slogan "he kept us out of war", failed to secure Senate approval for the key element of the post-war settlement, the League of Nations treaty. In part, this resulted from the personal animosity between Wilson, a Democrat, and Senator Lodge, a Republican from Massachusetts, the Senate majority leader. Wilson elected not to take any senior Republican leaders to the Paris peace talks after the war and the issue of the post-war role of the United States in the world became a partisan political issue.

Partially as a result of this bitter experience, a bipartisan consensus emerged during and after the Second World War. Senator Vandenberg, also Republican and Chairman of the Senate Foreign Relations Committee during the Truman presidency, made the famous statement that "politics stopped at the water's edge", implying that foreign policy was not to be a partisan issue. The risks to the nation's interests of having an incoherent and unreliable foreign policy – especially during the Cold War – outweighed the potential political gains.

To say that during the Cold War US foreign policy was bipartisan is, of course, not entirely accurate. The virulent anti-communism of the McCarthy period had more to do with domestic politics than foreign policy but clearly demonstrates a partisan element to the national security debate. Foreign policy differences also played a major part in presidential elections. For example, Eisenhower campaigned on a peace platform during the Korean War, and Kennedy argued the Republicans had paid insufficient attention to national defence, accusing his opponents of allowing a "missile gap" to develop between the United States and the Soviet Union. It is nevertheless accurate to say that there was no fundamental difference between Democratic and Republican foreign policy during the 1950s. Indeed, contrary to the presumed positions of his party, the United States under Kennedy pursued a much more aggressive foreign policy which in fact led to the Vietnam engagement.

Observably, then, continuity characterises US foreign policy more than disunity or changes of direction. Even the popular division of US policy into "multilateral" periods or "unilateral" periods is misleading. The real division in US foreign policy is between internationalists and isolationists and the internationalists have dominated both parties for a long time. The United States has traditionally viewed its national interests as consistent with the pursuit of global stability and taken a practical approach to this overriding goal. When the United States can obtain international support to this end, all the better; when it cannot, no major obstacle is presented so long as there is support in Congress for a particular course of action and it is consistent with national security. So against this backdrop, what role could the international community play in influencing the direction of US foreign policy towards accepting the constraints of international law? A prerequisite to answering this question is to understand the strategic culture within which the US foreign policy just described is formed.

Strategic culture

It is in politics that cultural conversations become most explicit: what ends should the nation pursue? What means should it use? On a spectrum of conversational explicitness, foreign policy is at the very high end because it concerns relations with outgroups, i.e. groups that serve the dual purpose of acting as a foil for national identity (we are not like them) and as a threat to national identity (we must resist becoming like them). Suffice it to say that it is only through definitions of the "other" that we can carve out a distinctive niche for ourselves (being us because we are not them).

Understanding US strategic culture – where strategic culture can be defined as a people's distinctive style of thinking and dealing with the problems of national security – is of course a crucial step in discussions of global security because of the nation's military and economic impact. Strategic culture, more often than not, is couched in explanations of war and conflict. It is fuelled by the construction and maintenance of identity boundaries and, as was indicated above, it invites a bipartisan approach in the determination of critical decisions in foreign policy. The stars and stripes on the lapels of both former President Bush and his successor Obama symbolised trust in "that greatest nation on earth". Notably, Bill Clinton already saw the United States standing alone as: "the world's indispensable nation".[7] "The President's job", Bush said in the context of his successful campaign for re-election in 2004, "is not to take an international poll; the President's job is to defend America". Such rhetoric, with its real world results, grows out of a phenomenon that Bill Clinton identified: in times of crisis and insecurity the American people want a leader that is "strong and wrong" rather than one who is "weak and right".

The American drive to construct a supra-global national identity may well relate to the lack of primordial identity in a settlers' society. In this connection, there is a uniquely American approach to strategy. But is this strategic culture predicated on deeply rooted cultural traits embedded in the American polity (read "American exceptionalism"), in a more short-term, secular historical experience devoid of the cultural element, or in a fusion of both? Strategic culture in the American context, it seems, is more the product of a 'micro culture' at work in the foreign policy circles than any meaningful identity crisis at the root of American society.

The American foreign policy establishment has traditionally underestimated and at times ignored the importance of cultural influence when dealing with the threats and opportunities of the world around them. American ethnocentrism at the foreign policy level is precisely the result of this failure to understand the value systems and cultural proclivities, indicia that could help to predict the tendencies of both their allies and enemies. It was during the Cold War that the need first arose to conceptualise strategic culture as an instrument of analysis. But while it could be argued that the constraints of bipolar rivalry largely nullified the domestic idiosyncrasies of nations, the reality today makes analysis of (American) strategic culture a major priority: the end of the Cold War logically allowed more artificial strategic cultures to give way to more culturally rooted ones, and hence it has become increasingly difficult to predict patterns of interaction in the international arena without examining national security and foreign policy in the framework of cultural influence. However, and this is the critical point in the framework of international security, a culturally rooted strategic focus is predicated on national security imperatives, and not *civilisational* ones.

The disturbing linkage between socio-political naiveté and socio-political power became the underpinning of American politics when the Bush administration quickly opted in the aftermath of 9/11 for an overly simplistic "us versus them" dualism ("Whoever is not for us is against us"![8]), which they immediately translated into the latest chapter of the story of "good against evil". Any attempt to analyse the causes of the 9/11 attacks through self-examination was seen as supporting the "enemy", and those who suggested such analysis were vilified and branded "unpatriotic". Lamentably, the United States has lost the moral ascendancy it inadvertently gained in the immediacy of the attacks and frittered away the opportunity to build a genuine domestic and foreign coalition that could have so easily emerged from the debris of 9/11. Instead, jingoistic, triumphalist rhetoric and a continuing tendency to see things in facile ways only served to feed the very Manichaeanism that has already created so many problems.

A clash of civilisations?

For instance, to speak of a "clash of civilisations" (Huntington) is to deny the fact that neither the West nor the Islamic world (a false dichotomy to begin with) are monolithic entities, but geographically and historically disparate groups of states with very real differences. More revealingly, it is extremely difficult to identify leaders of a civilisation and, from a practical standpoint, it is virtually impossible to actualise threats made in the name of civilisations (like declarations of a holy war or jihad) precisely because the only underlying institutions that could put them into effect are nation-states. Islamic "fundamentalism" is not a monolithic theology but rather a diverse ideology that manifests itself very differently in socio-political life in both positive and negative ways. For instance, the Ikhwan (the Muslim Brotherhood) has aligned itself with the monarchy in Jordan and plays a moderate (even constructive) role in some Arab countries. In contrast, Islamists are more radical in Egypt, Algeria and the Occupied Palestinian Territories (Hamas). The point is that in a diverse and often divided Islamic world there is little room for conspiracy or "group dynamic". Moreover, what counts is not fundamentalism but radical exclusivism, which provides the ideological foundation of exceptionalism: "Your (international) legal order is not mine". Fundamentalists are not necessarily terrorists, nor does the opposite hold. Hence, the propensity to lump fundamentalists into the category of "dangerous extremists or terrorists" is a self-defeating exercise: it both blinds one to the diversity of supposed foes and turns one into the same category that is being opposed.

As an illustration of how this facile error in analysis has real effects, it is only from a monolithic, non-nuanced perspective that the war in Iraq made more sense to the American war cabinet than focusing on a strategy of dismantling and destroying Osama Bin Laden and his network, although the latter always constituted a greater threat to the United States and the world than Saddam Hussein and his weapons of mass destruction (which in the end were never found). Iraq has become the least safe country of the twenty-first century. Hence, the American misadventure there may turn out to be the biggest strategic and tactical blunder since the Bay of Pigs fiasco. The quagmire that the Bush administration precipitated will in all likelihood have disastrous long-term consequences for US foreign policy, to say nothing of global security. Much irreparable damage has already been done. Once the machinery for the foreign policy implementation process is set in motion, it becomes difficult (and often politically risky) to dislodge, as the Obama administration has experienced.

The "War on Terror"

The initial post-9/11 reaction outside the United States was largely one of sympathy and concern, but expressed in different forms. Many Arab and Muslim countries, as represented by important spiritual and religious leaders in the Middle East, were quick to condemn the attacks, and make it clear that such acts were morally reprehensible and anathema to Islam. For some, though, there was also a feeling that the chickens had come home to roost: the United States through its sometimes blundering, violent, myopic and insensitive policies had brought this upon itself. There was also a more widespread hope that perhaps the gravity of the attacks had contributed towards galvanising US opinion into introspection, thus effecting positive change in US foreign policy. The sentiment, shared by many in the world community, was that the United States would finally take notice of the plight of other countries experiencing the same terrorism and unite nations in a genuine effort to defend the world against such violence. But nothing of the sort happened. The rational argument and nuanced analysis that could have (and should have) taken centre stage in mainstream US politics was largely ignored in the corridors of power. Those with political axes to sharpen won the day and helped pave the way towards a tragedy of missed opportunities.

Notably, the whole idea of a "War on Terror" is a misnomer and a gross misstatement: this is not a war that one could tangibly identify, let alone "win". Indeed, while the phrase is a soundbite, convenient for public consumption, the dynamics are complex – this is not a zero-sum game in which the "we win and you lose" scenario works. Moreover, the entity currently called Al Qaeda is less an organisation than an ideology. The Arabic word *qaeda* can be translated as "base of operation" or "foundation", or alternatively as a "precept" or "method". Islamic militants always understood the term in the latter sense. In 1987, Abdullah Azzam, the leading ideologue for modern Sunni Muslim radical activists, called for "al-qaeda al-sulbah" (a vanguard of the strong). He envisaged men who, acting independently, would set an example for the rest of the Islamic world, and thus, would galvanise the *umma* (global community of believers) against its oppressors. It was the FBI – during its investigation of the 1998 US Embassy bombings in East Africa – which dubbed the loosely linked group of activists that Osama Bin Laden and his aides had formed as "al Qaeda". It is worth mentioning in this connection that the whole concept of war as we have known it, tends to be changing. Conventional warfare is being replaced by terrorism, guerrilla warfare, piracy and low intensity conflicts (Van Creveld 1991: 192).

Although Bin Laden and his partners were able to create a structure in the dysfunctional state of Afghanistan that attracted new recruits and forged links among pre-existing Islamic militant groups, they never created a coherent terrorist network in the way commonly conceived. Instead, Al Qaeda functioned like a venture capital firm – providing funding, contacts and expert advice to many different militant groups and individuals from all over the Islamic world.

Through the UN-endorsed invasion of Afghanistan, the structure that had been built there was destroyed, and Osama Bin Laden and his associates have scattered or been arrested or killed. There is no longer a central hub for Islamic militancy, but the Al Qaeda worldview, or "al Qaedaism", used to grow stronger every day. This radical internationalist ideology – sustained by anti-Western, anti-Zionist and anti-Semitic rhetoric – has adherents among many individuals and groups, few of whom are currently linked in any substantial way to Bin Laden or those around him. They merely follow precepts, models and methods, which have become "popularised". They act in the style of Al Qaeda, but they are only part of Al Qaeda in the very loosest sense. That is why Israeli intelligence services prefer the term "jihadi international" instead of "Al Qaeda". Indeed, "jihadism" is seen as the major ideological threat to peace and security today.

Notably, jihadism as an ideology of terror does not stand on its own, but exists against a cultural, political and economic backdrop that deserves detailed analysis. One component of the breeding ground on which radical exclusivism can flourish is poverty (coupled with socio-economic inequality), which itself constitutes a human rights issue. This will be discussed further in Chapter 5. Another component of the global breeding ground for conflict and confrontation pertains to communication in the sensitive domain of religion and culture: the "sacred realm".

The "sacred realm": domain of polemics and polarisation

In many villages in the "Christian" West, but rarely in cities, people refrain from noisy operations on Sundays, such as cutting their grass or blowing away autumnal leaves. At stake is "Sunday serenity", to be respected by everyone, through the ages. The noise of church bells is accepted, however, practically during the whole day, as distinct churches have different times at which they call believers to their services. What we touch upon here are peaceful practices relating to the "sacred realm", a space only partly subject to public law and order. The term is used by, among others, city architects: aside from the private realm of houses and offices and the public realm of roads, parks and squares, there is a sacred realm of mosques, churches, temples, monuments and graveyards. Here the term will be used particularly in a figurative sense, as a field of orientation and focus, an area of beliefs, feelings and emotions, but also of rituals, symbols and words.

An open nerve

More than half a century ago there was already a growing feeling that the sacred realm would disappear before long. As Wright Mills (1959: 32–34, quoted in Norris and Inglehart 2004: 3) put it rather bluntly:

> Once the world was filled with the sacred – in thought, practice, and institutional form. After the Reformation and the Renaissance, the forces of modernisation swept across the globe and secularisation, a corollary historical process, loosened the dominance of the sacred. In due course, the sacred shall disappear altogether except, possibly, in the private realm.

While the trend towards secularisation continues in the West, this does not apply to the world as a whole. In their study *Sacred and Secular*, Norris and Inglehart (2004: 5) conclude that:

1. The publics of virtually all advanced industrial societies have been moving toward more secular orientations during the past fifty years.
2. Nevertheless, the world as a whole now has more people with traditional religious views than ever before – and they constitute a growing proportion of the world's population.

Clearly, all those believers do not accept a confinement of words and practices based on their religious views purely to the private realm. Far from having vanished, the sacred realm dominates the international news almost daily. It has become an area full of sparks that tend to set fire to the tinder of cultural tensions throughout the world. Yet, for "secularists" the view that the sacred realm should just evaporate into the private realm has assumed normative proportions: as something that just ought to happen. The cartoon drawings of the Prophet Mohammed that set off mass demonstrations all over the world in the first months of 2006, and that continue to have residual effects, are a case in point. Both the initial publication and the media hype that followed were far from spontaneous expressions of free thought and conscience.

We live, indeed, in a "symbolic society" in which spreading information through newspapers, (summarised) reports and oral accounts is largely replaced by electronic dissemination through symbols, images and words transmitted on the Internet by websites with instant video- and audiotapes (Elchardus 2002). Although as a result of processes of individualisation people are, in principle, more autonomous than ever before, the individual has actually become easy prey for media manipulation. Public anxiety, culminating in mass demonstrations, can be quite easily mobilised today, and this certainly applies to "religious" violence as well as to political violence. Illustrative of the absurd illogic – and thus the clear manipulation – at the roots of such violence were the attacks against Christian schools and hospitals in Pakistan, whereas both global and local Christian leaders had fully condemned the cartoons. On average 90 per cent of students and patients in the molested institutions were Muslim.

The reactions in the halls of power display a similar level of hysteria. In the Netherlands, a cabinet minister pointed to the consequences of democracy as an arithmetic method of political decision-making, implying that with a two-thirds majority, the constitution could be changed to introduce Sharia law. Subsequently, parliament devoted a full afternoon to a discussion of ways and means to block Sharia in the lowlands. Notably, of the current 7 per cent or so Dutch MPs who are Muslim (at least in origin), none advocates such a move. Is it, indeed, almost complete silliness that is gripping the world? What we are witnessing here may fairly be characterised as an open nerve. Evidently, the sacred realm has become an extremely shaky space, a breeding ground of clashing prejudice that is perhaps inimical to purely logical resolution.

The clash between "occidentalism" and "anti-Islamic secularism"

According to Edward Said (1978), "Western" thought has created a dichotomy, between the reality of the East and a notion of the "Orient" as backward and unaware of their own history and culture. *Orientalism* is a way of dealing with "the Orient" that confirms a relationship between Occident and Orient of power, domination and hegemony:

> Unlike the Americans, the French and British – less so the Germans, Russians, Spanish, Portugese, Italians, and Swiss – have had a long tradition of what I shall be calling Orientalism, a way of coming to terms with the Orient that is based on the Orient's special place in European Western Experience. The Orient is not only adjacent to Europe; it is also the place of Europe's greatest and richest and oldest colonies, the source of its civilisations and languages, its cultural contestant, and one of its deepest and most recurring images of the Other. In addition, the Orient has helped to define Europe (or the West) as its contrasting image, idea, personality, experience. Yet none of this Orient is merely imaginative. The Orient is an integral part of European material civilisation and culture. Orientalism expresses and represents that part culturally and even ideologically as a a mode of discourse with supporting institutions, vocabulary, scholarship, imagery, doctrines, even colonial bureaucracies and colonial styles.
>
> (Said 1978: 1–2)

Orientalism, then, is a style of thought based upon an ontological and epistemological distinction between "the Orient" and (most of the time) "the Occident". Intolerance and "us–them" divides tend to result from such contorted pictures of the other.

What we have been witnessing in the first decade of the new millennium is a new threat in this respect, based on mutual stereotyping: not so much Huntington's clash of civilisations, but rather a clash of collective prejudices: a collision between an ideologically coloured rejection of "the West" by "the East" and a similarly coloured rejection of "Islam" by "the West" as a monolithic, despicable religion. In both cases, the threat to human security lies in ideological manipulation of religion – or of its opposite, anti-religion – as a means of constructing opposing cultural identities in regard to which both sides claim irreconcilable incompatibility.

Buruma and Margalit (2004) use the phrase "religious Occidentalism" to describe the anti-Westernism espoused by radical Islamists. This ideology despises "the West" as a materialist capitalist society worshipping false gods based on a public-political order that allows a false dichotomy between the public and the private realm. (Incidentally, the ideological manner in which the Danish prime minister distanced not only the state, but also his government and his person from the cartoons issue – "those offended can file their applications with the judiciary" – did much to confirm that image.)

Strikingly, we find the term "Occidentals" already in the last lines of Edward Said's famous *Orientalism* (1978), albeit with a different connotation (Westerners as they see themselves, namely, as superiors). Said's scholarly work focuses, primarily, on academic studies. Today, however, Orientalism manifests itself as a secularist political ideology. The "other" against which it identifies itself is not so much the East as such, but Islam as a religion fundamentally incompatible with such crucial values and institutions as freedom, democracy, gender equality and the rule of law. When criticised from within the West such Orientalism is usually called "secularism" or even "secular fundamentalism" (Ekins 2002), even though the term "fundamentalism" is misleading in this respect, as will be argued below. Although, indeed, political in nature, it seeks connections with liberal political theory, arguing that without fully confining religion to the private realm, democracy becomes impossible. This view becomes increasingly prevalent in party politics in Europe as a growing number of liberal theorists enter the arena today, presenting their secularist views in newspaper columns, radio and television interviews, and presentations at political party gatherings.

It is this confrontation between contemporary Occidentalism and anti-Islamic secularism that has created a climate of intense sensitivity towards anything that might be seen as confronting ideological positions already taken. It is even possible that, had the prophet Mohammed cartoons not been published in a "Western" medium and had violent demonstrations not followed that "manifestation of freedom of expression", the conflict between Israel and the Arab Middle East might not have assumed the dimension of the Israel–Hezbollah war of 2006. Notably, in the social sciences it is impossible to confirm such assumptions; hence, such observations remain a matter of argued plausibility.

Thus, it is the constant "mediatisation" of touchy events, opinions and discourses that makes the new sensitivity so hazardous. There is an urgent need, therefore, to recognise this global ideological confrontation as a new threat in the first place, and to accept the new challenge to surmount it. In order to overcome the new battle of discourses, the first prerequisite is, indeed, to understand how it came into being. Towards the end of their mirror study *Occidentalism*, Buruma and Margalit (2004: 143) acknowledge the way in which Islamism has been influenced precisely by Western secularism:

> The Islamist revolutionary movement that currently stalks the world, from Kabul to Java, would not have existed without the harsh secularism of Reza Shah Pahlavi or the failed experiments in state socialism in Egypt, Syria and Algeria. This is why it was such a misfortune, in many ways, for the Middle East to have encountered the modern West for the first time through echoes of the French revolution.

This historical interpretation is confirmed by Sadik Al-Azm (2004: 27) in his perceptive essay on "Islam, Terrorism and the West Today":

> In fact, the modern European violent intrusion into Islamdom and Arabdom (starting with Bonaparte in 1798) created, in my view, a final, decisive and definitive rupture with the past that I can only compare with the no less final and definitive rupture effected by the violent Arab-Muslim intervention into the history of Sassanid Persia. And just as the history of post-conquest Persia stopped making sense without Arabs, Islam and their eruption on the local Farsi scene, similarly, the post-Bonaparte history of Arabdom stopped making sense without Europe, modernity and their eruption on the local Arab scene as well.

In other words, no Occidentalism is possible without its prior counterpart. Consequently from a Western perspective, the first challenge lies in conducting a critical self-analysis of what can be done to overcome Orientalism in its modern anti-Islamic secularist guise. The American introspection hoped for after the 9/11 attacks would be in this vein. The importance of this "liberating" mission was implicitly noted by Said (1978: 328), when towards the end of his study he concluded: "Without 'the Orient' there would be scholars, critics, intellectuals, human beings, for whom the racial, ethnic, and national distinctions were less important than the common enterprise of promoting human community." Noticeably, for "the Orient" one might also read "the Occident". While Orientalism served to justify bad colonial rule, it was particularly in the Arab world that Occidentalism ("the Americans", "the West") played the same part as justification of bad independent rule. The confrontation of those responsible for bad and corrupt government with their own angry masses already marks the second decade of the twenty-first century as testimony to the potential of upstream human rights in adverse environments.

A side-effect of the apparent conscientisation of the Islamic masses could well be its positive effect in terms of overcoming Western anti-Islamic prejudice. As Orientalism and Occidentalism appear to be two sides of the same coin, overcoming these might be seen as a joint challenge. Indeed, the remarkable events of early 2011 may be seen as a firm step in the direction of healing the global divide, too.

After this diversion into the religious reality – the sacred realm as a major breeding ground of conflict and confrontation – let us now return to that major challenge in respect of global realities today: how to reconcile US hegemony with an international political and legal order conducive to the realisation of human rights.

American security concerns and the international legal order

Naturally, the United States is looking for allies and coalitions in their confrontation with ideologically inspired terrorist networks, both to spread the costs of the "war on terror" and to help legitimise their actions. What is to be criticised, however, is the distance taken from an emerging international legal order predicated on human rights principles. Their reluctance to participate in international law institutions derives precisely from the home-grown contention that the rights of Americans are embodied in the US constitution and are subject only to local consent and national popular sovereignty. US non-ratification of international rights conventions and treaties establishing new institutions such as the International Criminal Court, however, runs counter to US interests in the long run and impedes efforts to build an international order based on international peace and justice. It was precisely this reflection which did, indeed, result in the Obama administration's new foreign policy strategy, after the mire of the Bush era. The challenge for the rest of the world in this connection is to harness and enhance that fragile and embryonic shift towards an international orientation taken by the Obama administration, based on the United States' own security concerns.

Understandable, indeed, as US unilateralism may be in the light of disappointments far from home – in the former Yugoslavia, for example, where Europe failed to take care of a problem in its own backyard – defending the United States today will require a substantial change in its strategic culture. To confront unilateralist national security discourse with an international human rights-based communication will not, however, have much effect. But it is precisely within the context of current concerns with international terrorism that the international legal order manifests its primary importance for the Americans themselves. To clarify what is meant here, it is helpful to understand the notion of policy *by-products*.

The term by-product signifies that which is not the primary, automatic or intended object of production; nevertheless, a by-product may be regarded as essential and even the primary purpose of a strategy. Let us take democracy as an illustration here. Notably, a democratic system implies constitutional rule and the acceptance of government by its citizens or, in other words, legitimacy. Indeed, for Fukuyama (1992), the advocate of liberal democracy as "the end of history", a regime is democratic when it is legitimised through the consent of the ruled. Here, democracy and legitimisation are synonyms. It is also possible to see legitimacy as an essential by-product of democracy (Van Gunsteren and Andeweg 1994). The term "by-product" means, indeed, that the "production" of legitimacy is not automatic – democracy does not equal legitimacy; nevertheless it is essential because without it democracy will lose its meaning. "Without the citizens' support, who recognise the regime as being legitimate, a political democracy cannot survive" (Van Gunsteren and Andeweg 1994: 100). A problem with "*pure* by-products" is, generally, that they cannot be aimed at, even where their production is regarded as essential. Thus, paradoxically, politicians in power cannot just aim at legitimacy, for example, through major efforts in public relations. Rather, they have to aim at the right policies and, if these are successful, they might produce "people's subjective perceptions" (Fukuyama 1992: 15) that constitute the regime's legitimacy.

It is also clear that American preoccupation with national security – a key element in their strategic culture – is of such centrality to their national discourse in respect of international relations that engaging it is essential. Ultimately, then, American endorsement of and enrolment in the international legal order must come as a substantial by-product of enhancement of their own national safety interest. As long as US primacy reigns supreme and it perceives its national security to be under threat, the United States is not going to be bogged down by international treaties or international law. Furthermore, no country in its present form is going to develop a defence capability that rivals that of the United States, and hence, would enable it to engage in pre-emptive actions on the global stage. (To do so would make it an automatic target of US military power.) What is abundantly clear, however, is that global interdependence has never assumed greater significance than it does today, especially in light of powerful destabilising non-state forces at work as part of the new "jihadism". It is precisely global chaos that international terrorism aims at, which requires a response, based on the rule of international law. Notably, the Obama administration has manifested an evident awareness that constantly "going it alone" threatens American security interests while making the United States and its citizens primary targets of jihad ideology. A parallel concern is that the international community would be rendered impotent without US support. Now that both sides appear to accept these realities, a common agenda has become viable. Indeed, in order to change the other's opinion, the first place to start might be self-analysis and introspection. In that spirit, let us now examine the role of the United Nations in the international political, legal and economic order.

United Nations reform

In respect of global legitimacy – indeed the crucial issue – a discussion of the right principles is a great deal easier than an examination of the right institutions. The United Nations receives a lot of well-founded criticism, and in this respect, it is worth listening to the voices of American scepticism. (Clearly, a focus on legitimacy implies not only that in view of their military supremacy the United States is not necessarily right but also that US policies are not necessarily wrong.) Inefficient and ineffective bureaucracies, irrelevant discussions, and endless procedures undermine the UN (for instance, recall the Chongwe case with which this study opened). Conspicuously, the veto system appears to have outlived its purpose in its current arrangement. Yet, institutions such as the Security Council cannot, of course, be scrapped. They are the tools we have. To critique those tools is not to eliminate them, but to reform and reinvent them; it is the only way towards progress in the endeavour to realise rights.

The critical point is that the right processes, the next major element in establishing legitimacy in the realm of global power, are necessarily connected with the United Nations, and it happens to be the UN itself that in its decision-making processes suffers from a lack of democratic legitimisation. This applies not only to the organisation as such, but also to connected agencies such as the World Trade Organisation. A widespread impression is created that whatever has been decided in the upper levels, corrections upstream are never possible.[9] Naturally, however, there is no alternative to the UN, so the only way forward is its effective reform.

At both the global and the local level, operational structures are needed for decent and credible ways of association with civil society. Despite reports following the agenda set in 2005,[10] there has been little progress in the efforts to reform the Secretariat. In January 2008 Secretary-General Ban Ki-moon outlined the broad fronts on which the United Nations would need to advance if it is to meet the challenges facing the member-states and their peoples in the twenty-first century. In areas like the environment, public health and human security, he argued, the world is facing threats and challenges that respect no boundaries. It is true, of course, that in the exclamation "Thank God for the death of the United Nations" sceptics, such as Richard Perle, have to be convincingly confronted. But that battle has to be fought with more than words alone; it is, indeed, high time for a revitalisation of the United Nations in line with its conventional and contemporary challenges. Hence, Kofi Annan's immediate reaction as UN Secretary-General to the Iraq invasion that bypassed the international community – "you stumble, you fall, you rise, and then you walk again" – missed the seriousness of the crisis in the international political order (Pronk 2003: 16). The position of the Bush administration was, indeed, confronted – not least of all from within the United States. But the (opportune) election of a former lecturer in human rights law to the US presidency does not imply that basic changes in the international system itself are no longer urgently needed. Now is the time to act, to take advantage of the embryonic shift in US strategic culture mentioned above.

A revitalisation of the UN is to be founded in the three grand projects with which the organisation was entrusted after the Second World War: international security, international justice (implying universal responsibility for the realisation of human rights) and international economic development. The primary challenge today is to integrate these ventures, from the three separated institutional settings of the Security Council with its international political focus, the General Assembly and the human rights institutions with their juridical focus, and the United Nations Development Program, the specialised and development agencies and the Bretton Woods institutions with their economic focus, towards a more integrated approach aimed at each of these named arenas.

When the Roosevelt Foundation in Middelburg (NL) gives out its biannual "four freedoms awards", it nominates not only a prize winner for each of these – the freedom of speech, the freedom of worship, the freedom from fear and the freedom from want – but also a fifth one: for the four together.[11] In that light the Security Council might move from just dealing with human security (and from that perspective with human rights and human development only incidentally) to integrate these concerns into the fullness of its mission. In the Human Rights Council (HRC) and other human rights institutions, international security and development considerations will have to be made explicit rather than influencing the decisions in effect from behind the scenes. (Notwithstanding the use of juridical terminology in line with the rather absolute language of international human rights law, the HRC, to all intents and purposes, is an international political body and should act as one.) Corresponding to the new orientation of the United Nations Development Program (UNDP), the international financial institutions (IFIs), too, will have to accept their role as principal actors in respect of international human rights obligations, as we shall further discuss below (pp. 167–171).

Another major challenge lies in the huge deficits in the three distinct areas of that international mission: international security, international justice and international development. Consequently, a re-engineering of each of these seems well in order. Let us address them now in turn with emphasis both on their deficiencies and on steps in the right direction, focusing primarily on outcome.

Addressing the international security deficit

The international security deficit expresses itself in endless manifestations of intra-state collective violence. Grave instances of complete failure of the international community come to mind here, including Rwanda and Srebrenica. Now that the *casus belli* with regard to Iraq has shifted *ex post facto* from weapons of mass destruction to gross and systematic human rights violations, it is high time to develop an international strategy on humanitarian action and intervention, and to restructure the Security Council accordingly. A first step in this direction has already been taken with the shift in emphasis in respect of state sovereignty: from the right to control people within the state's territory to the responsibility to protect them. In 2001 an International Commission on Intervention and State Sovereignty published a report titled "The Responsibility to Protect" (International Development Research Centre 2001).

The United Nations World Summit of September 2005 embraced this responsibility to protect:

> Each individual State has the responsibility to protect its populations from genocide, war crimes, ethnic cleansing and crimes against humanity. This responsibility entails the prevention of such crimes, including their incitement, through appropriate and necessary means. We accept that responsibility and will act in accordance with it. The international community should, as appropriate, encourage and help States to exercise this responsibility and support the United Nations in establishing an early warning capability.
>
> (Outcome document ¶ 138)

In the next paragraph the international community, through the United Nations, also recognises its responsibility "to use appropriate diplomatic, humanitarian and other peaceful means, in accordance with Chapters VI and VII of the Charter, to help protect populations from genocide, war crimes, ethnic cleansing and crimes against humanity" (¶ 139). Security Council Resolution 1674 (adopted on 28 April 2006) reaffirmed these provisions and committed itself to taking action to protect civilians in armed conflict. In February 2008, Secretary-General Ban Ki-moon appointed a Special Adviser for the Responsibility to Protect (R2P in UN SMS jargon) at the Assistant Secretary-General level.

The responsibility to protect constitutes an important shift in the international law doctrine of sovereignty. This principle no longer means "the right to control" people and borders at all costs, but now implies the duty to protect civilians, especially from genocide, war crimes, ethnic cleansing and crimes against humanity. When a state fails to protect its own civilians, that responsibility then falls on the international community in three phases: to prevent, react and rebuild in countries affected by mass suffering and atrocities.

R2P admirably recognises and addresses the root causes of civil conflict in order to prevent atrocities, framing *prevention* as the foremost duty. It is also the broadest responsibility, as activities that positively contribute to the stability and well-being of a country and its people help to prevent future civil conflict and mass human suffering. The protection of human dignity in line with the golden triangle of human dignity realisation (Figure I.2) should be interpreted as the centrepiece of these efforts towards prevention.

Prevention efforts may fail, however, which calls for intervention through a range of reaction options, the large majority of which are non-violent, including targeted sanctions and political pressure from neighbouring countries. If military intervention becomes necessary, it must satisfy the "force majeure" threshold, which implies that large scale loss of life must be imminent or actually happening, before any action can be authorised. It must also meet the "threshold criteria", which include such things as "right intention" and "reasonable prospects of averting suffering". In order to prevent abuse of a doctrine of humanitarian intervention by powerful states, military action for peace with justice against a "sovereign" state, beyond Chapter 7 of the United Nations Charter and hence without authorisation by the Security Council, has not been regulated in international law. Yet, it may be accepted in practice through acquiescence by the international community, meaning tacit *ex-post* approval by the Security Council in the first place. The intervention of NATO allies in Serbia/Kosovo is a case in point.

Finally, R2P recognises that without effective rebuilding measures that establish the rule of law, good government and reconstruction, regions recovering from violent conflict are likely to remain confronted with civil strife. This means that development and poverty reduction programmes like education, health, water and food security projects, as well as injustice response programmes like peace building, human security and refugee assistance projects, are encompassed within this new international doctrine.

Since the relevant record of the Security Council is not particularly impressive so far, it is too early to come up with a final assessment here. Yet, the shift from useless references to human rights in Geneva- or New York-based, powerless fora to the day-to-day security agenda of the Security Council might be seen as a first step towards that long-needed global perspective for oppressed peoples. But, it should not be seen as simply an extension of the human rights mission as conceived in legal discourse. R2P plainly confronts the international community with the need to strategically conceptualise human rights as an active discourse in close connection with the two major ventures that form the other points of the golden triangle of human dignity realisation (Figure I.2): human security, as based on F.D. Roosevelt's freedom from fear, and human development, as tuned towards FDR's freedom from want.

Addressing the international justice deficit

As we have observed already, the realisation of human rights suffers from a huge *deficit* too, one that is all too often submerged in the general euphoria and ritualised lamentation of human rights declarations, conferences, committee meetings and workshops. Despite the International Criminal Court (confronted by the Bush administration with its "Hague Invasion Act"), one of its aspects is the almost worldwide struggle that has to be fought against impunity of state-related violations of civil and political rights. In a persuasive article titled "World Governance: Beyond Utopia", Stanley Hoffmann (2003) submits a strong *plaidoyer* for a world court on human rights. To achieve this goal, however, will require a huge investment of time, money and patience; in the meantime, however, the habitual ineffective rituals and mantras of the Geneva- and New York-based institutions definitely call for substantial reforms.

After 65 years it is, indeed, high time to assess the UN's human rights machinery as such. For that purpose, the total investment in the *international* mechanisms may be compared with all resources made available for *local* realisation. Such an evaluation might focus on each of the four major elements of the global human rights deficit in particular: the struggle against impunity, overcoming the public–private divide, realising the rights of the poor and protecting collectivities. The latter two challenges will be more specifically examined in Chapters 5 and 6. In the present analysis of global realities we now turn to the failure of attacking poverty through international development.

Addressing the international development deficit

"The years since 1980 have ... seen ... an extraordinary systematic increase of inequality" (Galbraith 2002: 23). Inequality in income and wealth has risen everywhere. Indeed, the international development deficit manifests itself in gigantic inequalities both between countries and between people(s). There is no single country in the world in which the current trend is towards decreasing relative poverty and in the world as a whole the figures are truly alarming: at the turn of the millennium, the richest 5 per cent of people received one-third of total global income, whereas the bottom 5 per cent received only 0.2 percent, meaning a ratio of 165:1 (Milanovic 2007: 40). In fact, even the most unequal countries in the world remain very far from manifesting such an incredible degree of inequality.

As far as global structures of production, finance and trade are concerned, there appears to be an almost complete lack of corrective mechanisms working towards global equity. The point is, of course, that there still exists a striking dichotomy between economic globalisation and the lack of global political control. What *The Economist* noted in 1930 is still true today: "our achievements on the economic plane of life have outstripped our progress on the political plane to such an extent that our economics and our politics are perpetually falling out of gear with one another" (11 October: 652). Conceptually, the foundation of the United Nations as a universal intergovernmental organisation for security, justice and development may, indeed, be characterised as one of the few "breakthroughs in twentieth century politics, regardless of how successful it has been in practice" (Bassin 1994: 1), but world government remains an illusion. In its effects on the economies of the South, the negative consequences of the colonial mega-intervention continue to play their part. The ways in which the former colonies have been linked to international monetary, financial and commercial structures tends to be accompanied by a negative net capital flow and sudden disturbances in entitlement positions. During the 1970s and the 1980s the share of sub-Saharan Africa in world trade dropped from 3.8 to 1 per cent, while foreign direct investment (FDI) also declined substantially (UNDP 1992: 37). In the same period global losses through trade protection, immigration barriers and increasing debt burdens amounted to ten times the aid developing countries receive. During the last two decades of the twentieth century the least developed countries have seen their share of world trade reduced from 0.6 per cent to 0.3 per cent; in fact, FDI bypasses more than half of all developing countries (United Nations Development Programme 1997: 9). Towards the end of the last century, the interest on the debt, which the South pays to the industrialised nations, became more than twice what it received in official development aid (Harrod 1992: 34). Admittedly the years 2001–2007 have been quite successful for sub-Saharan Africa in terms of FDI (International Monetary Fund 2009: 11) as well as sales and exports (IMF 2009: 87/96), but both FDI and sales and exports have considerably declined again as a result of the global financial crisis of 2008.

In the second edition of Thomas Pogge's *World Poverty and Human Rights* (2008), the fundamental data concerning world poverty have not shown any change for the better since the book first appeared (2002), despite substantial global economic growth. The number of undernourished people appears to be stagnant: almost 800 million in 1996, 830 million in 2006. Particularly disturbing is the number of daily deaths due to poverty-related diseases; this amount still stands at one-third of the total (with over two-thirds of these being children under five). Behind that frightening figure lies a distribution of income that leaves no more than 1.2 per cent to the poorest 46 per cent of the global population. Pogge argues that the rich part of our world is not only failing to contribute possible solutions to the predicament of the global poor but is actually a decisive part of the problem. This view is based on the existence of a functioning global political-economic order in which the OECD governments participate directly as well as through the international financial institutions that they dominate in both treaty negotiations and actual policies.

Particularly convincing is Pogge's response to "four easy reasons to ignore world poverty": futility (any effort to do something would be no more than a drop in the ocean), jeopardy (eradicating world poverty would demand an investment that the rich societies cannot bear), perversity (it would lead to overpopulation and hence to more poverty-related deaths in the future) and over-optimism (thanks to concerted global efforts there is already sufficient progress in tackling world poverty). The latter is probably the most dangerous blinker today due to the MDGs' shift of perspective to the year 2015, while based on merely soft commitments at world summits.

Clearly then, globalisation has its downside – processes of exclusion – with the ensuing risks of social disintegration. This pertains to whole regions and countries but also to more than one billion individual human beings who live in entirely marginalised conditions.

Now it is true that socio-economic inequality and the lack of protection against poverty and destitution have always plagued the global economy. But the idea was that global free trade would result in increased general welfare. The subsequent trends towards increased inequalities would be addressed at the national level by the creation of a welfare state, which would work towards distributive justice through the necessary income transfers. Three comments are in place here. First, in the countries in which such mechanisms for social justice did work, their effects have lost impact. Second, the majority of global citizens live in countries in which such corrective mechanisms have never worked. As Murshed has forcefully argued, these low-income economies "have become caught up in the wave of globalisation sweeping through the world" while besides "being intrinsically vulnerable, they face new constraints in the processes of trade, technology transfer, investment and international finance" (2002: 28). And third, globalisation confronts the world rather bluntly with the lack of global mechanisms for distributive justice. Consequently, national economies get increasingly affected by economic globalisation (De Gaay Fortman and Klein Goldewijk 1998). There are regional as well as global supra-state trade arrangements. But these have the character of structured interventions in people's entitlement positions – affecting prices, for example – rather than assuming the nature of entitlement systems in their own right.

The major challenge in this respect lies with the North, where per capita Gross Domestic Product (GDP) in purchasing power parity (PPP) is more than one hundred times that figure in the poorest countries in Africa. In respect of this enormous geographical disparity, development assistance appears at best to play a highly marginal part. An empirical study on the effects of official development assistance (ODA) in Africa shows that ODA does not correlate with poverty reduction (Arimah 2004, five years later confirmed by Moyo 2009; see also Collier 2007). This means, of course, that income poverty is not significantly affected by donor activity (aid) and reduction. There is a strong correlation, however, between national expenditure on health and education and poverty alleviation (Arimah 2004). But the question remains how far the donor countries have developed an institutional ability to combat poverty in their development assistance efforts.

The highest priority, as formally recognised already at the outset of the development co-operation era, is not aid but trade, in the sense of rectifying long-standing and long-ignored injustices in the international economic order. However, the "New International Economic Order" which was the subject of two special sessions of the United Nations in the 1970s did not materialise. Indeed, the rights dimensions of poverty have international consequences that have been neglected far too long. The connection between human development and the realisation of human rights is too clear, too compelling for current schemes for reform not to be taken seriously. At the beginning of the new millennium, these were concisely summed up by Yilmat Akuz (2000 quoted in Mshana 2002). After the outbreak of the global financial crisis, the following issues have become even more topical:

- Establishing an international credit insurance corporation designed to reduce the likelihood of excessive credit expansion.
- Creation of a board of overseers of major international institutions and markets, with wide-ranging powers for setting standards, and for the oversight and regulation of commercial banking, securities, businesses and insurance.
- Forming a global mega-agency for financial regulation and supervision – a world financial authority – with responsibility for setting regulatory standards for all financial enterprises, both off-shore as well as on-shore entities.

- Creating a genuine international lender of last resort, with discretion to create its own liquidity.
- Formation of an international bankruptcy court in order to apply an international version of Chapter 11 of the United States Bankruptcy Code for orderly debt workouts.
- Management of the exchange rates of G3 currencies (the yen, the euro and the US dollar) through arrangements such as target zones.
- The Tobin Tax proposal to curb short term-volatility of capital movements and exchange rates while at the same time collecting significant funds for development and the attack on poverty.

Meanwhile a global financial crisis hit the world in 2008, with major effects on developing countries in general and sub-Saharan Africa in particular.[12] This crisis might well have been avoided had the proposals mentioned above been followed. Additionally, many constructive proposals have been formulated to make the necessary changes in the World Trade Organisation's (WTO) arrangements. However, in spite of all progress made since the UN's foundation, all these proposals are still far from being effectively implemented.

Naturally, a review of global political economy would be unfinished if it neglected the environmental crisis that manifests itself globally in, among other things, climate change through carbon dioxide emissions. In response, the United Nations have taken laudable institutional initiatives (Schrijver 2010). Yet, the mandate of the United Nations Conference on Environment and Development in Rio de Janeiro (1992), as confirmed by the World Summit on Sustainable Development (Johannesburg 2002) and incorporated in the United Nations World Summit 2005 Outcome Document is rather ambiguous. The United Nations Climate Change Conference of 2009 (the Copenhagen summit) did not in any way strengthen global authority to respond to climate change. The Cancún summit of 2010 did result in an ambitious final document although that still lacks teeth.

This flawed international mandate emanated from a General Assembly resolution that stressed the sovereign right of states to develop their own resources pursuant to their own policies. The only limitation was that their activities must not cause environmental damage to areas beyond their jurisdiction. Thus the challenge of environmental sustainability continues to be set in the context of a world of sovereign states. However, it is precisely in such a setting that the environmental crisis developed.

Actually, the redistribution of risk, rather than the redistribution of wealth and resources, continues to dominate the international agenda. Too often, the South is supposed to mitigate the effects of environmental threats and vulnerabilities in the North. Its contributions to the CO_2 problem, its supply of energy to the industrialised world and its portion of global pollution are all examples of that trend. In such a setting, the follow-up meetings to the Rio conference could not produce much institutional progress.

Thus, the real challenge remains with national implementation of global guidelines. In respect of environmental sustainability it is particularly the North

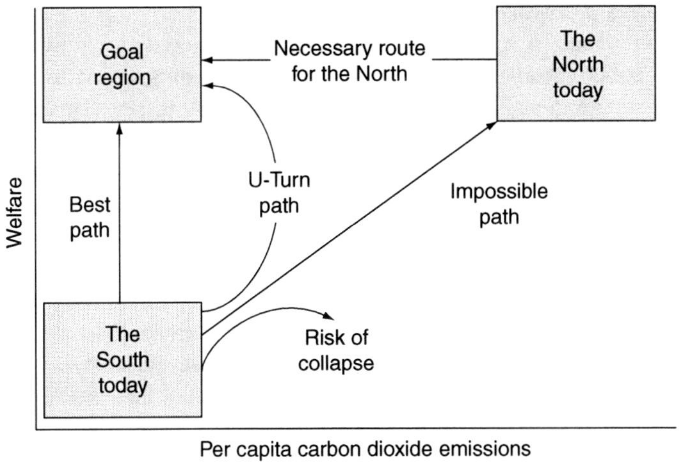

Figure 3.1 Achieving the sustainable energy goal.

that would have to take the lead, as a graphic presentation illustrated already in the early 1990s (Netherlands Ministry of Foreign Affairs 1993: 24) (see Figure 3.1).

The obvious lesson is that policies for redistribution of risks are bound to cause trouble for the world as a whole, including the framers of such policies themselves. For those who did not yet believe this socio-psychological truth, the failure of the follow-up conferences on sustainable development may have opened their eyes. These times are unique in the sense that survival has become a genuinely global undertaking that requires reorienting "economistic" value systems. The challenge is to connect the material to the moral, to tie growth to sustainability and to link production with human development. This means a revitalisation of public interest in a genuinely global sense (A. Young 2008).

Concluding reflections

Notably the United Nations 2005 World Summit Outcome Document, although primarily concerned with the unsatisfactory achievements in respect to the Millennium Development Goals (MDGs; pp. 146–147), referred to the "interdependent and mutually reinforcing pillars" of sustainable development as economic development, social development and environmental protection. "Feeding the ... poor and vulnerable populations in Africa, while preserving the natural resource base and the environment", Akin Adesina put it, "is one of the most pressing development challenges of the twenty-first century" (Toenniessen *et al.* 2008). While pointing at the factual issues, those two comments miss the link with international justice. Indeed, climate change has its human rights implications too, which tend to be neglected (e.g. Salih 2011). In the current mechanisms for international justice, for example, there is no recourse for climate displacees (Van Bommel 2010).

The challenge, then, is to find combined strategies to combat environmental crises, global poverty and exclusion in an integrated setting tuned to international security, international development and international justice. This does not only involve state representatives in their conference buildings. All sections of the global population, all types of actors – individual citizens, corporations, non-governmental organisations and states – will have to work together to reorient civilisation. There is a growing demand today for "a new consciousness". "What is required is a systems shift, a new holistic view of the world we live in" (Leiserowitz and Fernandez 2008).

As to the integration of the United States in the international political order, a different style in international politics is required at all levels: a style tuned to consultation and involvement of people rather than geopolitical manoeuvring, and dealing primarily with the real threats, such as lack of water, rather than just outward manifestations of power, like possession of weapons of mass destruction. Naturally, confronting the deficits in global governance also demands a willingness on the part of the better angels of the US foreign policy establishment to embrace an internationalist agenda.

Within an international setting tuned to negative as well as positive peace, then, a special position for the United States with its impressive power in terms of military, financial and human resources remains unavoidable. Essential in that respect is a legal framework based on a re-engineering of international principles regarding sovereignty and the prohibition of violence. The ancient principle of proportionality is also important in this connection: even justified interests are not to be pursued with means that cause disproportionate damage to individuals and groups outside of the actual conflict. In this respect certain lessons are to be learned.

Finally, it has become obvious that in the international order's current predicament much more is at stake than just international security in a narrow sense. Indeed, it is not merely a revision of the Security Council and a discussion on the prohibition of violence between states that are part of the agenda, but also the role of the United Nations in conflict prevention. Working on that agenda, it is not only the realism of the United Nations' founders that may offer profound inspiration but their ideals, too. No matter the overwhelming importance of realising reform on the global plane, such advances mean little without effectively tackling local environments that are adverse to the realisation of human rights as well. The major challenge in this respect lies in an effective operationalisation of R2P. See further Chapter 6, p. 199.

4 Local realities

Strife and struggle

The world is very much more complicated than the arguments.

Hedley Bull (1961: 212)

Gross human rights violations in an adverse environment

In Rwanda between April and June of 1994, more than 800,000 people were killed (Prunier 1995: 265). The image of a river turning red with blood suddenly became a horrifying reality as the Kagera was stained with the blood of thousands of victims, almost all belonging to the Tutsi tribe. As a result of this intra-state violence, more than two million persons fled their country, many of them merely to die abroad in refugee conditions. In the (then) Zairian refugee area of Goma, the number of deaths was so great that priority had to be given to burying the dead rather than treating the sick. Despite peace accords, the ensuing war in that region has continued uninterrupted, showing no signs of resolution (see below, p. 196).

Incomprehensible as such horrors may be, the killings were not unanticipated. Indeed, the "early warning" system worked. The United Nations was indeed already present in the country with a peace-keeping force. It was, rather, in early *action* that the real challenge to international inertia manifested itself. As Prunier noted regarding "the causes and probable consequences" of the Rwandan genocide, "one is struck by a feeling of predictability" (1995: 346). In that light the international reaction to the crisis in Rwanda was entirely incomprehensible. Precisely when it became clear that the killings were the beginning of a genocide of frightful proportions, the United Nations – already in Rwanda to monitor an insecure truce between the government and the Rwanda Patriotic Front (RPF) – decided to reduce its force of 2,500 to a mere 270 lightly armed soldiers. Thus, rather than starting a massive peace-enforcing operation, the community of nations decided to abandon its failed peace-keeping mission.

In order to better understand the failure of the international community to intervene in an effective way to prevent the bloodshed in Rwanda, it is necessary to examine the setting of the international human rights mission as well as the environment in Rwanda that preceded the killing. Let us examine the set-up of the human rights mission first. The "international venture for the protection and

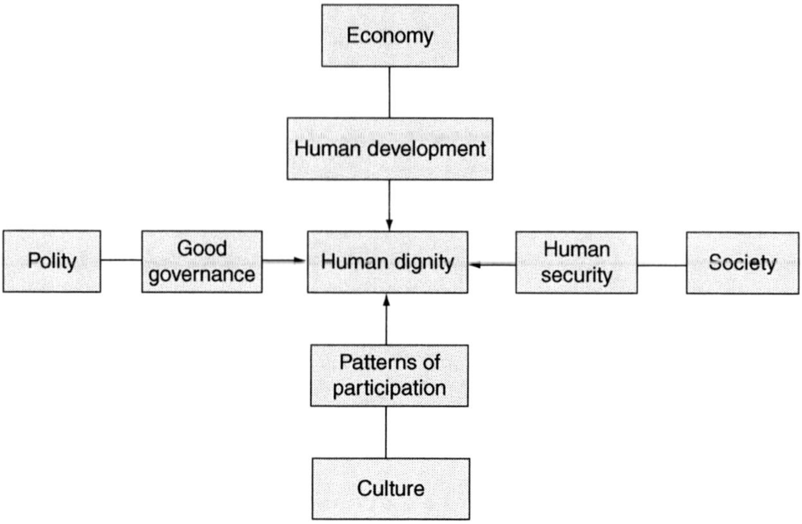

Figure 4.1 An environment enabling human rights realisation.

promotion of human rights" – as it is usually called, rather softly, as noted above (p. 46) – tuned as it is towards enforcement and protection of legal rights, relies upon the existence of environments that are already "enabling" from a political economic perspective, implying a well functioning economy, good government and a strong judicial culture. Such a setting may be graphically depicted (see Figure 4.1).

Yet, the reality is that more than half of the global population lives in what comes closer to a "disabling" environment for the realisation of human dignity: misallocation of resources, extreme social and economic inequality and exclusion, violence in and among communities, corruption, anarchy and cultures of domination and submissiveness. Such an environment is schematically represented in Figure 4.2.

In such an adverse or "disabling" environment, a system that is tuned towards the legal enforcement of rights is obviously of little use. Human rights enforcement as currently practised by the UN thus has a severely limited capacity to protect human dignity in adverse environments, precisely where the grossest human rights abuses are most prevalent. Let us now examine the situation in Rwanda in 1994 as "typical" of such adverse environments.

Rwanda is a densely populated country whose resource-base offers its people insufficient income-generating opportunities in an insecure coffee culture and virtually no employment in industry and commercial services such as tourism (Trouwborst 1994: 348). As there was little productivity, there was also little effective taxation. Official development assistance was therefore the major source of public investment. In such an environment, state power becomes the

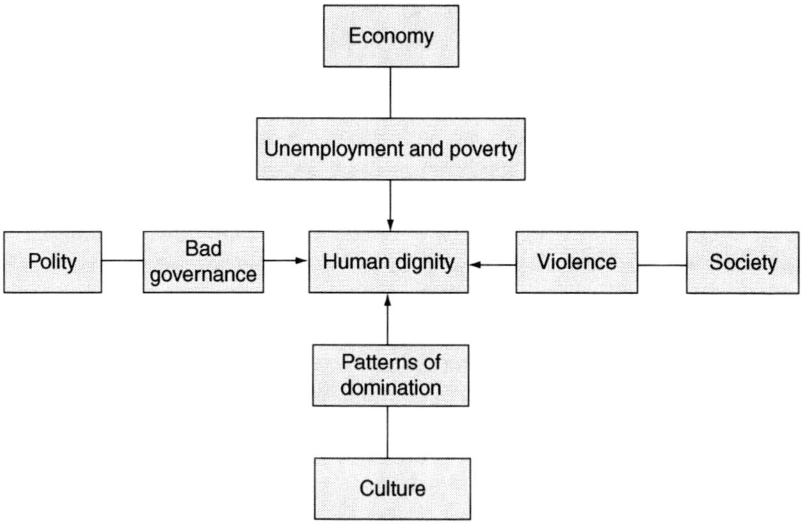

Figure 4.2 An environment adverse to human rights realisation.

"dominant social good" in the sense that those who have it "can command a wide range of other goods" (Walzer 1983: 10). Under those conditions, politics predictably takes the form of a fierce fight for entitlement positions arranged by the state, resulting in a system of governance rooted in corruption.

Rwanda's population is ethnically divided, around 90 per cent Hutu, 9 per cent Tutsi and 1 per cent Twa. After independence the regime became Hutu-based with the Tutsi excluded. Economic deterioration in the years preceding the genocide provoked a growing resistance to the Habyarimana administration (Hutu-based with its roots particularly in the Northwest). Between 1986 and 1989 international coffee prices fell by around 50 per cent. In 1989, due to severe balance of payments problems and a strongly increased foreign debt, the government accepted and began to enforce the structural adjustment prescriptions of the International Monetary Fund and the World Bank. As a result the currency was strongly devalued. Any possible positive effects of this measure on exports were, however, completely offset by a further fall of the coffee price on the world market (Dupont and Marijsse 1994: 340–341). A high rate of population growth (±3%) also placed increasing pressure on the land.

After the fall of the Berlin Wall in November 1989, international pressure on one-party states also affected the regime in Rwanda. Consequently, on 5 July 1990, a process of democratisation was announced. The following month the Rwanda Patriotic Front, a political and military organisation of refugees from earlier intra-state violence in 1959, invaded the country from the north. The government's reaction to the growing external pressure was not just to announce the end of the one-party state, but also to curtail its expenditure on education and health in order to mobilise more soldiers and import more military equipment. The ruling elite and all those dependent on them through family ties and patronage politics feared they might be deprived of their privileged entitlement positions. The majority Hutu population was mobilised to attack their Tutsi compatriots – often their own neighbours and/or brothers and sisters in the same church – in order to defend their entitlements with a fanatic paramilitary called Interahamwe (those who fight together) in the vanguard. Through Radio Mille Collines – alias "Radio Machete" – the Hutu population was incited to see the Tutsi as "cockroaches" that "should be crushed". Eventually, internal and external pressure for multi-party democracy in an adverse economic, political and socio-cultural environment resulted in the degeneration of politics into war and genocide.

Clearly, the global as well as local failure to create the conditions necessary for an adequately functioning market economy led to a type of politics focused entirely on the fight for positions in the state sector as bases for otherwise lacking entitlement positions. And it is precisely because politics took this form that institutions indispensable in path dependent development (relating to economies of scale, complementarities and externalities, North 1990) were not created. In cases of high conflict susceptibility like Rwanda in the 1990s, development aid provided in its conventional state-oriented patterns merely tends to increase the privileges of those in power, thus feeding and entrenching the root problems rather than helping to solve them. Blindly following conventional aid patterns in such situations is thus not only unproductive, but counterproductive. External assistance of a different nature – more oriented towards an improved infrastructure (economic-technical, legal, administrative, etc.) – might assist in breaking the catch-22 situation of a malfunctioning economy and politics in the form of a fierce and violent fight for state-related entitlement positions. Yet, the international reaction to the conflict made no attempt to provide the Rwandan population with new economic perspectives. Where intra-state conflict is rooted in serious problems of resources sharing within an economic structure that offers insufficient opportunities for the whole population, both preventive diplomacy and post-conflict peace-building will have to address these socio-economic constraints. Only on that basis can the military political aspects of the struggle be resolved.

The Rwandan genocide may also serve to illustrate the social and political, if not also economic, limitations of structural adjustment programmes imposed from above. Based on pure and in itself indisputable macro-economic logic, such schemes tend to display a lack of concern for the political and social fabric of the societies in which they have been applied and also to neglect global causes of economic crises. As a result, their economic performance is highly questionable, too (Bello and Cunningham 1994).

Prunier concluded his impressive historical account of the genocide as follows: "The whole system went wrong for reasons which at first were economic and then turned politico-cultural" (1995: 350). Unfortunately, however, at the pre-genocide stage the international community made no attempt to address the global and local socio-economic context of the conflict; instead, it merely sent some "peace-keeping" troops and engaged in "peace-making" efforts to bring parties together and start a process of political reconciliation.

Rwanda is a catastrophic example, but we must acknowledge that the worst violations of human rights most commonly occur in such adverse environments. Usually, these involve whole populations in a situation of civil war, like the people of the Darfur region in Sudan. In response to such dreadful events, international authorities trying to enforce human rights tend to focus on judicial measures against the culprits. Thus, the International Criminal Court in The Hague has indicted a number of high officials in Sudan, including its Head of State Omar al-Bashir (ICC 2009). No matter the justification for that decision, it offers little expectation of peace and security to those directly affected by the bloodshed, including millions of displaced persons. For those people hope lies only in a drastic change of their whole political-economic environment.

A "stylised" fact

There is no phenomenon on our globe today that does more to create feelings of anxiety and insecurity than intra-state war. The cases of Afghanistan, Iraq, Sri Lanka, Democratic Republic of the Congo, Somalia and Sudan are just a few among many that come quickly to mind. Often, such conflicts are described as "ethnic" or "religious" in nature. For example, observers tracing the history of the genocide in Rwanda sometimes describe Hutu–Tutsi relations as principally based upon primordial ethnic differences (Van Putten 1994: 5).[1] Those who see intra-state war today primarily as ethnic conflict, will, however, find it difficult to answer two crucial questions:

1 How to explain that the same people who are now engaged in violent conflict can in other times live in peaceful coexistence?
2 How is it possible that in other parts of the world other peoples with more substantial cultural differences can live peacefully together in the same nation-state?

Such questions become less difficult to answer when, with Claude Ake, we see violent upsurges of ethnic identity and consciousness as an expression of "the multiple crises of economy, polity and society" (1994: 51). In conflict analysis, perhaps more than in any other field of social sciences research, one has to accept that the "polity and the economy are inextricably interlinked" (North 1990).

Though international criminal law has penalised "crimes against humanity", acts which from a normative angle are regarded as inhuman are nevertheless committed by human beings. Indeed, intra-state collective violence is a highly complex problematique, if only because it often faces us with incomprehensible facts. Consider, for example, the way in which during the Rwandan genocide otherwise "normal" men and women killed their neighbours, including the elderly as well as babies. This is, indeed, one reason why in the social sciences one can never aim at Isaiah Berlin's ideal of all natural science:

> a system of propositions so general, so clear, so comprehensive, connected with each other by logical links so unambiguous and direct that the result resembles as closely as possible a deductive system, where one can travel along wholly reliable routes from any point on the system to any other.
>
> (1997: 21)

Yet, as acts committed by human beings, crimes against humanity do fall within the research mission of the social sciences, as both *obiectum quod*, the empirical object of studies, and *obiectum quo*, the core perspective that is taken. But contrary to the natural sciences, in the social sciences we have to accept the lack of real facts that allow us to establish undeniable truths like determining the formula of water as H_2O. The collective violence observed in Sudan is distinct from that in Iraq, or in Bolivia or wherever. Differing circumstances led to each of these. What can be established are merely "stylised facts" in the sense that violent conflict as a stylised phenomenon (internationally identified on the basis of more than 1,000 deaths per annum) tends to occur in a particular setting. That environment tends to be characterised by:

1 extreme pressure on resources;
2 huge socio-economic inequalities; and/or
3 lack of a social contract.[2]

This correlation is depicted in Figure 4.3, while connecting intra-state collective violence with a poor economic structure in general.

The evident question is: what explains this "stylised" fact? To this end it is important to distinguish between economic process, economic structure and economic order. The *economic process* is the actual way in which goods and services are produced, distributed and consumed. Its performance (in flow variables, implying quantities calculated over a period of time such as a year) is measured through Gross Domestic Product (GDP) per capita. In countries with a low average income there tends to be a much higher incidence of conflicts entailing gross and systematic human rights violations.

Yet, the economic process as such does not provide any means to determine why this correlation exists. Behind it, though, is the *economic structure*, which consists of the whole of a country's productive resources in relation to the needs

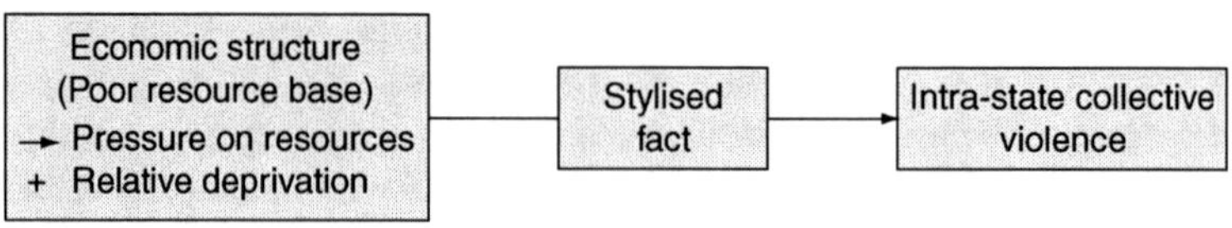

Figure 4.3 Intra-state collective violence as a stylised "economic" fact.

of its population. Productive resources are land and other natural resources, capital goods (factories, roads and other physical infrastructure such as harbours), labour (in terms of both the size of the workforce and its skills) and technical and organisational expertise. Although vital in determining a country's productive potential, these stock values are difficult to measure,[3] but it is clear that an undeveloped and vulnerable economic structure results in extreme pressure on economic resources.

However, even a strong productive potential, resulting in a relatively high GDP, is not a sufficient guarantee for a conflict-free economy. Nigeria, for example, has developed its oil resources in such a way that GDP grew at very high rates. Yet, the result has been increasing political violence. To understand why, we must examine the *economic order*: the institutional and organisational framework within which economic activity takes place. Its essence is the pattern of distribution and control of economic power, both within and without the polity. Since the role of the state is crucial in this respect, we must ask: is it effectively established, is it powerful in the sense of a capability to execute its policies and to collect taxes, is it based on the rule of law and connected to a democratic polity with a strong civil society? If not, the economic order is likely to manifest "relative deprivation".

So it is clear that in countries with a weak economic structure and a malfunctioning economic order, the environment tends to be highly conflict prone. The next question is: how do these economic circumstances lead to the actual process of preparing psychologically for war and mobilising forces for that purpose? Thus, two theorists offer an explanation: the economist Theodore Robert Gurr (1970), and the sociologist and political scientist Charles Tilly (1978).

Relative deprivation theory

Gurr's magnum opus, *Why Men Rebel* (1970), is based on the frustration-aggression hypothesis that Dollard, Doob, Miller, Mowrer and Sears presented in a pentagraph written in 1939. Gurr argues that collective frustration, lying at the roots of collective violence as it does, arises from relative deprivation, meaning a noticeable discrepancy between "value expectations", the goods and conditions of life to which people believe they are entitled, and their "value capacities", the goods and conditions they think they are capable of getting and keeping. The foundation of his theory, then, is that the potential for collective violence varies strongly with the intensity and scope of relative deprivation (Gurr 1970: 24; Dugan 2003).

For individual economic subjects, "acquirement failure" – to use the terminology already introduced (Figure 1.1) – has to do with their lack of access to resources through poor entitlement positions. But if acquirement failure is structural, it is seriously affected by the economic structure at the macro level. Relative deprivation, then, has its macroeconomic roots in a weak economic structure combined with an economic order that produces huge socio-economic inequalities. To enhance a country's economic structure, development is the prescription, in the normative sense of improving a country's productive potential in relation to its people's essential needs. To realise social justice in the sense of a more equitable distribution of income and wealth, however, democracy might help.

Not surprisingly, given these relationships, current international political thinking in regard to the resolution and prevention of intra-state violence manifests itself in a peace–democracy–development triad. Research in this triad reveals some evidence that states with appropriate institutions for representation of citizens and for the implementation of civil and political rights are relatively well off economically (Scully 1988), while we observed already that countries with relatively high levels of welfare are less conflict prone. Such static comparisons are, however, of limited significance. One problem is that in order to reach a stage of rather stable and legitimate government, countries have to go through processes of democratisation. We must keep in mind that very few states were created on the basis of homogeneous populations[4] and that global developments today work against national cultural homogeneity. In his post-Cold War paper, "Why Minorities Rebel" (1993), the same Gurr has noted that democratisation implies an increasing manifestation of communal demands. If the new regimes fail to accommodate these, "the ensuing civil wars will add to the diffusion of communal conflict and to the floods of refugees who will create future communal tensions" (1993).

As Gurr implies, the success or failure of processes of democratisation cannot be detached from processes of development related to the aspirations of communal entities. Hence, there is a need for closer examination of the socio-economic context of intra-state war and the ensuing gross and systematic human rights violations. In an economic-political sense, then, in line with Gurr's observation, collective intra-state violence may be seen as strategic action by collectivities in pursuance of their claims to certain livelihoods: "the acquirement problem" as discussed above (Chapter 1, p. 25).

Issues of acquirement, then, often follow crucial processes of change in the economic order. But before going any deeper into such processes, let us first further focus on the socio-psychological background to relative deprivation theory.

The frustration–aggression hypothesis

Gurr bases his economic-psychological explanation of the correlation between collective violence and the state of the economy on the so-called frustration–aggression hypothesis. This consists of a twofold assertion:

1 "the occurrence of aggressive behavior always presupposes the existence of frustration"; and
2 "existence of frustration always leads to some form of aggression" (Dollard *et al.* 1939: 8).

While the first proposition is still generally accepted, the latter is no longer seen as a valid assumption. In order to understand why, we have to look first at the concepts themselves.

Aggression is a form of behaviour intended to cause harm to those towards whom it is directed. Behind it, the hypothesis states, is a state of mind characterised by dissatisfaction with goals that were not achieved, "an interference with the occurrence of instigated goal-response at its proper time in the behavioral sequence" in the learned terminology of Dollard *et al.* (1939: 7). Malcontent from that interference, as Lorentz has put it rather bluntly, drives "the fighting instinct in beast and man which is directed against members of the same species" (1966: 20).

Obviously, here we find ourselves at the interface of brain, mind and consciousness on the one hand (the inner engine) with structural factors behind violence among peoples on the other hand (the outer engine.). This is, above all, the realm of those who study human behaviour as a matter of instincts and drives, the dominion of psychologists, in other words. It was Freud who proposed to approach aggression as a major instinct derived from what he calls Θάνάτος, the innate drive directed against the self. As Ερος, the other major drive, which happens to direct us towards life, usually wins, we turn our aggression outward. Through what Freud calls κάθάρσίς – acting as observers to violence, for example, or finding an outlet in the milder displays of anger – the aggressive urge, he suggests, may be diminished in emotionally purified and calmed states of mind (Dugan 2003; Campbell 1993). In such ways endless violence among human beings may be avoided.

Yet, while those who regard aggression as basically a matter of nature tend to ascribe a cathartic effect to the milder expressions of the instinct, empirical research does not substantiate that premise, as Dugan has noted (2003). Apparently, couples who quarrel most are also the most likely to engage in physical violence and "the best predictor of an individual's likelihood of criminal violence this year is his criminal violence last year" (Dugan 2003: 2). Notably, this observation corresponds fully with the positive correlation between civil war in the past and today. Thus, past outbreaks of collective violence between Serbs and Croats, to mention just one specific example, have not taught those peoples a lesson in peace-making but rather created a breeding ground for continuing and often escalating acts of aggression against one another.

Fortunately, however, the issue is not solely one of human nature. Beside those who regard aggression basically as a matter of instinct, there are two other schools of thought in respect to aggression: those who see it as externally stimulated and those who focus on learned aggression. Naturally, other disciplines come to the fore here (Dugan 2003: 1). Indeed, the frustration-aggression hypothesis is induced, as co-author Neal Miller (1941) commented two years after publication of the study launching it, from commonsense observation, from clinical case studies, from a few experimental investigations, from sociological studies and from the results of anthropological fieldwork. Not surprisingly, then, Miller himself already qualified the assertion that the existence of frustration always leads to some form of aggression as

> unfortunate from two points of view. In the first place it suggests, though it by no means logically demands, that frustration has no consequences other

> than aggression. A second objection to the assertion in question is that it fails to distinguish between instigation to aggression and the actual occurrence of aggression.
>
> (1941: 337)

The latter point was taken up by Berkowitz. He argues that, although "every frustration increases the instigation to aggression", which he terms "anger", every frustration does not necessarily result in aggression (1980: 136). Aggression results only when "there are appropriate cues or releasers" (1980: 122). The point is that between frustration-induced anger and aggression another variable appears to play its part: interpretation of one's malcontent in terms of actual response. Indeed, individuals may learn to respond to frustration and anger in non-aggressive ways.

Obviously, alternative ways of handling anger may well be learned through experience as well as transference of methods and values by those exerting an influence on the continuous processes of cultural development and personality formation. It is not just nature, but nurture, too, that plays a role here. Thus, while the impetus to human aggression may, indeed, lie in external stimuli, people may also discover more creative ways of handling their dissatisfaction than just destructive aggression. Conversely, aggression, too, may be learned behaviour, as Erich Fromm (1973), for one, has concluded from studies of so-called primitive societies. He observed that in societies with similar external indicators, some were "characterized by much interpersonal violence, destructiveness, aggression and cruelty", while the majority were life-affirmative societies, in which "there [was] a minimum of hostility, violence or cruelty among people, no harsh treatment, hardly any crime, and the institution of war [was] absent or play[ed] an exceedingly small role" (1973: 17). This would, indeed, provide an explanation of the already mentioned correlation between violent conflict in the past and civil war today: those peoples have learned to respond aggressively to feelings of frustration and the resulting anger.

Evidently, the three approaches must be seen as not so much distinct schools of thought but rather as different perspectives. Frustration-driven aggression, in other words, is a matter of nature (instinct), nurture (external stimuli) and culture (learned aggression but also learned alternatives to aggression). But enough now on socio-psychological analysis; let us further analyse collective violence in its political-economic setting.

State–society relations

While colonialism brought with it an administration in miniature which functioned fairly efficiently, both its objectives and its means were determined by the interests of the "motherland" (De Gaay Fortman and Mihyo 1993: 137). With independence and the transfer of that administration, two problems invariably arose: first, the absence of bodies and policies aimed at promoting local development and, second, the fact that the new administration was not sufficiently keyed to local cultural patterns. Here lies *one* cause of the disintegration of the state which has played a role in so many instances of intra-state violence.

The colonial legacy

The political situation in the South often bears the traces of a colonial legacy in other respects as well. Thus, Sri Lanka, Rwanda and Burundi are still suffering from the consequences of the positive discrimination of Tamils and Tutsi respectively, which was practised by the colonial power. The extended period of violent conflict in Uganda might likewise have been prevented under a different political construction than that left behind by the British. Where a nation-state is not rooted in cultural homogeneity – as is the case in most countries – a centralised government and a parliamentary democracy patterned on the Westminster model do not appear to contribute to political stability. Even in those cases where, after a period of one-party rule, countries have been able to make a fresh start, they clung to the Westminster model with a kind of Anglo-Saxon single-mindedness. Zambia and Malawi are examples which spring to mind, while South Africa is a welcome exception. The susceptibility of South Africa to intra-state violence was undeniable. Hence, it was not without reason that the process of democratisation there was ushered in by a relatively long period of reconciliation and ultimately the system that emerged was a political construction capable of keeping the forces of disintegration under control.

In Angola, by contrast, things went decidedly wrong. There the United Nations strove to emulate the success of the Namibia operation while disregarding the totally different circumstances. Thus, it was decided that preparations for the elections should begin at once. In a throwback to the days of the Cold War, the conflict in Angola was viewed in political-ideological terms, with insufficient regard for cultural factors, notably the fact that the Ovimbundu felt that they had no say under a Mbundu-dominated MPLA-government. Despite the mutual suspicion among people of different tribes that made it imperative that the elections should be preceded by a process of reconciliation, the UN forged ahead.

Obviously, then, contemporary state–society relations cannot be understood in the context of the South without due regard to the colonial legacy in respect of governance and a contextualised view of the missteps in the (often hasty) withdraw of the colonial powers.

Past conflict and (counterproductive) intervention

In many countries in which we witness instances of intra-state violence today, there has been violent conflict in the past. Major examples are the Balkans and the region of the Great Lakes in Central Africa. Reminiscences of recent killings are especially likely to ignite new violence. Strikingly, research among refugees has shown that memories of past conflict are kept alive, particularly in the camps (Malkki 1992). Hence, there is every good reason to promote either a return of refugees to their old homes or a full integration elsewhere (such as has happened with Hutu refugees in Tanzania, for example), from not only a humanitarian angle, but from a conflict-prevention angle too.

As discussed already in Chapter 3, the history of the US/UK invasion in Iraq has shown the enormous risks that such intervention carries, particularly the risk that the environment thereby created will be disabling rather than enabling from a human rights perspective. Unfortunately, the history of development assistance provides countless examples of counterproductive interventions, too, notably in the case of military aid. For example, between 1983 and 1991 Afghanistan received US$500 worth of arms for each man, woman and child in the country with little attention to the long-term effects of such an influx of weapons into the country. Civilian aid is also often counterproductive, mainly because the political and cultural aspects of the recipient country are not taken into account. Large infrastructural projects, for example, such as the construction of irrigation dams, often cause great unrest among population groups who find their access to the means of production blocked.

In much the same way, diplomatic intervention in the former Yugoslavia had the opposite effect to what was intended. The premature recognition of Croatia as an independent state, with no regard for the consequences which this would have for Bosnia, was a fatal blunder. It is possible that the peace plan for Bosnia drawn up by the mediators Vance and Owen failed because American diplomats had given the Bosnian President Izetbegovic the impression that his government could count on military intervention.

Doubtless many other examples of counterproductive interventions could be added to the list. For our purposes, however, the above instances will suffice. Notably, what is expected of states in the relatively peaceful North is not that they "do good". As Sheik Muhammad Abduh put it already more than a century ago in his lectures in London: "Do not attempt to do us any more good. Your good has done us too much harm already!" (Abduh 1890). The primary challenge is rather to take responsibility for a state of the world in which global conditions contribute significantly to structural harm.

Law and order

Strikingly, Gurr has suggested that a regime's coercive potential (read: "dictatorship") should be regarded as a factor that might mitigate a country's conflict susceptibility (1970). The explanation is simply that dictatorships possess a capacity to suppress all kinds of dissidence, including resource mobilisation for entitlement defence on the basis of distinct collective identity. This observation clearly relates to the risks inherent in fast processes of democratisation in the transitional periods referred to above.

Gurr's observation is not, however, the whole story. Actually, what we often observe in conflict-sensitive societies is a "dual state". Usually processes of law are just "normal", but as soon as the regime deems that "security interests" are at stake, it arbitrarily interferes in those processes. In other words, that a state appears to be governed by the rule of law as codified in legislation is not necessarily a strong indicator of its conflict susceptibility. In the dialectics of law and power, a shift in the direction of power is far more often indicative of a susceptibility to violent conflict. In South and Central America during the 1970s and early 1980s, the impunity resulting from such shifts in power (perpetrators of crimes who are connected to state power go unpunished) has contributed significantly to revolutionary violence. In Sri Lanka, to cite another example, the civil war started in 1982 after Tamil leaders had been lynched inside prison, and consequently the whole Tamil population lost whatever was left of their trust in the rule of law. An administration's capacity to truly govern without discrimination indeed appears to be decisive in creating and maintaining its citizens' trust in the rule of law and the absence of the capacity to govern without discrimination is a strong indicator of a country's conflict susceptibility.

Notably, while our "stylised" politico-economic fact tends to hold in countries confronted with civil strife culminating in collective violence with gross and systematic violations of human rights, naturally the correlation is not a rigid causal relationship. A major challenge in the social sciences is, indeed, to explain the exceptions to a presumed connection.

One explanation lies in the notion of relative deprivation itself. In Zambia, for example, the fall of the copper price in the 1970s and 1980s, resulting in a fall in GDP of more than two-thirds, did not lead to intra-state collective violence as the economic deterioration affected the different ethnic communities all in the same way. Suppose President Kenneth Kaunda's government had especially protected the Northern Province (where he was born and whose Bemba speakers form the country's largest tribal community), opposition forces might have been mobilised in the other provinces, possibly resorting to political violence. Instead, even though there was significant deprivation, it was "relatively" the same for both non-dominant and dominant collectivities, resulting in frustration but not aggression.

It is in this connection that we touch upon Charles Tilly's theory, which focused attention upon the mobilisation of individual resources for collective ends (1978). At the roots of political violence stands collective action, for which people have to be mobilised on the basis of common interests against the state. A particular challenge in this context is to explain the breakdown between "routine collective action" (e.g. electoral rallies, peaceful protest) and "nonroutine collective action" (e.g. rebellion, collective violence, riots). Participants must find a collective motivation to free themselves from the restraints on violent behaviour, both moral and physical, that the public-political community normally imposes upon its members. The idea of a "social contract" is crucial here, in the sense of a state regarded by citizens as "their own", based on its capacity to govern according to the rule of law and to maintain law and order nondiscriminately. Here Gurr enters the picture again.

The core issue to which Gurr (1970) called attention, remember, concerns perceived discrepancies between people's value expectations and their value capacities. This leads him to the hypothesis that the potential for collective violence varies strongly with the intensity and scope of relative deprivation among members of a collectivity. Economically, this results from a weak and vulnerable economic structure and a malfunctioning economic order, as we have already seen.

The state appears to play a pivotal role in this respect, in its influence on people's value capacities through provision of basic public services like health and education, in its protection of private and institutional entitlement systems and in the way in which it directly or indirectly arranges and rearranges entitlements. One of the major factors here is the state's own juridical structure: is the government centralised or does it take the form of a (con)federation? In the relationship between Russia and Chechnya, for example, this aspect appears to have played a decisive part. The structure of party politics within the country is also of crucial importance. Political democracy must be seen as an ongoing process. In this process the separation of powers and the possibility for a continuous development of checks and balances tend to be of more significance than periodical elections. Indeed, there are frightful instances of post-conflict elections followed by a resumption of violence (e.g. Angola in 1992, see above, p. 113).

From a human rights-conducive angle then, certain institutions play a crucial role in suppressing a country's susceptibility to collective abuse of power:

- a functioning legal system, which provides a juridical basis for the government to maintain law and order, to execute its policies and to collect the necessary taxes;
- an independent, competent and accessible judiciary in order to achieve the necessary checks and balances;
- a free press that serves to guarantee transparency in all use of power; and
- a professional central bank, which is not subordinate to politics so that the currency is stable and enterprise can thrive.

If post-conflict processes of democratisation do not begin with a period of national reconciliation and the establishment of such institutions, but rather with immediate elections, there will be a risk that the political conflict will escalate into full-fledged warfare. As we know, this is precisely what happened in countries like Angola (the already mentioned elections of 1992) and Rwanda (the preparation for multi-party elections in 1994).

It is, indeed, not only democracy, but also such concepts as "rule of law" and "good governance" that must be seen as processes. "Responsive governance" means not only taking one's own citizens seriously, but also continuously structuring the market economy for the benefit of all. This includes the creation of a social and juridical infrastructure. Douglass North speaks here of "path dependent development" (1990), by which he means the institutional basis to take due account of economies of scale, complementarities and externalities in production. If this fails, people will conclude that productive activities are not worthwhile and will then focus their economic energy on redistributive activities. In such a situation the stakes in politics become so high that the political struggle may deteriorate into war as a continuation of politics by other means, which is itself a continuation by other means of the economic search to satisfy people's value capacities.

Another factor which is clearly of importance in regard to conflict susceptibility is political leadership. Notably, political leaders confronted with the failure of policies designed to solve social problems often undertake to do "something grand". The political temptation to wage war, in particular where the government is lacking in democratic calibre, has been exemplified in the Falklands War between Great Britain and Argentina. More research is needed to establish the extent to which a country does indeed get the leadership it deserves in the sense that bad and irresponsible leadership is not just co-accidental but related to certain other structural factors. Crucial institutional factors in relation to the cultivation of good political leadership seem to be substitutability of power in processes of government formation and control of power through strong mechanisms of accountability. Failing these, elections are not only worthless but counterproductive in that they provide a mask of legitimacy for otherwise illegitimate rule. "Civil society" in the sense of a strong institutional landscape between the family and the state is also crucial in this regard. A strong state requires a strong civil society; a strong democracy needs strong individuals in the sense of citizens who cannot be easily cheated, whether individually or collectively.

In Africa it is particularly the churches that have significantly expanded their activities into the realm of civil society. Indeed, in Zambia, Kenya and Malawi they were at the roots of a democratisation process. In Rwanda, however, bad political leadership in the years preceding the genocide went together with irresponsible behaviour on the part of church leaders, contributing to collective ethnic prejudice.

Ethnic differentiation is a culturally constructed rather than a primordial factor, but it is no less important for that. The ethnic differences which groups of people experience are often the object of political and religious manipulation. In Rwanda, as we saw, the situation was seriously corrupted by propaganda ("Radio Machete"), and the same can be said of the former Yugoslavia. In this respect the support of free and independent media is one form of constructive intervention. Such media are grounded in a strong civil society.

The foundation of a well-functioning civil society lies in education. In this respect, the situation in Africa worsened substantially at the end of the last century. The strong relationship between deteriorating economic conditions and the quality of education must be made explicit and effectively addressed. Staff/student ratios of over 1:100 are not an exception, even at university level. An improvement of such conditions exerts a positive effect on conflict safety only, though, if it coincides with a rise in employment opportunities for young graduates. In this connection one might bear in mind that in Sri Lanka violence started with extremist political mobilisation of well educated youngsters with few employment prospects in both Sinhala and Tamil circles.

External interventions aiming at conflict prevention, then, should be directed towards strengthening organisations that play a constructive role in civil society.

At the government level, efforts may be made aiming at mediation and reconciliation of the opposing factions ("preventive diplomacy"). These could be complemented by development assistance designed to create and improve institutions which render a social market economy more viable. Thus, development cooperation may return to its starting points from the 1960s: "institution-building" and "institution-strengthening". As mentioned above, development aid that is not directly tied with these institutional objectives is not only wasted, but often counterproductive. As discussed in the previous chapter, the main challenge continues to lie in reform of the global politico-economic order.

Indicators

In terms of policy the challenge in finding the necessary indicators in regard to local realities is not just early warning but *early action*. Although naturally, there are no genuine "causality data" (Murshed 2010), early warning indicators already exist, for example, in the observations of foreign envoys all over the world, in figures collected by the United Nations and its specialised agencies, and in the fact-finding work of international nongovernmental organisations such as the International Crisis Group. In its 1994 *Human Development Report*, the UNDP already identified a number of countries in a severe state of crisis. The major issue is how to react to these warnings. If, indeed, the roots of conflict are to a significant extent of an economic-political nature, the challenge becomes to link political strategies aimed at reconciliation to intervention of a politico-economic nature.

Naturally, however, it remains crucial to get indications of conflict susceptibility at such an early stage that politico-economic intervention is still possible. From such an "early early" warning perspective, there is a natural interest in indicators of a country's susceptibility to intra-state violence and the preceding and ensuing gross human rights violations that accompany it. Indeed, as a basis of early action (intervention by whatever peaceful and/or military means) an assessment is needed in respect of a country's conflict susceptibility. Furthermore, concrete studies are called upon to examine which institutions could be conducive to peaceful interaction in specific regional and national contexts, whether in pre-conflict, post-conflict or relatively conflict-free situations. In order to appreciate the complexity and importance of this task more specifically, let us return to the stylised fact explained above.

Human development and the democratic factor

At the bottom of the Human Development Index (HDI) ranking,[5] as provided by the United Nations Development Programme (UNDP) in its annual *Human Development Report* we generally find countries engaged in intra-state collective violence, such as Zimbabwe, DR Congo, Niger, Burundi, Mozambique (now at a peace-building stage), Guinea Bissao, Chad, Liberia, etc. (HDR 2010). Moreover, in an analysis of *Democracy, Power, Genocide, and Mass Murder*,

Rummel (1995) found only one political indicator of "democide" (genocide, massacres, extrajudicial executions, etc.): totalitarian power. Indeed, Gurr's mitigating factor – the state's coercive potential to suppress dissension – relates only to the short term; in the long term, dictatorship naturally calls for collective resistance and revolution.

Democracy, Rummel concluded, is inversely related to democide. "That power kills is the primary and, for domestic democide, singular general explanation of democide … and the more democratic [a society is] the less domestic collective violence" (emphasis in the original, 1995: 25). Hence, in trying to assess conflict susceptibility one might think of combining the UNDP's annually computed HDI with a kind of "human freedom index" (HFI) as calculated in the *Human Development Report* 1991.[6] To a certain degree, this combination of factors may help to discriminate between high and low "armed conflict"-prone countries.

The problem, however, is that countries cannot become established democracies just like that. Furthermore, the mere fact that certain countries show positive indicators for levels of welfare and democracy does not warrant the conclusion of continued peaceful interaction in the future. For example, what would happen with the established democracies in rich countries should their incomes be halved in a relatively short period? Within one decade, such a decline has manifested itself in several African countries. After the end of the Cold War, even more marked income downfalls have taken place in new states such as Armenia, Azerbaijan, Georgia and Tadzhikistan. These states have certainly been beset by internal strife. But here, too, one cannot simply pass judgment from an observation of erupting violence in just one dimension of social activity.

Thus, the issue of indicators involves more than just the question of why intra-state armed conflicts have emerged in the so-called Third (and former Second) World, whereas in this respect the First World has been relatively conflict-free in the period 1945–1992. The exceptions to this stylised fact require explanations too. More or less counterfactual cases like Mexico, Northern Ireland, the former Yugoslavia and Sri Lanka make this clear. Allowing for the possibility that democracy and high levels of development are not necessarily unconditional safeguards against the occurrence of collective violence, we need a dynamic view on institutions rather than comparative static analysis. It becomes pivotal when conducting concrete case studies, then, to grasp two separate but closely intertwined concepts:

1 differences in institutional structures and the way in which these are related to behaviour and outcome; and
2 the social forces that through some mechanism propel or block institutional change.

One possible way, then, to conceive of a possible indicator of intra-state violence is a measurement of human security, which is also connected with relative deprivation.

Human security

Security has to do with the many threats people face in their lives. In a broad sense it entails safety, protection against disaster and a dimension of prevention: a minimisation of threats to human (co)existence. Thus, it means freedom from disaster, anxiety, attack and violent disruption of what is considered a "normal" life. These correspond to FDR's freedoms from want and fear. Yet there may be as many perceptions of a "normal" life as there are people on our planet. Notably, each period in human history seems to be preoccupied with its own specific interpretations of security (Rothschild 1995). For example, during the Cold War there was a nearly exclusive emphasis on security between states, whereas now there is much more emphasis on the security of collectivities within the state. Essentially, then, security is a contested concept. Contradictions pertain to relations between defence and security, between individual, national and international security and between violent means and peaceful ends (Buzan 1991).

In response to such contradictions and interdependencies, Tinbergen and Fischer (1987) had already proposed to couple the issues of welfare and security in addressing these as a combined "problematique". The *Human Development Report* 1994 of the UNDP is also indicative of a new notion of security between people rather than just states. Specifically, the report attempts to unite the two pillars of security: freedom from want and freedom from fear. Components of this notion of human security concern the economy, food, health, the environment and personal, community and political security.

The army

Armies are supposed to promote external security. The latter, however, can never be seen in isolation from internal resistance to violence, as related to people's own assessment of the quality of their lives. Hence, military expenditures must always be weighed against other things on which the limited public funds might be spent, such as health-care and education.

Processes which result in the militarisation of government tend to make a country more susceptible to intra-state violence. Military regimes usually give priority to the purchase of weapons, and this requires foreign currency which has to be earned by export. Not only economic development, but also the political system is regulated from on high, while the legal system is subordinated to the battle against the "enemy from within".

An indicator in this context is the percentage of the national budget allocated for military expenditures. Military aid usually entails years of largely counterproductive intervention. Support for an existing conversion programme (from arms production to civilian manufacture) might be seen as an example of constructive intervention, and the same applies to programmes for voluntary destruction of weaponry accompanied by employment schemes for those leaving the army.

Finally on the matter of "early early warning", the United Nations Development Program (UNDP) perceives "development" as a process of extending the

Table 4.1 Analysing local susceptibility to intra-state collective violence

Conflict = **And its roots in:**	**Perceived**	**Incompatibility of**	**Interests**
Society	• Socially open or closed • Role of ideology • Us–them divides • Collective prejudice	• Pluralism • Systems of power-sharing • Quality of group leadership • Social mobility • Protection of non-dominant collectivities	• Group recognition and group rights (rights of collectivities) • Collective (in)equality (systemic discrimination)
Culture	• Freedom of expression • Ways of voicing dissent and criticism • Role of media • Cultures of dominance and submission (e.g. patriarchy)	• Freedom of worship • Fundamentalism vs. tolerance • Multiculturalism • Quality of religious leadership	• Cultural identities • Religious convictions • Voice • Cultural rights
Polity	• Do citizens regard the state as their own or do they feel that the state owns them? • Democratisation? • Legitimacy of power formation and execution	• Social contract • Democratic institutions • Quality of political leadership • Rules of law with a fair and functioning legal system • Role of the army	• Access to political power and to public goods • Citizenship and political rights • Legal protection
Economy	• Trends and expectations in economic growth/stability and in (perceived) entitlement positions	• Employment • Poverty and vulnerability • Empowerment and rights • Scope for collective action (from resistance to reform) • Land reform • Development	• Income and wealth (distribution) • Pressure on and access to resources • Economic and social rights • Entitlement systems and social protection

range of people's choices, while security means that these choices can be freely and safely exercised over time. The challenge remains to connect the two in one new paradigm for "sustainable human development" that encompasses human security and human rights. Meanwhile case studies remain an obvious prerequisite in any attempt to concretely assess conflict prone environments. Table 4.1 provides a tool that may help in such analyses. It looks at conflict in its generally accepted nature of "perceived incompatibility of interests", implying columns referring to collective perceptions, factors influencing (in)compatibility (dispute settlement) and group interests. These are to be examined in the context of society, culture, the polity and the economy.

Thus, the table contains 12 boxes, each with elements influencing a country's susceptibility to intra-state violence. In this tool for concrete case studies one row – which has so far not been touched upon in this chapter – relates to culture and the role of religion. We shall now turn to this important element in contextual human rights research.

The impact of culture and religion

Culture may be seen as "a characteristic arrangement of customs, objects and behaviours which are linked to learned, shared and flexible rules, values, norms and ideas through which people respond to their surroundings" (Gasper 1994). People experience the world outside through a sort of filter which serves to classify, interpret and assess the stimuli in their environment to which they then respond. This process "follows patterns of learned actions and reactions which have developed over the course of time in specific circumstances. It is this interaction … that engenders cultures and produces such a wide variety of them" (AIV 2005: 7).

People function as members of many different groups: in their families, at work, in areas of leisure, in religious or secular contexts, as residents of a village, city or country, and as citizens of the world. Each of these groups has its own way of filtering external experiences and impressions, to the extent that its members share certain ideas, knowledge and experience. "That common basis gives the group and its members their characteristic identity, which overlaps with other identities they may have" (AIV 2005: 7).

In respect of human rights realisation, culture functions as both a resource and a constraint. As a resource it sustains convictions and commitments towards fundamental rights based on universal human dignity. As a constraint it tends to manifest itself in exclusive views and cruel practices that are often religiously justified. One might think here of ethnic discrimination, religious intolerance based on collective prejudices against "unbelievers" and inhumane practices such as female genital mutilation. Culture and religion also affect leadership. A concern was, for example, the impact of irresponsible religious leadership in conflict prone contexts such as Northern Ireland, Serbia, Rwanda and Sri Lanka, where it appears to have fostered violence.

The problem of cultural receptivity

Naturally, a cultural filter and the feelings of identity it creates are shaped primarily within the (extended) family. Patriarchy, for example, is characterised by male dominance and female dependency and a focus on "masculine" values. Further research may reveal to what extent such a micro context should be seen as a breeding ground for cultures of violence. (Strikingly, in Northern Ireland women had to play a notable part in order to engage in processes of peace.) At any rate, an important aspect of the micro-order would appear to be its involvement in the transference of values, often within a religious setting.

Above all, in respect of human rights realisation a focus is needed on cultural receptivity to the values behind these rights in the local *meso*-context. Indeed, spiritual roots of a culture of human rights have to be found in different social and cultural contexts.[7] Hence, in accepting their responsibility for the implementation of human rights, states and the international human rights movement are well advised to look for religious and other types of moral support for efforts made within the environment of their specific jurisdiction in addition to the international setting. An example of such an effort is the Cairo Declaration on Human Rights (1990). This is, however, not unproblematic, as the effort to connect the Islamic world with global human rights explicitly declared that all rights and freedoms mentioned are subject to Islamic Sharia, which affects universality, particularly in respect of freedom of religion and the position of women.

Naturally, it is not just within an Islamic context that cultural receptivity happens to be challenging. Particularly problematic in the setting of the United States, for example, is the principle of recognition of need – social justice – that lies behind articles 22 to 25 of the Universal Declaration of Human Rights (United Nations 1948) and the International Covenant on Economic, Social and Cultural Rights (United Nations 1966b). The struggle for social justice appeals to people's sense of solidarity and collective responsibility. But in the context of a settlers' society like the United States – a country that has such a dominant influence on global culture – it is individual autonomy rather than social justice that dominates legal and political thinking. ("Your well-being is not my concern. I made it. It's up to you to make it on your own!") As we all know, this type of politico-legal thinking is not confined to that particular country, as the whole culture underlying economic globalisation tends to be generally based on possessive individualism[8] rather than social justice.

Indeed, the real issue is not the universality of the human rights idea per se but a universal reception of that idea. No culture, in the sense of a way of life transferred from one generation to the next, is fully receptive to the notion of universal human dignity and equality. It is an illusion to think that this idea might be simply disseminated by means of readable material. Indeed, the human rights project cannot escape confronting deeper questions such as "Who is the human being?" and "What is freedom?" (Mufazzar 1994).

To illustrate: in some Western countries, liberal policies on pornography are legally regarded as a consequence of the basic freedom of expression (press freedom). Such a view exemplifies the shortfall of human rights as a secular religion connected to a universalist legal system with clearly defined procedures and institutions. Yet, there is no way to escape the necessity of weighing one person's freedom to express against the freedom of others to regard certain expressions as dehumanising, repugnant and hence intolerable. There are, indeed, comprehensible reasons to justify the decriminalisation of the production, distribution and consumption of pornography, but human rights is definitely not one of them. The difficulties that this misuse and misunderstanding of human rights causes are used elsewhere to construe human rights as not universal at all, but rather as a caricature of Western thinking.[9]

A glance through the jurisprudence of the European Court of Human Rights reveals a surprisingly large number of cases in which criminal suspects and convicted persons invoke certain articles in the European Convention for the Protection of Human Rights and Fundamental Freedoms (Rome Treaty of 1950) in regard to criminal procedure. This is not unimportant: the protection of everyone against the abuse of power, including criminals, constitutes the core of human rights. (Often after liberation from tyranny, the formerly oppressed have to get used to the idea that torturing their former oppressors would mean violating the same human rights on which they based their struggle.) Yet it is clearly not the jurisprudence of the European Court in Strasbourg that is going to provide the human rights project with the necessary cultural roots in Europe itself let alone the rest of the world. The main challenge everywhere is the realisation of fundamental freedoms and sustainable daily livelihoods. The Human Rights mission bases this upon the notion of universal respect for human dignity. Contextualising this foundational value in diverse cultures and contextualising strategies to overcome diverse cultural constraints may well enhance universal acknowledgement of human rights.

Indeed, the very idea of universality signifies also responsibility for the realisation of fundamental rights of people elsewhere. Rapidly increasing global inequalities illustrate, however, the lack of global mechanisms to correct injustices, as we saw already in the previous chapter. The phrase "everywhere in the world" as used by President Franklin D. Roosevelt in his "Four Freedoms Address" and subsequently endorsed in the Universal Declaration of Human Rights now requires primarily implementation rather than new standard-setting. Thus, whatever view one takes on the question of universality of human rights norms, there definitely is a universal problem of receptivity.

Notably, cultural receptivity is not a one-way process from existing and unchanging human rights norms towards their integration in certain specific cultures. Since the ratification of the Universal Declaration of Human Rights, non-Western cultures have exerted a growing influence on formulations of rights in new charters and covenants. This has meant a shift in emphasis towards duties, also in regard to communities, economic, social and cultural rights, and collective rights. In further attempts to objectivise human rights, non-Western views on justice may play an increasing role. Although an individual-centred and rights-oriented view lies at the roots of the historical process of formulating international human rights standards, a growing moral universality will require receptivity to alternative approaches to justice. In regard to economic and social rights a predominance of non-Western (communitarian) thinking is already noticeable. As Virginia Leary has said:

> Despite its contemporary Western origin dating to post Second World War, the antecedence informed by the earlier life of World religions and moral philosophies, the concept of human rights must now be recognised as a universal term accepted through the world. But the concept is a dynamic and evolutionary one that has recently been extended to cover many aspects of human dignity not contemplated under the traditional Western rubric of human rights. Western influence, dominant in the origin of the development of international human rights norms, is now only one of a number of cultural influences on the development of international human rights standards. Its contribution to the development of human rights has been great, but it has not been unique, and other cultures have made and are making significant contributions to our collective conception of human dignity.
>
> (Leary 1990: 29–30)

It is noteworthy in this respect that whereas in their Western historical context human rights developed as a protective concept – to defend the autonomy of individual citizens against threats coming particularly from sovereigns (states) that would try to extend their power into the citizens' own realm – in the cultural context of Africa, Asia and South and Central America the human rights idea is of a much more emancipatory character: a struggle for truly universal human dignity through realised rights of the have-nots. While our analysis already disclosed that human rights are highly action-oriented, this applies particularly to the situation in developing countries:

> Human rights have often been functioning as the rights of the privileged both at the world level and also in national and local societies. But the dispossessed, the underprivileged, and that is the majority of the world, they regard human rights as instruments of liberation and emancipation.
>
> (Leary 1990: 30)

In such a context human rights are used as a legal resource as well as a political instrument for social change while playing their part particularly in the struggles of social movements (see Table 1.1).

From a human rights perspective, then, culture indeed acts as a two-sided sword. On the one hand, the cultural filter through which people experience the outside world is indispensable in terms of sustaining that global faith in universal dignity and equal rights. On the other hand it may double as a serious constraint to that faith. Let us now first examine the former aspect of culture. Generally, this concerns the need for Faith (with a capital F) in the sense of a transcendental worldview in which the belief in universal human dignity is grounded. In this connection a distinction may be made between religion and faith.

Why human rights needs faith

The term religion stems from the Latin *religio* in the sense of a bond. While religion may manifest itself as doctrine, rules and hierarchies, faith refers to authentic conviction and concrete commitment. It is the Muslim scholar Abdullahi An-Na'im in particular who has suggested shifting the debate on "religion and human rights" from textual interpretations of prescriptions and proscriptions to the actual understanding and practice of belief (2004). In the present study "faith" as proclaimed in the foundational human rights documents is written with a small f, whereas "Faith" signifies a transcendental belief to drive, sustain and inspire that faith in human dignity and its associated values of liberty, equality and solidarity, which were proclaimed in Article 1 of the 1948 Universal Declaration of Human Rights (see Figure I.1).

The Declaration was followed, as we saw (above, pp. 44–45), by numerous international covenants, conventions, protocols and declarations of the General Assembly of the United Nations in texts with a lesser immediate appeal. Although in a legal sense the universality of human rights is now almost undisputed and a great deal of political consensus on the human rights' idea exists as well, there are still serious difficulties in realising these rights. Obviously, their inclusion in legal texts is in itself insufficient. It is often precisely in states with the most serious human rights violations that we find the most elaborate and high-sounding constitutional clauses on fundamental freedoms and entitlements. Accessible procedures of a supranational nature have been effectively created only in Europe. But in order to bring a case before the European Court of Justice, all local remedies must have been exhausted. This may take a long time and it may also require a considerable investment in lawyers' fees. Hence, contentious action, however important as a remedy for human rights violations, has to be accompanied by socio-cultural and political action aiming at cultural receptivity (De Gaay Fortman 1995).

Yet, in the period following the adoption of the Declaration, the human rights project was interpreted, as we saw, as a juridical challenge to legislate and to create procedural provisions for judgment of individual and state complaints. On the basis of an intrinsically neutral attitude towards the culture, regime, religious beliefs and the level of prosperity in the country concerned, human rights violations, it had been concluded, would have to be denounced everywhere.

As we know, the acceptance of that responsibility for protection of the human dignity of everyone requires more than just a legal basis, no matter how universal that foundation may be. Indeed, the ratification of treaties, the establishment of courts of human rights and the development of human rights jurisprudence is not enough. The moral grounds for a conviction upon which responsible behaviour rests have to be constantly nurtured on the basis of a worldview. Insofar as the notion of human rights is to be sustained in individualism, it is "responsible" individualism that matters. This is evidently not the same as "possessive" individualism. Yet the former may easily degenerate into the latter.

It is exactly those cultures in which possessive individualism has strong roots – and that includes the global village as such – which experience great difficulty with economic and social rights, as early as the stage of standard-setting. While individualism may offer a sufficient moral foundation for respecting everyone's fundamental freedoms, it is inadequate as a basis for accepting other people's needs as grounds for justified claims. Economic, social and cultural rights presuppose not just free individuals but a community that accepts responsibility for the fulfilment of everyone's basic needs.

The liberal-democratic idea – according to Francis Fukuyama the end of the history of ideas (Fukuyama 1992) – fails here. In the ideal type of a free market economy the weak find no structural protection against unemployment, disease, disability and old age. For good reasons, dependence on the charity of the strong was considered unsatisfactory. In many industrialised countries measures such as workers' protection, compulsory education, professional training and health protection constituted a structural attempt towards the realisation of economic and social rights. The social struggle that led to such achievements was nurtured by Faith in the sense of a set of ideas transcending individual existence. (In this sense socialism, too, may be regarded as Faith.)

Friedrich Hayek, the godfather of neo-liberalism, once wrote a book under the title *The Mirage of Social Justice*. It is only a negative notion of freedom, he feels (keep your hands off other people's property, allow everyone her liberty) that can be more than a mirage. Hence, for a vision on social justice we have to look elsewhere.

John Rawls is well known as a philosopher who has attempted to construct political principles of justice applicable to any society that tackles not just the problem of freedom, but the problem of inequalities among people as well (Rawls 1972). His "non-normative" theory is based on a hypothetical social contract between citizens who, behind a "veil of ignorance" regarding their relative success or failure in acquiring entitlement positions, decide what is socially "fair". This is not the place to review that theory critically, but it is clearly noteworthy that Rawls' rational-liberal theory of justice failed him when he tried to construct a political "law of peoples" that would legitimate human rights on the basis of reason only (Rawls 1999). For one thing, he feels compelled to abandon the three egalitarian features of his theory of justice: the fair value of political liberties, fair equality of opportunity and the difference principle.[10] Thus, his human rights concept deals only with civil rights and excludes political and socio-economic rights, let alone the rights of collectivities. His argument then implies that even representatives of hierarchical societies, committed in a rather absolute sense to certain ideologies and religions, placed behind a veil of ignorance (the basic assumption in hypothetical contract theory) would accept the same "law of peoples", including basic civil rights, possessed by democratic societies. But why would they? As Stanley Hoffmann reasons (1995: 54):

> Are societies whose governments are dogmatically committed to ideology or religion likely to respect basic human rights at all? Since there are no free elections, how would we know that their "system of law" meets "the essentials of legitimacy in the eyes of [their] own people"? Whatever the answer, what is clear is that Rawls's law of peoples has been shaped so as to appeal to a purely hypothetical group of peoples.

The fallacy lies in the parallel Rawls seems to draw between an "overlapping consensus" of comprehensive doctrines that endorse a single conception of justice within a democratic political culture, and an "overlapping consensus" of societies based on very different political conceptions of justice. Such different societies could only endorse a very weak "law of peoples" (Hoffmann 1995: 54).

Hence, for a stronger "law of peoples" one has to look beyond "non-ideal theory" (Rawls). Indeed, we cannot escape the search for the conceptual roots of human rights within the various religions themselves. Research done by Wronka would point to a preliminary conclusion that the idea of one person's responsibility for satisfaction of another person's needs is common to all world religions (Wronka 1998). An example is the Bible, in which *tsedâqâh* implies acknowledgement of the claims of the poor, purely on basis of their need. Thus, the connection with religion may provide the necessary cultural basis for the struggle for economic, social and cultural rights. Notably, apart from all sorts of political and economic constraints to the implementation of human rights, there also exists a major obstacle in the cultural resistance to norms and values implying that people are responsible for the well-being of their fellow human beings. A "culture of contentment" predominates in the post-Cold War era, paralysing the global "haves". In this connection Christopher Lasch spoke of a rebellion of the elites and the betrayal of democracy (Lasch 1994 (posthumous)). With so many people excluded from a decent existence, the human rights project suffers from structural – day-to-day – violation; this is the core of its deficit.

In terms of human rights realisation, then, the true issue is of a moral-cultural nature: how do people see each other? One way of seeing people in daily hardship, living in distant countries (or in any other socially or spatially constructed category), is as a threat. It is the problems of ecological destruction and migration in particular that might convince the world's rich of the need for a global care system for the benefit of the poor (De Swaan 1988). A second way of viewing the deprived is as victims to whose welfare massive relief operations might be directed within the framework of modern charity. It is doubtful, however, whether either or both these ways of seeing other people will provide sufficient inspiration and motivation for global collective action for social justice. But there is a third way of viewing them: as fellow human beings, i.e. as people with the same dignity and fundamental rights. A crucial question arises here: What is the basis of humankind's belief in liberty, responsibility, equality and the value of human life per se? The response to that query cannot be universal as not all men and women share the same basic convictions.

For the three Abrahamic religions – Judaism, Christianity and Islam – Faith means trust in one God, creator of heaven and earth. He is respected as the One who endowed the human being with reason and conscience, and hence continues calling people to do justice, establish peace and respect life in the whole creation, which may be graphically represented as in Figure 4.4.

This Faith-based anthropology is reflected in Article 1 UDHR, albeit with two exceptions: there is no mention of God, or of nature. As to the first, the *universality* of the Declaration requires, as we saw, faith-based identification with its principles and values from the perspective of plural religious constituencies, including those who see the source of reason and conscience not in God but in humanity itself.[11] Hence, the founding fathers of the Declaration (with founding mother Eleanor Roosevelt in the forefront) refrained from any deeper grounding of that faith in the dignity and worth of the human person, which the preamble reaffirms. The second absence has to do with the times: just after the Second World War had shown the extent to which human beings could violate human dignity; to fight and prevent such injustice was the sole focus in the new international justice venture.[12] Had a global faith-based document as the UDHR been adopted today, a connection with human responsibility towards nature would certainly have been part of it.[13]

Although, as noted already, Faith-based approaches to human rights cannot be of a universal character, these distinct perspectives do not necessarily affect the universal nature of human rights as such. At the same time, such linking to the sources of faith in the equal dignity and worth of wo/men and their inherent freedoms and responsibilities may play a vital part in establishing a genuine global human rights constituency. A striking illustration of a faith-based endorsement of human rights as in essence God-given came from the Roman Catholic bishops in Latin America. Notably, in his encyclical *Quanta Cura* with its annexed *Syllabus of Errors*, Pope Pius IX had censured the idea of inalienable

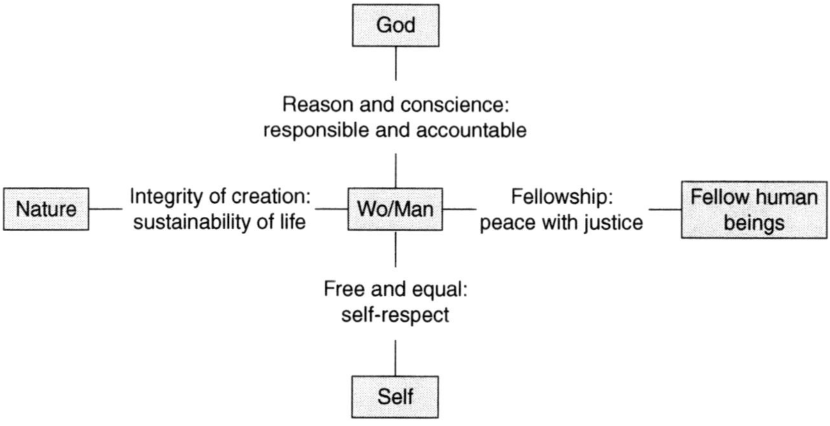

Figure 4.4 An anthropology common to the three Abrahamic religions.

human rights (1864). Yet, although that denunciation has never been formally withdrawn, in 1992 the Latin American bishops fully endorsed the human rights idea as follows:

> The equality of all human beings, created as they are in the image of God, is guaranteed and completed in Christ. From the time of his incarnation, when the Word assumes our nature and especially through his redemption on the cross, He demonstrates the value of every single human being. Therefore Christ, God and man, constitutes also the deepest source and guarantee for the dignity of the human person. Each violation of human rights is contrary to God's plan and sinful.
>
> (CELAM 1993: 164)[14]

In this statement the Christian faith is seen as the deepest foundation of all human rights. It illustrates how faith-based approaches to human rights may even lead to a complete synthesis of two missions that are separate in origin and principle. In order to secure actual protection of human dignity, connections between secular settings of human rights and Faith-based views on their grounds are, indeed, crucial. The belief in human equality, for example, is sustained by Faith-based assumptions that all human beings spring from the same origin.[15] An Islamic source for the belief in equality and the need for fellowship is Surah 49: 13: "O mankind! We created you from a single (pair) of a male and a female…!"[16]

Faith, then, requires first (re)*confirmation*, or (re)affirmation as it is called in the preambles of both the UN Charter and the Universal Declaration of Human Rights. These documents, in other words, represent not only a conviction but also a commitment: walk the talk! "Free and equal in dignity and rights" requires individual self-respect, structural incorporation of respect for each and every human being in the institutions of society, and actual day-to-day protection against abuse of power over others. Indeed, right after their faith-based affirmation of human rights, the Latin American bishops expressed a deep concern about daily abuse. These rights, they note, are however grossly and systematically violated from day to day:

> not only by terrorism, repression and attacks … but also through the existence of extreme poverty and unjust economic structures which result in extreme inequality. Political intolerance and indifference in regard to the situation of general impoverishment reveal a general contempt for concrete human life on which we cannot remain silent.
>
> (CELAM 1993: 165)

Hence, as a "pastoral action line" the bishops request the realisation of human rights in an effective and courageous manner

> based on both the gospel and the social doctrine of the Church, by word, action and cooperation, and in that way to commit ourselves to the defence

> of the individual and social rights of human beings, peoples, cultures and marginalised sectors of society, together with persons in a state of extreme vulnerability and prisoners.
>
> (CELAM 1993: 165)

Unquestionably then, the fellowship that human beings are called upon to establish is not just a matter of envisioning the others as free and equal creatures but also of doing justice and living together in peace. Indeed, as argued already repeatedly above, the gist of the whole international human rights venture might be much more tuned to realisation rather than just to the intricacies of setting standards, making reservations, declaring new rights and interpreting specific articles.

Second, Faith implies *accountability*. "Reason and conscience" call for a self-image based on responsibility and with that accountability towards all those affected by public as well as private decision-making. As a matter of faith, and hence of transcendental inference, human beings are accountable. Consequently, power becomes authority, based on principles and standards to protect life in dignity. Notably then, protection of all those over whom power is exercised – a core idea in the international venture for the realisation of human rights – is a Faith-based requirement.

Indeed, in a moral political sense the principal question in respect of those living in daily hardship is not "What problems will these people cause?" or "What can we do for these poor devils?" but "How can their rights be realised?" The way in which such questions are put is related to socio-political concepts of freedom. Does freedom mean easy access to video and audio equipment? Does it mean earning a high income so that one can have a wide choice of goods while opting for many things at the same time? Does freedom imply not making choices that exclude other options – indeed, never committing one? Or does freedom mean choosing one particular path and staying loyal to that choice in the sense of a real commitment. For the latter, a conviction is required that directs people's attention to more than the mere satisfaction of their own wants. Human rights, in other words, primarily implies a conviction and a commitment that needs local realities, which continuously sustain and nurture that engagement through spiritual beliefs and practices transcending pure egotism and power-based instincts.

Why religion needs human rights

Religion embodies institutionalised connections with transcendental bases for morally justified behaviour. From a reality beyond direct human experience, moral standards are set with "eternal" pretence. Does this mean that respect for truly universal human dignity is inherent in all religion? Practice shows it does not. First, the religious message itself may contain discriminatory elements. This applies particularly to situations in which, apart from the religious core of the message, its cultural setting is also authorised and made absolute. Religion may then sanctify a whole people or caste and hence will come into conflict with the principle of human equality. The enactment of apostasy as a serious crime is a clear indication of a general attitude of considering a particular religion as being above human rights (Van Krieken 1993). Generally, such a belief is based on tradition and on interpretations of Holy Scriptures, which are not indisputable.

In the human rights mission, religion played its part right from the start, in two ways. First, freedom of worship (or non-worship) is one of the fundamental human freedoms. Strikingly, realisation of this freedom is particularly problematic in a multi-religious context as absolutism easily permeates organised Faith. Second, religion, with all that belongs to it, i.e. beliefs and institutions, also falls under the universal norms of the Declaration. People determined to discriminate or even kill others for religious reasons, collide with human rights. Stunningly, the assassin of the Israeli Prime Minister Rabin said he had been acting on "God's orders". Indeed, resistance to fundamental rights that obtain for everyone, such as the right to life, may be based on religious convictions too. These are usually grounded in "verbalism" (a normative doctrine of method according to which judicial interpretation of authoritative texts should aim at establishing the original meaning of the text without any regard to context [De Gaay Fortman 2010: 11]).

Indeed, fossilisation of a certain cultural context from the past runs the inherent risk of incompatibility with current human rights standards. Moreover, contemporary religion may be subject to socio-political manipulation. For instance, right after the Rwandan genocide Justin Hakizimana, an elder in the Presbyterian Church, observed that the church and the government had become too close:

> The church went hand in hand with the politics of Habyarimana. We did not condemn what was going on because we were corrupted. None of our churches, especially the Catholics, has condemned the massacres. That is why all the church leaders have fled, because they believe they may be in trouble with their own people.
>
> (McCullum 1995: 73)

The corruption of religious institutions here described is a gradual process that may strongly embarrass people retrospectively. This was strikingly expressed in the reaction of Reverend Mugamera, who lost his whole family (his wife and six children) in the Rwandan bloodshed:

> Why did the message of the gospel fail to reach the people who were baptised? What did we lose? We lost our lives. We lost our credibility. We are ashamed. We are weak. But, most of all, we lost our prophetic mission. We could not go to the President and tell him the truth because we became sycophants to the authorities.
>
> We have had killings here since 1959. No one condemned them. During the First Republic, they killed slowly, slowly, but no one from the churches spoke out. No one spoke on behalf of those killed. During the Second

> Republic there were more killings and more people were tortured and raped and disappeared; and we did not speak out because we were comfortable.
>
> Now there has to be a new start, a new way. We must accept that Jesus' mission to us to preach the gospel means that we must be ready to protect the sheep, the flock—even if it means we must risk our lives for our sisters and brothers. The Bible does not know Hutu and Tutsi; neither should we.
>
> (McCullum 1995: 75)

Who would deny a crucial role to human rights in such a new start after genocide? Indeed, religion per se appeared to be insufficiently equipped to deal with the politically inspired processes of exclusion (us, not them!), thinking of others as enemies, demonisation and final extermination.

Religion, then, appears to be subject to both ideologisation and institutionalisation. Human rights, on the contrary, put the human being above ideology and the dignity of the individual person above the organisation. Consequently, the Pope's question to Soviet leader Gorbachev, as formulated in an exemplary story, "Mr. Gorbachev, this glasnost of yours, as I understand it (hopefully correctly), is an idea for just outside the church?" has to be answered in the negative. Religion needs human rights – including the fundamental freedom to critique power.

After the genocide of April 1994 the United Nations High Commissioner for Human Rights attached an immediate priority to Rwanda. Training programmes for human rights monitors were set up all over the country. Would such a response lead to better protection against ethnicism, structural discrimination and genocide than the teaching of the churches had apparently failed to offer? A sceptical undertone is already detectable in the question itself. The global human rights project possesses its own institutions: intergovernmental and nongovernmental centres, complaints procedures with commissions, committees and courts of law, training programmes and academic teaching courses. Human rights are already seen as a "global religion" (Korzec 1993) and that is meant in an institutional sense as well. The real challenge is, however, to get the global faith in a dignified existence for everyone, rooted in all hearts and minds.

Justifications for continuing violations of human rights in the name of religion tend to come from alliances of politicians with radical exclusivist religious leaders as opposed to the moderate religious establishment – be it Jewish, Christian, Muslim, Hindu, Buddhist or whatever religion. Religion is, indeed, subject to strong political manipulation. The strategic question is how to avoid clashes between religion and human rights effectively. Notably, generalised statements on the superiority of human rights to religion may provoke violent reactions, as UN Special Rapporteur Gáspár Bíró experienced in Sudan. His remark on the subservience of Islamic Sharia law to human rights in conformity with the *lex posterior* principle[17] provided the Sudanese government with an excellent opportunity to switch from a defensive to an offensive position, denouncing his observations as blasphemous.[18] That whole incident was illustrative of the tremendous challenges of rooting the global human rights mission in distinct local realities.

This will not always be possible without periods of sharp confrontation with the powers that be, including religious leaders.

Combating cultural rules and practices that violate human dignity

The realisation of human rights may also be more directly confronted with cultural obstacles. In terms of internationally accepted human rights standards, the intolerability of practices such as female genital mutilation (FGM) and the prohibition of apostasy, for example, is indisputable. Yet, the next question remains how to combat such culturally driven violations of basic human dignity. Of course, once decisions have been taken on principle, strategy is the next challenge.

Indeed, clear identification of the cultural (often religiously justified) rules and practices to be combated from a universal human dignity perspective is not the main problem. What is urgently needed is a re-examination of strategic approaches. The first issue that has to be looked into is whether to contest the rule or practice from without or rather from within. As regards FGM, there has been an over-emphasis on criminal proscription as a stick and development aid as a carrot. Indeed, as a result of pressure on the part of donor agencies such as American AID most African states with sizeable Islamic majorities now have legislation that criminalises FGM. Yet, reality does not seem to be considerably affected by criminal investigation, prosecution and punishment. What really counts is how people look at their own culture, as Isatou Touray explains in a collection of studies titled *Hermeneutics, Scriptural Politics and Human Rights: Between Text and Context.*

> [Culture] is an area of contestation regarding women's sexuality and autonomy over their bodies. Culture has many faces and does not exist in isolation from other discourses that shape its various contexts. The term "culture" refers to the various practices and ways that societies choose to pattern themselves. Symbols and rituals, tradition, language, dress, food, behavior, and ethics mediate these practices. Other factors such as gender, class, religion, wealth, position, and laws also influence them. The laws can be written, unwritten, or based on consensus of the people. Depending on all the factors that shape it, culture as a social construct can be acceptable or unacceptable. As we know, cultural practices can be either positive or negative as seen from distinct perspectives.
>
> Some aspects of African cultures are beautiful and hence Africans have good reason to be proud to show them everywhere. However, it is also necessary to look at one's own culture with a critical eye in order to locate the axis of gender inequalities and subordination, and to examine how religion is used to shape women's sexual rights and autonomy. The practices of female genital mutilation, early or forced marriage, and gender-based violence both at a community level and at a household level are features of many cultures. These practices are gender-specific and if women do not

> bring them to the public domain, little or no attention will be given to them. Even feminist activists sometimes try to gloss over these negative issues. Indeed, patriarchal resistance can be so strong that some, eventually, give up the fight or take on compromising views, to allow the perpetuation of these practices. These are the areas of female subordination, however, and I am of the view that the conditions of African women can be improved only if there is a general acknowledgement that cultural practices can, indeed, contribute to gender inequality and oppression. Many women and children suffer in silence, not because they accept what is happening to them, but because their culture sanctions it. Many times there is no cultural space available for these victims of cultural oppression to express their objections. It is particularly in the practice of female genital mutilation that the culture of silence prevails.
>
> (Touray 2010: 237–238)

There is an unmistakable lesson to be learned here: when it comes to such intolerable practices, universality of human rights has to be built primarily from within, through sophisticated methods of human rights education. Accordingly, in countries such as Senegal, the Gambia and Mali women show others pictures that demonstrate what FGM physically involves. A subsequent strategic element concerns the link with religion. In the case of FGM, interpretation of Quran'ic texts from a gender-conscious perspective appears to result in new ways of understanding what is actually meant, including contemporary implications. It also suggests various strategies that can be employed to improve the debate on women's rights issues from a religious standpoint. Touray's study (2010) explains how misinterpretations of Islam have resulted in sexual mutilation of over 33 million women and children in Africa and beyond, while she also provides examples of ways in which women's rights organisations and feminist activists may strategise in regard to these rights using the sacred text as well as human rights conventions to move the agenda.

Indeed, culturally rooted ideas and practices are not uncommonly founded in (mis)interpretations of texts in Holy Scriptures. In the same collection of studies, Ali Mirmoosavi of Mofid University in Qom (Iran) writes on the highly intricate theme of "The Quran and Religious Freedom. The Issue of Apostasy". After carefully analysing the relevant texts he arrives at the following conclusions:

> The Qur'anic scriptures establish a general principle that can be described as the Qur'anic principle of religious freedom. The main rule is that "there is no compulsion in religion", which rejects any pressure on belief. Yet, in connection with other verses that put some limitation on belief, this principle cannot justify religious freedom in its broad dimensions.
>
> The issue of apostasy is the most controversial issue which increases the gap between Islam and religious freedom. According to the Qur'an apostasy does not mean just simple changing of religion or disbelief. It implies to change religion after confidently believing and because of an unjustified

> motivation, usually concerning treason. However, the Qur'an does not directly impose any worldly punishment for apostasy. This deduction discloses a possibility for reconciliation between the Qur'an and religious freedom.
>
> Freedom of religion was not compatible with past Islamic society where citizenship was based on religious belief. The jurist decrees and punishment of apostasy, which conflict with freedom of religion, are based past society and reflect those conditions. The current transformation of society and state leads to different jurisprudence which should be compatible with new conditions. Modern Islamic society experiences a completely different life in the globalized world of political, economic and security interdependence. Freedom of religion in this world is not only the legitimate right based on several arguments, but also a necessary condition for peaceful and stable life. Even though traditional interpretations can justify themselves as the best ones, pragmatic necessities cancel and frustrate these interpretations. These pragmatic necessities lead Muslim jurists to appeal to some facilities that can reconcile their jurisprudence with freedom of religion.
>
> (Mirmoosavi 2010: 141–142)

Evidently, efforts such as those undertaken by Islamic scholars like Isatou Touray and Ali Mirmoosavi, arguing on a common ground and confronting religious rules and cultural practices incompatible with universal standards of human dignity from within, are of foremost importance. Indeed, the international human rights movement would not be wise to confine its vital mission to legal, case-by-case approaches, attacking intolerable manifestations of culture and belief merely from the outside. In a contemporary context of globalisation and religious pluralism, strategic sophistication is called for, not least in the intricate domain of religion, culture and human rights.

To conclude this analysis of the economic, political and socio-cultural aspects of local realities, a tool is presented here to enhance contextual analysis that focuses specifically on constraints as well as resources for human rights' realisation (see Table 4.2).

Thus, we have used the definition of human rights to create three columns: human dignity, power and protection, and the functioning of law. Combining these with four rows – each depicting a crucial aspect of the nation-state – this results in 12 squares with elements determining the environment in which human rights would have to be realised.

Using such a contextual tool in concrete analysis of local realities, it is important to realise that the distinct factors and conditions mentioned are not all of the same significance. Indeed, there are strong empirical and theoretical indications, as discussed above, that our "stylised fact" (Figure 4.3) and the quality of state–society relations play a principal part among factors affecting the enabling or disabling character nature of human rights' environments. Local realities, moreover, must be thoroughly analysed but they cannot be taken for granted. Beyond the legal protection of interests, human rights have transformative

Table 4.2 Analysing local realities in respect of human rights realisation

Human rights = **And its roots in:**	**Human dignity**	**Protected against abuse of power**	**By law**
Society	• Distinctive collective identities/ collective prejudices • Acceptance of distinct collective entities (minorities)/us–them divides	• Pluralism/social mobility • Power-sharing • Quality of group leadership • Collective equality/systemic discrimination	• Group rights (rights of collectivities)
Culture	• Cultural and religious freedom/ diversity • Recognition of the individual/ individual freedom • Customs and traditions • Language/history • Gender equality/sexism/patriarchy	• Subordination/submission • Public–private divides • Religious and ethnic leadership • Fundamentalism/tolerance • Multiculturalism/monoculturalism	• Cultural rights • Voice (free expression)
Polity	• Citizenship/political awareness • Conscience publique/individualism • Participation/clientelism	• Social contract • Democracy/tyranny of the majority • Quality of political leadership • The state: functioning or failing	• Rule of Law/public order • Access to political power and to public goods • Civil and political rights
Economy	• Sustainable livelihoods/poverty as deprivation (absolute and relative) • Indigenous knowledge/subsistence methods/productivism • Socio-economic inequality	• Employment opportunities/economic vulnerability/socio-economic security • Pressure on and access to resources • Land reform • Development and its organisation	• Economic, social and cultural rights • Entitlement systems and social protection

power, too (see Table 1.1). In "disabling" environments more than anywhere else, that emancipatory function gets activated. Evidently, more than from above human rights emerge from local realities: inclusive human dignity asserted by victims of violation. It is, indeed, precisely in adverse realities that human rights may develop into a motivating and inspiring force of great weight. Notably, the twenty-first century's second decade has already shown signs of developing into an era of global emancipation.

5 Realisation

The rights of the poor

No one can be developed; people develop themselves.[1]

Joseph Ki-Zerbo (1999: 114)

Development *with* poverty

At the beginning of the new millennium, two new international strategies were adopted that were meant to spell the end to a long period of economic development without poverty reduction. One was the acceptance of the so-called Millennium Development Goals (MDGs); the other focused on "pro-poor growth" (PPG). As an instrument to bring about PPG, countries desiring multilateral and bilateral loans and aid were supposed to draft Poverty Reduction Strategy Papers (PRSPs).[2]

During a meeting organised by the African Learning Group of the Economic Commission for Africa to discuss this new conditional financial facility, its lack of genuine focus on the poor was aptly explained.[3] As pointed out in the report on the meeting:

> *Incorporate the voice of the poor*: It was stressed that the poor do have spokespersons, but that the poor are not really given the chance to express their needs. As a Sierra Leonean representative explained, "I can assure you that their priorities will be totally different from what we list as priorities in our PRSPs. Their priorities will definitely be food on their tables or in their villages, improved housing—they are living in deplorable conditions. But we, the spokespersons will come out with grander priorities, which at the end of the day may not even meet their needs. We therefore need some kind of introspection between governments and civil society organisations".

Ludger Nyoni, the Chairman of the Tenants' Association in Tanzania, voiced the opinion of the poor at the conclusion of a "Poverty Policy Week" organised by the Chair of the PRSP Steering Committee:

> I was sitting waiting to hear something new from the researchers but there is nothing Mr Chairman ... Some years ago I attended a similar meeting under

> this same roof and what we have been hearing today is the same as what we were told during that meeting. What I expected, was to be told the implementation of what we discussed way back in 2000; the achievements and where we have hit snags so that we can think of how to overcome the snags.
> (quoted in Nyanje 2002: 9)

Mr Nyoni then summarised some of the factors causing poverty: conditions attached to the loans ("giant institutions which get their money from poor people's contributions but are very discriminatory in giving loans to poor people"), lack of adequate housing schemes and unfair distribution of the national wealth. "We are cracking our heads", he concluded, "but factors which cause poverty are obvious to each and everybody".[4] In contrast to that simplicity in respect of the causes of poverty, his colleague from the Tanzania Family Association pointed to the complexity of poverty alleviation strategies, with the result "that many people did not know how they fit into the equation" (Nyanje 2002).

"Can Anyone Hear Us?"

At the turn of the millennium the World Bank also published its *World Development Report 2000/2001: Attacking Poverty* (World Bank 2001). Before publication it had submitted a draft for debate on the Internet. In terms of communication it was a great success: in a chapter-by-chapter discussion through electronic messages, thousands of people all over the world responded to the invitation to present comments and views. Summaries of chapters as well as of the discussion itself were provided week by week. For the seriousness, depth and width of its poverty analysis, the Bank received praise from all corners. Indeed, it had come a long way from its previous narrow focus on income, poverty and quantitative analysis – the number of people living on less than the purchasing power parity (PPP) of one or two US dollars per day[5] – towards a multi-dimensional view of poverty in the light of strategic notions such as empowerment. In terms of criticism, however, two related issues were prominent: the "appropriation" of an alternative development jargon without accompanying changes in policies and action, and the lack of critical examination of the international financial institutions themselves (Chambers 2001).

The draft report had been preceded by a study undertaken by the Bank's own social scientists in collaboration with other scholars: *Voices of the Poor*. Part I is based on a review of 81 Participatory Poverty Assessments (PPA) mandated by the Bank itself in 50 different countries in the course of the 1990s. Its subtitle is most appropriate: *Can Anyone Hear Us?* (Narayan 2000a). Indeed, these "voices of the poor" had been shouting out for quite some time. Now that they had been analysed and published together in one forcefully written study, the question re-imposed itself all the more forcefully: are development actors prepared to listen? Joseph Stiglitz, then still the Bank's Chief Economist, concluded: "We now need to expand our conceptions of poverty focusing on income, expenditure, education, and health to include measures of voice and empowerment. That is the challenge that the poor make to us."

Crying Out for Change is the title of Part II of *Voices of the Poor* (Narayan 2000b). This study, based on comparative fieldwork conducted in 23 countries in 1999, collected and examined the voices of over 20,000 poor women and men. Here elements of powerlessness and ill-being are brought together in one "many-stranded web" (2000b: 249). This might be graphically represented as in Figure 5.1, below.

Naturally, the public environment in which poor people have to sustain their daily livelihoods is principally the same as for all human beings: the economy, society/culture, basic services, the polity and provisions to secure law and order. But all five major realms confront them with adverse conditions, as Figure 5.1 depicts the findings of the *Voices of the Poor* studies.

Analysis on the adverse environments in which people live in daily hardship is used in the World Development Report on "Attacking Poverty". What remains lacking, however, is a conceptualisation of human rights obligations with regard to poor people's daily livelihoods, especially in light of the power relations behind "a pronounced deprivation of well being" (the Bank's new definition of poverty). Thus, the Report's treatment of *empowerment* – a crucial element in its three-pronged approach of attacking poverty through opportunity, empowerment and security – is still full of such weak aspirational terms as "improve",

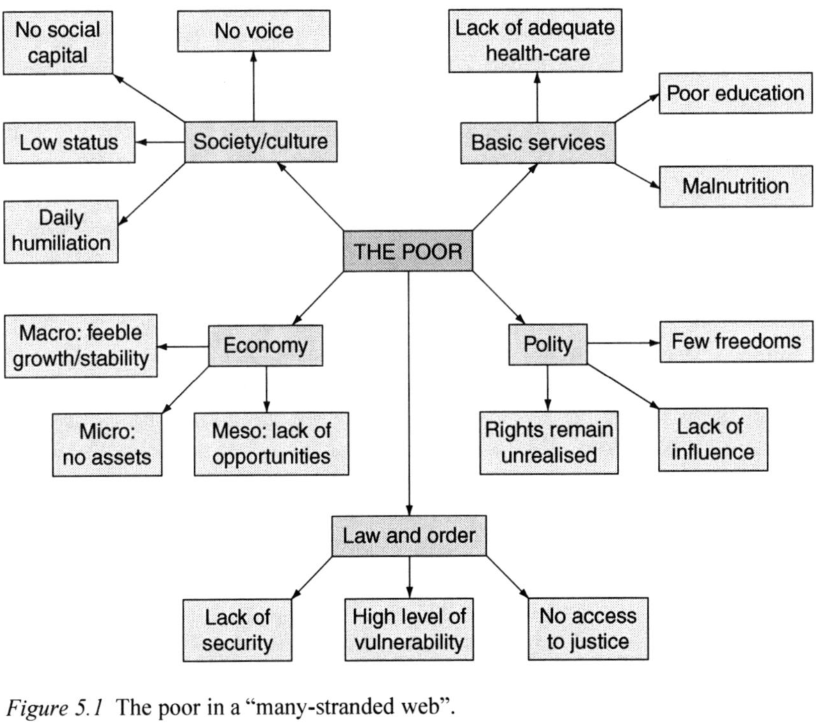

Figure 5.1 The poor in a "many-stranded web".

"promote", "help" and "facilitate". In their foreword to *Voices of the Poor*, World Bank President James Wolfensohn and British Minister for Overseas Development Clare Short drew the conclusion that a majority of the world's poor "feel they are worse off and more insecure than in the past". Yet, the World Development Report refrained from a critical assessment of the Bank's own role in the deterioration of poor people's lives and of its own responsibilities in the follow-up of the *Voices* study. Notions such as responsibility and accountability, in other words, were not yet applied to the international financial institutions themselves.

The issue, then, remains: (abuse of) power and (lack of) protection. We therefore have to examine why poor people generally lose out and do not tend to gain from the global economic drive to ever-increasing productivity.

The economy as a system of power

Economic life is as much filled with power as a hedgehog with spines, as a political economist once aptly observed (Lambers 1971: 63). This obviously concerns not just political power derived from the enforcement capacities of the modern state, but also economic power, based on access to and command over resources used in the production, distribution and consumption of goods and services. Yet, mainstream economists do not usually focus on power but on flows of goods and services, including resource use, and on financial flows linked to such processes. Notably, the discipline of economics began with Adam Smith's description of a "natural order of things" in which an invisible hand coordinates the economic activities of agents through the working of "free competition" in a perfect market (Smith 1900 [1776]: 290ff.).[6] Consequently, economic subjects may be seen as mere price-takers, lacking as they do any degree of economic power. This natural economic order was presumed – an "ideal type" – and theory was developed to explain its operations.[7] Although later theory did recognise certain fundamental imperfections in market structure – defects in the channelling of information and mobility and divisibility of resources – the study of economic power remained largely confined to power over price.

Institutional economists stand out for having taken a broader view on power, examining the functioning of real-life institutions in the context of history, culture and geography (Lekachman 1979). In their analyses neither the economic structure (the whole of economic ends and means in the sense of all factors of production, in relation to all public and private wants) nor the economic order (the institutional and organisational framework within which economic activity takes place) are taken for granted (treated as *data*: given and unchanging). Indeed, the economy is seen as a system of power, which governs whose interests are to count, not only in resource allocation but also in the distribution of income and wealth (Samuels in Lekachman 1979: iii).

Once economic power is recognised as a fact of life, the challenge becomes to study not just structures of power, but also modes of dealing with normative aspects of both its existence and its use. A primary problematique lies in the formation of economic power. This is the subject of an impressive body of economic literature, particularly in industrial economics and antitrust policy aiming at the artificial creation of a perfectly competitive economy (De Gaay Fortman 1966). More fundamentally, inquiries must be made into the *sources* of economic power, a core focus in political economy since the days of Karl Marx. A related problematique is the relationship between economic and political power. This tends to be a little more complex than Rosa Luxemburg's view that in reality "political power is nothing but a vehicle for the economic process" (Luxemburg 1971 [1913]: 452). Modern network analysis thus examines intertwined connections between executives and directors of multinational corporations and persons occupying influential positions in public life (Heemskerk 2002).

The economy is, then, conceived here as a system determined not just by the formation and distribution of power, but also by ways and means of control. The principal issue through the ages is the relationship between state and market. In an economy dominated by large corporations, limitations are set with regard to mergers and other types of economic concentration. Indeed, competition policy is regarded today as increasingly important. This has to do with the growing reluctance of the state to intervene directly in the market economy. The "Rhineland model of capitalism" that came into existence in continental Western and Northern Europe during 200 years of economic industrialisation and socio-political emancipation is under increasing pressure (Albert 1991). This mixed type of economic order consists of an effective state guaranteeing an adequate administration of justice and capable of producing and financing collective goods and services, together with social cohesion, corporate responsibility and social protection through welfare policies (De Gaay Fortman and Goldewijk 1998: 35ff.). While finding their rationale in a fight against misuse of public power, privatisation and deregulation obviously limit the possibilities of control. In both the developing world and the former socialist economies, such shifts in the distribution and means of controlling economic power were already being effectuated before a "market-augmenting state" (Olson 2000) had been created and effective socialisation of the market economy could have taken shape.

Productivism and the poor

Thirty years ago the Brazilian government – a military dictatorship at the time – proclaimed a development strategy consisting of three consecutive stages: "productivismo", "distributivismo" and "desenvolvimento social" (social development). Not surprisingly the whole process remained confined to the first stage in one of the most unequal countries in the whole world.

Unfortunately, the tendency to focus on just allocative power while disregarding issues of distribution and control, has pervaded the realm of economics as a discipline, too. Indeed, the fad has become to separate the economic from the political, assigning blame for persistent poverty particularly to the latter. "The consequences can be disturbing", Graham Pyatt observed, "not least when economists are tempted … to argue that the development problems of particular countries are essentially political, by which they mean institutional, the inference being that they are beyond the reach of sensible economic policies" (2002: 1). The problems are not uncommonly the result of *insensible* development policies, following from a purely productivist approach to economic development without any regard to effects on the daily livelihoods of the poor. The history of "development-induced displacement", mega "development" projects implying the forced eviction of people from their lands, is particularly illustrative of this approach (Dwivedi 2001: Ch. 1). Michael Cernea, an expert of the World Bank itself, noted the following eight sub-processes converging in impoverishment: landlessness, joblessness, homelessness, marginalisation, increased morbidity, food insecurity, loss of access to common property, and social disarticulation (1995: 251–252). Yet, to both recommend and enforce policies, programmes and projects that lead to such enormous deteriorations in people's entitlement positions is still the order of the day. For hundreds of millions of people development means not a right but a threat, as is aptly expressed in the title of Irene Hadiprayitno's study of development policies in Indonesia: *Hazard or Right? The Dialectics of Development Practice and the Internationally Declared Right to Development* (2009). Not surprisingly then, a study of *Human Rights and MDGs in Practice* (Office of the High Commissioner for Human Rights 2010: 31) concludes, among other things, that "states and the international community need to ensure that development projects do not cause more harm than good". It is rather problematic, in other words, to delegate realisation of the economic, social and cultural rights of the poor to "development" no matter its consequences in respect of concrete entitlement positions.

"Productivismo"

Behind all "development-induced" disasters in the lives of the poor lies what might be called "productivism": an overwhelming focus on increasing productivity in general and labour productivity in particular.[8] Now we know, of course, that the basic snag in the calculation of output over input lies in externalities: decisions are taken on the basis of a calculation of resource inputs that excludes costs to both people and the environment not charged through the market, and a calculation of output that neglects not only the problem of final waste but also the social aspects of consumption. But there is more to this influential ideology.

Structurally, the "progress of opulence" finds its roots in division of labour and specialisation, and the application of technology tuned to economies of large-scale production. It was Adam Smith who, early on, pointed out the structural dynamics of continuously increasing productivity through applied inventions (machines that "facilitate and abridge labour"), specialisation and exchange (1900 [1776]: 4). However, such *processes* not only influence overall prosperity (which is commonly acknowledged), they also affect people's working conditions (a fact to which international development still seems blind). Take Smith's well-known example of the pin factory, in which division of labour results in a thousand-fold increase in productivity and production. Certainly, an artisan producing complete pins just by himself is not likely to rejoice in the forced transition to monotonous labour on the conveyor belt: hence the development of trade unions and their role in so called "productivity agreements", aiming at a fair distribution of the benefits of increased specialisation (Flanders 1970: 85–88). Furthermore, continuously increasing labour productivity implies that workers will be laid off and hence have to move from one occupation to another, rendering them vulnerable to major changes in their entitlement positions. Indeed, people's daily livelihoods are dependent on their opportunities to be productive in combination with the concrete activities they perform. Consequently, except for subsistence economies in which people produce simply to satisfy their own primary needs, there are the questions of employment and remuneration: the issue of "exchange entitlement" in the terminology of Amartya Sen (1981).

A formidable driving force towards ever-increasing labour productivity rests in the organisation of exchange through a system of markets and prices. Rising productivity reduces costs per unit of production and hence increases profit. At the same time it improves a firm's position in the continuous struggle for an increasing share of the market. Employment within the firm can be maintained only if production increases at the same rate as productivity. In stagnant or even shrinking markets this implies a fierce competition for market shares.

Adam Smith, as we saw, used the metaphor of the "invisible hand" to depict the organising power of this whole productivist dynamic of working for constantly rising labour productivity. Although regarded as the backbone of economic growth and with that the wealth of nations, it is not without "side-effects", to put things mildly. In the context of "limits to growth" there has been discussion of not only physical limits (nature and the environment) but also social and cultural limits. The latter still have to gain their place on the political agenda. Homer-Dixon (2002) has pointed at "the relentlessness of this technological replacement", occurring in all industries and economic sectors at the same time, including the service sector that used to act as a reservoir for labour which had become redundant in other sectors. Such processes force workers to be continuously retrained and re-skilled while looking for new employment opportunities either within their current firm or without. Workers who cannot meet the cognitive and skill requirements for new types of jobs will become unemployed or, at best, will have to accept low wages. He concludes:

> Without remedial action, society will polarize between, on one hand, a shrinking but ever-richer economic elite of hyper-cognitively-adept workers who run the ferociously productive technologies of our economy but who are unwilling to consume all its products and, on the other, an expanding mass of technologically displaced workers who can't generate enough demand to consume the economy's bounty.

Notably, the argument applies in the first instance to the workforce in the countries of the Organisation for Economic Co-operation and Development (OECD).

Before economic globalisation these workers could largely be considered as a labour aristocracy within the global context. Today, from this angle, there tends to be an economically motivated outcry against immigration.

Coming to the position of the global poor now, strikingly, whatever terminology is used – "poverty alleviation", "poverty reduction", "poverty eradication" or "the attack on poverty" – productivism remains the driving ideology behind economic policies. The reason lies partly in the inner logic of productivism as an economic system itself: meeting its "side-effects" requires public spending and that in turn means a need for even more economic growth. But it also has to do with the usual conceptualisation of poverty in policy circles as a macroeconomic phenomenon, to be measured by the number of people – or even the proportion of that number in relation to the whole population – living on less than one US dollar purchasing power parity (PPP) per day. In the title of a paper, Pyatt pointed the finger in the right direction: *Poverty versus the Poor* (1999).

Poverty reduction strategies

Research today has moved far beyond the money metric centred on income poverty. There is, indeed, a growing focus on the lives of the poor in more than just one dimension. The OECD's Development Assistance Committee (DAC)'s "Guidelines on Poverty Reduction", which set out the five interrelated and interactive dimensions of poverty depicted above in Figure 5.1, are illustrative of this fact: society/culture (no voice, no social capital, low status, humiliation); basic services (lack of health-care, poor education, poor nutrition); economy (macro: lack of growth and stability, meso: lack of opportunities, micro: lack of income and assets); polity (rights unrealised, few freedoms, lack of influence); and law and order (no access to justice, lack of security, high level of vulnerability) (OECD/DAC 2001: 39).

In a memorandum to the Netherlands government, the Advisory Council for International Affairs (AIV 2003) has shown how these five dimensions connect the macro, meso and micro levels of poverty. The question of how to translate such sharp analyses into what the AIV calls "targeted development policy", however, remains.

At the international donor-driven level we find the two "approaches" today towards effective poverty reduction, already mentioned at the outset of this chapter. Concerning the first one this study can be brief: the Millennium Development Goals (MDGs) are just internationally endorsed objectives to be reached in 2015. The targets aim to halve the proportions of the global population suffering from lack of means towards decent daily livelihoods and lack of access to essential public services. As such, these goals signify targeting long-term macroeconomic poverty rather than the lives of the poor today. While it is true that the targets now include health, education, basic amenities, reproductive health and environmental sustainability – and hence transcend approaches based on notions of pure income poverty – as a strategy this approach lacks clear mechanisms and instruments for implementation, as its intermediate assessment revealed. The

MDGs are, indeed, just development goals assumed to influence policies, particularly in the field of development cooperation. The effects of efforts to monitor progress towards these goals remain unclear. What action has been taken, for example, in response to country progress reports? Clearly, additional standards will have to be set that concern people's daily livelihoods here and now, while benchmarking is likely to have an impact only where coupled with mechanisms for monitoring and implementation. Five years before the target year 2015 a shift in the international focus from the MDGs towards "rights-based" approaches was, indeed, already noticeable. "The Millennium Development Goals are failing the world's poorest people because governments are ignoring and abusing their human rights", Amnesty International markedly declared when heads of states met at a UN summit in New York to review progress on the MDGs (20–22 September 2010).

Pro-poor growth

The second approach towards poverty reduction is "pro-poor growth". This was launched in the context of the poverty reduction strategies of the World Bank and the International Monetary Fund, while not being unrelated to their practice of conditional financial facilities. Contrary to the order of the words, however, growth remains its first focus. "Overall economic growth", the *World Development Report on Poverty* notes, "is crucial for generating opportunity" (2000/2001: 7). The DAC Guidelines on Poverty Reduction also start off by stating that economic growth is an absolute necessity for poverty reduction. While that conventional starting point is becoming increasingly qualified – with "pro-poor" as the latest fashion – it seems useful first to critically examine the view that economic growth should be seen as an absolute requirement for poverty reduction.

The benefits of economic growth as a strategy for poverty reduction were forcefully elaborated in a research paper by Dollar and Kraay of the World Bank's Joint Working Group on Poverty Reduction. Still interpreting poverty in terms of income coupled with a money metric quantitative approach, the two produced data indicating that macroeconomic aggregates and averages show growth as distribution-neutral. In that case a policy conclusion follows by definition: growth reduces poverty. There is, however, good reason to assume that things are more complicated. Statistically, for one thing, it appears that the lower one defines the poverty line (poverty in this case understood as lack of income), the less growth helps to reduce poverty. To illustrate: if the dividing line between "poor" and "not poor" is drawn on a definitional basis which implies that one-third of the population is poor, then growth does less to combat poverty than when – by the definition used – two-thirds of the population are poor (Pyatt 1999). Indeed, as pointed out by Ravi Kanbur – the principal coordinator of the *World Development Report 2000/2001* study who later dropped out of the World Poverty Report team – there are several fundamental types of disagreement in macroeconomic poverty studies, including inappropriate simplification of its definitions and measurements (Kanbur 2001).

Strikingly, while in the past 93 per cent of the world's poor people lived in low-income countries (LICs), it is estimated that in 2007 three-quarters of the world's approximately 1.3 billion poor people lived in middle-income countries (MICs) and only about a quarter of the world's poor – about 370 million people live in the remaining 39 low-income countries, which are largely in sub-Saharan Africa (Sumner 2010: 1). Indeed, growth may be accompanied by increasing inequality and marginalisation to such an extent that people already excluded become worse off. This applies particularly in times of inflation as they tend to lack possibilities of passing the effects of rising prices on their purchasing power on to others. Hence, to discuss growth and poverty while ignoring (re)distribution does not seem to result in meaningful analysis. A more sophisticated study has been undertaken in this connection by Kakwani and Pernia. Pro-poor growth, they argue, "requires a strategy that is deliberately biased in favor of the poor so that the poor benefit proportionally more than the rich" (Kakwani 2000: 3). Based on this conceptual starting point, they develop an indicator that shows growth to be pro-poor when it results in a redistribution in favour of the poor. In a practical application to Asian economies, however, they found that this indicator would not reflect "pro-poor growth" in any of the subject economies. Faced with a consequential pressure to adjust their criteria,[9] they then labelled growth with an equalising effect "highly pro-poor" and growth accompanied by a moderately worsening inequality "pro-poor". *Anti-poor* is the term they used for growth in which the growth effect on the income of the poor is more than offset by the rise in inequality.

Evidently, the use of such macroeconomic calculations based on averages and aggregates is rather limited. What is important, though, is the admission that growth is not necessarily neutral, let alone pro-poor; it can also be anti-poor. Not everyone, to use a metaphor, rises with the tide; indeed, many drown. In terms of "poverty reduction" one conclusion is obvious: actors should focus first of all on stopping anti-poor growth. We shall return to this issue later, but the basic point is that growth implies change, including change in people's entitlement positions as rooted in the entitlement (sub)systems to which they are connected. Hence people's concrete entitlements can also be negatively affected. This has been the case in structural adjustment policies which, while aiming at the right economic conditions for growth, may use measures with immediate consequences in terms of increasing hardships for the poor (e.g. the cutting of food subsidies, Hunt 1996: 196ff.). Hence, economic policies aiming at certain effects on the macro level should always be assessed with regard to their microeconomic distributional effects too.

In an IMF/World Bank publication on poverty reduction Ames *et al.* note on policies aimed directly at income redistribution: "As these topics pertain more to political economy than exclusively to macroeconomics, they are beyond the scope of this pamphlet". This comment aptly illustrates the problem: treating macroeconomics as if it were somehow "divorceable" from politics. How can politics be "beyond the scope" when it is central to the problem? In this volume, then, a brief look at pro-poor growth from a political

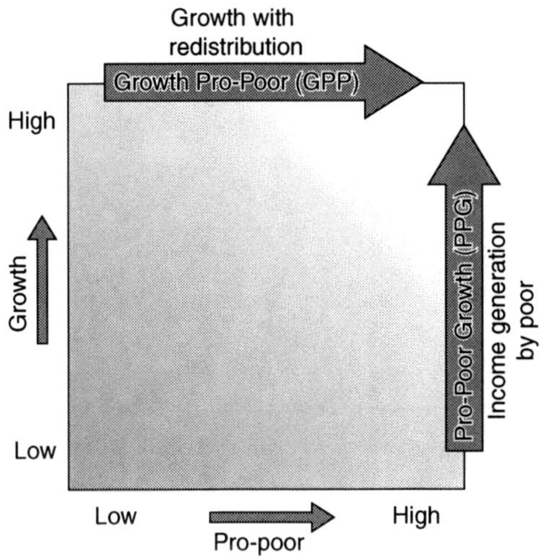

Figure 5.2 Poverty reduction: Growth Pro-Poor versus Pro-Poor Growth.

economy perspective seems more than appropriate. For that purpose a matrix may illustrate the problematique (see Figure 5.2).

This figure confronts rates of economic growth (GDP per capita), from very low to very high, with tendencies supportive of the daily livelihoods of the poor, from zero (negative is also possible as already noted) to highly beneficial. Thus, a number of different situations fit into the picture, while the ultimate objective, obviously, is to get into the upper right corner: a very high growth rate combined with protective and distributive mechanisms highly favourable to the poor. Two arrows point in this direction: one aiming at improving distribution in favour of the poor by increasing productivity (income-generation), the other at increasing the effects of growth on poor people's daily livelihoods. The crucial point here is that the focus of the strategies concretised in the Poverty Reduction Strategy Papers (PRSPs), which have become fashionable as a starting point for new policies of both the government and the donor community, is on the horizontal rather than the vertical arrow: in other words, growth pro-poor instead of the proclaimed pro-poor growth. Notably, growth pro-poor – defined minimally as growth that does not *worsen* income distribution, nor the poverty head count – may well be meaningful with regard to poverty reduction. However, it is pro-poor growth just as much as growth pro-poor, if not more, that has had a radical effect on the elimination of poverty in Europe. Indeed, the role of public goods – free access to health and to education during compulsory school age – cannot be underestimated. This did, indeed, provide the poor with an opportunity to accumulate assets.[10]

To illustrate the need for genuine *pro-poor* growth, though, a figure may be presented that reflects some findings during a field trip to Tanzania (see Figure 5.3).[11]

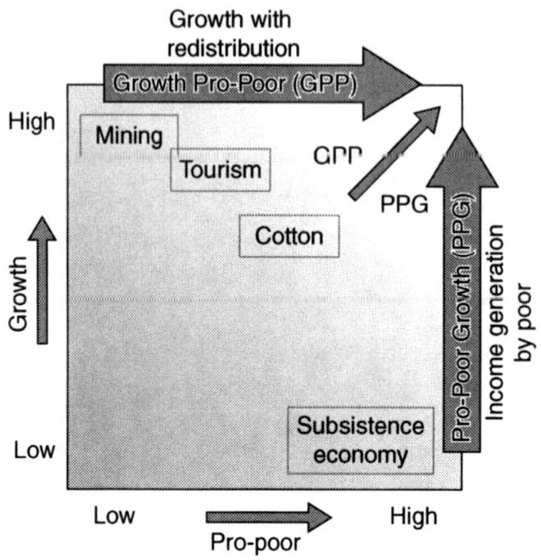

Figure 5.3 A (sub)sectoral approach to poverty reduction in Tanzania.

In Tanzania the "Growth Pro-Poor" focus on the national economy appeared to have taken a *general* economic perspective in the sense of aiming at the promotion of an "enabling environment" for attracting and gaining foreign exchange. This meant a concentration on the mining and tourism sectors, implying a high growth rate but little direct effect on poor people's daily livelihoods. Notably, for a reduction of poverty in Tanzania the IMF estimated in 2005 that a sustained high growth rate of GDP would be required of at least 6–8 per cent per annum over the next decade (International Monetary Fund 2006: 36). Pursuing such a policy puts particular emphasis on creating a climate conducive to foreign direct investment. Naturally, this tends to benefit sectors already manifesting increasing productivity which, in the Tanzanian case, means mining and tourism in the first place. Subsequently, the strategy requires redistribution of benefits to the poor. This is done through increasing expenditure on health and education, in general, rather than focusing particularly on accessibility to the poor. What such a policy lacks, then, is any concrete focus on those sectors where the poor have stakes. Although 80 per cent of the population is dependent in some way on agriculture, the feeling among actors was that this mega "sector" is generally neglected in the "Poverty Reduction Strategy" (PRS) process. But an environment that is genuinely pro-poor growth – rather than just a growth pro-poor framework – of course requires a set of policies for specific sectors in which the poor have stakes, aiming at improved opportunities for income-generation. A first point of attention in such a strategy would be the *subsistence economy*, a generally neglected subsector in which labour productivity is very low whereas distributive effects are optimal. Policies might aim at both a better quality of subsistence production itself and increasing productivity

– through customer-friendly forms of mechanisation, for example – resulting in a surplus. The latter requires not only measures to ensure that demand is coordinated with the supply of produce not consumed by the peasants themselves, but also efforts to prevent disruptions in distribution networks. The horizontal path represented by such policies, however, tends to be neglected.

In actual fact, the horizontal arrow may also, regrettably, point backwards. Harrod, in his path-breaking *Power, Production and the Unprotected Worker* speaks of "brutal intervention against subsistence farmers to make them produce a surplus" (1987: 48). As was already noticeable in the 1970s, moving peasants out of subsistence agriculture into commercial production, which the World Bank used to see as its primary agricultural objective, cannot be considered an unequivocal objective for development policy. *Cotton is the Mother of Poverty* is the title of an appalling account of forced cotton production in Mozambique, imposed by the Portuguese colonial power (Isaacman 1996). Obviously, this refers to the export crop driving out all subsistence production. In the former British colonies the pressure was milder, but nonetheless compelling. "Subsistence adversity" is, indeed, a term born of experience. Paradoxically, in projects resulting in "development-induced displaced" populations, such as the construction of huge dams for power generation, whole villages tend to get moved to places where the inhabitants may only see the electricity passing over their heads, while large-scale irrigation projects often also imply that local people lose their access to water. As the Bank itself has attested:

> Social disruption is inevitable in large-scale irrigation projects ... Local people often find that they have less access to water, land and vegetation resources as a result of the project. Conflicting demands on water resources and inequalities in distribution can easily occur both in the project area and downstream ... altering the distribution of wealth.
>
> (Technical Paper 140, in McCorquodale 1999: 743–744)

In order to prevent such "disruptions", or, in less concealing language, forced evictions, *ex ante* social impact studies are now seen as an essential element in the decision-making process. Yet, the mere prevention of anti-poor growth should not be mistaken for the adoption of pro-poor strategies.

In the Tanzanian context, cotton can be placed somewhere in the middle of Figure 5.3, implying a median level of both productivity and distributive capacity. Doubtless, it is a subsector relevant to the poor in Tanzania; it is primarily produced by smallholder farmers who cultivate between 0.2 and 2.0 hectares per year. Approximately half a million families with five million people are involved in cotton production in Tanzania[12] and, according to the Tanzania Cotton Board,[13] around 11 million are dependent on cotton production to some extent (i.e. about one-third of the whole population). A true pro-poor growth strategy, then, would attempt to overcome certain constraints in Tanzanian cotton production such as an acute shortage of pesticides and other agricultural inputs due to structural adjustment (monetisation of inputs), poor farming methods, the heavy debt burden incurred by the rather weak cooperative societies, poor infrastructure, an inadequacy of experts in the country and, as a result of all this, a sharp decline in cotton quality. While in the first decade of this century such measures were indeed taken, a current "pro-poor" constraint appears in poorly organised market structures with power imbalances between small producers and buying agents. Linking peasants to information that is daily available on the Internet might help here.

Not surprisingly, the global economic crisis seriously affected the Tanzanian cotton sector. In 2009/2010 a stimulus package that raised the price of cotton by 22.2 per cent over just a few months, together with a lowering of the price of cottonseed by 100 per cent and a further subsidy on the price of insecticides, appeared to effectively facilitate the survival of Tanzania's cotton farmers.

However, even if all the constraints on the supply side were overcome, problems would persist on the demand side due to global injustices. The United States pays its cotton farmers US$2 billion a year in subsidies while farmers in other countries of the North receive an additional US$3 billion. The result is frequent overproduction with serious negative effects on prices. In fact, overproduction caused cotton prices to fall to about one-third of their peak in the mid-1990s. The International Consultative Council on Cotton estimated the price of cotton would go up 26 per cent if the US authorities were to discontinue farm subsidies.[14] Notably, Africa is particularly vulnerable with little textile production and hence most of its cotton exported as fibre.[15] Indeed, the many millions that African producers lose as a result of regular falls in market prices are directly related to subsidies in the North.

While the cotton subsector in Tanzania continues to offer ample opportunities for genuine pro-poor growth, in the sense of a strategy starting from the daily livelihoods of the poor themselves, the major obstacles are, indeed, not merely domestic, but related to a demand side that is largely determined in an international economic order in which Tanzania is in a posture of almost complete dependence. A striking asymmetry exists in this context between the policies the North pursues domestically and what the international financial institutions force upon the South: within the global territory of the Organisation for Economic Development and Cooperation (OECD) there are subsidies, social protection, countercyclical macroeconomic management, regulation of markets and correction of outcomes whereas developing countries are faced with directives to abolish such "free market inimical" measures.

Surprisingly, neither these international aspects nor the local constraints on the supply-side figure highly on policy-making agendas. What we are touching upon here is a *justice* gap. Indeed, productivist approaches to poverty tend to neglect the inequities determining the daily misery of the poor. These are well known: research reveals them time and again. Yet, strategies for poverty reduction still tend to conceptualise the effort as a positive-sum game, neglecting the needs for protection, redress and reform. As illustrated in the stories at the outset of this chapter, the mindsets of the poor and the perspectives of strategists charged with addressing their predicament are so out of sync that they seem, at times, to be almost at odds.

Pyatt finished an analysis of inequality as the "seed of conflict" with the observation that, in a society that lacks an effective redistribution system, wealth and income inequalities are likely to increase with growth, "and growing numbers may find themselves caught in a poverty trap" (1999: 27). Hence there exists, it must be concluded, a fundamental incompatibility between productivism as a driving force in the global market economy and "pro-poor" as a forthcoming attitude towards the poor. Indeed, the operation of markets in light of initial endowments creates the condition of the poor; hence Pyatt's argument. The search for non-productivist, justice-focused approaches to poverty is thus not only justified, but necessary.

Towards rights-based strategies

The logic of Pyatt's argument is that, "if the economy continues to grow, then the income and wealth inequalities will grow" (1999: 28).[16] Although they are unacceptable to many citizens, he concludes, ever-growing inequality and poverty are endemic within a capitalist society that lacks an effective redistribution system (1999: 27). Unfortunately, this applies to the global economy in the first place. Global inequality as measured by the ratio of upper over lower quintiles in income distribution is around three times higher than that in the most unequal individual countries (approximately 100 times globally versus approximately 30 times for Brazil).[17] With aid only marginally counterbalancing net financial flows from South to North ("water flowing upwards"[18]), we cannot speak of an effective global system of fairness and justice, rule of law and protection of the weak under the prevailing economic relations. Hence, for any credible global anti-poverty strategy, the international economic order will remain the first item on the agenda.

Indeed, it is not just what is needed in a local setting, as stressed by the exclamation of the Tanzanian tenants' representative quoted at the outset of this chapter, but also the requirements of an international economic order that are well known and hardly need much further research. Thus, in a search for pro-poor strategies, the primary question is: where do we find an impetus towards concrete policies and action aiming at effective protection of the poor in processes of economic change, effective redress where poor people get harmed in their legitimate interests and reform tuned to improvement of the entitlement positions of the poor? What kind of ideas, in other words, can set people in motion? Indeed, the almost continuous flow of ideas embodied in new technologies has to be matched with "ideas about social organisation, especially about reforming and building institutions", as Homer-Dixon has put it (1999: 109). It is in this context that the "rights approach" has come to the fore.

"People are turning more and more to the law—including international human rights law—to claim their rights", the *Human Development Report* of the United Nations Development Program observed in its edition on "Human Development and Human Rights" (UNDP 2000). The terminology used here is a bit unclear: what has to be claimed is access to resources necessary to acquire what people need. Rights are abstract acknowledgements of such claims. In order to get one's claims *honoured* the rights acknowledging them would have to be *asserted*. But will that help? In other words, will "rights-based approaches" be conducive to poverty eradication? Let us, once again, turn to the *Voices of the Poor* studies that had been commissioned by the World Bank.

Participation

When asked what she saw as the main finding of those studies, which had been undertaken under her guidance, Deepa Narayan's response was: "Participation!"[19] The crux, in other words, lies in development processes that include rather than exclude the weaker and more vulnerable sections in society. Apparently stimulated by the appointment of a Special Rapporteur on the "Right to Development" to the UN Commission on Human Rights[20] (14 years after the UN General Assembly Declaration on "The Right to Development"), the World Bank decided to take this right as a new guideline to its policies.[21] The new element which the Declaration, already recognising notions in respect of human dignity, added was "free and meaningful *participation* in development and in the fair distribution of the benefits resulting therefrom" as it had been stipulated in the UN General Assembly Declaration on the Right to Development (41/128, 4 December 1986, emphasis added). In the Bank's development efforts this clause would seem to imply, among other things, a persistent focus on participation from the grassroots and on distributional equity. The point is made, rather strongly, in the tenth guideline of "A Human Rights Approach to Poverty Reduction Strategies", drafted under the auspices of the United Nations High Commissioner for Human Rights:

> A human rights approach to poverty reduction also requires active and informed participation by the poor in the formulation, implementation and monitoring of poverty reduction strategies. The international human rights normative framework includes the right to take part in the conduct of public affairs. This is a crucial and complex human right that is inextricably linked to fundamental democratic principles. A democratic social order based on constitutionalism and free and fair elections is an essential prerequisite for enjoyment of this right. However, effective participation by the poor requires more than a functioning democracy. It calls for specific mechanisms and detailed arrangements at different levels of decision-making that help to overcome the impediments that the poor, and marginalized groups in general, face in playing an effective part in the life of the community.
>
> (Hunt 2002)

Putting participation first, it becomes clear that the rights approach, while being non-productivist, is not anti-productivist either. What matters is that increasing productivity no longer operates as the central moving force of a system driven by return on capital investment, but gets tuned to income-generating opportunities for the poor themselves. Where people are considered to be central as human beings with rights, macroeconomic policies ensuring a growth-conducive environment are reduced to the status of side-conditions while the question poses itself forcefully: growth by and for whom? Indeed, the right to development signifies not only protection against anti-poor policies and measures (Hadiprayitno 2009), but also legitimates the struggle for "pro-poor growth" in the sense of upstream growth, as against merely growth pro-poor (interpreted as merely growth with some redistribution). It is crucial that the injustices lying at the roots of denied needs be addressed. Behind the structural non-implementation of economic, social and cultural rights rest complicated social, political, economic and cultural structures. An effort has to be made to understand and expose the roots of economic injustices. A relevant tool may be the entitlement systems analysis that was advanced in Chapter 1 (see Figure 1.1). As set out there, that methodology is based on using the notion of entitlements not as synonymous with rights embodied and implemented in positive law (Sen 1981) but as *legitimate actual* access to resources and command over goods and services. Now the point is that poor people lack concrete entitlements in the sense of opportunities (understandably a crucial notion in the *World Development Report 2000/2001*) to engage in activities on the basis of which they can claim their basic necessities. In line with Sen's analysis of poverty and famines, this may be called entitlement failure.

Even basic rights must be contextualised. In this connection it is imperative to examine people's own perceptions of what they are due in terms of fundamental freedoms and basic entitlements. This cannot be simply deduced from the internationally declared standards. For instance, in the perception of rural women in Bangladesh, an obvious requirement of a decent life appears to be "private wash places". Such a perceived entitlement can be determined only inductively, in communication with the poor themselves.[22] Obviously, rights-based approaches will have to combine the two methods in spelling out the implications of human rights at national and local levels.

Economic and social rights

Of course, when it comes to strategies for the implementation of the rights of the poor, the word "approach" is rather weak. It could make a "human rights approach" sound like the latest fashion in launching ideas on development strategies. If the poor have rights – and doubtless they do, no less than any other human being – then there is no new "approach" thinkable that could deny or ignore these rights. Indeed, much more than an approach, human rights is first of all a conviction and a commitment. Hence, for actors adopting "rights-based approaches", there will be no way back.

Remarkably, however, the *Voices of the Poor* studies fail to explicitly mention economic, social and cultural rights. Insofar as powerlessness and exclusion are critically discussed, only civil and political rights – such as freedom of speech, the right to participate in democratic decision-making and freedom of association – are brought forward. These might, indeed, be seen as "empowerment rights": enabling people to exert public pressure through collective action in order to have their socio-economic interests duly represented and realised. It becomes apparent, then, that although economic, social and cultural needs refer directly to the sustainability of people's daily livelihoods, these interests tend not to be expressed as rights.

Somehow, the lack of economic rights language among the poor themselves, too, is not surprising. Rights are interests protected by law, as discussed earlier, and the poor tend to live in areas in which formal legal systems are malfunctioning and thus may not conceive of themselves as legal actors. If, however, "law and order" means an adequately functioning system to enforce security of the person, stability of possessions and the keeping of promises, as was argued above (p. 11), then this is precisely one of the poor's urgent needs as expressed in the World Bank studies. Instead, not protection but abuse by police and other state officials appears to typify their lives, as revealed in *Crying Out for Change* (Narayan 2000b: 281ff.). "An effective modern police force is needed to maintain order by enforcing the law, dealing with potentially disorderly situations, and attending to citizens in distress", the World Bank's report noted (World Bank 2001: 103).

A second snag with regard to the use of rights language, also explicated already in Chapter 1 (p. 33), is that law normally functions as a way of protecting already obtained freedoms and entitlements. But in the case of human rights in general, and economic, social and cultural rights in particular, the declaration of rights precedes actual attainment. Take, for example, the summary of the "rights of the poor" in article 25 of the Universal Declaration of Human Rights of 1948 (UDHR):

> Everyone has the right to a standard of living adequate for the health and well-being of himself and of his family, including food, clothing, housing and medical care and necessary social services, and the right to security in the event of unemployment, sickness, disability, widowhood, old age or other lack of livelihood in circumstances beyond his control.

Strong and compelling language, indeed, but what does it mean for the world's poor? The international community responsible for such "rights language" appears to be unable to guarantee its enforcement. Indeed, the structural non-implementation of the rights of the poor is part of the huge *deficit* in the global endeavour for the realisation of human rights. This is remarkably reflected in the softness of language used with regard to poverty: "poverty alleviation", "poverty reduction", "pro-poor growth", etc.

In this respect, it is important to note that the strong language of the Universal Declaration of Human Rights became more specified and at the same time weakened in the subsequent covenants. This manifests itself particularly in the notion of "progressive realisation" with regard to economic, social and cultural rights,[23] a phrase also adopted in the *Human Development Report* 2000, which has human rights as its special theme (UNDP 2000: 70). The background to that coinage is that non-implementation may be rooted in lack of available resources. Yet the realisation of economic, social and cultural rights may be more about *distribution* of resources than their "availability". An endeavour to realise these rights, then, can become a highly confrontational affair since efforts towards their implementation challenge existing power structures. While the *Human Development Report* 2000 follows earlier UNDP terminology as to the need for promoting "a rights-enabling economic environment" (118–119), the day-to-day reality of adverse ("disabling") conditions when it comes to implementation of people's basic human rights is not dealt with. It is evident that international development, the UN's conventional response to conditions of material misery, has not succeeded as a means of reducing the number of absolute poor, let alone tackling poverty as a relative phenomenon.

The DAC Guidelines on Poverty Reduction observed an "increasing focus on the "rights approach" which links empowerment to international agreements on human and political as well as economic, social and cultural rights".[24] As an anti-poverty strategy, this has been advocated by both international organisations like UNDP and international nongovernmental organisations like ActionAid. But it was with the publication of UNDP's *Human Development Report* 2000 on the theme of human development and human rights, that Kofi Annan's appeal for a "mainstreaming" of human rights received a real conceptual response.[25] Undeniably, the persistent efforts towards integrating development, security and governance through a compelling focus on the human being – human development, human security and human rights – constitute a major achievement of the *Human Development Reports*. It is, indeed, basic human dignity that links the three together (see Figure I.2).

To genuinely understand the meaning of a rights approach to the predicament of the poor, we first have to elaborate what was earlier said on the meaning of rights (p. 34). Since rights imply protection by law, the first priority becomes a functioning legal order. Law, as argued in the introduction, implies order in the public-political community, and hence protection of people (personal security), their property (stability of possessions) and their deals (*pacta sunt servanda*). In this respect a rights approach is not particularly new to the science of economics. Indeed, "property rights" have become closely connected with political economy. Yet, the focus tends to be on stability and security in respect of allocative power rather than on distributive mechanisms. *Power and Prosperity* is the illustrative title of a book by Mancur Olson (2000). Pyatt, however, referred to rights in another meaning when he argued that the stability of a society that lacks an effective redistribution system "depends on a compact which guarantees certain rights".[26] What he means here is rights to health and education and a system of social protection. The aspect of rights that has to do with order, in other words, must also be supplemented with justice, procedurally implying at least the Rule of Law.

This is not to say that a mere legal order as a prerequisite for a functioning economy would be irrelevant in the lives of the poor. On the contrary, *Voices of the Poor* showed clearly that poor people live in adverse environments in which both the economy and the legal order are dysfunctional and are not in any way conducive to the realisation of their basic interests. Hence, a functioning legal order with common access to justice is, indeed, a first implication of a rights approach.[27]

However, even in a well functioning legal order rights will not automatically be realised. The primary responsibility for implementation of subjective rights rests as it always must with the legal subjects. Indeed, it is these rights-holders themselves who would have to come into action. This applies to human rights, including the rights to decent livelihoods, no less than others. The second element in a rights approach, therefore, is concrete legal activism, or, in social science terminology, quiet encroachment into the status quo as reflected in positive law. An enlightening illustration is the *Grootboom* case in South Africa.

Asserting the right to shelter

The strongest legal foundation for the rights of the poor in our world today is the South African constitution. Consequently, much more straightforwardly than elsewhere, cases in that country concerning affirmative rights will obtain a "human rights" label as has been illustrated already in *Treatment Action Campaign* (pp. 72ff).[28] Yet, such constitutional incorporation does obviously not automatically create the relevant entitlements for everyone, transforming have-nots into haves in a flash. Indeed, even in the landmark case *Grootboom* v. *Oostenberg Municipality and others* (2000), the Constitutional Court of South Africa emphasised that neither section 26 of the constitution (on Housing) nor section 28 (1c) (on Children and the Right to Shelter) gave any of the respondents the right to claim shelter out of the blue.

Grootboom concerned 900 homeless adults and children who had constructed shacks on land not belonging to them, but not in current use either, and in that way acquired roofs over their heads while, as a by-product, attracting public attention to their constitutionally guaranteed right to adequate shelter (section 26).[29] Their subsequent eviction – by mandatory court order – left the respondents homeless, giving rise to their claim for housing based on two provisions of the constitution that guarantee the right to adequate housing for all (section 26) and especially for children (section 28(1c)[30]). The court, then, had to address the essential dilemma of enforcing an affirmative right embedded in the constitution when there are clear constraints in clauses such as "reasonable legislative and other measures", "within its available resources" and "progressive realisation" in reference to what steps the government must take to ensure the implementation of the right. The High Court of the Province ruled that the government had taken adequate steps for progressive realisation of the right to housing, but the state was still responsible to house the children under section 28 along with one parent. Against this judgment the government appealed to the Constitutional Court.

Judge Yacoob immediately set the stage, stating that socio-economic rights were enforceable in South African law as they are embedded in the Bill of

Rights, which is justiciable. The only question, then, was *how* to enforce them. The discussion that followed stressed the importance of reading the rights in their particular context, whereby the court went to great lengths to extend the scope of the right to housing, constrained as this was by terms such as "reasonable" in respect of the duties of the government. Judge Yacoob (*Grootboom* 2000, ¶44: 34) observed:

> To be reasonable, measures cannot leave out of account the degree and extent of the denial of the right they endeavour to realise. Those whose needs are the most urgent and whose ability to enjoy all rights therefore is most in peril, must not be ignored by the measures aimed at achieving realisation of the right. It may not be sufficient to meet the test of reasonableness to show that the measures are capable of achieving a statistical advance in the realisation of the right. Furthermore, the Constitution requires that everyone must be treated with care and concern. If the measures, though statistically successful, fail to respond to the needs of those most desperate, they may not pass the test.

In concluding that there was a deficiency in the state's programme for realising housing for the homeless, the Court's mandatory order demanded that this deficiency be addressed. This ability of the judiciary, then, to look into the context of the claim and weigh the perceived violation against the objectives of the rights is quite unique. In the end, human dignity as the founding principle of rights was considered essential in reaching a "just" conclusion. Judge Yacoob (*Grootboom* 2000, ¶83: 61) put it as follows:

> But section 26 is not the only provision relevant to a decision as to whether state action at any particular level of government is reasonable and consistent with the Constitution. The proposition that rights are interrelated and are all equally important is not merely a theoretical postulate. The concept has immense human and practical significance in a society founded on human dignity, equality and freedom. It is fundamental to an evaluation of the reasonableness of state action that account be taken of the inherent dignity of human beings. The Constitution will be worth infinitely less than its paper if the reasonableness of state action concerned with housing is determined without regard to the fundamental constitutional value of human dignity. Section 26, read in the context of the Bill of Rights as a whole, must mean that the respondents have a right to reasonable action by the state in all circumstances and with particular regard to human dignity. In short, I emphasise that human beings are required to be treated as human beings. This is the backdrop against which the conduct of the respondents towards the appellants must be seen.

Indeed, the case ended in a mandatory court order stipulating that the South African government secure alternative shelter for Irene Grootboom and the 899 other poor and vulnerable individuals that had been removed from their squatter compound. Yet, after more than ten years, this order – so highly praised in human rights circles – has only been partially executed, while Irene Grootboom herself has already passed away. It is therefore clear that, whatever the potential of the judiciary to become a powerful engine for the realisation of human rights, the struggle cannot be restricted to the courts. It is indeed fortunate that these rights play a part not just as legal resources, but also as political instruments, as illustrated in Table 1.1. Indeed, as argued extensively in Chapter 1, no use of political power can be considered as being legitimate unless it is exercised in conformity with international standards for the protection of human dignity. Concretely, this means that when the primary actors – those living in daily hardship themselves – are confronted with insurmountable obstacles in their daily efforts to secure sustainable livelihoods, the duties of other actors are activated. This applies not only to the power of the state, but to that of all actors, including corporations, as the UNDP *Human Development Report* 2000 duly noted (De Gaay Fortman 2000a). Actors become accountable duty bearers: here lies the crux of upstream struggles to realise human rights.

Evidently, then, there is an important third general element in rights-based strategies (next to efforts to realise the rule of law and judicial activism): political activism.

Notably, despite the deficiencies in terms of immediate positive effects for the Grootboom group, the requirements with regard to the state's housing programmes and policies, as stipulated by the Court in *Grootboom*[31] did have public effect. Indeed, these detailed criteria are now used to develop the necessary political instruments tuned to realisation of economic, social and cultural rights. Highly relevant in this respect are the design, implementation and evaluation of the government's own social programmes, the focus and design of applied research in general and entitlement systems analysis in particular, and advocacy projects by civil society organisations (Liebenberg 2000b: 22).

Access to safe water in the light of rights, entitlements and claims

Guaranteeing access to safe water is generally regarded as part of basic services and as such a public responsibility. Consequently, privatisation of water delivery is a human rights issue in two distinct ways. First, it implies an institutional change that will tend to impinge on existing access to water. While basic water entitlements are supposed to be protected by human rights law, this is likely to influence implementation. Second, access to safe water is an entitlement, which, although obviously linked to basic human dignity, is still far from being realised for everyone. The point here is that privatisation tends to affect human rights as a transformational mission, too. Hence, not surprisingly, water issues receive a great deal of attention in human rights debate. Indicative in this respect are two articles in subsequent issues of the *Netherlands Quarterly of Human Rights*, one on access to water as a human right (Tully 2005) and the other on that right in the light of "the human rights-based approach to development" (Filmer-Wilson 2005).

Notably, as international implementation of the standards tends to be extremely weak – *vide* the usual fate of "concluding observations" of the various Treaty Bodies with regard to both country reports and complaint cases – the whole emphasis in the downstream human rights venture tends to be on further specification of rights and duties. In the case of water this approach resulted in the proclamation of a "human right to water" as being inherent in the ICESR. Indeed, in General Comment No. 15 the United Nations Committee on Economic, Social and Cultural Rights declared water straightaway as being "indispensable for leading a life in human dignity". As such it "is a prerequisite for the realization of other human rights" (2003: 1).

Without indulging in any further effort to first establish a certain measure of conceptual clarity, the Committee immediately took the following position:

> The human right to water entitles everyone to sufficient, safe, acceptable, physically accessible and affordable water for personal and domestic uses. An adequate amount of safe water is necessary to prevent death from dehydration, to reduce the risk of water-related disease and to provide for consumption, cooking, personal and domestic hygienic requirements.
>
> (2003: 1)

In what follows in this General Comment we encounter an endeavour that seeks to combine deductive reasoning – rights derived from positive international law that would have to be implemented – with inductive efforts to determine what people require in order to sustain their daily livelihoods. Indeed, the two approaches get completely mixed up, as becomes evident in the following statement:

> The Committee notes the importance of ensuring sustainable access to water ... as it is required for a range of different purposes, besides personal and domestic uses, to realize many of the Covenant rights. For instance, water is necessary to produce food (right to adequate food) and ensure environmental hygiene (right to health). Water is essential for securing livelihoods (right to gain a living by work) and enjoying certain cultural practices (right to take part in cultural life). Nevertheless, priority in the allocation of water must be given to the right to water for personal and domestic uses. Priority should also be given to the water resources required to prevent starvation and disease, as well as water required to meet the core obligations of each of the Covenant rights.
>
> (2003: 2)

The Committee's declaration – which actually fell beyond its mandate – culminated in a General Assembly declaration on "the right to safe and clean drinking water and sanitation as a human right that is essential for the full enjoyment of the the right to life and all other human rights" (UN 64/L63/Res.1 of 28 July 2010). A first conceptual question in this respect is of course whether such a proclamation is really required. A Universal *Declaration* of Human Rights (UDHR) had already been passed in 1948, which subsequently has been endorsed to such an extent that its core articles in respect of the protection of basic human dignity are generally seen as customary international law (Klein Goldewijk and De Gaay Fortman 1999: 7). It includes, *inter alia*, the right to a standard of living adequate in terms of health and well-being (article 25). Article 12 of the ICESCR defines the right to health as "the right of everyone to the enjoyment of the highest attainable standard of physical and mental health".[32] As the specification of what that entails in article 12, para. 2 under 1, 2, 3, and 4 is obviously not limitative the United Nations Committee on Economic, Social and Cultural Rights might well have addressed water entitlements in its previous General Comment on the right to health (No. 14).

Yet, in General Comment, No. 15 the following reasoning is employed:

> The right to water clearly falls within the category of guarantees essential for securing an adequate standard of living, particularly since it is one of the most fundamental conditions for survival ... [It] is also inextricably related to the right to the highest attainable standard of health.
>
> (art. 12, ¶1)

In downstream international human rights, representing – just to recall – those quarters that are primarily concerned with the protection of human dignity from the perspective of international standard-setting and supervision, issues discussed include the question whether sets of claims that have not been explicitly recognised in legally binding documents, might nonetheless be seen as "inherent", "tangential" or "implied" rights (Tully 2005: 37). Evidently, the Committee opted for the inherent position, connecting the "right to water" primarily to article 11 (adequate living standard, with particular emphasis on housing and food) and article 12 on health. But it found more links:

> The right [to water] should also be seen in conjunction with other rights enshrined in the International Bill of Human Rights, foremost amongst them the right to life and human dignity.... The right to water has been recognized in a wide range of international documents, including treaties, declarations and other standards. For instance, Article 14, paragraph 2, of the Convention on the Elimination of All Forms of Discrimination Against Women stipulates that States parties shall ensure to women the right to "enjoy adequate living conditions, particularly in relation to [...] water supply". Article 24, paragraph 2, of the Convention on the Rights of the Child requires States parties to combat disease and malnutrition "through the provision of adequate nutritious foods and clean drinking-water" ... The right to water has been consistently addressed by the Committee during its consideration of States parties' reports, in accordance with its revised general guidelines regarding the form and content of reports to be submitted by States parties under articles 16 and 17 of the International

Covenant on Economic, Social and Cultural Rights, and its general comments.

(¶4)

Thus, the newly declared right to water would appear to stand on firm juridical ground. Nevertheless, this whole downstream venture of declaring ever new rights is faced with three critical limitations:[33]

1 Protection of human dignity by law assumes – recall – "law and order" in the sense that law functions as a way of guaranteeing security of people in their person, in their possessions and in their deals (implying that *pacta sunt servanda*), and settling disputes based upon conflicting interests in an ordered manner. However, in many a politico-juridical setting the role of universalist state law is rather constrained.
2 The values behind human rights norms have to be "received" in the sense of a cultural reception of the law (see pp. 123–126). In reality there tend to be serious politico-cultural constraints, although these may well differ depending upon the concrete context.
3 Human rights norms do not reflect all core aspects of justice in the same way. It is particularly in respect of the principle of equality as more than just formal equality of all before the law that their meaning is rather limited. The reason is that inalienable subjective rights tend to be formulated in a rather absolute manner: everyone has the right to…, whereas the struggle for social justice has to be directed against substantive socio-economic inequality that is of a relative nature. Indeed, human rights appear to function inadequately as a normative instrument in combating growing socio-economic inequality.

A review of these limitations with regard to water instigates the following brief comments:

1 Luckily, law is more than just state law, official courts and enforcement agencies. If, indeed, the realisation of fundamental norms binding the use of power were purely dependent on formal legal processes, in many environments deficits in the enforcement of crucial standards would be much worse. Fortunately, however, law can also work through informal mechanisms or, in the terminology introduced in Chapter 1 (p. 37), as *living law*. While "law" manifests itself as regulation of power, living law has the nature of "anti-power". For example, through protest and resistance the building of a dam that would cut people off from their existing water supplies may actually become impossible even if it had been incorporated in an official act of parliament (see Dwivedi 2001). In a similar vein, agencies supplying water to households may be forced to tolerate tapping off practices that are not based on any formal contract. Notably, entitlements protected by living law may well be affected by privatisation policies.

2 Politico-cultural reception of access to safe water as a human rights issue is bound to require collective action. Indeed, in many a politico-economic context the transformation of declared rights into conclusive rights with guaranteed freedoms and entitlements for everyone, calls for long and enduring struggles. As for civil and political rights it is the political order that has to be confronted. In the case of economic, social and cultural rights it is the entitlement (sub)systems that lie behind structural non-implementation which would have to be changed and that means a confrontation with the economic powers that be.

3 Notably, in struggles for access to water and sanitory services a core issue is socio-economic inequality. While in international human rights standards the principle of substantial rather than just formal equality is poorly embedded (De Gaay Fortman 2003: 161–162), religion-based views on justice tend to take a much deeper and more encompassing perspective. Reference may be made, for example, to Christian social thinking as developed in both the Roman Catholic Church and the Ecumenical Movement (De Gaay Fortman and Goldewijk 1998: Ch. 3). Indeed, integration of the principle of equitable distribution – posited by the UN General Assembly resolution on the Right to Development (UN A/RES/41/128 of 4 December 1986) – requires an embedding of human rights struggles in pertinent religious settings rather than just in secular human rights discourse (see also above, pp. 126–131).

Actually, all three observations point to a need for more than just downstream efforts that spell out all possible implications of human rights in terms of access to water. An upstream human rights perspective appears to be essential. This requires, first of all, some basic understanding of the meaning of rights in processes of acquiring basic necessities such as safe water and sanitary services.

Perusing general comments of the committees supervising the implementation of the various covenants and conventions, as well as the vastly increasing bulk of literature discussing these, one is struck by a rather fundamental confusion in human rights terminology. Evidently, terms as "rights", "entitlements", "access" and "freedoms" are used both as synonyms and as elements of a cocktail in which they can be freely mixed.

In General Comment No. 15 of the United Nations Committee on Economic, Social and Cultural Rights water is principally classified as a right but generally discussed as an entitlement. Crucial is the statement already quoted at the onset of this subsection: "The human right to water entitles everyone to sufficient, safe, acceptable, physically accessible and affordable water for personal and domestic uses." Again, one question has to be asked first: do rights really *entitle* people? If that were generally true, why then do so many people in our world today lack "sufficient, safe, acceptable, physically accessible and affordable water for personal and domestic uses"? It would be preferable to speak of entitlement failure in that respect: 1.2 billion persons on this earth suffer from lack of access to potable water, not because resources are lacking but as a result of deficient entitlement.[34]

A natural response to such terminological criticism could be: "It is true that entitlements following from rights do not always materialise but that means no more nor less than that rights are often violated. Unfortunately, this applies above all to human rights in general and to economic, social and cultural rights (ESC rights) in particular." Should one conclude, then, that ESC rights are rights without remedies? Indeed, in much of the literature we find comparable arguments. Rather typical for much human rights discourse in the United States, for example, is Wronka's distinction between "rights as ideals", "rights as enacted" and "rights as realized" (1992: 28–30). Thus, General Comment No. 15 would simply constitute the beginning of a process, moving from the proclamation of a right to water as an ideal through enactment in national legislation towards realisation of the entitlements necessary to acquire safe water from day to day.

This view would seem to imply that those lacking access to safe water and sanitary services would have to wait first for local enactment. However, it is precisely in respect of their transformational role that human rights may operate as a powerful weapon before any local legislation has been effectively enacted. Notably, people's struggle is tuned to daily acquirement in the sense of sustainable livelihoods, rather than abstract rights. Subjective rights constitute neither more nor less than a commitment towards legal protection of related interests on the part of those holding them. Thus, in case of dispute the owner of a thing will invoke her property right. In fact, ownership implies abstract acknowledgement of claims based on the right-holder's interests. Entitlements, in contrast, refer to concrete protected opportunities to satisfy one's needs. Indeed, what makes entitlements meaningful, recall, is *actual* legitimate access to specific resources and *actual* legitimate command over definite goods and services. Entitlement is concrete, in other words, while the qualification "legitimate" refers to authoritative protection. Naturally, concrete titles may well find such authoritative protection in rights, as is clearly the case when owners who actually possess a property, use it to acquire what they need. It is on the basis of entitlements that we may claim what we require in terms of daily livelihoods. Hence, "rights-based" action against poverty and destitution will have to focus on entitlements in the first place.

Rights-based action

Subsequent to these two case studies on adequate housing and access to safe water respectively, the elements of concrete rights-based action against poverty may now be summed up as follows:

1 Poverty is to be viewed as *deprivation* ("a pronounced deprivation in well being" as the World Development Report has defined it [World Bank 2000b]), or, in the words of the UNDP, "a brutal denial of human rights" (UNDP 1998). Hence, unlike the good willing goals for development in the new millennium, rights-based action is *normatively loaded*: it confronts the

status quo in which poverty as human rights deficit has its roots. As such, this differs from development-oriented approaches based on striving for progress (interpreted as pure "positive-sum games").

2 The focus of a rights-based strategy is not on poverty as some abstract and generalised phenomenon – the number of people who have to survive on less than the purchasing power of so much per day – but on *the poor* in the sense of all people living in daily material hardships, here and now. Indeed, the centre of attention is and should be people's needs rather than the state's resources.

3 Those living in daily hardship are *people with rights*. Economic, social and cultural rights are meant to offer people protection in activities aimed at satisfying their basic human needs. Hence, the injustices that lie at the roots of denied needs have to be addressed. Behind non-implementation lie complicated social, political and economic structures. An effort has to be made to understand and expose the roots of economic injustices that lie within these structures. The point is that poor people lack concrete entitlements in the sense of opportunity[35] to make legitimate claims. Acquirement failure therefore has to be analysed in its connections to flawed entitlement positions (see Chapter 1 and Figure 1.1).

4 Rights entail responsibilities. Indeed, *individual responsibility* takes a predominant place among the values and principles upon which the idea of a universal legal protection of fundamental freedoms and basic entitlements for each and every individual right is based. By speaking freely, for example, it is individual human beings themselves who implement the fundamental freedom of expression. In the same way the poor themselves have to be seen as primary actors in their own cause and in their own right. In other words, the primary duty-bearer regarding a person's right to shelter is that person herself. Conceptually, this view has certain consequences with regard to the way in which human rights are approached: upstream, to start with, and only then in connection with international and national downstream mechanisms.

5 With regard to implementation, then, a core notion in rights approaches is *accountability*, meaning that institutions and persons exercising power (actors, in other words) become duty-bearers. In situations of non-implementation the challenge is to identify duty-bearers and to specify their duties. In cases of concrete violations, that may be quite evident. In Zimbabwe, for example, when President Mugabe ordered people's shacks to be bulldozed down while destroying their possessions, simply because he wanted their squatter compound out of sight during a state visit by Queen Elizabeth II in 1991, the duty-bearer was easily identifiable: the state. The *Grootboom* case that we examined above also illustrates how economic, social and cultural rights become justiciable once a certain actor has engaged in concrete action affecting people's daily livelihoods.

6 However, apart from case-by-case violations, we are also often confronted with situations of structural non-implementation of the rights of the poor. In such a context accountability implies a duty for actors to engage in policies

that meet standards of appropriateness following from internationally declared human rights. Here lies the conceptual basis for "budgeting rights". The normative component guiding the execution of power by all actors implies that the use of power can be seen as legitimate only if international human rights standards are followed. Hence, rights-based action has to track not just inputs and processes, but follow-up, in terms of outcomes, in order to determine whether duty-bearers have met their obligations. For this purpose specific standards have to be set within a context that is not merely local but also international. The United Nations system for the realisation of human rights has established principles, institutions and processes based on internationally accepted requirements for the protection of human dignity. In light of the UN failure to prospectively provide resources and establish a mandate for follow-up, the time has come now to address unjust outcomes as well, in the first place at the global level itself. Indeed, rights-based approaches will remain rather meaningless if not tuned to responsibilities for global injustices.

Implications for the international financial institutions

Notably, as powerlessness – together with vulnerability and voicelessness – is seen as the institutional root of poverty, the effort to attack poverty implies a confrontation with the powers that be. Hence, much more is required than just suitable analysis combined with goodwill. What recognition of the rights of the poor entails will now be examined in respect of current challenges to the IFIs, with a primary focus on the World Bank. The starting point is that the responsibility for realising human rights is universal and hence concerns all actors, whose decisions affect people's lives, including the IFIs.

At the time when the World Bank published its *Voices of the Poor* studies, Human Rights Watch had noted "positive steps" of the IFIs "to address human rights issues" (2001). The IMF, it was felt, "has also begun slowly to change in ways that will help integrate human rights in the global economy". Indeed, human rights based criticism of its projects has been acknowledged by the World Bank for some time already. An Inspection Panel deals with complaints from people negatively affected by World Bank projects; cases have to be based on alleged contravention of the Bank's own rules and guidelines.

In the world of development assistance, this is understandably seen as a breakthrough. Yet, while the publication "Accountability of the World Bank: The Inspection Panel Ten Years On" emphasised the Panel's broad investigative powers and its impartiality (World Bank 2003), there remains reason for criticism, too. The Panel's three members are appointed by the Executive Directors for non-renewable periods of five years. Although its actual work is not subject to executive interference, the Panel must receive approval from the Executive Directors before it can begin an investigation. It is the Executive Directors, moreover, who resolve any conflicts between panel findings and staff responses. Missing from the Panel's mandate are also:

> specific powers normally associated with open, independent investigations, such as holding meetings with government officials where the complaint originated; conducting public hearings and site visits in the immediate and surrounding areas of the project; requesting written and oral submissions from affected peoples and NGOs; and hiring outside expert consultants to conduct studies.
>
> (Hunter and Udall 1994)

Worse still, the Panel's Investigation Report does not contain recommendations for actions that should be taken by management (World Bank 2009: 41).

What is needed, moreover, is a clearer recognition that the so-called disruptions constitute human rights violations. Would recognition of the IFIs' role as duty-bearers in regard to human rights, one might wonder, indeed make a difference? What, in other words, is the meaning of the currently fashionable term "rights-based approaches" in respect of the international financial institutions?

In this respect, it seems useful to follow the six elements in respect of rights-based strategies outlined above:

1 Poverty is systemic non-acquirement rooted in existing power structures. With its emphasis on the poor's lack of assets and their need for empowerment, the *World Development Report 2000/2001* (World Poverty Report) has made this abundantly clear. As poverty is to be seen as deprivation in the sense of a brutal denial of human rights, the existing order in both its political-economic and its legal aspects will have to be confronted, locally, nationally and in an international context. Indeed, the primary challenge is to identify concrete obstacles to the realisation of economic, social and cultural rights for each and everyone. Notably, these are to be found first and foremost in an unjust international economic order. From the international financial institutions, a constant effort in awareness-raising as regards global economic injustice is required.

2 As the human rights focus is on the poor in their daily hardships here and now, Millennium Development Goals (MDGs) oriented towards objectives to be reached in 2015 are insufficient and sometimes even counterproductive. While it is true that these goals include health, education, basic amenities, reproductive health and environmental sustainability, to mention a few, and hence transcend approaches based on notions of pure income poverty – this strategy still fails to meet the imperative requirements of human rights standards. The MDGs are, indeed, just development targets assumed to influence policies, particularly in the field of development co-operation. The results found in a study monitoring progress towards these goals in the light of human rights standards are "not particularly encouraging" (OHCHR 2010: 30). Clearly, additional standards have to be set that concern people's daily livelihoods here and now while operational from at least a political-economic perspective.

3 The World Poverty Report (World Bank 2000b)[36] did examine the structures behind poverty. A crucial part is Chapter 5: "Expanding Poor People's Assets and Tackling Inequalities". Indeed, poor people do lack assets; that is precisely the point. The report observes that "markets do not work well for poor people" (79), and that inequalities are rooted in, among other things, unjust distribution of public resources. In regard to the latter "the power of the state to redistribute resources, especially in services that create assets, such as education, health, and infrastructure is underscored". In analysing how redistribution might be achieved, dilemmas between economic effectiveness and social justice come to the fore. While the report recognises that naturally the poor themselves must be seen as the major actors in strategies to improve their resource base, the question remains how Bank and Fund will support them in these struggles.

This brings us to the crucial issue of empowerment. The issues brought out by the *Voices of the Poor* include: the need for support of poor people's organisations, working with the state to change rules that hinder poor people's trade and exchange in markets while simplifying and registering property rights (De Soto 1999), supporting social impact analysis, and creating local empowerment funds for learning and networking. What is still urgently needed is concrete analysis of the PRSPs, the processes by which the papers are drafted, and their implementation.

Another critical issue with regard to "rights approaches" is social protection. The WDR sees vulnerability as a central element in the lives of the poor and hence calls for structural measures to enhance security. In a social protection strategy paper entitled "From Safety Net to Springboard", this is further elaborated (World Bank 2001). With regard to the poor the challenge lies in informal social risk management requiring possibilities for risk-reduction and micro-insurance services in the informal economy. Among the major obstacles mentioned are gender-based violence and constraints on women's access to productive resources.

4 The *Voices of the Poor* studies also reveal what the poor themselves see as their due. Clearly, an effort must be made to connect these "inductive rights" to standards and mechanisms reflecting internationally declared rights. One notable priority lies in police reform and access to justice (Chambers 2001). Other obvious "inductive" rights concern basic amenities, some space for privacy, health and education.

5 In an updated version of its World Poverty Report (World Bank 2000b) the World Bank might write the omitted Chapter 12 in its WDR 2010/2011, applying the preceding analysis to its own policies and programmes (Chambers 2001). In other words, it has to take responsibility for its own role as a major duty-bearer in regard to human rights implementation. It is within the framework of its own policies and actions – PRSP processes, for example – that these duties become activated. Civil and political rights may be mentioned first here, as it is precisely lawlessness and abuse of empowerment rights that tends to typify the social and political context in which poor

people live. Naturally, the international financial institutions cannot be expected to establish suitably functioning law and order, but doubtless that does imply a responsibility to do what is in their power to ensure the rule of law in a real sense. Supporting regimes that ignore poor people's rights and deny them access to justice, for one thing, disregards their responsibility as human rights duty holders. Law and order, let us remember, has three major constituent elements: security of the person, stability of possessions and the keeping of promises (*pacta sunt servanda*). Where such an environment is lacking, all actors, including the IFIs, absolutely must tune their primary efforts towards creating these fundamental conditions of good governance, for where these conditions are not present, further efforts fail. It is therefore within this framework that these international actors have to do their business and their policies certainly must not be permitted to act against the establishment of these conditions.

With regard to the obligations of the IFIs in the field of economic, social and cultural rights, two observations may be made. First, their duties must be seen as including the removal of institutional obstacles towards implementation of these rights. This applies in a direct way when the IFIs are themselves directly responsible for the impediments, as in the case of their own projects and policies, for example. Generally, *ex ante* human rights impact assessments must be seen as imperative and a matter of due course. When, on the other hand, it is the state that is primarily responsible for structural obstacles towards human rights implementation, the IFIs may reasonably be expected to exert pressure on the state to remove these. Indeed, anti-poor policies and programmes constitute active and ongoing violations of human rights. As to the types of institutional obstacles that exert a negative influence on poor people's daily livelihoods, both *Voices of the Poor* (Narayan 2000a and 2000b) and the ensuing World Poverty Report (World Bank 2000b) contain clear analyses of the deeper roots of poverty. It is now time to translate these into practical guidelines. Notably, when poor people are engaged in processes to create structural opportunities of acquiring life necessities, these international financial actors have a human rights-based responsibility to support and assist.

6 In terms of human rights obligations legitimacy, not legality, is the key word. In fact, it is precisely where legal systems malfunction and the use of legal resources has become problematic that the function of human rights as standards of legitimacy becomes activated: confrontation of abuse of power with norms based on protection of human dignity. Government housing policies, to come back to the issue in *Grootboom* (pp. 158ff.), must be based on the right of everyone to live in a decent house, and government budgets should reflect the priority given to the satisfaction of people's housing needs. In fact, any use of power that is relevant with regard to the implementation of people's human rights has to be monitored and the information thus gained must be acted upon, else the monitoring means little.

To monitor the use of public funds, for example, a new indicator of effects on poor people's daily livelihoods might be developed: the "purchasing power of the poor" ("PPP", in a sense different from its current meaning as purchasing power parity). The money needed for a basket of essential commodities within a set timeframe would indicate fluctuations in the purchasing power of the poor. With this indicator, analysis of state expenditure for different purposes and at different levels (national as well as local) could serve as an instrument to pin down accountability for violation of the right to a decent living standard. This "PPP" might also serve as a standard in determining whether IFIs have developed and implemented appropriate policies. The next step, then, is to find innovative strategies to address violations of the right to a decent living standard. In themselves, indicators do no more than bring violation and non-implementation out into the open. Hence, in strategies for the implementation of economic, social and cultural rights, they should be linked to analyses of entitlement systems and processes behind actual acquirement such as those discussed on pp. 25ff. It is these power relations and the role of law in processes of exercising power that determine (non)-implementation of economic, social and cultural rights. In this connection the UNDP *Human Development Report* 2000 has rightly noted "the call for developing indicators that extend beyond current legal obligations" (92).

Finally on this score, as major actors responsible for human rights implementation, the IFIs should have an open eye for informal mechanisms of enforcing human rights standards, or, in another terminology, "living law" (see above, Ch. 1, p. 37). It is precisely in situations where formal legal systems are not functioning adequately that these international actors may find opportunities for informal ways of protecting basic human dignity. And while external monitoring and regulation of the IFIs regarding their human rights obligations is certainly crucial, it is equally clear that no matter how intense these efforts may be, it is their own internal enforcement mechanisms that are likely to remain major instruments for realisation of these duties.

Economic justice

While justice is a rather abstract term indicating that society has a responsibility to enforce what is right, we need ingenuity in its concretisation in clear objectives and goals.[37] A primary concern is distributive justice. In the context of the economy, this means an equitable distribution of and access to economic resources ("economic justice"[38]). In the 1970s the World Bank proposed as a new paradigm – as against development as just economic growth – "redistribution with growth" (Chenery 1974). In actual practice the resulting policies fell into the category of what was called "growth pro-poor" rather than "pro-poor growth" (pp. 146ff). The latter orientation was reflected in Irma Adelman's title "Redistribution Before Growth" (1979). The crux of that paper is in her theory of economic policy: "for equitable growth, *at each stage of the development process*, access to the critical factor of production should be redistributed *before* its productivity is improved".

The argument is that "if the need for redistribution is *anticipated* and acted upon, the social suffering involved in the developed-country process can be greatly reduced in developing nations and the time-scale before equitable growth can take place can be greatly accelerated" (1979: 165, emphases in original). Empirical evidence for the success of this strategy she found in, for example, Israel, Japan, Singapore, Taiwan and South Korea. In the latter, land reform preceded productivity growth in agriculture resulting in greater distribution of the benefits of increased productivity to the poor, in stark contrast with a country like India, where the Green Revolution was introduced without such a preceding redistribution of access to land, which has resulted in continuing rural poverty. Unfortunately, in the donor-driven world of development strategies Adelman's pro-poor policy advice has been largely neglected. It is, however, reflected in the report to the Dutch government on pro-poor growth, written by the Advisory Council for International Affairs (AIV 2003). In this policy advice, growth and social justice are married in an approach that stresses the need to link growth with emancipation. Since it points to processes of development from below, the term "emancipation" does seem to be more appropriate than "redistribution".

In the international human rights venture terms like "emancipation" and "transformation" are not part of the jargon. Not just in respect of civil and political rights but regarding economic, social and cultural rights as well, the focus is on the state and its responsibilities "to respect, to protect, and to fulfil" in a world of "equal" states. To support processes of emancipation of those living in daily hardship and transformation of the societies in which they are embedded, falls outside that frame of reference. Yet, it is particularly upstream struggles that would have to be supported. Moreover, a shift in focus towards non-state actors was long overdue. While in the current century that is getting increasing attention, beginning in academia (Jägers 2002), the approach remains non-committal. "Corporal social responsibility" (CSR) for example (Lambooy 2010), while meant to structurally incorporate the public interest into the corporate world, is only rarely connected with firm sanctions on non-compliance, although one of its constitutive elements concerns the internationally recognised standards of the International Labour Organisation (ILO). A second element regards environmental sustainability. Here again, the struggle is upstream in the first place, primarily confronting non-state actors. A remarkable case in point is *Gbemre*.

Gbemre

Gas flaring is a huge problem for people in the Niger Delta and beyond, as it is also a significant source of greenhouse gases. Notably, for many years, Shell has been promising to stop flaring gas in Nigeria. But year after year, it continues to break this promise.

Not surprisingly, then, oil production in Nigeria has regularly given rise to court proceedings on environmental damage. Amongst these, the case of *Gbemre and Others* v. *Shell Petroleum Development Company Nigeria Ltd and Others* (2005) was remarkable in two respects. The case was brought up by the

Iwherekan community with support of the Nigerian NGO branch of Friends of the Earth (Lambooy 2010: 411–412). First, the Court had no trouble whatsoever in granting leave to Jonah Gbemre to institute proceedings in a representative capacity not only for himself, but also "for each and every member of the Iwherekan Community in the Delta State of Nigeria". Indeed, there was no discussion whatsoever in the judgment on juridical intricacies such as legal personality. Second, the decision against the defendants, who had continued flaring gas in the course of their oil exploration and production activities, explicitly mentioned "the right to a clean, poison-free, pollution-free and healthy environment". This is based on an interpretation of the "[c]onstitutionally guaranteed fundamental rights to life and dignity of the human person" in conjunction with Articles 4 (right to life), 16 (right to enjoy the highest attainable physical and mental health standard and duty for states to take the necessary measures to protect the health of their people) and 24 (people's right to a generally satisfactory environment favourable to their development) of the African Charter on Human and Peoples' Rights as well as certain national procedural rules.

However, *Gbemre* flopped in 2007 after Justice Nwokorie had been removed from the case. Yet, it is still noteworthy from a political economy perspective. On 10 November 1995, Ken Saro Wiwa and eight of his companions in MOSOP (Movement for the Survival of the Ogoni People) were hanged after a trial that had met with worldwide indignation on account of gross violations of due process rules. This was the time of the reckless tyranny of General Abacha. In those days, writ petitions such as Gbemre's did not even reach the courts; the applicants would be dealt with in a brutal and extra-legal manner. (On the notion of anti-law see p. 20.)

Gbemre shows, in the first place, that the struggle for public justice is inherently action-oriented. It is, indeed, through upstream action that human rights may trigger judicial law development. Yet, no matter how important judicial law development may be, from a civilisational perspective there is another, primary struggle: founding, grounding and nurturing the rule of law.[39] Sadly, amidst complicated jurisprudential efforts to bring positive law to a higher level of both sophistication and civilisation, all can suddenly be set aside when unrestricted power takes over completely.[40] Indeed, since the judicial case-by-case approach to human rights realisation has its obvious limitations, *Gbemre* also points to the need for political operationability of human rights standards.

The crucial role of institutions

Notably then, economic justice requires a firm institutional base. In an Economics Focus on the *Roots of Development*, *The Economist* mentioned the current stress on "the importance of long-lived 'institutions' that are conducive to growth": political stability, property rights, legal systems, patterns of land tenure and so on (Economics Focus 2002). It then discussed a working paper by Easterly and Levine that examined the relative importance of sound and stable institutions in comparison with two other factors: competent policies and favourable geography (2002). *The Economist* concludes: "The results are intriguing. Institutions turn out to matter most—but that is putting it mildly. Geography and policy, as influences in their own right, turn out to matter not merely less than institutions but, roughly speaking, not at all" (2002: 86). Institutions, then, matter immensely. Notably, we are concerned here with institutions that promote productivity growth in the first place; hence the emphasis on institutions to protect private property and curb the power of the state. Institutions represent rules, as North has put it, namely, the set of political, economic, social and legal ground rules – such as constitutional and criminal law, economic laws like property rights and the law of torts and contract – reflect "the rules of the game of a society and consist of formal and informal constraints constructed to order interpersonal relationships" (North 1990: 3; North 1994). Within such a general framework, various organisations and institutional arrangements have developed to structure relations both inside and with the outside world. In this connection, we touch again upon Sally Falk Moore, who speaks of the institution as a "semi-autonomous field" that applies to both the formal and the informal economy (1983: 55–56). Indeed, at a lower level, too, there is a moulding of human conduct by formal and informal rules as agents are also part of these lower level entities (De Gaay Fortman and Kortekaas 1998).

If institutions are so important as roots of genuine development, then a primary challenge for development economics is "how to get from bad to good institutions?" (Economics Focus 2002). In a "vital economy" perspective – the term is Bernard Shaw's – a preceding question must be answered: what makes an institution bad or good? It is the rights focus that compels us to answer that question not solely in respect of productivity but with regard to distributive mechanisms as well. Indeed, it is high time to review all relevant institutional arrangements both internationally and at the local level from the perspective of the rights of the poor. The primary focus on rights has direct consequences concerning current "rules of the game" such as debt issues, agricultural subsidies, and trade rules. This is well reflected in the way in which *Terra Viva*, the daily journal of the International Press Service reports regularly on concerns in international and local development, namely, under the heading "Rights". In local environments this kind of scrutiny of existing institutions as rules (North 1990) would do well to start from what research analyses have revealed as constraints and obstacles in the lives of the poor. The starting point for such enquiries is pro-poor growth in a real sense, meaning productivity increasing strategies embarked on by the poor themselves. Credit systems might be recalled here as an example of an industry in pressing need of institutional reform.

Implications of inaction or non-interference can be much more easily determined than those relating to effective protection and genuine pro-poor growth; this is a general difficulty in non-laissez-faire approaches. Naturally, an institutional scrutiny based on the rights of the poor is not value-free. For one thing, this makes a full application of Hernando De Soto's research findings less simple than he assumes. In his latest book, *The Mystery of Capital*, De Soto comes to a total amount for the assets possessed by the poor that would imply an average of

US$8,000 per person (2001: 33). How can this be reconciled with the *Voices of the Poor* studies, which conclude that one of the primary causes of poverty is that the poor lack assets? The point is that these are just possessions in a de facto sense, but with the holders lacking any kind of title (usually including entitlements based on institutional protection). De Soto's calculations, in other words, include the shacks constructed by Irene Grootboom and the likes. What he correctly deplores, then, is the fact that poor people's access to their own assets is not protected by rights, which makes it practically impossible for them to borrow, invest or accumulate. Assets such as a piece of land with a squatter's shack on it cannot be used for further accumulation because there are no titles protected through the modern, universalist legal system. It is a mistake to think that this would be just a matter of overcoming bureaucratic constraints. Registration of titles primarily requires a process of quiet attainment of legitimacy for an originally illegal status quo. This is likely to involve confrontation with precisely the powers that have denied the poor their titles in the first place.

Finally in this context, it should be emphasised that the rights approach is inherently non-violent. Rights, as interpreted in this study, are interests protected by law, and law is a way of dealing with conflicts of interests in a non-violent manner. Hence, no matter the degree of economic injustice reflected in the distribution of land in Zimbabwe, Mugabe's way of sacrificing the rule of law to tackle that, has been totally at odds with a rights approach.

Once one has determined what makes an institution bad or good, *The Economist*'s question on how to get from bad to good institutions still has to be answered. This brings us to our final point: the importance of upstream action, starting from those struggling to sustain their daily livelihoods themselves and focusing primarily on those actors that exercise power relevant to poor people's daily livelihoods. Notably, opportunities for self-help approaches do exist, requiring self-confidence on the part of the poor. Yet such approaches should be "considered as complements, not as alternatives, to accessible public services and the redistribution of income and wealth" (Berner 2002).

Although the actual changes in the World Bank's policies with regard to the poor are undeniably noticeable, the change in attitude at the level of the top leadership, as reflected in the *Voices of the Poor* studies and the *World Development Report 2000/2001* (World Bank 2000b), is to be regarded as just the beginning of involvement in a process towards meaningful rights-based strategies. Indeed, pro-poor growth in a genuine sense might be conceived as not just a new conditional facility; it also constitutes a change in mindset. Reform always begins with different attitudes and then still takes a long time. What the new mindset, tuned primarily to the poor themselves in their daily struggles for survival, might well lead to is a change of focus within the IFIs from a productivist orientation towards mega projects and programmes with harmful effects on communities of the poor, to keeping an open eye to the self-organising and self-government capabilities of local peoples.[41]

At the outset of the new millennium Pyatt ended his sombre account of growing inequality as the "seed of conflict" with a nostalgic reminiscence of the

World Bank's response in the 1970s that had been characterised by "redistribution with growth broadly interpreted to include land reform, and a steady flow of foreign assistance". However, he continued, "that is no longer the official position. Does anyone have a coherent alternative?" (Pyatt 2002: 29). It might well be argued that today such a new vision, based on rights, is gaining ground. But what is beginning as a change of mindset still has to become embodied in institutional change, too. There is no doubt that this requires the institutions of good government in the first place, as Greg Mills has forcefully argued in his *Why Africa is Poor. And What Africans Can Do About It* (2010). His main point concerns African leadership and its incredible record of bad governance, to which the African electorates have become apathetic. In that light his recipes are disappointing, however, focusing on Asian tigers as shining examples on the one hand, and large scale commercial economic opportunities in Africa itself on the other hand, namely, agriculture, mining and tourism.[42] All three areas he envisages as requiring huge investments in order to increase productivity. Yet it is precisely capital-intensive sectors of production that have shown to be rather sensitive to bad governance.

Actually, there is no alternative to processes of emancipation working their way through the whole matrix of Table 4.2. These might well start from rights' awareness. Perhaps it is not so much in terms of productivity growth but primarily in emancipation from bad leadership that the African grassroots may learn something from people in other parts of the world. As we see it, the lack of progress in democratic emancipation in Africa – and even its retreat (Diamond and Plattner 2010; Easterly 2010: 38) – is a major cause for concern. In the next chapter, while focusing on the protection of collectivities, we shall touch upon the dialectics of democracy, too.

6 Realisation

The rights of collectivities

Wrong does not cease to be wrong because the majority share in it.

Leo Tolstoy (1987 [1908]: 158)

Of minorities and minarets

On 29 November 2009, Switzerland accepted a people's initiative to amend Article 72 of its constitution (on Church and State) with a third section:

The construction of minarets is prohibited.

This decision resulted in not only ongoing debate within the country itself, but also an international outburst of indignation, not least in countries in which freedom of religion is categorically more problematic than in the pricey republic of the conjurors. The Islamic Republic of Iran, for example, summoned the Swiss ambassador to account for the Islam-inimical decision of his people. The dominant feeling within Europe was one of astonishment: this had happened in a country with an impressive political history of peaceful coexistence between people of different cultures and creeds; a state based upon a decentralised system of government; a constitution embodying fundamental rights, including both equality before the law and freedom of religion and conscience; and a fair record of international human rights compliance. Stunningly, all such observations had also been made in the debate in both houses of the national parliament in Bern, where the people's initiative had to be validated before it could be put to the popular vote.

Although the ban was immediately challenged in the European Court of Human Rights in Strasbourg, the socio-cultural background of the decision, its actual content and its international status, are not our major concern here. Above all, the change of the Swiss constitution may be seen as illustrative of the contemporary human rights problematique, not only from a substantive perspective, but also with regard to certain procedural aspects.

The decision was taken with a turnout of 53 per cent and a majority of 57.5 per cent. Hence, the initiative passed even though less than one-third of the electorate had actually voted in its favour; yet, such were the rules of the game. The point is that, in the Swiss system of public-political decision-making, assurances against the popular whim are not sought in qualified majorities – such as the two-thirds majority in the second parliamentary reading of a proposal for constitutional change required in the Netherlands – but in the authority of the federal assembly to validate or invalidate an initiative that had secured the requisite number of more than 100,000 signatures.

When a people's initiative meets the formal requirements, the federal assembly has to discuss two proposals from its governing council: one on validation and one on endorsement. If the initiative is validated but not endorsed, it will be put to the popular vote with a recommendation from parliament to reject it. This is precisely what happened in the case of the minarets. Both validation and the recommendation to reject the people's initiative were accepted with huge majorities.

Article 139, § 3 of the Swiss constitution sets out the grounds for invalidation:

> If the initiative fails to comply with the requirements of consistency of form, and of subject matter, or if it infringes mandatory provisions of international law, the Federal Assembly shall declare it to be invalid in whole or in part.

Since the proposed constitutional change had been formulated in clear and unequivocal wording, the discussion in the Federal Assembly naturally concentrated on its compatibility with "mandatory" provisions of international law, *ius cogens* in other words. The obvious question posed by this course of events, albeit rarely discussed, is "How on earth could the *Bundesrat* (the Federal Council) recommend validation and the *Bundesversammlung* (parliament) approve that"? This query is all the more striking if one considers the initiative's multiple infringements of positive law, which the *Bundesrat* had already enumerated in its proposal to parliament. Incompatibilities were noted in respect of Switzerland's own constitution: the equal treatment requirement and the non-discrimination principle (Article 8), freedom of religion and conscience (Article 15), and guarantee of ownership (Article 26). Furthermore, the initiative was considered to be in breach of Articles 9 (freedom of thought, conscience and religion) and 14 (the non-discrimination principle) of the European Convention on Human Rights. The United Nations Covenant on Civil and Political Rights was considered violated in respect of freedom of thought, conscience and religion (Article 18) and the prohibition of governing with distinction to religion (Article 2).[1] Stunningly, the Swiss Federal Council did not regard any of these violations of international human rights norms as a contravention of *ius cogens*. What then, one might wonder, is the meaning of that phrase? Remarkably, this has not been catalogued, let alone unequivocally determined, although there is general agreement on prohibitions against aggressive war, crimes against humanity, war crimes, maritime piracy, genocide, apartheid, slavery and torture. The way in which the Swiss government treated the matter – shocking as it may be –

is nevertheless generally in line with states' practice of interpreting the question of infringement of *ius cogens* according to their own authority (Stüssi 2008).[2]

In the parliamentary debate on the proposal, two observations stand out. One is the reference to other states that had limited the construction of religious edifices. Indeed, it is not surprising that the issue of compliance with *ius cogens* is judged in respect of actual states' practice, which in quite a number of countries tends to be rather restrictive when it comes to Christian churches. (Incidentally, as one of the delegates ironically remarked, the canton of Vaud – "reformed" until 2003[3] – repealed its prohibition of Catholic church towers only in 1930; strikingly, after 80 years of erecting Catholic towers, the majority of the inhabitants of its capital Lausanne are today Catholic.) More amazing from a contemporary perspective is the delegates' overwhelming adherence to their citizens' "democratic right" to take majority decisions on their constitution by popular vote. As this freedom entails the responsibility to watch over the realisation of that charter's fundamental rights, the Swiss government's action raises the question of minorities' protection in the context of majority rule, an enigmatic and controversial problematique in current human rights debates.

Democracy as majority rule

Notably, democracy's way of handling conflicts of interests in a public-political community is not simply majority rule. To illustrate, consider Abraham Lincoln's definition – government of, by and for the people – as a starting point. Government of the people means not only self-determination but *representative* government; government by the people signifies *participatory* government; and government for the people may be seen as *accountable* government. The three concepts are obviously interrelated, as they are all connected to principles in the formation, use and limitation of political power. Thus, democracy implies that public-political power be representative, participatory and accountable to both the majority and the minority if it is to be legitimate.

Even when confined to just the representative component of democratic government, majority rule entails, in fact, three basic principles:

1 decisions rest on majorities;
2 dissenters acquiesce; and
3 majorities respect and protect minorities.

As to the operation of the first principle, it is well known that when it comes to highly contested issues, simply counting heads without any preliminary process of consultation and persuasion is not conducive to peaceful government. Thus, although the will of the majority is the basis for upholding the decision, a connection with the democratic prerequisite of participatory government is essential to the decision's legitimacy.

The second principle naturally presumes that the rules of the decision-making game have been followed, both in the formation and in the execution of political power. "When the majority has once spoken, it is the duty of the minority to submit", Tocqueville noted already in 1835 in his *Democracy in America* (428). Minority compliance exemplifies the rule of non-violence, implying that opposition, protest and resistance be confined to civil disobedience, though even that method of non-violent confrontation of government and the laws enacted by parliament already tends to be politically destabilising. In practice, the smooth acceptance of majority decision-making by dissenting minorities requires an adequately functioning rule of law, based on an accessible and independent judiciary within the context of limited government respecting and protecting people's fundamental interests by law.[4]

This brings us to the third principle, which has been strikingly worded in the European Court of Human Rights' *Grand Chamber* judgment in the case of *Sørensen and Rasmussen* v. *Denmark*: "[D]emocracy does not simply mean that the views of a majority must always prevail: a balance must be achieved which ensures the fair and proper treatment of minorities and *avoids any abuse of dominant position*" (2006: 26, emphasis added). Yet, this is perhaps the most problematic aspect of democracy in our world today as minorities still tend, poignantly, to be unprotected,[5] precisely at a time when nations become increasingly heterogeneous. Notably, peaceful settlement of disputes arising from conflicting interests flows from this third principle and requires not only participation in decision-making by all concerned, but also a well-functioning rule of law both to protect minorities' interests and to gain their acquiescence in decisions taken by the majority.

Minority rights: for what purpose?

Returning to the Swiss people's initiative, the religious issue as such – constructing a minaret as a culturally specific type of tower connected to an already existing edifice of worship – is obviously rather trivial compared to the *collective discrimination* that such a constitutional prohibition directed towards Muslims entails. Strikingly, this decision was taken in a country with only four existing minarets, where the great majority of Muslims were secular refugees from the former Yugoslavia. In conflict studies – a research area to which human rights studies would be wise to become more intimately connected – it is common knowledge that state policies, measures and actions, negatively directed at specific groups whose public-political position is already problematic, tend to induce political violence. Remarkably, however, criticism on the Swiss people's initiative ignored any reference to minorities' protection.

Incidentally, reference is made to minorities in Switzerland's own constitution in Article 70, § 2 in the context of languages (qualified by the adjective "indigenous") and in Articles 109 and 110 in respect of tenancy matters and employment policies (which have to take appropriate account of "the justified interests of minorities"). Notably, these clauses stipulate respecting equality before the law as the overriding principle. The fundamental prohibition of discrimination, in other words, remains the primary concern.

In the European setting, a Charter for Regional or Minority Languages (ECRML) was adopted in 1992 under the auspices of the Council of Europe to protect and "promote historical, regional and minority languages" in Europe. As a regional security body, the Organisation for Security and Cooperation in Europe seeks to identify ethnic tensions and to set standards for the rights of persons belonging to minority groups. In 1998 a European Framework Convention for the Protection of National Minorities entered into force. In Article 1 it declares that "[t]he protection of national minorities and of the rights and freedoms of persons belonging to those minorities forms an integral part of the international protection of human rights, and as such falls within the scope of international co-operation". The ensuing articles refer, again, to "persons belonging to national minorities". In actual legal and political practice, however, this Convention plays no part.

At the global plane, a Sub-Commission (of the Commission on Human Rights; since 2007 called the Human Rights Council) had been set up for the Prevention of Discrimination and the Protection of Minorities. There was consensus right from the start that it had "singularly failed to make any contribution towards the protection of minorities" (Humphrey 1968: 869), for more reasons than just its low place in the UN hierarchy.[6] In 1992 the United Nations adopted the Declaration on the Rights of Persons Belonging to National or Ethnic, Religious and Linguistic Minorities. This document stipulates in Article 2, § 1:

> Persons belonging to national or ethnic, religious and linguistic minorities (hereinafter referred to as persons belonging to minorities) have the right to enjoy their own culture, to profess and practice their own religion, and to use their own language, in private and in public, freely and without interference or any form of discrimination.

In this wording, the question whether a minaret is a matter of culture or religion is obviously not decisive. As a declaration adopted by the UN's General Assembly it is, however, not regarded as internationally binding, let alone *ius cogens*.

Since 2005 the UN also has an "Independent Expert on Minority Issues" who regularly issues statements (e.g. on "early attention to minority rights as a key tool for stability and conflict prevention", 20 October 2010).

As to Treaty law, Article 27 of the International Covenant on Civil and Political Rights (ICCPR) provides that

> [i]n those States in which ethnic, religious or linguistic minorities exist, persons belonging to these minorities shall not be denied the right, in community with other members of their group, to enjoy their own culture, to profess and practise their own religion, or to use their own language.[7]

In its General Comment No. 23 the Human Rights Committee has observed that this Article establishes and recognises a right which is conferred on *individuals* belonging to minority groups. Yet the Committee's jurisprudence has shown that, in practice, Article 27 can be used to address some of the problems affecting indigenous collectivities, namely those related to internal aspects of self-determination. In this connection, the minorities' right to "enjoy their own culture" includes "a particular way of life associated with the use of land resources, [e]specially in the case of indigenous peoples. That right may include such traditional activities as fishing or hunting and the right to live in reserves protected by law" (CCPR General Comment No. 23 1994: ¶7). The Committee's jurisprudence on Article 27 has also confirmed that economic activities may come within its scope if they are an essential element of a minority community's way of life. There is, however, no international enforcement in human rights treaty law; this remains dependent on the success of efforts within national jurisdictions.

In situations of intra-state collective violence wherein the state has shown itself consistently unable to protect a minority, which constitutes a majority in a specific area within the national territory, some scholars speak of "an emerging right to autonomy within international law" (Sydenham 2004). Whether regarded as *lex ferenda* or not, such a "right" is still far from being *lex lata*.

Obviously, then, international minorities law appears too weak to play any effective part in the actual protection of people suffering from abuse by others in dominant positions, to draw on the terminology of the European Court of Human Rights. This inherent weakness begs the question whether efforts to protect such people should focus on properly defining and strengthening "minority rights", which seems to be the major trend in modern human rights law, or be directed towards a search for alternative approaches.

The minority problematique in a political economy perspective

There is nothing normative in the notion of a minority; it is just a residual category in respect of the idea of majority rule. Nevertheless, as Tocqueville pronounced in his seminal work (1945 [1835]: 265):

> [t]he moral authority of the majority is partly based upon the notion that there is more intelligence and wisdom in a number of men united than in a single individual, and that the number of the legislators is more important than their quality.[8]

True as this may be, majorities are fortunately *not* primordial categories. Hence, the starting point in our analysis must be *majority construction* as something beyond simply assembling and counting votes. Indeed, if majorities were merely incidental outcomes of political debate, majority rule would not be problematic in its consequences for dissenters, as the latter might be as "floating" in taking sides as those consenting in the issue at stake. This, however, is not the case. Institutional attempts at majority construction, such as the formation of political parties, are natural; in this connection electoral systems merit particular attention with regard to their exclusionary consequences. Strikingly, in the "Westminster" constituency system, the excluded ("minority") parties joined together may well constitute a majority. In the United Kingdom, for example, a majority of the popular vote seldom brings a party into power, while often the party with the most seats garners support from not much more than one-third of the population. In reality, then, it is the *rules of the game* that count more than "the will of the people".[9]

Thus, first-past-the-post may well lead to permanent or at least long-term exclusion from power, even for groups with firm roots in society. The practice of power-sharing becomes particularly crucial in this respect. Although it is a concern usually falling beyond the scope of human rights, attaining ample participation in government for national collectivities often acts as a prerequisite for political stability and peace.[10] The way in which Nelson Mandela managed to secure (Zulu-based) Inkhata participation in the first South African post-apartheid government of 1994 provides a striking illustration. On the other hand, the constituency system in certain Commonwealth countries has led not only to continuous government by the same political party[11] but sometimes even to one-party parliament.[12] In evidently non-homogeneous nation-states this is likely to result in a structural minority problematique. Hence, it is not without reason that heterogeneous Switzerland uses a model of political power formation that guarantees a fair amount of power-sharing among the parties representing the citizens' interests at all distinct levels of government. Ignoring the concerns behind power-sharing may have disastrous consequences, particularly in a post-conflict peace-building stage.

The socio-cultural basis of political party formation is a second aspect of majority construction that may be tricky in its effects on exclusion. This applies particularly to racial, ethnic, tribal, religious or other types of party formation based on an exclusive collective identity, whether formally or informally organised. Particularly in such settings, power-sharing tends to become imperative. Indeed, the Northern Irish exclusion of Catholics from power – for whatever kinds of reasons – has been highly conducive to civil strife. Even when religious and/or ethnic majorities rotate – as in some island states of the Caribbean[13] – majority rule based on collective identity construction may affect entitlement positions of persons belonging to the minority temporarily out of power.

In addition to the political conditions necessary for democracy's capacity to establish legitimate government, there are also *economic* prerequisites of majority rule. In his exposition on *The Economic Prerequisite to Democracy* (1981), Dan Usher's concern was with the distributive effects of democracy as a system of government. His book "is a study of how society protects democratic government by entrusting the economy with a task that the legislature can never perform – the task of assigning the major part of income and other advantages" (1981: ix). His worry is "conflict over assignment" in societies governed on the basis of majority rule. "For democracy to survive", Usher feels, "there must be a prior agreement among citizens on a set of rules for assignment that voters and legislators will not lightly overturn". He refers to this as a "system of equity", defined as "a set of rules for assigning income and other advantages independently of and prior to political decisions arrived at in the legislature" (1981: viii–ix). The protection of people's entitlement positions regardless of their political preferences and affiliations comes to the fore here. A particular challenge in this connection is to prevent poverty and unemployment from affecting the same people all of the time.

Based on the three points made above – that majorities are not primordial but *constructed*, that they do not necessarily represent an *actual* majority position and that they are subject to multiple forms of manipulation and *political* pressure – it becomes increasingly clear that majority-minority relationships are not the key problematique in the formation and execution of political power. The real issue is construction of dominant positions based on collectively exclusive elements and the actual abuse of such positions. In South Africa, for example, the apartheid regime was based on minority rule; political support for the Afrikaner regime by a majority of all voters would not have legitimised the creation and abuse of that white dominant position. In Guatemala, to mention another example, it is still the indigenous majority that suffers from discriminatory exploitation. Obviously, then, numerical inferiority is not an adequate criterion for establishing what constitutes a "minority" in a legally normative sense. As Mohamed Salih has put it:

> The case of dominant minorities makes us realize that minorities are not the passive recipients of majority oppression, nor incapable of oppressing others. To that extent minorities are social entities, a construction of a social reality and their position in the polity of the nation-state. Nevertheless, on the whole, history has so far shown that there are more oppressed than oppressive minorities in the world.
>
> (2003: 109)

Strikingly, there is no internationally enacted definition of the term "minority". Francesco Capotorti, United Nations Special Rapporteur, in the context of Article 27 of the International Covenant on Civil and Political Rights (on rights of "persons belonging to ethnic, religious or linguistic minorities"), proposed the following text:

> A group numerically inferior to the rest of the population of a State, in a non-dominant position, whose members – being nationals of the State – possess ethnic, religious or linguistic characteristics differing from those of the rest of the population and show, if only implicitly, a sense of solidarity, directed towards preserving their culture, traditions, religion or language.
>
> (1979: 96)

"A group numerically inferior to the rest of the population of a State" is not only arithmetic nonsense, but also neglects the primary background of the minority problematique: abuse of dominant positions that are based on exclusivist collective identities.

Notably, people corresponding to Capotorti's definition do not usually identify as such. Still struggling with the meaning of minority rights, this author's eyes were opened when at a conference in Brunei – an Islamic Sultanate with an ethnic Malay dominance – no single participant reacted in the affirmative on the question if there were "persons belonging to a minority" present. Yet, on the follow-up query "Are there any Chinese among us?" many responded in the affirmative. "Christians?" Many, again. Indeed, why would one identify as a minority person while there would be nothing to gain from such self-identification and a lot to lose in terms of daily security.[14] Indeed, the Chinese in Brunei, or the Christians for that matter – to a large extent overlapping categories – wish for security above all else. This happens to be attainable by these groups only through complete identification as citizens of the land: citizenship above minority rights, in other words.[15] Naturally, the Chinese citizens of this Malay-dominated state cherish their distinct language; obviously Christians desire freedom of worship in that Islamic Sultanate. But while they do want to preserve "their culture, traditions, religion [and] language", their need is first and foremost for human security in the sense of freedom from fear, which is best attained through indisputable integration in the nation-state.

It is true that Brunei is not a democracy, but neither is it a ruthless tyranny. Constitutionally as well as socio-culturally, ethnic Chinese and religious Christians are accepted and protected. Since that first encounter in Brunei almost two years ago, the question has often been put to international students at Utrecht University: "Who of you belongs to a minority?" The response from this sample, admittedly limited, reveals that a positive answer is given only by refugees and by those whose collectivity had already organised itself as a political power (e.g. Roman Catholics in Northern Ireland).

A second flaw in Capotorti's definition lies in the phrase "whose members ... possess ethnic, religious or linguistic characteristics differing from those of the rest of the population". The verb "to possess" creates the impression that there is a kind of primordial distinctiveness about minorities and ignores their construction through identity-based majority formation. Incidentally, in Article 2 of the UN Convention on the Prevention and Punishment of the Crime of Genocide, a similar disregard of anthropological wisdom emerges, as it defines genocide as meaning certain specific "acts committed with intent to destroy, in whole or in part, a national, ethnical, racial or religious group, as such". This way of putting things creates the impression that such entities exist regardless of their construction and definition either by themselves or by people in dominant positions.[16]

In the final part of Capotorti's definition, the element of self-identification does receive emphasis, as it stipulates that people manifest "a sense of solidarity, directed towards preserving their culture, traditions, religion or language". But would not already declared human rights such as freedom of religion and cultural rights suffice here? It is true that in practice "cultural rights" have been treated in a step-motherly fashion, but that should be no reason to refrain from operationalisation of this already declared category of rights.

Protection of cultural freedoms and entitlements through cultural rights

The problem with cultural rights as distinct from other categories of human rights is that there is no further concretisation based on specific values related to human dignity. In respect of economic rights there is the right to a decent living standard, for example, while in regard to civil rights there is a specification in the prohibition of torture for instance. But "cultural rights" are typified as "an aspiring human rights principle, under discussion and maybe under development" (Ketscher 2007: 219). This far from encouraging characterisation is based on the vague and inadequate incorporation of these rights into the international venture for the realisation of human rights. "As a legal figure", Ketscher started her inquiry, "'culture' is unclear" (2007: 221), and she ends with the conclusion that "Culture as such does however not enjoy a notable legal status" (234). In her review of United Nations instruments and mechanisms this gloomy statement is well substantiated. Indeed, it corresponds with other sources such as the Final Report of a fully-fledged "Congress on Cultural Rights and Human Development" held in Barcelona in 2004.[17] Neither Article 27 of the Universal Declaration of Human Rights (UDHR) which declares the rights of everyone to participate in the cultural life of the community, to enjoy the arts and to share in scientific advancement and its benefits, nor the corresponding Article 15 of the International Covenant on Economic, Social and Cultural Rights (ICESCR) appears to have resulted in meaningful human rights legislation, let alone supervisory mechanisms. In her study "Towards a Right to Cultural Identity" Donders comes to the conclusion that "freedom of cultural identity", as she calls it, has not really taken shape beyond "soft law" declarations (2002: 341). Yet, like similar indistinct "rights", cultural identity may well play the role of a general principle of law.[18]

Despite the unsatisfactory incorporation of cultural rights in national and international legal systems, from the perspective of ordinary women and men these rights do relate to their daily lives. Think, for example, of those who have the graves of their dear deceased in a cemetery. Notably, in Chicago people who had their departed relatives buried at St Johannes Cemetery (founded in 1849 by German immigrants) have been engaged in judicial efforts to stop the City from taking over their suburban graveyard (promising to move the graves to another cemetery) in order to build a new runway as well as another terminal for O'Hare International Airport.[19] Although legally the whole case appeared to centre on a clause in the Religious Freedom Restoration Act proscribing eligibility for federal funding of plans that would "substantially burden religious exercise", along with the applicants depicting themselves as "religious plaintiffs", it obviously concerns protection of a *cultural* entitlement. Aside a graveyard's possible connection to religion and/or religious institutions, relatives are undeniably involved in its accessibility. Indeed, few would deny that this is a cultural issue closely related to basic human dignity.[20]

Hence, instead of "religious exercise" the law in question might have used the phrase "cultural practice" as a category of entitlements that ought not to be "substantially burdened". I see two reasons why this has not been done. First, there is the American public-political identification with religion while culture is rather seen as a purely private affair. Second, cultural practice is not regarded as something intrinsically legitimate, and hence worthy of legal protection. The latter may well represent a worldwide feeling. Female genital mutilation, to mention just one particular practice by way of example, is resisted precisely on account of women's human dignity. As explained already in (pp. 122ff) Chapter 4, in regard to human rights culture is a two-edged sword.

Another obvious feature of *St. John's cemetery* is its collective aspect. A nearby cemetery concerns the life of a whole community; hence, it is their collective dignity that is at stake. This tends to be typical of cultural rights in general. In the cemetery there is a connected church that possesses legal personality.[21] But whether or not applicants constitute a legally recognised entity, what concerns them affects not merely a collection of disconnected individuals but a whole group of people. Although collective rights tend to be heavily contested even in human rights circles proper,[22] for those who feel their communal human dignity affected, collective action is a natural response. Today both lawmakers and judges manifest a growing recognition of these collective aspects of human dignity protection.[23]

The point, then, is that human rights oriented efforts for the protection of cultural freedoms and entitlements are to emerge from practice, as is not unusual in human rights struggles. "We Filipinos learned human rights not from books", an activist under the Marcos regime once put it. "We were oppressed, and we had no choice but to fight back. In that very struggle we discovered the rights we had lost" (Contreras 1996). In a similar vein, an indigenous people's representative who spoke of a fundamental right to "be guaranteed an education which respects and strengthens our cultural heritage", immediately referred to the background of that assertion: "gross and systematic violation of the rights of peoples belonging to particular groups" as "a perennial component of social relations through the world" (Dodgson 1994). Hence, while from a modern human rights perspective a term such as "cultural heritage" is far from clear, to those living in realities denying any collective sense of belonging, it is entirely plain. The same applies to such communal needs as a history of their own (Fesneaux 1976).

The irony of collective equity

Collectivities, so much has become clear now, have a genuine human dignity-related interest in public-political protection of certain freedoms and entitlements that are common to the group as a whole. Quite evidently, however, minorities are far from fixed objective categories and their identification is subject to extensive politicisation, but neither is the "minority" issue a mere chimera in the sense of an issue that could just be ignored. It remains a reality determined by abuse of entrenched dominant positions, resulting in disqualification and discrimination of collectivities regarded as different in the sense of inferior. In the public-political community, deeply rooted patterns of socialisation of people in terms of majoritarian superiority and minoritarian inferiority are not likely to be eliminated by one stroke of the pen, nor even by enacting rights. Notably, in the social as well as the legal sciences, it is not wise to begin working from existing scholarly models and conceptualisations; the challenge is rather to study how people behave in the real world. Hence we have to start from reality on the ground and then attempt to connect our findings to human rights – upstream analysis, in other words[24] – rather than the downstream approach starting from the legal texts, which so often prevails in academic human rights research.

In the real world the "minority" problematique appears to be part of the general setting of "us–them" divides, manifesting itself in three distinct ways: collective prejudice against people associated with certain constructed categories, discrimination against members of such "groups" (not rarely culminating in the most serious of crimes) and systemic inequalities.

Evidently, legal systems do not provide an effective instrument to deal with collective prejudice. The challenge here lies in human rights education, a huge effort tuned to majority acceptance of differences and the creation of an environment in which "minorities" can feel recognition as well as inclusion. As concluded from a survey in Finland, a country in which the foremost issue is language:

> [t]he best laws are useless if the acceptance of the majority is prerequisite to the laws' successful implementation. In this sense, human rights education would be a valuable tool for the fostering of an environment of acceptance. Human Rights Education is vital to spreading of information about minorities and their special needs, including teaching the importance of recognizing differences to change practical living conditions, even though the protection given by law seems to be perfect.
>
> (Mahler 2009: 201)

In regard to individual rights of persons belonging to a "minority", education's utility lies primarily in the struggle for equal treatment. In a society with a strong juridical culture such as the United States, law played an obvious part in getting rid of much systemic discrimination. It must be acknowledged, however, that such laws were the result of long and contentious political struggles that are not over, even in a country that, at least domestically and for its own citizens, has a long history of struggling to realise the rule of law. But when the laws are not observed, national legal systems can deal with disputes only if cases come from recognised legal personalities, or, in practice, individuals. In regard to such individual cases of discrimination, domestic law may provide certain remedies, though these are inherently unsatisfactory because they tend to be only partial and reactive in response to discrimination that is systemic and pervasive. This is to say nothing of countries where the juridical culture is deficient.

In the international setting direct remedies are lacking. Thus, with all due respect for the Committee on the Elimination of Racial Discrimination (CERD) that receives occasional individual complaints and scrutinises state reports in which it makes useful comments and policy recommendations, the lack of effective mechanisms for direct enforcement tends to reduce its role to merely commenting on the effectiveness of national institutions. Nevertheless, where national instruments are completely lacking because specific forms of discrimination have not been established as human rights violations – such as castism and discrimination against certain non-recognised "minorities" – international human rights may still play its part in bringing issues to the fore and mobilising shame.

It should be clear from the prior discussion that what law has to offer regarding efforts to rectify systemic inequities is inherently limited. This complicated problematique is a matter of policies in the first place, as I have discussed in earlier work (De Gaay Fortman 2002). With that in mind, let us focus now on the "minority" issue in its contextual connection with intra-state collective violence, starting with an attempt to draw lessons from a frightful episode in European history: collective oppression, persecution and resistance in France in the epoch between the rise of Protestantism and the French Revolution.

That period of religious strife began with the Reformation, which questioned the public-political monopoly of the Roman Catholic Church in Western Europe. In France, as in other countries, that church had been established as the sole institutionalisation of Christianity. The suppression of those who adhered to the reformed faith, the so-called Huguenots, amounted to what would now be called crimes against humanity and certainly acts of genocide as well. As the Protestant resistance had organised militarily, the almost 300 years of intra-state collective violence included religious wars and war crimes on both sides.

While always a minority in the entire kingdom of France, the Huguenots were geographically concentrated in an area south of the Loire and especially in the crescent stretching from La Rochelle through the southern provinces of Guyenne, Languedoc and Dauphiné to Geneva. In the cities under their control, it was the Roman Catholics who had to suffer from collective discrimination and humiliation. The Edict of Nantes (1598) brought a short period of relative peace based upon a certain degree of power-sharing that allowed the French Protestants to garrison some 200 towns. Huguenots acquired access to royal offices, legal redress before special royal courts (known as *chambres de l'édit*), and the right to establish their own academies. Royal letters (*brevets*) accompanying the Edict granted subsidies for their troops, pastors and schools. In most of France, however, Protestants were granted only limited rights of worship.[25] Thus, rather than extracting religion from state power, the Edict launched a kind of religious cleansing of the kind we still find today in a city like Belfast.

Collective minority recognition is the inevitable consequence of majority entrenchment through public-political establishment. Yet, a major lesson from that French history, which still is to be learnt, is that its side-product may well be a worsening of the divide. Politically organised and internationally recognised "minorities" stand at the roots of new processes towards majority construction in the sense of their gaining dominant positions that might well be abused. For instance, after the war of 1998 the Albanians in Kosovo lost no time in transforming themselves from an abused minority into an abusive majority. It is of course acknowledged that collective human "cleansing", that repulsive phenomenon of the twentieth century, is definitely not the answer to the "minority" problematique. Nevertheless, in this connection an *irony of collective equity*[26] can be empirically detected: with each supposedly equitable solution to one minority problematique, new majority minority divides manifest themselves resulting in new iniquities. The former Yugoslavia provides a striking illustration of this tendency. As to the insoluble puzzles to which intolerance in a heterogeneous nation-state may lead, Belgium represents an off-putting illustration.

Notably, in the negotiations leading to the pacification of the Nantes Edict, the Huguenots had formulated three major demands:

1 guaranteed freedom of worship for the Protestant (Reformed) religion in the whole Kingdom of France without any restriction as to time and place;
2 guaranteed equal access to office, whatsoever; and
3 guaranteed security for all citizens of the reformed faith.

(Van Enk 2009: 334)[27]

The failure to grant these guarantees had forced the Huguenots to further organise as a strong minority, dependent on auto-protection. This resulted in collective political and military organisation. Where they were in control they adopted policies of discrimination against the Catholics in their turn. Under Louis XIV they were crushed; the Edict of Nantes, although registered by the legislatures in 1598 as fundamental and irrevocable law, was revoked in 1685. Protestantism was declared illegal; as a result, the following century until the French Revolution was a time of unrestrained anti-Protestant tyranny, persecution and oppression. Hundreds of thousands of Huguenots fled hearth and home (Kaplan 2007: 159–169).

It is instructive here to pay heed to the second Huguenot request, which amounts to equal economic opportunities. The lack of perspective resulting from politico-economic exclusion has proven to be a major factor contributing to intra-state violence – both then and in the present. Adam Smith's observation in his *Inquiry into the Nature and Causes of the Wealth of Nations*, already mentioned at the outset of this study (p. xx), might still be taken as a starting point here: "commerce and manufactures gradually introduced order and good government, and with them the liberty and security of individuals" (Smith 1900 [1776]: 313) As a structural basis for peace and political stability, this presumes non-discrimination in trade and employment, too.

Notably, we are touching upon the golden triangle of human dignity realisation again: human rights, human development and human security (Figure I.2). Equally indeed, the third Huguenot demand obtains: protection of everyone against violence. This may still be seen as the most important function of the state: law and order (see above, pp. 114ff), aiming at the *equal protection of all* who find themselves on the territory in respect to:

1. their *person*, implying not only protection *against* the state[28] in the sense of security of person as stipulated in Article 3 of the UDHR, but also protection *by* the state against criminality;
2. their *goods*, implying solidity of entitlement positions, which is both more and less than the right to own property as such (article 17 UDHR); and
3. their *deals*, implying the execution of contracts (*pacta sunt servanda*) through an "exact administration of justice". (Smith 1900 [1776]: 540)

Obviously, then, in respect of collectivities' protection too, human security requires a strong state based on an inclusive social contract and commitment to the rule of law. The guarantees the Huguenots sought are the basic due any citizen should expect from the state. Beyond these prerequisites, is there any specific role for "minority rights"?

A misconception

Minority rights do not find much of a basis in the Universal Declaration of Human Rights, that foundational document, which has assumed the character of chapter 1 of a virtual global constitution. Consequently, in efforts to conceptualise these "rights" there was little ground to start from. Actually, two international missions have been confused here: collective rights and the rights of collective entities, usually called group rights or minority rights.[29] Collective rights are rights which by nature can be enjoyed just collectively (Dinstein 1976). Self-determination is the most familiar example; today it is particularly the right to a healthy environment that comes to the fore. In the UNESCO setting of pronouncing ever new rights, a declared "right to cultural diversity" may be mentioned (Donders 2002). In practice such "rights" play the part of principles (*regulae iuris*; see Chapter1, note 26), both in the realm of politics and in litigation.

Group rights are a different matter; here the legal subject is a collective entity no matter the character of the rights claimed. Since rights protect interests by law, they grant abstract acknowledgements of claims based on these. It is often argued in this connection that only individuals can be human beings and hence enjoy human rights.[30] This, however, is not the issue. There is no compelling reason why the subject of such legal protection could not be a collectivity. The practical prerequisite of creating rights for collectivities would be "merely" that the groups be granted legal personality.[31] As human beings live in community with others, there are definitely collective aspects to the need for human dignity protection, as has been clearly recognised in the UN human rights venture. In the case of ethnic and religious groups – the categories usually referred to in international human rights documents concerned with minorities – this has generally not been the case. The real issue is not, however, whether collectivities might be recognised as legal personalities, but whether doing so is an effective strategy in protecting the human dignity of the individuals in these groups.

While, indeed, international human rights law could universally declare all individual human beings to possess legal personality and has actually done so – equal in inalienable rights – with regard to a general category of "groups" this would obviously be unwise. To the degree that this project is pursued it is distracting, confusing and even counterproductive. This holds true for two central reasons. First there is the unavoidable problem of definition, as discussed above, whether the group is a minority, a majority, a people or an indigenous group. There exists no consistently reliable *legal* methodology for limiting – defining – the membership composition of groups in a public law context.[32] The human rights bodies and the human rights instruments do not share a single definition of "minority". To imagine that a useful and reliable legal definition of "minority" will emerge seems a naïve dream. Instead, the obvious result of granting special or extra rights such as rights of self-government or secession, or even mere special protection of already existing rights, to vaguely defined and ultimately illimitable "groups" is that groups – however defined – will multiply and compete in the political arena in an attempt to take advantage of such rights. This generally has led towards, rather than away from, greater political strife. But this is, of course, only the first problem.

Second – and this impediment applies more generally to the narrow conception of human rights as mere rights in the sense of abstract legal acknowledgement of interests – even if legal personality were granted to collectivities, the lack of an international court of human rights seriously hampers the realisation of judicial remedies related to those rights they may assert. So the question remains whether an international legal discourse still is to be seen as an effective way to achieve the aim of equal protection for all as far as the collective aspects of human dignity are concerned.[33] Indeed, the same doubt persists about whether modern state law could provide the right machinery for such protection.

There are, certainly, states that have incorporated constitutional clauses for the protection of minorities. A striking example is Macedonia where, in 2001, after a period of serious civil strife between the ruling Macedonians and the structurally excluded Albanians, a new constitution was enacted as part of a peace accord. This involved deletion of references in the constitution's preamble suggesting that persons belonging to minorities are second-class citizens, as well as enshrining 15 amendments designed to give greater rights to the country's ethnic Albanians. There is no general reference here to "minority rights", but specific clauses are enacted to protect the position of a designated category of citizens, identifiable by their common language. Notably, in response to the peace accord, the leader of the political party of Albanians welcomed the constitutional changes with the following words: "We repaired the constitution and now we have to repair the mentality that created ethnic conflicts" ("Macedonia Adopts a New Constitution" 2001).

Yet, Macedonia is a shining exception. Actually, in constitutional documents we tend to find more references to arrangements for the protection of the majority than to minority rights. Does not the term "minority rights", then, create mere illusions? In other words: isn't it a major misconception?

Majority entrenchment

Constitutions, as we know, embody rules on the authority of states to maintain public order through law; they tie the exercise of power to moral norms. This is reflected in the notion of a social contract: behind state law, as a way of stipulating legal obligations, lies the virtual state-citizens' agreement to form one public-political community. Thus, the term is used here not as a philosophical idea, but rather, in line with conflict theory. As was already explained in Chapter 4, intra-state collective violence finds a breeding ground in two major factors: structural socio-economic inequalities and lack of an adequately functioning social contract.[34] The latter implies, first, that there be not a failing but a functioning state and, second, that citizens in general look upon this state as theirs. Naturally, this requires legitimate government, too, in the sense of an administration ruling on the basis of the principles, institutions and processes that are regarded as "right", as well as commonly acceptable outcomes (De Gaay Fortman 1998b).

Even where majority construction, as a way of privileging a defined segment of the public community to the exclusion of other "groups", has an emancipatory background, it remains a problematic practice. A characteristic example is Malaysia, where Article 153 of their constitution grants the Head of State responsibility for safeguarding the special position of the Malay and other indigenous peoples, collectively referred to as "Bumiputra", meaning the sons of the land.[35] The Bumiputra actually form a majority within Malaysia, but have historically been at the bottom end of the economic ladder.[36] The discriminatory arrangement that Malaysia's constitution entails may be seen as a carry-over of laws made by the British colonial power to protect the Malay from being overpowered by the immigration of Chinese and Indian workers into Malaya. Indeed, behind the construction of the Bumiputra as a majority at independence is a period in which income inequalities corresponded to a socio-economic dissimilarity between Chinese and Indians on the one hand and ethnic Malays on the other. In actual practice, Article 153 has created a distinction between Malaysians of different ethnic backgrounds, resulting in the implementation of affirmative action policies which only benefit the majority Bumiputra.[37] This entrenchment of a division between the Bumiputra and other groups is one cause of ongoing political tensions.

No matter their intelligibility and their historical origin, such entrenched dominant positions[38] are not only susceptible to abuse; they also institutionalise sensitive us–them divides, thus affecting the susceptibility to conflict of the nation-state as such. Their legal starting point lies in public-political establishment of one specific religion, origin, language or any other grouping in a way that may well marginalise or exclude people who do not share the established characteristics. Such establishment of a dominant position for one particular collective entity may be either formally embodied in the constitution or informally entrenched in daily decision-making. As this may well be seen as the crux of the whole "minorities" problematique, let us now turn to the international venture for the realisation of human rights in that light.

"Minority" protection in a juridical/judicial perspective

Notably, the way in which the protection of "minorities" has been conceptualised in legal instruments and mechanisms has placed great emphasis on the second foundational principle of human rights: the quest for fundamental rights. The major flaws that affect "minorities" protection can be traced to this overreliance on judicially enforceable rights as such. International mechanisms for the realisation of human rights were set up as if the emancipatory struggles preceding adoption of the legal model had already been definitively concluded with the victory of the allied forces in the Second World War. That model is based on three stages: standard-setting, supervision through monitoring of compliance and enforcement. Its capacity to enforce international human rights law, however, is terribly weak, as was noted already in Chapter 2. So the responsibility for implementing all those internationally *declared* rights still rests basically at the national and local level. In respect of minorities, however, the nation-state is precisely the level at which the struggle for equal protection faces the greatest challenges.

"Minorities" protection in Universal Periodic Reviews

Monitoring of state compliance with regard to the protection of "minorities" is clearly flawed, as a summary survey of the recently created Universal Periodic Reviews (UPRs) in the Human Rights Council (HRC) reveals. Strikingly, in respect of a country such as Burundi, wherein it has consistently been the Tutsi minority that has abused its dominant position, no substantive questions on minorities and minority rights were asked (HRC 2009a). The same applies to the sessions concerning the Czech Republic, India, Indonesia, Philippines, Pakistan, Uzbekistan and the Democratic Republic of the Congo,[39] to mention just a few other examples of states facing evident challenges in the protection of distinct collective entities.

The substance of the recommendations that the countries having come up for review by their "peers" have received is equally revealing. The whole process, as it is conducted, fully deserves the title that UN Watch gave its recent evaluation of the process: "Mutual Praise Society" (2009). Here are three illustrations from the review sessions. First, a suggestion from the United Kingdom to Poland: "[C]onsider forming twinning relationships or partnerships with countries that have been through a process of legal reforms on minority issues to work closely with them on the legal, technical and institutional challenges involved in introducing change" (HRC 2008f: 7–8). Is there anyone in Geneva who believes that such advice was really conducive to minorities' protection in the country under review? And what to say about Myanmar making the following recommendation to Malaysia:

> [C]ontinue to share and extend its experience and best practices in the efforts in developing comprehensive policies and strategies for the advancement of indigenous groups which focus on uplifting the status and quality of life of the community via socio-economic programs.
>
> (HRC 2009b: 8)

In the words of the Malaysian poet Cecil Rajendra: "Can the blind see for the dumb? Can the dumb talk?" (1987: 30–31).

Quite astonishing, finally, is the following proposal that Mexico made to Sri Lanka:

> Continue to strengthen its activities to ensure there is no discrimination against ethnic minorities in the enjoyment of the full range of human rights, in line with the comments of the Committee on Economic, Social and Cultural Rights, the Committee on the Elimination of Racial Discrimination, the Committee on the Right of the Child and the Committee on the Elimination of Discrimination Against Women.
>
> (HRC 2008g: 20)

Poor Tamils; poor Muslims! As treaty-based human rights law hardly offers effective protection of minorities against abuse by those in dominant positions, the UN charter-based mechanism appears to provide no solution either. While not utterly without effect, these mechanisms are least effective precisely in those countries where the protections they promise to collectivities are most necessary. Indeed, another paradigm must be found.

Yet a crucial point remains, already noticed repeatedly in this study: despite its obvious flaws, the international human rights mission did create a strong notion of global legitimacy, which is particularly precious as there is no global government. Indeed, no use of power can be considered legitimate if it violates international standards on the protection of human dignity. It is here that we find a genuine prospective vision for substantial improvement in the relevance of human rights in respect of collectivities' protection.

"Minority" protection in an integrated human dignity perspective

Human dignity, as discussed in the Introduction, refers to the inherent worth of each and every human being, simply as an innate consequence of human existence whether or not an individual person is herself convinced of that.[40] Inherent is, indeed, the adjective used in the preambles of both the UN Charter and the UDHR, meaning that human dignity is a matter of being rather than having, and hence implying that it cannot be taken away. Yet, it is worth emphasising here that some people have been denied the enjoyment of these rights merely because of their group identity, whether that is imposed from without or within. It is violation, then, more than preconceived group rights that governs the problematique. Thus what has been conceptualised as "minority rights" – rights protecting minorities – must be reconceptualised as based not on minority status, but as already internationally established rights protecting universal human dignity in its collective aspects too.

Naturally, that Muslims in Switzerland can no longer connect minarets to their mosques is just a minor issue compared to the major violations of human dignity which other "minorities" have to suffer. Yet, the formal incorporation of that prohibition into the Swiss constitution despite all national, regional and international law to the contrary is indicative of a world in which offensive action based on us–them divides tends to prevail over legal protection of collectivities. The validation of the people's initiative by the Swiss national parliament also constitutes a striking illustration of the systematically weak incorporation of human rights into positive law (see above, pp. 178–179).

A frightful case in point is the civil war that has raged in the Democratic Republic of the Congo since the Rwandan genocide of 1994. This conflict, in which the fighting factions are mainly based on ethnically identified collectivities, has already cost the lives of almost six million people. Since the formal peace agreement of 2003, it is particularly the eastern region that remains prey to gross and systematic violations of human rights. In such a context, crimes against women tend to abound, too (Mibenge 2010). A United Nations peace force is apparently unable to provide military protection to civilians, let alone force an end to the atrocities. A limited legal response comes from the International Criminal Court in The Hague, which since its start in 2002 has indicted a few military commanders responsible for major human rights violations in Eastern Congo. None of these cases has so far led to a conclusive judgment. In the meantime, the political economy of that war appears to be based on illegal mining and selling of coltan, gold and other minerals. While legal deterrence does not offer much in terms of staunching the flow of blood, political-economic intervention holds much more promise as a way to end the carnage. That reality is well known, but not acted upon despite some forceful advocacy by civil society organisations such as the Netherlands Institute for Southern Africa (NIZA).

Overall, then, the picture is grim. Yet, before coming to final conclusions on human rights and collectivities' protection, there is one more recent development that warrants attention: the progression of indigenous rights.

Indigenous rights

In 2007, after an astonishing 22 years of preparing a text, the United Nations General Assembly adopted a strongly worded Declaration on the Rights of Indigenous Peoples. This document contains clear statements on vital issues such as self-determination and access to lands, territories and resources. These include not only cultural rights (Article 11) but also strong provisions on land rights. Thus, Article 26 declares:

> 1 Indigenous peoples have the right to the lands, territories and resources which they have traditionally owned, occupied or otherwise used or acquired.
>
> 2 Indigenous peoples have the right to own, use, develop and control the lands, territories and resources that they possess by reason of traditional ownership or other traditional occupation or use, as well as those which they have otherwise acquired.

3 States shall give legal recognition and protection to these lands, territories and resources. Such recognition shall be conducted with due respect to the customs, traditions and land tenure systems of the indigenous peoples concerned.

Four states, all with historically oppressed indigenous populations far outnumbered by later settlers – Canada, the United States, Australia and New Zealand – voted against this declaration. All four have since then endorsed it, New Zealand with the following qualification:

> In moving to support the Declaration, New Zealand both affirms those rights and reaffirms the legal and constitutional frameworks that underpin New Zealand's legal system. Those existing frameworks, while they will continue to evolve in accordance with New Zealand's domestic circumstances, define the bounds of New Zealand's engagement with the aspirational elements of the Declaration.

This reservation is in line with the expressed views of many countries that had already voted in favour of the declaration.[41] At the time of its adoption, concerns were also expressed on the lack of a clear definition of the term "indigenous". The consensus was that this would have to be decided at the national level. Indeed, an international rule on who is indigenous and who is not would conflict with the general trend towards self-identification as the only reasonable way to determine allegiance with collective entities, such as race and ethnic group. But when socio-cultural groups within a nation-state self-identify as "indigenous people" just like that, the whole declaration loses its meaning. In fact, this appears to be happening already in Bolivia (Pallares-Burke 2006) as well as Iran (Kymlicka 2008: 16–17). Political mobilisation amongst ethno-cultural groups in Africa, based on (a contested meaning of) "indigenousness", similarly illustrates the difficulties inherent in relying upon a normative, all-encompassing legal definition of this concept (Ndahinda 2009). The same problematique, in regard to the construction of "minorities", is threatening to be overshadowed by the desire to identify as "indigenous" rather than as "a person belonging to a minority". While some scholars may "hope to develop a more adequate legal framework" (Kymlicka 2008: 31) as the path forward, such an approach is not available because of the inherent problems attending such legalistic definition, whether the object of the definition is "minority" or "indigenous".

Meanwhile, the actual problematique of indigenous peoples conspicuously follows from operations of multinational companies endorsed by government policies that make them victims of development (Hadiprayitno 2010). Thus, while language and culture remain important elements in the protection of human dignity in its collective aspects, a primary need today is protection against so-called "development" and its consequences in terms of sustaining daily livelihoods, particularly insofar as these are based on access to land. Oddly, the human rights mission is not of much use here as it has uncritically opted for an understanding of development as inherently positive, culminating in the UN declared "Right to Development". With this observation we are getting to the crux of the matter: to move beyond such blinkered analysis – to achieve a *life-world* understanding of the meaning of human rights as opposed to a policy analyst's. Legalistic questions about the definitions of "minority" and "indigenous" must be put to the side. Instead of focusing on enforcing rights based on legal status – which evidently engenders legal battles over status while the rights go unrealised for decade after decade – human rights must be envisaged and implemented in a wider human dignity perspective, including sustainable *human* development and human security.

Operationalising R2P

People learn human rights not from books but in the actual struggle for the protection of their dignity against abuse of power. Here lies the clue to a new conceptualisation of what was meant by "minority rights", too. The key issue is a fundamental shift in how to identify the collective subject in need of protection.

As a normative category entitled to international protection, a minority should not be seen as just a group of people in a non-dominant position with access to particular rights, but rather as a collective entity in need of public-political protection against abuse of dominant positions; *identification through violation*, in other words, rather than legally recognised, seemingly primordial characteristics. To determine abuse of dominant positions, the standards of international human rights law may well serve, meaning primarily the norms of *ius cogens* such as prohibitions of aggressive war, crimes against humanity, war crimes, maritime piracy, genocide, apartheid, slavery and torture, and generally the Universal Declaration of Human Rights that was proclaimed by the United Nations General Assembly in 1948:

> [A]s a common standard of achievement for all peoples and all nations, to the end that every individual and every organ of society, keeping this Declaration constantly in mind, shall strive ... to secure their universal and effective recognition and observance, both among the peoples of Member States themselves and among the peoples of territories under their jurisdiction.

While this approach to the "minorities" problematique provides sufficient clarity for integrated policy responses, it cannot form a basis for *judicial* protection as the legal subject is, and will remain, indefinite. Indeed, the collectivities in need of public-political protection, so called "minorities", are not primordial categories but collective entities arising out of (deficient) political practice. As such they will benefit from a shift of resources from (quasi-)juridical action towards policies supporting political-economic transformation. After a meaningless start down in the UN hierarchy with the Sub-Commission for the Prevention of Discrimination and the Protection of Minorities, it is high time now to take the security of national collectivities seriously. A new mission might well need a new name. Conceivably, then, a Sub-Council for Protection of National Collectivities might be established directly under the Security Council, the only UN body with real teeth, to operate according to the principles of the newly conceived "Responsibility to Protect" (R2P, see pp. 95–96).[42] The normative background for such a new institutional setting lies in the genealogy of universal human dignity rather than that of fundamental rights, and in established global legitimacy rather than declared universal legality. Indeed, in order to effectively protect collective victims of abuse of dominant positions, this whole mission will have to be rooted in not merely human rights, but in the full triangle of human dignity, including human security and human development. In this respect UN Security Council Resolution 1973 (2011) on the creation of a "no-fly zone" in Libya may well be seen as a breakthrough. In that text, the Council authorises member states "to take all necessary measures ... *to protect civilians and civilian populated areas under threat of attack*" over Libya (emphasis added), excluding only "a foreign occupying force". Notably, in previous UN terminology reference to repression of a civilian population used to be connected with a qualification of such behaviour as "threatening international peace and security in the region" (see, for example, Resolution 688 (1991)). In the light of Article 42 of the UN Charter, which authorises all military action that "may be necessary to maintain or restore international peace and security" such wording was understandable. In Resolution 1973 (2011), however, the language is fully R2P-based, with an ensuing focus on crimes against humanity committed against a State's own population. Thus, almost five years after Resolution 1674 (2006) in which the Security Council committed itself to R2P-based action in order to protect civilians (see p. 95), this new principle of international law can be regarded as a fully legitimate foundation for validating international military action.

Finally, then, there is nothing wrong with rights, including group rights in the sense of "rights of collectivities". Yet, there are conceptual and contextual difficulties in pursuing efforts to realise such rights. The term "minority", both as a label and as a concept, does not assist in any way toward overcoming those obstacles: it is here that we encounter a major misconception. What is required now is first to reconceptualise the mission in terms of collective human dignity protection, and second to move that venture from the UN mechanisms for the "promotion and protection of human rights" to an international environment truly conducive to their realisation.

Conclusion

The quest for realisation

> Justice and power must be brought together, so that whatever is just may be powerful, and whatever is powerful may be just.[1]
>
> Blaise Pascal (1863: 298)

Human rights as battleground

Laguna de Bay is a salty lake not far from Manila, the capital of the Philippines. On its shore are fishing villages. The catch in open waters is primarily for local consumption. However, a boom in urban demand for lake fish in the early 1980s resulted in the establishment of fisheries through exploitation of fish pens. For commercial purposes "waterlords" from Manila have affixed nets to the bottom of the lake, in effect trapping "their" fish in these private ponds, privatising what was once the commons (see Chapter 1, note 13). The small fishermen at the lakeside could not afford the investments required to construct their own fish pens. As a result only about a third of the lake is accessible to the locals; the rest is exploited by rich individuals from Manila with strong connections to government. But every once in a while a typhoon sweeps the water across the lake and the fish are "liberated" from the private ponds. "Today God is with us", the local fishermen say. But what about tomorrow? Should the lives of these poor villagers remain forever limited by the status quo of inequitable access to basic (communal) resources? Should things always stay as they are? Or might God be assisted in righting the wrong, in line with the title of that French movie *Dieu a besoin des hommes!* ("God needs people")?

Traditional fishermen have now organised in cooperatives to advocate dismantling the big fish pens owned by the Manila-based investors. The aim is a fair allocation of the area accessible to the locals. This struggle for greater access to the lake is, counterintuitively, a fight against legality (as embodied in the status quo) in favour of legitimacy (a generally held conviction on what is right and wrong) and human rights play a crucial part here. With the support of NGOs the villagers have become aware that they have rights related to protection of their basic human dignity. Human rights may, in other words, transform a clash of interests as protected by different power positions into a struggle for public justice. Hence, in adverse environments the primary meaning of human rights is to recraft common standards of legitimacy. Cultures of passivity, determinism and submission may thus give way to new forms of initiative and resistance.

At stake in such cases are not just ordinary subjective claims in the sense of personal interests protected by law. Human rights protect freedoms and needs so basic that their denial puts human dignity itself at risk. What may seem from the outside to be a simple conflict of distinct interests protected by diverse power positions is thus placed in a normative context, confronting both interests and the use of power with values attached to human dignity. Where positive law does not yet acknowledge fundamental freedoms and basic human needs, human rights are most crucial for their strength as principles of legitimacy.

At the roots of systemic denial of people's dignity-related freedoms and entitlements, this study has argued, lie gross injustices in the formation, distribution and use of economic and political power. Hence, rather than a mere moral discourse, human rights is best conceptualised as an arena of struggle. In that light the real question to be tackled is *strategy*: ends and means tuned to overcoming constraints to realisation. It is, indeed, not the core of the human rights mission, universal human dignity, which must be seen as problematic. As David Kennedy noted in an article, which deserves much more response from within "the human rights world" itself, "[t]here is no question that the international human rights movement has done a great deal of good". He identifies that "good" as:

> freeing individuals from great harm, providing an emancipatory vocabulary and institutional machinery for people across the globe, raising the standards by which governments judge one another, and by which they are judged, both by their own people, and by ... the "international community". (2002: 101)

Yet, Kennedy wonders whether the "international human rights movement" must now be seen as "part of the problem": "The strong attachment of the human rights movement to the legal formalisation of rights and the establishment of legal machinery for their implementation makes the achievement of these forms an end in itself" (2002: 110). To the reader of the present volume, the setbacks he mentions will not sound unfamiliar: a mission that became legalised, bureaucratised, secluded in pretensions and promises it cannot deliver, and isolated from the world of politics and economics in which the most vital battles for justice are fought. Indeed, these flaws all have to do with the ways and means in which the mission has been conceived, institutionalised and de-contextualised.

The international human rights venture, this study demonstrated, was *conceived* without due regard for its foundational "faith" in universal human dignity, nor for the essentially political nature of a mission grounded in declared rather than conclusive rights. It was also confusingly *institutionalised* through a pretentious legal system subservient to international politics. And in its doctrinal implementation of standardised strategies all over the world it became *de-contextualised*, without due regard for the specificity of concrete socio-cultural and politico-economic environments.

Based on a review of ten specific flaws,[2] Kennedy advocates "a pragmatic reassessment of our most sacred humanitarian commitments, tactics and tools" (2002: 115). This study has focused on adverse environments confronting people in distress: the poor and displaced, the vulnerable, victims of violent conflict; all those living in conditions of grim hardship, in short. In that light, let us focus this reassessment of commitments, tactics and tools on three ways in which the global human rights mission affects daily efforts to have fundamental freedoms and entitlements respected and protected, namely, deepening, widening and uplifting such struggles. These correspond, as we shall see, with a strategic focus on reconceptualisation and contextualisation, and a quest for innovative ways of institutionalising the human rights mission.

The struggle is deepened

First, then, let us reassess "our commitments". Human rights *deepen* struggles for the protection of fundamental human interests by putting these in a normative (moral-political) setting: the quest for respect and protection of human dignity as a matter of public justice, implying the confrontation of power with basic rights of human beings and fundamental principles of legitimacy. Indeed, people fighting for access to safe water are not just involved in a struggle for economic power that will give them better access to goods and services. The denial of their basic needs for clean water must confront society with its own values when their efforts are framed within the context of human rights. This has immediate political implications in respect of public policies and their execution as well as to business decisions. In Chapter 5, for example, we touched upon the phenomenon of development-induced displacement of people, as in the construction of giant dams for electricity generation (p. 151). The essential critique of purely "development"-oriented approaches to human deprivation and destitution, as concluded in that chapter, is that the primary basis for public and private decision-making should not be development per se, but human dignity as the foundation of people's basic freedoms and entitlements.

Notably then, the struggle for universal human dignity is a matter of principles, prospectively and not just in judicial hindsight. These are values of primary importance – *principium*, after all, means beginning – in determining policies and actions. The juxtaposition is with interests: *Between Principles and Interests* Van der Kooy titled one of his books (1956). Power is the means by which people realise their interests, and principles, grounded in universality and human dignity, are meant to guide both the use of power in endeavours to realise interests and the resolution of disputes arising out of conflicting interests.

Power and violence

A first issue in this respect is the power of government. Although its "monopoly on physical violence" is often advanced as the essence of government (Weber 1964 [1947]: 154), in her "Reflections on Violence" Hannah Arendt strongly objected to this conventional characterisation:

> Power is indeed of the essence of all government, but violence is not. Violence is by nature instrumental; like all means, it always stands in need of guidance and justification through the end it pursues.... Power is..., as the saying goes, "an end in itself".
>
> (1969: 14)

Arendt is referring here to power formation, inherent as that is to the very existence of political communities: power "springs up whenever people get together and act in concert, but it derives its legitimacy from the initial getting together rather than from any action that may follow" (1969: 14). However, whereas the initial social contract may continue to legitimate a form of power, violence needs continuous justification in the present. An example of such an immediately legitimating cause is self-defence, "because the danger is not only clear but present, and the end to justify the means is immediate" (1969: 14).

It is true, Arendt admits, that violence can defeat power, but only at a high price:

> Nowhere is the self-defeating factor in the victory of violence over power more evident than in the use of terror for purposes of maintaining domination ... terror is not the same as violence; it is rather the form of government that comes into being when violence, having destroyed all power, does not abdicate but, on the contrary, remains in full control.
>
> (Arendt 1969: 20)

Indeed, the opposite of violence is not non-violence but power: "Power and violence are opposites; where the one rules absolutely, the other is absent" (Arendt 1969: 20). Violence never springs from power but it often springs from rage, the mad fury as a collective instinct that Sartre had referred to, and that expressed itself in the slave revolts and the rebellions of the oppressed. Yet, Arendt comments:

> [R]age is by no means an automatic reaction to misery and suffering as such; no one reacts with rage to a disease beyond the powers of medicine or to an earthquake or, for that matter, to social conditions which seem to be unchangeable. Only when there is reason to suspect that conditions could be changed and are not, does rage arise. Only when our sense of justice is offended do we react with rage ... The point is that under certain circumstances violence, which is to act without argument or speech and without reckoning with consequences, is the only possibility of setting the scales of justice right again. (Billy Budd striking dead the man who bore false witness against him is the classic example.) In this sense, rage and the violence that sometimes, not always, goes with it belong to the "natural" emotions, and to cure man of them would mean nothing less than to dehumanize or emasculate them.
>
> (1969: 20)

Thus, Hannah Arendt's enlightening discourse on power and violence brings us back to the deeper layers of human dignity protection: the rhetorically abused yet indispensible concept of justice. Justice and power must be brought together, as Blaise Pascal stated already some 150 years ago (see the epigram that begins this chapter). This must be the essence of any effort to deepen the struggle for realisation of equal dignity and rights. Indeed, the reconceptualisation that this requires may start from the preamble to the UN Charter and Article 1 of the Universal Declaration.

Justice as a human need

In his grassroots work for peace building, John Paul Lederach of the Conflict Transformation Program in the United States touched upon the "justice gap" (1999). This is the consequence of inadequate efforts to develop a peace-building framework that not only reduces direct violence but also produces public justice. The point is that in all situations of violent conflict, there are original injustices that lie at its roots. The reason hostilities can be ended is generally that those involved realise that the violence of war is even worse than the original injustices. But at the time that they cease active hostilities, they will also expect these original injustices to be dealt with. Expectations are raised that life will not continue to be as before, but that there will be an improvement, a public path towards justice. Notably, justice has very much to do with the outcome of the use of power, and hence with daily freedoms and livelihoods, with people's needs and the recognition of these. The "root conflict", in Johan Galtung's terminology (1998), has to be addressed in order to prevent future conflict. Its essence is injustice.

Justice is both normative and compelling: it refers to what is right from such a perspective and to such an extent that it ought to be enforced. It is often seen as an ideal, a set of values that provide direction to public policies, for example. But in the context of our final focus on strategies for the realisation of fundamental rights, what matters is justice not as merely an ideal of law-making, but as a human need: a functional necessity in any viable "social contract", including the (virtual) global compact. Our attention is drawn here to Durkheim's "The Division of Labour in Society" (1893) as interpreted through Anne Rawls (2003). Indeed, rather than just advocating socio-political consensus as opposed to the Marxian focus on conflict arising from inner contradictions in society, Durkheim appears to emphasise *conflict* as a foundation for consensus. Thus, justice is the foundation of what keeps the public-political community together. In the setting of our search for innovative strategies, this view is very much on point:

> [P]ersons in a division of labour society have the right not only to conflict, but to combat, in order to preserve their interests … If the right of combat is restricted in the interests of consensus, and conflict eliminated through force, then, according to Durkheim, the society will fall into a state of

> constraint that violates the prerequisites for solidarity in the division of labor, creating a deep internal contradiction and endangering its survival.
>
> What is necessary is that through exercise of the *right to conflict*, and participation in self-regulated practice, members of society achieve, from moment to moment, the consensus that they need to go on.
>
> (Rawls 2003: 298, emphasis added)

That "right to conflict" might be conceived as an abstract acknowledgement of the legitimacy of fighting for the realisation of one's essential interests, that is, for justice. Recognition and protection of fundamental interests or, in modern words, "human rights" is the key term. Hence, where an environment conducive to the realisation of human rights has not been established – where conflict has been eliminated through force rather than negotiation and consensus – people's right of combat would be activated. Naturally, this is quite distinct from a "right to violence". The latter "right" cannot exist since the cause of protecting human dignity excludes any entitlement to the use of force. Indeed, the distinction between conflict and violence is fundamental.

In Amartya Sen's comparative study on famines (1981) the right to conflict is triggered in case of a below-minimal acquirement of food. An "entitlement failure" is said to occur when the actual obtainable food bundle falls below this minimal norm. His analysis aims at explaining the phenomenon of famine rather than some type of conduct that might stem from it; hence people are assumed to remain passive under the entitlement failure a famine signifies. Indeed, in the cases that Sen analysed people did endure starvation without attempting to change the prevailing formal set of entitlement rules. In conflict analysis, however, such a set of entitlement rules is no longer treated as given and unchanging. In particular, the social repercussions that might well follow from a case of entitlement failure should also be considered, especially as they might develop over time. As Keynes has warned: "Men will not always die quietly. For starvation, which brings to some lethargy and helpless despair, drives other temperaments to the nervous instability of hysteria and to a mad despair" (1920: 213). The obvious lesson is that while existing entitlement positions and the power relations on which these are based must be thoroughly analysed, they cannot be taken for granted. Beyond the legal protection of interests, human rights have transformative power, too (see Table 1.1). In "disabling" environments more than anywhere else, that emancipatory function becomes activated. Evidently, rather than as a product of international initiatives human rights emerge from local realities as inclusive human dignity asserted by victims of violation (Tables 1.1 and Figure I.4). It is, indeed, precisely in adverse realities that human rights may develop into a motivating and inspiring force of great weight.

What, then, are the implications for our focus on human rights realisation? How do human rights, marshalled in the political arena of conflict, *deepen* the struggle to protect human dignity? By creating a normative setting in which power may be exercised in pursuit of justice without resort to violence. Indeed, justice as a basic need and a right to conflict, activated by failures to guarantee fundamental freedoms and essential entitlements, entails a context of human malcontent which has certain normative features. People should be perceived, then, as individuals with equal dignity in a normative context that may trigger Durkheim's right to conflict.

The struggle is widened

Second, let us reassess "our tactics". Human rights imply that the fight for recognition of fundamental interests is *widened* to the whole community to which they relate. When people's fundamental freedoms and their essential needs are denied, human rights-based strategies broaden that struggle for liberty and livelihood to involve the whole surrounding environment: agents of government, development and peace organisations, women's and environmental groups, and businesses. Indeed, where fundamental needs meet rights, "actors" become "duty-bearers". It means that these fundamental rights must be integrated into all activities of such institutions as principles guiding policies and activities, not just incorporated into specific human rights programmes and projects. This is what the United Nations calls "mainstreaming". The idea behind mainstreaming is that questions concerning realisation of primary objectives must be taken seriously "in central, mainstream, 'normal' institutional activities and not simply left in a marginalised, peripheral backwater of specialist mechanisms and institutions" (Charlesworth 2005: 1). In a UN setting this concept has been first applied to gender equity. In respect of human rights, we should like to broaden it to involvement of the whole public-political community to which those right-holders, whose fundamental freedoms and entitlements are at stake, relate.

Shifting the focus of realisation strategies to not just state-based institutions, but extra-governmental activity at the local level as well, including the corporate world, requires approaches which may differ depending on the nature of the interests at stake. For those involved in struggles for actual protection through civil and political rights, the natural focus is on legal resources. Efforts for the realisation of economic, social and cultural rights, in contrast, are naturally oriented to extra-legal action. Action first, legalisation later (and often as a result of action) seems to characterise successful strategies in the latter case. But in both instances a primary focus must be on the whole socio-cultural and politico-economic environment in respect of its conduciveness to human rights realisation (see Table 4.2). To frame it in terms of this study's enquiry: in an endeavour to widen the struggle for realisation of human rights, *contextualisation* is a condition sine qua non.

States should of course be confronted with their positive obligations to provide basic public services to all and to guarantee adequate living standards. Here, "budgeting rights" may work as an effective tool (see p. 25). But economic, social and cultural rights may also serve as a weapon to fight concrete state interventions that result in abuse of people's basic entitlements. Furthermore, where duty-bearers can be clearly identified, concrete violations of economic, social and cultural rights may also be addressed in litigation as has been illustrated in quite a number of cases discussed in Chapters 2 and 5.

Human rights thus imply rights-based approaches to exclusion, deprivation and displacement. Here lies the basis for transformative action and resistance against the status quo. However, in nurturing such grassroots action, civil society organisations and other actors assisting in these struggles should be aware of and sensitive to the circumstance that people's feelings of self-respect may be expressed in types of discourse different from human rights language. Indeed all cultural and spiritual sources that might serve to trigger right-holders' action, must be exploited. What matters is not the wording but the effectiveness of the action elicited. Naturally, it will always be wise to communicate in a discourse close to those on whose agency the mission is dependent.

Markedly, we are still only at the beginning of efforts to develop strategies to implement economic, social and cultural rights in particular. In terms of focus and vision, methods and strategies, multiple actors and diverse levels, the recognition of these rights requires new commitments to concerted action based on new tactics. In awareness, in practice and in law, these rights gradually mature. Concretely, this suggests linking practical actions against displacement and poverty with human rights concepts and issues, developing a political culture of human rights, which includes economic, social and cultural rights. Like Amnesty International's "mobilization of shame" with regard to violations of civil and political rights, what is intended here is to evoke a deeply felt concern for other people's livelihoods.

Such processes of conscientisation regarding human rights as responses to "a pronounced deprivation of well-being" (World Bank 2000b) should be driven by a primary focus on basic human needs. When people in need see themselves as right-holders and those in power recognise their duties, the fight against poverty and destitution is put in a civilisational perspective in the sense of a widening of the common good. Accordingly, in polity, economy and society alike, it is high time to mainstream human dignity at the centre of concerted agendas. The new shift in emphasis from sovereignty as freedom from external interference towards sovereignty as responsibility to protect all those whose essential interests rely on public justice as connected with the power of the state, may be seen as a significant step forward (see pp. 94–96).

The struggle is uplifted

Finally, let us reassess "our tools". The struggle for recognition and protection of everyone's human dignity is uplifted to the international level as these standards are universal and connected with recognised international responsibilities. The adjective "universal" in the term "universal human rights" points to responsibility. Indeed, we recognise today as a universal responsibility the duty to protect those whose unmet needs imply a violation of their basic dignity. The human rights mechanisms established by the United Nations are rooted in that universal human responsibility for the implementation of fundamental freedoms and basic entitlements. Yet, no matter how important this international venture for the protection of human rights may be, it will have real significance only when connected to what we have identified as the first two elements of transforming the struggle: human rights as principles of legitimacy and local community involvement beyond those whose basic human dignity is directly affected. The vision presented in this study shifts the emphasis from alleviating the consequences of oppression, hunger, malnutrition, infant mortality, reduced life expectancy and illiteracy (adaptation in other words) towards a focus on people and their life conditions as rooted in institutions, processes and outcomes that will have to meet fundamental standards of legitimacy (i.e. mitigation).

It is the universality of human rights as internationally accepted standards of legitimacy that makes it possible to *also* mobilise international support in struggles against their violation. International pressure through reporting by the United Nations Special Rapporteur for Housing, for one, may well contribute to processes of acquiring actual recognition of people's housing needs. Notably, it is often international organisations and nongovernmental organisations rather than states, which fight side-by-side with those carrying out their responsibilities in UN compliance mechanisms.

It is in this connection that a shift in the allocation of scarce resources becomes inevitable. The enormous expenses involved in the existing organisation of international criminal justice cannot be validated by a simple reference to the saying "justice has no price". Justice means "righting the wrong", which is more than just bringing the suspects to trial, no matter how crucial that may be. It also involves the lives of the survivors and the bereaved, the environments in which these people have to generate new conditions for daily sustainability of their livelihoods, and the creation of a generally more conflict-safe society in which the economy functions and law rules. Public justice – the juridical principle of righteousness in the land – cannot be separated from economic effectiveness as the principle by which scarce resources must be effectively allocated to optimally satisfy human wants (see above, p. 16).

In the current era, one further observation is pertinent. Without a doubt, the twentieth century was the age of modernity. An almost invincible belief in technological as well as social engineering and the "constructability" of society prevailed. Out of this have come the law-driven model for the protection of fundamental freedoms and the "developmental" perspective on realising people's basic entitlements. In the process, the deepening of daily struggles for freedom from oppression and sustainable livelihoods through human rights as universal principles of legitimacy has been lost. In fact, post-modernity, with its mistrust of principles as such, implies a further defeat: no objective standards of legitimacy are recognised any longer, and human rights get buried in cultural relativism.

The way out of the sterile debate between legal universalism and cultural relativism may well be found in a contextual approach which starts from the universal standards proclaimed in the Universal Declaration of Human Rights as the foundational document for the global human rights venture. Strategically, this focus acknowledges the diverse roots of human rights in different social, cultural and religious contexts while linking local practices and languages of human dignity and rights to the international standards and mechanisms for human rights implementation: upstream approaches seeking connection with the downstream UN venture (Figures I.3 and I.4 respectively).

Human rights are often discussed as tools that have to be taken up and mastered. If that had been the purpose of this study, we might have focused only on the opportunities for and constraints to implementing all declared human rights. But in a real sense that is where this book began. The focus on people and the realisation of basic freedoms and needs in their own unique environments carried us to the core of strategies for implementing human rights: universal human dignity. It cannot be gained or lost, though of course it can be seriously hurt and violated. Universally inclusive human dignity is the global "faith" sustaining the struggle for realisation, which finds its wellspring in deeper sources, flowing from a diversity of worldviews and religions.

Uplifting the human rights struggle to the level of global justice requires more ingenuous ways of institutionalisation than the current circus of councils, commissions and committees with tedious documents deliberated in lengthy meetings. In this study the focus has not been on problem-solving and legal or socio-economic engineering but on people faced with the violation of their basic human dignity; how they themselves experience their struggles for freedom, equality and sustainable livelihood; and how the international human rights mission might come closer to their daily environments. One point is clear: coming closer to people in their daily pursuit of liberties and livelihoods is the most productive perspective for the realisation of human rights in the twenty-first century.

Notes

Introduction: rights, realities and realisation

1 Out of discontent with ongoing political corruption and the new President's role therein, Dr Chongwe had resigned from his cabinet post as Minister of Justice. Not long thereafter he founded a new party and organised an Alliance of opposition parties. Dr Kaunda's United National Independence Party (UNIP) was the major participant in that Alliance.

2 See also Arts and Mihyo (2003). The term is now used by the United Nations High Commissioner for Human Rights, too. See their press release of 12 April 2010 on "A Massive Human Rights Deficit".

3 He attributes these failings in part to the economic crisis, its effects on the middle class in Western democracies and its concurrent influence on the attitude of "political realism" adopted by their leaders.

4 Other efforts to connect human rights to national and local ethics and customs, which combine empirical and anthropological approaches with dialogue with an emphasis on tangible results, such as the "Receptor Approach" advocated by Zou and Zwart (2011) might be seen as a step in the right direction. Rather than gazing backward such efforts could move from the UDHR forward, as long as the borderline with cultural relativism is not crossed. See in this volume, pp. 123–126, on the problem of cultural receptivity.

5 For this narrative see, for example, Lynn Hunt (2007). Notions of cultural imperialism vis-à-vis the imposition of "Western" human rights norms on non-Western peoples often arise in relation to this narrative. See Ignatieff (1999: 34–38) for a strong refutation.

6 Paulus libro secundo ad edictum, *Corpus Iuris Civilis*, De diversis regulis iuris antiqui, D. 50, 17, 106. See also 122: Gaius libro quinto ad edictum provinciale: "Libertas omnibus rebus favorabilior est".

7 A typical "anti-Western" source for the declaration of freedom is Ho Chi Minh: "Rien n'est plus précieux que la Liberté et l'Indépendence".

8 Today we read "sister and brotherhood" or *fellowship*. Obviously, the underlying principle is solidarity. In the global venture for human rights, this constitutes the basis for so-called solidarity rights such as the right to a healthy environment. Besides solidarity, one can also read here an urge not to engage in aggressive behaviour – endangering peace and stability – as the human rights instruments were adopted immediately after the Second World War.

9 For a full discussion of human dignity as a core principle in human rights, see Klein Goldewijk and De Gaay Fortman (1999).

10 Not surprisingly Justice Brennan (1990 quoted in Wermiel 1998: 233) saw the death penalty as "wholly inconsistent with the constitutional principle of human dignity".

11 Susanne Baer has constructed another triangle, in which dignity, liberty and equality are interrelated (Baer 2009). It seems preferable, however, to conceive of human dignity as the core value, to which three interconnected human rights values are all related.

12 For a more detailed discussion of these limitations, see De Gaay Fortman and Salih (2003).

1 Rights: the dialectics of power and protection

1 Cf. Max Weber: "Macht bedeutet jede Chance, innerhalb einer sozialen Beziehung den eigenen Willen auch gegen Widerstreben durchzusetzen gleichviel worauf diese Cance beruht" (Weber 1976 [1922]: 28).

2 The term "social contract" is interpreted here, in the public policy sense of a state regarded by citizens as "their own", based on its capacity to govern according to the rule of law and to maintain law and order non-discriminately.

3 For different political ways of dealing with economic power, see De Gaay Fortman (1981: 161–181).

4 With regard to the Netherlands, for example, one may refer to the Act of Desertion (Placcaet van Verlaetinghe) of 1581 in which it is stipulated that God did not create the subjects for the Sovereign's pleasure but, on the contrary, the Sovereign for the benefit of the subjects – in order to rule them with law and reason.

5 The world is certainly more complex than reflected in Karl Marx's phrase "Right can never be higher than the economic structure of society and the cultural development conditioned by it" (Marx 2009 [1875]: 21). See in this volume, p. 20.

6 For the original text in Greek, see Thucydides (Θουκυδίδης), *Historia Belli Peloponnesiaci*, I. Matthias Stahl (ed.), Lipisiae: Ex officina Bernhardi Tauchnitz, MDCCCCX, pp. 46–50.

7 Thucydides, V.89.

8 For additional reading on Thucydides, see also Bedford and Workman (2001) and Chittick and Freyberg-Inan (2001).

9 "Human nature being what it is", in Thucydidean terminology (Kokaz 2001: 39).

10 For a discussion of morality in the twentieth century, see Glover (1999).

11 The term *integrity* in regard to law was coined by Dworkin (1986).

12 On anti-law in general, see Carbonnier (1961).

13 Another verse describing law as an expression of existing power relations, relates to the common good:

> *The Law locks up the man or woman*
> *Who steals the goose from off the common*
> *But lets the greater villain loose*
> *Who steals the common from the goose.*

14 For additional reading, see Deflem (1996).

15 Female infanticide, for example, and genital mutilation are typical lifeworld practices in contravention of human rights that hence have to be fought primarily in a lifeworld setting.

16 On law-finding, see Koopsmans' excellent revision of G.J. Wiarda's (1999) gem entitled, *Drie typen van rechtsvinding.*

17 Samuels' view comes down to the belief that all subjective rights are merely fictions. This view was taken by Bentham who stated:

> The word right is the name of a fictitious entity: one of those objects, the existence of which is feigned for the purpose of discourse, by a fiction so necessary that without it human discourse could not be carried on. A man is said to have it, to hold it, to possess it, to acquire it, to lose it. It is thus spoken of as if it were a

> portion of matter such as a man may take into his hand, keep it for a time and let it go again.
>
> (as quoted in Olivier 1973: 50)

Today this view is taken by legal positivists, who refuse to discuss law in substantially normative terms.

18 A citizen who wishes to make use of her rights to a subsidy or welfare allowance has to cross at least five different barriers:

1 She should know that there is such a scheme.
2 She should know where to get information about that scheme.
3 She should overcome any embarassment in collecting the information.
4 She should be able to understand the information (the brochure) and to apply that to her own situation.
5 She should fill in the forms while going through the whole bureaucratic procedure.

One particular cause of trouble arises during the moment of applying. In an investigation into take-up of benefits in the Netherlands, Filet found that no less than 30 per cent of the respondents were of the opinion that they had submitted a formal request for social welfare while the civil servants concerned felt they had just supplied information (quoted in Van Oorschot and Kolkhuis Tanke 1989: 9).

19 The term *universalist* denotes an orientation towards legal security based on equality of all people before the law and equal treatment of equal cases.

20 The "International Bill of Human Rights" is an informal name given to the International Covenants on Civil and Political Rights and Economic, Social and Cultural Rights respectively and the UN General Assembly resolution on the Universal Declaration of Human Rights.

21 For example, the principle behind art. 17 UDHR (United Nations 1948) that declares the right to property.

22 For example, the principle behind art. 21 UDHR (United Nations 1948) on the right to participate in government. Cf. the *regula iuris* "Quod omnes tangit debet ab omnibus approbari", as formulated in the *Corpus Iuris Canonicis* (SEXTI DECRETAL., LIB. V, TIT.XII., DE REGULIS IURIS, Bonifacius VII, Regula XXIX).

23 See Chapter 4, pp. 103–138.

24 Joseph Wronka (1998), for one, sees human rights as a process from "rights as ideals" via "rights as enactments" to "rights as exercised".

25 For the full list of manifestions of the human rights deficit in distinct domains of law versus power see p. 36 and Chapter 2, note 13.

26 In that way collective rights, too, can play their part. Thus, as an enlightening principle the right to a healthy environment, for example, or the right to development, may well determine a court case.

27 While the term "living law" is used in different meanings I use it here in the sense of *informal* processes of setting, monitoring and enforcing norms pertaining to order and justice within a certain community.

28 Obviously, slave-owners feared that non-compliance would imply a considerable risk of slave revolts and hence jeopardise the whole social system.

29 One of the most striking developments in this respect is the incorporation of human rights clauses in the general principles of transnational corporations. Shell International, for one, not only adopted such a human rights clause in its own code of conduct but also deleted the phrase "Shell is not involved in politics". While, naturally, party politics is a different matter, the universal responsibility for the observance of human rights implies that no actor in business can stay out of politics. The whole discussion on corporate responsibility and human rights was sparked off particularly by Shell's traumatic experiences in Ogoniland (Idowu 1999). See also the discussion on *Gbemre* in Chapter 5 pp. 172–173.

30 A German legal concept that refers to constitutionally guaranteed human rights that are assertable against not just public authorities but also non-state entities. See Netherlands Institute of Human Rights (SIM) database, "Thesaurus", Online. Available at: http://sim.law.uu.nl/sim/thesaurus.nsf/0/31597e464322af31c1256643004604f5?Open (accessed 23 July 2009).

2 Rights: the dialectics of international norms and national practice

1 The trial ended in a conviction. On 26 July 2010 the UN-backed Cambodia tribunal sentenced Kain Guek Eav ("comrade Duch"), senior member of the Khmer Rouge, to 35 years in prison in its first verdict three decades after the Maoist "Killing Fields" revolution tore Cambodia apart. On 16 September 2010 four more former Khmer Rouge leaders were put to trial.

2 On 17 March 2006, Lubanga became the first person ever arrested under a warrant issued by the International Criminal Court. The Trial commenced on 26 January 2009, but has been stayed twice in the meantime due to circumstances that according to the Trial Chamber amounted to denial of justice in this case. The last stay was lifted by the Appeals Chamber on 8 October 2010 and the trial is soon to be resumed. According to the Court's website as of March 2010, there are open investigations into six situations: Uganda, the Democratic Republic of the Congo, the Central African Republic, Darfur, Sudan and the Republic of Kenya. Fourteen arrest warrants and three summons to appear have been issued by the Court, five individuals are in custody, seven are at large, one is deceased and against one the Pre-Trial Chamber refused to confirm the charges. The joint trial of Germain Katanga and Mathieu Ngudjolo Chui, also of the Democratic Republic of the Congo, began on 24 November 2009.

3 See, for example, Héctor Olásalo Alonso, *The Role of the International Criminal Court in Preventing Atrocity Crimes through Timely Intervention: From the Humanitarian Intervention Doctrine and Ex Post-Facto Judicial Activism to the Emerging Notion of Responsibility to Protect and the Preventive Role of the International Criminal Court*, Inaugural Address on Accepting the Utrecht University Chair in International Criminal Law and International Procedure with Special Reference to the International Criminal Tribunals, Utrecht, 18 October 2010. While sketching an ideal picture of the ICC, this address refrains from any kind of critical assessment. For an exception see Apori Nkansah (2010) whose research compares the tribunal approach in Sierra Leone with the Truth and Reconciliation Commission approach in South Africa. See also Kamira Clarke (2009).

4 *Vienna Declaration and Programme of Action*, World Conference on Human Rights, Vienna, 14–25 June 1993, confirmed at the United Nations 2005 World Summit, 14–16 September 2005, that was a follow-up summit meeting to the United Nations' 2000 Millennium Summit, which led to the Millennium Declaration of the Millennium Development Goals (MDGs).

5 No one can be a judge in his own case.

6 See Case of the International Court of Justice Concerning the *Barcelona Traction, Light and Power Company Limited (New Application: 1962) (Second Phase) Belgium* v. *Spain*, ICJ 1970, Rep. 3.

7 Bangladesh, Cameroon, China, Cuba, Djibouti, Jordan, Mauritius, Mexico, Nigeria, Russian Federation, Saudi Arabia, Senegal and Uruguay are the countries contemplated.

8 The other major international human rights treaties are the Convention on the Elimination of all forms of Racial Discrimination (in force 4 January 1969), the Convention on the Elimination of all forms of Discrimination Against Women (in force 3 September 1981), the Convention Against Torture, and Other Cruel, Inhuman or Degrading Treatment or Punishment (in force 26 June 1987), the Convention on the Rights of the Child (in force 3 September 1990), the International Convention on the Protection of

the Rights of All Migrant Workers and Members of Their Families (in force 1 July 2003) and the Convention on the Rights of Persons with Disabilities (in force 3 May 2008), and the Convention on Enforced Disappearances, which has not yet entered into force.

9 These are the Committees under respectively the International Covenant on Civil and Political Rights (called the Human Rights Committee, or HRC, to be well distinguished from the Charter-based Human Rights Council), the Convention on the Elimination of Racial Discrimination (CERD), the Convention Against Torture (CAT), the Convention on the Elimination of All Forms of Discrimination Against Women (CEDAW) and the Convention on Migrant Workers (CMW). With regard to individual complaints under the International Covenant on Economic, Social and Cultural Rights (ICESCR), on 10 December 2008, the General Assembly unanimously adopted an Optional Protocol, which provides the Committee competence to receive and consider communications. The Optional Protocol was opened for signature at a signing ceremony in 2009.

10 Cf. the Chongwe case, pp. 1–2.

11 Normand and Zaidi (2008: 322) state: "the human rights system was designed from the start not to be enforced except through political means at the behest of powerful states".

12 Rights, as we saw, signify abstract acknowledgement of interests implying protection by law. Human rights refer to interests directly connected to human dignity, namely, fundamental freedoms and basic entitlements. To "protect human rights", then, means protecting the protection of these fundamental interests by law. Obviously, such discourse weakens the mission.

13 Recall:

- impunity of state-related perpetrators of human rights abuse, such as government officials, politicians, prison officers, policemen and members of the armed forces;
- human rights violations committed under the cover of the "public–private divide" such as domestic violence against women and children;
- structurally failing protection of "minorities", giving rise to collective violence and internal and external displacement of whole groups of people; and
- structural non-implementation of the human rights of those living in situations of extreme poverty and marginalisation.

14 In this respect, both the Charter and the Declaration give some clue in terms as "the dignity and worth of the human person" and "the inherent dignity." For a concise reflection on the meaning of human dignity see Klein Goldewijk and De Gaay Fortman (1999: Chapter 5).

15 Notably, it is not being argued here that the rule of law requires that such acts be outlawed. In any legal order the capacity to enforce and the flaws of prosecution in a context of privacy are serious issues that must be well taken into account. The point is merely that such non-interference is unrelated to human dignity as a foundational principle of human rights. The human dignity element behind article 19 lies in the necessity of truth against power.

16 In respect of the three elements typifying American exceptionalism (Chace 2004) – hegemony (and with that the idea of expansion), unilateralism ("going it alone") and pre-emptive strike – particularly problematic has been the expansion of the notion of "pre-emptive strike" by former US President George W. Bush, to include preventive strikes aimed at eliminating a presumed threat before it becomes imminent. See further Chapter 3, pp. 81ff.

17 The downstream-upstream terminology in respect of human rights strategies was presented in the Introduction, pp. 11–13.

18 See the Judgment of the International Court of Justice in the "Tehran Hostages case", 24 May 1980, ICJ Reports 1980, p. 42, par. 91.

19 The possibility of a right of secession in a territory that is treated in such a way so as to make it an oppressed entity was acknowledged as early as 1920 in the *Aaland Islands* case brought before the League of Nations. The League established an "International Commission of Jurists" to investigate the dispute arising from the desire of most inhabitants of the Islands to seek union with Sweden instead of Finland. While the Jurists concluded that self-determination was not on "the same footing as a positive rule of the Law of Nations" at the time, they also conceded that such a right may arise where "a manifest and continued abuse of sovereign power" effectively alienated a territory from its administering state. This concept is now known as *carence de souveraineté* (Crawford 2006).

20 Janse's (2008) instructive article reviews a number of recent publications on the rule of law and its "exportability" by "donor states" to "recipient countries".

21 For a lucid explanation of this jurisprudential doctrine as applied by the ECtHR, see Wilhelmina Thomassen (2006), former judge of the Court. For a general overview of the doctrine in international law, with special reference to the International Court of Justice, see Shani (2006).

22 The constitution allows the executive branch to exert broad wartime powers, but the President gains moral legitimacy when he acts with the express support of the legislature. See Justice Jackson's concurrence in *Youngstown Steel*. Jackson divided Presidential authority in relation to Congress into three categories, ranked in descending order of legitimacy: (1) cases in which the President was acting with express or implied authority from Congress, (2) cases in which Congress had thus far been silent, and (3) cases in which the President was defying congressional orders.

23 The US initially accused Hamdan of conspiracy and providing material support for terrorism, but the initial charges against him were dropped in June of 2007 (Prieto 2009). Without being charged, he was nonetheless kept in US custody as an "unlawful enemy combatant". In July of 2008, he was recharged and a special military commission found him guilty of providing material support to Al Qaeda. At the same time, he was cleared of two counts of conspiracy. He received a five-and-a-half-year sentence and was credited with five years already served. In November 2008, the United States transferred him to his native Yemen to serve out the remainder of his sentence and Yemeni authorities released him in January of 2009.

24 El Masri is a German citizen whom the CIA allegedly abducted in Macedonia and transported to Afghanistan, where he (and others) were reportedly detained and tortured for several months.

25 After President Obama's election Mr Specter switched parties, becoming a Democrat.

26 The Kingdom of the Netherlands had concluded a bilateral treaty with the United States to station American cruise missiles on Dutch soil in order to counterbalance the stationing of Soviet SS 20 missiles in the German Democratic Republic. After parliament had ratified the treaty, a private foundation, entitled "Cruise Missiles No!" started a court case against the bilateral treaty, referring to international human rights standards. It had been submitted to a Court of Appeal after the court in first instance had declared the case inadmissible since the private foundation was not considered as having an appropriate interest in the matter. The Appeal Court admitted the case but declared itself incompetent to judge it. But before the Supreme Court ("High Council") could review that judgment in the final instance, American cruise missiles were no longer to be stationed in the Netherlands thanks to subsequent new agreements between the two superpowers following Soviet president Gorbachev's *novoye mushleenye* (new thinking).

27 *Lex posterior derogat legi priori*: posterior legislation derogates to prior laws.

28 Naturally, those who campaign on such issues are not the ones who are calling this process the politicisation of judicial decision-making. Rather, they seek connections with legal theories that produce politically desired results, such as textualism.

29 In his *De la déclaration de volonté. Contribution à l'étude de l'acte juridique dans le code civil allemand 1901* (preface p. ix) R. Saleilles speaks of a "Progrès juridique universel", quoted by J.H.A. Lokin (2006: 19).

30 Ibid., pp. 26–27. However, the view that "rules are rules" still breaks into political discussions every now and then, as in the case of the Dutch Minister of Immigration who in parliament appealed to this maxim in the case of an MP who, she stated, by lying about her name and birth date had *ipso facto* lost her nationality (16 May 2006). "I simply conclude", the Minister said, apparently not aware that by "simply concluding" she created legal consequences that without such a deduction from the facts of the case would not have come into being. Indeed, the Minister could have chosen to ignore the history of Ms Hirsi Ali's acquisition of her Dutch citizenship in view of the legal principle of *estoppel* (*venire contra factum proprium* or in the Dutch legal context "rechtsverwerking") since an organ of the state had already twice endorsed her credentials as a member of the States-General.

31 Lord Phillips of Sudbury in The House of Lords, 20 December 2005: "Lord Denning never got to the House of Lords ... because he was too *activist* for their Lordships" [my italics]. (By interruption he was corrected by Lord Goodhart: "Lord Denning did get to the House of Lords and then he went down a step to become Master of the Rolls at the Court of Appeal"), Lords Hansard 2005, Column GC 262. In his autobiography Denning (1979: 287) himself explains this step down as follows: "I was too often in a minority. In the Lords it is no good to dissent. In the Court of Appeal it is some good." Denning's apparent strategy was to confront the law lords with innovative judgments from a lower instance.

32 Naturally, Denning himself did not deny the legality principle. As he put it in a case concerning law abidance by the Trade Unions (Denning 1957 quoted in Kirby 1999b):

> The law should be obeyed. Even by the powerful. Even by the Trade Unions. We sit here to carry out the law. To see that the law is obeyed. And that we will do. A subject cannot disregard the law with impunity. To every subject in this land, no matter how powerful, I would use Thomas Fuller's words over three hundred years ago "Be you ever so high, the law is above you".

33 An example of legal common sense is the rule that everything that has come into being through certain causes, can also be dissolved by the same causes ("Omnis res, per quascunque causas nascitur, per easdem dissolvitur"): X 5,41,1 (*Corpus Iuris Canonici*: DECRETAL. GREGOR. IX LIB. V, TIT. XLI., DE REGULIS IURIS, CAP. I). General principles of justice may be illustrated by the rule that without guilt there can be no punishment. ("Sine culpa, nisi subsit causa, non est aliquis puniendus"): VIo 5,12, reg. 23 (*Corpus Iuris Canonici*: SEXTI DECRETAL. LIB. V, TIT. XII., DE REGULIS IURIS, Bonifacius VIII, Regula XXIII).

34 "Qui sentit onus, sentire debet commodum, et e contra": Vol 5,12, reg. 55 (*Corpus Iuris Canonici*: SEXTI DECRETAL. LIB. V, TIT. XII., DE REGULIS IURIS, Bonifacius VIII, Regula LV).

35 Papinianus libro tertio quaestionum: "Nemo potest mutare consilium suum in alterius iniuriam", *Corpus Iuris Civilis*, DE DIVERSIS REGULIS IURIS ANTIQUI, D. 50, 17, 75. In private law a similar rule is "Venire contra factum proprium". From a comparative perspective one might also refer here to the common law principle of *Estoppel*.

36 Broom (in Kersley 1969) argued that

> whenever the common law gives a right or prohibits an injury, it also gives a remedy. If a man has a right, he must, it has been observed, have a means to vindicate and maintain it, and a remedy if he is injured in the exercise and enjoyment of it, and, indeed, it is a vain thing to imagine a right without a remedy, for want of right and want of remedy are reciprocal.

37 Janet Hiebert (2006) contrasts such a culture with "a growing concern about the protection of civil liberties arising from 'a series of policies and decisions in which the rights of individuals have been overridden in the assumed interests of public policy' ". See the analysis on an emerging human rights culture in this volume, pp. 75–76.
38 For an excellent summary of the case and what it involved see, for example, Laurie Kazan-Allen's (2002) compilation. In the subsequent Barker case (Lunney and Oliphant 2008: 237–241) the law lords modified Fairchild and created a new concept of proportionate liability by limiting liability of employers to the proportional amount of time an employee had been working in the firm in question, thus laying the insolvency risk with the workers. (If a firm in which they had worked had gone out of business, it had become impossible to claim the proportion for which it had been liable.) To correct this inequity the (Labour) government then introduced the *Compensation Act 2006*, which actually legislated Fairchild.
39 Take, for example, the way in which Lord Denning was rebuked by Viscount Simonds when in his first (turning out to be dissenting) opinion in the House of Lords – in 1958 – he had argued that it would be unsatisfactory not to consider "some questions and authorities which were not mentioned by counsel":

> My Lords, I must add that, since writing this opinion, I have had the privilege of reading the opinion which my noble and learned friend, Lord Denning, is about to deliver. It is right that I should say that I must not be taken as assenting to his views upon a number of questions and authorities in regard to which the House has not had the benefit of the arguments of counsel or of the judgements of the courts below.
>
> (Denning 1979: 288)

40 In terms of individual claims I would speak here of an entitlement, protected particularly by the right to health and the right to a decent living standard (De Gaay Fortman 2006c).
41 The right to development is based on UN General Assembly Resolution 41/128 of 4 December 1986. It stipulates, among other things, the duty of states to adopt development policies that aim at "free and meaningful participation in development" and "the fair distribution of benefits" resulting from development. Through a certain period of regular practice, supported by *Opinio Iuris*, principles formulated by the General Assembly may acquire the status of general principles of law. Another example is sovereignty over national resources (Schrijver 1997).
42 Whereas in a country like the Netherlands ratified treaties have an immediate direct effect (for example, the *Cruise missiles* case discussed above), in other countries, generally those with common law systems, national incorporating legislation is required for treaties to have effect. Even in those systems, however, the judiciary will on occasion consider the ratified treaty in its interpretation of the law.
43 *Boehm* v. *Superior Court*, 178 Cal. App. 3d 494 (1986).
44 As an amusing aside, the Court ordered that all legal costs were to be paid by the government.
45 In cases in which protection of the public interest is at stake, it is not necessary that immediate victims of alleged violations bring the cases to court.
46 Collective rights tend to be heavily contested even in human rights circles themselves. See, for example, Jack Donnelly (1990). Formally, the legal basis of collective rights in general is already rather weak, and that applies to the right to a healthy environment in particular, originating as that does from the UN Stockholm Declaration on the Human Environment of 16 June 1972, a typical specimen of so-called "soft law". A more recent source, of a regional as well as consensual nature, is the Additional Protocol to the American Convention on Human Rights in the Area of Economic, Social and Cultural Rights, ("Protocol of San Salvador") of which Article 11 states: "Everyone shall have the right to live in a healthy environment". According to Article 14 of the Norms on the Responsibilities of Transnational Corporations and Other Business

Enterprises with regard to Human Rights approved by the UN Sub-Commission on the Protection and Promotion of Human Rights [UN Doc. E/CN.4/Sub.2/2003/12/rev.2 (2003)] transnational corporations and other business enterprises are responsible for the health and environmental impact of their activities, while the commentary to the article states: "Transnational corporations and other business enterprises shall respect the right to a clean and healthy environment." See also Chapter 5, p. 172.

3 Global realities: conflict and confrontation

1 The invasion of Iraq had been a longstanding project of "The New American Century", a think tank with which George W. Bush's foreign policy advisors were closely associated.
2 When the Charter was adopted human rights were considered to be "a secondary issue" (Stanley Hofman 2003: 28). The subservience of human rights to international security considerations has led to shameful manifestations such as Idi Amin's speech to the General Assembly in 1975 (in his incredible capacity as President of the Organisation for African Unity) and the continuing occupation of the Cambodia (Kampuchea) seat by the Pol Pot regime even after that frightful tyranny was removed from power.
3 "As long as there is one terrorist scheming against us, the United States considers itself as being in war" (George W. Bush), quoted by Van Ham (2003).
4 Rwanda 1994 and Srebrenica 1996 are cases that immediately come to mind here, as is Darfur (Sudan), a story of genocide that has not yet ended.
5 See Chapter 1, p. 21. For an often used model to establish degrees of legitimacy in an international context see Thomas M. Franck (1990).
6 In international legal practice, in case of *force majeure* ("quod est illicitas lege necesitas facit licitum" meaning that in reality there is no other way) the international community may legitimise the action through acquiescence ("qui tacit consentire videit"). Actually this happened in respect of the Indian invasion of East Pakistan although India itself never appealed to the legitimacy of a "humanitarian" intervention. Another instance is the NATO intervention in Serbia-Montenegro in order to protect the Albanian Kosovars from Milosevic's tyranny. In this case a Security Council resolution had not been sought because it would have been blocked by a Russian veto.
7 Second inaugural Address, President Bill Clinton, 20 January 1997.
8 Notably Jesus had formulated this aphorism also the other way round, and hence more modestly: "Whoever is not against us, is for us!" (Mark 9: 40).
9 See the discussion of upstream and downstream strategies in the Introduction, pp. 11ff.
10 See the Secretary-General's report *Investing in the United Nations* of March 2006 and the *Comprehensive Review of Governance and Oversight within the UN*, of June the same year.
11 Among those who have received this award is Nelson Mandela (2002).
12 "Africa has 27 million more people in Poverty Following Crisis" [press release] Businessweek, 30 March 2010. Available at: www.businessweek.com/news/2010-03-30/africa-has-27-million-more-people-in-poverty-following-crisis.html (accessed 1 November 2010). See also International Monetary Fund (2009).

4 Local realities: strife and struggle

1 For a comment on stories about a Tutsi-people invading the land of the lakes from Ethiopia and Sudan see Trouwborst (1994).
2 Lack of a social contract signifies a certain deficiency in state–citizen relations, a "fact" as imprecise as things may get in the social sciences. The term "social contract", recall, is to be interpreted in the public policy sense of a state regarded by citizens as "their own", based on its capacity to govern according to the rule of law and to maintain law and order non-discriminately.

3 This is why it is so problematic to develop a yardstick for the "green" national income, for example. The qualification "green" refers to ecological stock values while national income is measured over time, i.e. as a flow variable.

4 In this connection the degree of homogeneity may be conceived as the extent to which citizens identify with their state in terms of national-cultural identity.

5 The Human Development Index (HDI) combines Gross Domestic Product (GDP) per capita (the usual economic process oriented yardstick) with health indicators such as average life expectancy and education indicators such as the national literacy rate. There is also a separate "Multidimensional Poverty Index" (UNDP 2010: 161–163).

6 The HFI exercise in the HDR 1991 was based on an index developed by Charles Humana. It rated performances in the realisation of six civil and political rights. At a following UNDP general meeting in Kuala Lumpur (1992) it came under severe criticism of developing countries and was subsequently abandoned.

7 Michael Ignatieff (1999) signals a political crisis, a cultural crisis and also a *spiritual* crisis in human rights, as discussed in the Introduction to this volume (4).

8 Possessive individualism is the driving force of what Tawney (1920/1948) called "the acquisitive society":

> Such societies may be called Acquisitive Societies because their whole tendency and interest and preoccupation is to promote the acquisition of wealth. The appeal of this conception must be powerful, for it has laid the whole modern world under its spell.... It is an invitation to men to use the power with which they have been endowed by nature or by society, by skill or energy or relentless egotism or mere good fortune, without inquiring whether there is any principle by which their exercise should be limited.... It assures men that there are no ends other than their ends, no law other than their desires, no limit than that which they think advisable.

9 Naturally, the same applies to the construction of a "right to insult".

10 This "difference principle" stipulates that inequalities can be tolerated only if "they are to be to the greatest benefit of the least advantaged members of society".

11 A proposed amendment to the preamble of the UDHR by the Netherlands delegate Father L.J.C. Beaufort OP, referring to recognition of human rights as "based on man's divine origin and immortal eternal destiny" (Morsink 1999: 288), was rejected as being contrary to the universal nature of the Declaration. Accordingly, the Declaration makes no mention of religion as a possible basis for these fundamental rights. For the Saudi Arabian delegate, the fact that it began and ended with the human being, without any reference to God, was mentioned as his country's main reason to abstain.

12 The UN Charter's preamble opens with the purpose "to save succeeding generations from the scourge of war, which twice in our lifetime has brought untold sorrow to mankind".

13 Actually, there are accounts of references to God and Nature in earlier drafts of the UDHR. See Perry (1998: 110).

14 (CELAM 1993: 164):

> La igualdad entre los seres humanos en su dignidad, por ser creados a imagen y semejanza de Dios, se afianza y perfecciona en Cristo. Desde la Encarnación, al asumir el Verbo nuestra naturaleza y sobre todo su acción redentora en la cruz, muestra el valor de cada persona. Por lo mismo Cristo, Dios y hombre, es la fuente más profunda que garantiza la dignidad de la persona y de sus derechos. Toda la violación de los derechos humanos contradice el Plan de Dios y es pecado.

15 Cf. Perry (1998: 13).

16 See, for example, Ali Salman, *Human Rights and Islam: Some Points of Convergence and Divergence*, online essay accessible at www.renaissance.com.pk/octvipo2y1.html (accessed 9 April 2009).

17 "Lex posterior derogat legi priori": posterior legislation derogates to prior laws.

18 In 1994 Gáspár Biró, UN Special Rapporteur on Sudan presented a critical report on human rights abuse in that country, in which he indicated inconsistencies between the international human rights Conventions (to which Sudan had been a signatory party since 1986) and some provisions of Sudan's Criminal Act of 1991 that follow the Sharia law. Sudan's ambassador in Geneva then circulated a letter at the Commission on Human Rights UNCHR alleging that portions of the report "represent a vicious attack on the religion of Islam" and accusing him of making a "vicious attack on the religion of Islam". He alleged that the report "contained abusive, inconsiderate, blasphemous and offensive remarks about the Islamic faith". See www.jihadwatch.org/2008/07/calling-a-spade-a-spade-jihad-genocide-slavery-and-sharia-law.html (accessed 10 November 2010).

5 Realisation: the rights of the poor

1 "On n'est pas développé; on se développe."

2 Actually, the Poverty Reduction Strategy Papers (PRSPs) were meant as basis for a new facility for debt relief offered to Highly Indebted Poor Countries (HIPCs). The international financial institutions had responded to the criticism on their structural adjustment policies by including a social impact assessment in the decision-making process. In order that possible social effects might be brought to the fore the new lending facility was based on Poverty Reduction Strategy Papers, to be drafted as outcomes of an open and transparent process involving civil society.

3 African Learning Group on the Poverty Reduction Strategy Papers, *Summary Report of the First Meeting 5–6 November 2001, Economic Commission for Africa*, United Nations Conference Center, Addis Ababa, Ethiopia, p. 5.

4 For an excellent summary of the policies required, see Murshed (2002: 10–12).

5 Purchasing power parity (PPP) looks at what one US dollar can buy in the local context, focusing on a standardised basket of consumer goods.

6 Notably, St Augustine, in his *De Civitate Dei*, had introduced the notion of a "*justum pretium*", embodying elements of both opportunity costs and fairness.

7 It is in this type of economic thinking that *homo economicus* has his roots, implying a rational, purely utilitarian human being. However, while in undergraduate textbooks a utility function tends to be treated as a function of private consumption only, in advanced work today it is not uncommon to introduce customs, values and even altruism. In Amartya Sen's work an individual's well-being is not a matter of maximising personal pleasure but related to personal capabilities. These include much more than the capablity to derive utility from consumption. See, for example, Sen (1993) and Sen (1999: 74ff.).

8 The term *productivism* is a neologism. What is increasingly used, however, is the corresponding adjective. Claus Offe, for one, speaks of "the productivist syndrome" (*A Non-Productivist Design for Social Policies*, mimeograph 2002).

9 As revealed by Pernia in a presentation to the Wilton Park Conference on *Poverty Eradication: Responses by the International Organisations*, 6–9 September 2001.

10 See Murshed (2001: 11). He describes a public good as

> something that is not non-rivalled and non-excludable. Unlike private goods, this means that an individual's ability to consume a public good is not related to individual capacity to pay, and other people's consumption does not detract from his/her consumption. Examples include national security, law and order, but also many aspects of education and health.
>
> (2001: 4, n. 2)

11 This was a mission to Tanzania by the Pro-Poor Growth Working Group of the Advisory Council for International Affairs (AIV). For its report see the Annex to the AIV Advisory Report on Pro-Poor Growth, The Hague: AIV, 2003.

12 http://allafrica.com/stories/200209270255.html (accessed 29 November 2010).
13 www.tancotton.co.tz/index.html (accessed 29 November 2010).
14 Report in *Terra Viva Europe* of 9 October 2002, pp. 1 and 5.
15 www.corpwatch.org/news/PND.jsp?articleid=2615 (accessed 29 November 2010).
16 Pyatt's model uses a variety of capital (vintage capital).
17 See the *Human Development Reports* (HDRs) of the United Nations Development Program (UNDP).
18 See Griffith-Jones (2002: 4ff.). Notably, aid is not power-neutral, despite all efforts towards Southern "ownership".
19 Interview in *Internationale Samenwerking*, August 2002.
20 In 2007 transformed into the Human Rights Council.
21 See two papers by Alfredo Sfeir Younis, the Bank's Special Representative to the United Nations and the World Trade Organisation, Geneva, September 2000 (unpublished).
22 At a Conference on Poverty Eradication, Wilton Park, Winston House, September 2000 Robert Chambers gave this example.
23 Article 2.1 of the ICESCR declares:

> Each State Party to the present Covenant undertakes to take steps, individually and through international assistance and co-operation, especially economic and technical, to the maximum of its available resources, with a view to achieving progressively the full realisation of the rights recognised in the present Covenant by all appropriate means, including particularly the adoption of legislative measures.

24 *DAC Guidelines on Poverty Reduction*, Paris: OECD, June 2000, Volume I, 1.4.2, No. 59.
25 United Nations Development Programme (2000).
26 Ibid.
27 See also Juan Pablo Molina Berrizbeita, *A Case for the Human Right of Access to Justice*, Coventry: University of Warwick, 2002 (mimeograph).
28 See also Ramcharan (2005: 144–153).
29 26. Housing. Everyone has the right to have access to adequate housing. The state must take reasonable legislative and other measures, within its available resources, to achieve the progressive realisation of this right. No one may be evicted from their home, or have their home demolished, without an order of court made after considering all the relevant circumstances. No legislation may permit arbitrary evictions.
30 28. Children. Every child has the right … to basic nutrition, shelter, basic health care services and social services.
31 The Constitutional Court held that these must:

- be comprehensive, coherent and effective;
- be reasonable within the social, economic and historical context of widespread deprivation, and within the availability of the state's resources;
- give special attention to the needs of the most vulnerable;
- be aimed at lowering administrative, operational and financial barriers over time;
- allocate responsibilities and tasks clearly to all three spheres of government;
- be implemented reasonably, adequately resourced and free of bureaucratic inefficiency or onerous regulations.

32 Article 12 ICESCR declares:

1 The States Parties to the present Covenant recognize the right of everyone to the enjoyment of the highest attainable standard of physical and mental health.
2 The steps to be taken by the States Parties to the present Covenant to achieve the full realization of this right shall include those necessary for:

   1 The provision for the reduction of the stillbirth-rate and of infant mortality and for the healthy development of the child;

2 The improvement of all aspects of environmental and industrial hygiene;
3 The prevention, treatment and control of epidemic, endemic, occupational and other diseases;
4 The creation of conditions which would assure to all medical service and medical attention in the event of sickness.

On this right to health see, for example, Toebes (1999).

33 For a more detailed discussion of these limitations see De Gaay Fortman and Salih (2003).
34 See Sen (1981). Problematic is, however, that Sen identifies entitlements with rights, meaning "legal rights" as opposed to the "moral rights" that we know as *human* rights. In the *Human Development Report* 2000 – which is substantially based on Sen's conceptual work – the terminology has moved towards "abstract" rights and "concrete rights". In my view a significantly more comprehensible way to address the issues involved in structural non-implementation of human rights is through a clear distinction between (abstract) rights and (concrete) entitlements. See also De Gaay Fortman (2000a).
35 Understandably a crucial notion in the World Poverty Report (World Bank 2000b).
36 World Poverty Reports used to be published once every ten years. The theme of the World Bank's World Development Report 2010 is Climate Change. A new World Poverty Report might be expected in 2011.
37 For a discussion of "the ingenuity gap" see Homer-Dixon (2000).
38 Commonly, the terms "economic justice", "social justice" and "distributive justice" are used interchangeably.
39 In the time of King Charles I of England, as a prerequisite to legal practice, one had to study law and the legal method for seven years to be versed in all intricacies of the common law system. In the same period a case was decided in favour of the King's complete discretion to dispense with any laws if deemed fit because, as one of the concurring judges, *R.* v. *Hampden* (1937 quoted in Robertson 2005: 49), declared: "The law is of itself an old and trusty servant of the King's; it is his instrument … it is common and most true that *Rex* is *Lex* … The King cannot do wrong".
40 The World Congress of the International Academy of Comparative Law at Utrecht University in July 2006 took place just after the Middle East had been set on fire and civilians lost life and good in a flash, without any perspective of judicial remedies. It was mentioned only in the corridors those days, while we privately signed petitions to stop the slaughter on the Internet. Yet, during the public sessions too we were bound to feel the dialectics of law and power in our hearts and stomachs. But what can lawyers do except to continue living and acting from a belief in law as a global civilising mission?
41 This point has been forcefully made in Wunsch and Olowu (1995).
42 See also Mills' presentation at a forum hosted by the Cato Institute in Washington on 6 October 2010. Online. Available at: http://rickreviewsbooks.blogspot.com/2010/11/author-interview-greg-mills-discusses.html (accessed 27 November 2010).

6 Realisation: the rights of collectivities

1 See the message of the Federal Council on the People's initiative "Against the Construction of Minarets", Federal Council 08.061, 27 August 2008, and the Deliberations on that proposal, Federal Parliament 29.11.2009, VH 08.061.
2 The author describes how "the decision to hold the proposed ban on minarets as valid is equally as legal as holding it invalid" (144) based upon the conflicting *ius cogens* rights to freedom to practice one's religion and the right to self-determination.
3 Through the new constitution, the Reformed Church lost its established status to become a public institution on the same footing as other religious institutions.

4 It is in this respect that Tocqueville warned against a tyranny of the majority:

> I do not say that there is a frequent use of tyranny in America at the present day; but I maintain that there is no sure barrier against it, and that the causes which mitigate the government there are to be found in the circumstances and the manners of the country, more than in its laws.
>
> (1945 [1835]: 272)

5 This is part of the huge "human rights deficit" that still abounds after more than 60 years of the international venture for the realisation of human rights, as discussed already frequently in this volume. M.A. Mohamed Salih has reflected on the political aspects of this deficit in an essay titled "Minorities and the Political in the Human Rights Deficit" (2003).

6 The evident toothlessness of efforts to protect minorities at the international level is not a recent development. The League system itself, involving bilateral treaties that were essentially unenforceable, and which was abused by Nazi Germany, was one reason for the lowly status given this sub-commission (Humphrey 1968: 870). Since 1999 the sub-commission is known as Sub-Commission on the Promotion and Protection of Human Rights.

7 It might be observed in passing that even where treaty-law is "binding", states have often declared reservations that make the language of the treaty essentially ineffective in that state. For instance, Turkey has insisted on a definition of "minority" as indicating only "non-Muslims", a definition dating from the Treaty of Lausanne under the League system. Such reservations make legal enforcement of treaties empty (Oran 2007).

8 R.A. Dahl (1989) defends majority rule on the grounds that it maximises self-determination, is more reasonable than any other way of public decision-making, it is one way to check whether an assertion is true and it maximises utility. Salih (2003: 117) rightly observes that in respect of minority groups with no influence on the polity of the dominant "nation", the relevance of these considerations is questionable.

9 It is also worth mentioning in this respect that political consensus is the result of multiple negotiations and cost-benefit analyses, and does not necessarily, much less reliably, represent the *authentic* position(s) of the parties which form the numerical majority of votes. Not that all votes and positions are bought and sold, but they are not all represented by the "consensus of the majority" either.

10 Political participation does, however, have its costs, especially as it tends to require some degree of assimilation, which is precisely what non-dominant collectivites are often resisting (Toivanen 2004: 197).

11 In Botswana, for example, the Botswana Democratic Party has reigned with huge majorities since independence. That these are based on free and fair elections is not in doubt.

12 This has happened in St. Vincent and the Grenadines and in Lesotho, for example.

13 Trinidad and Tobago, for example, and Guyana.

14 Reeta Toivanen (2004: 108) has found similarly surprising results among minority groups in Germany.

15 For an examination of the advantages of citizenship rights, see Paulina Tambakaki's *Human Rights or Citizenship?* (2010).

16 For an examination of minority construction in Darfur, see Costa (2008).

17 Published by UNESCO, Paris 2004.

18 Ibid. See De Gaay Fortman (2001: 10–11) for a similar conclusion in regard to the right to development.

19 See *Village of Bensenville et al.* v. *Federal Aviation Administration*. U.S. App DC 05–1383 (2006) The 2:1 majority dismissed the case against the FAA on the ground of "mere approval or acquiescence" in another actor's decisions. This other actor is the City of Chicago.

20 In its Appeals decision in the case of *St John's United Church* v. *City of Chicago* (03 C 3726) the 7th Circuit affirmed the district court's decision that refused to enjoin the city from acquiring the cemetery. Since the Supreme Court denied certiorari that seems to be the end of the matter.

21 In the American jurisdiction this is not essential, as there always remains the possibility of a class action suit.

22 See, for example, Donnelly (1990). Formally, the legal basis of collective rights in general is already rather weak.

23 In countries that lack procedural figures such as public interest litigation (India) or class action suits (North America), there appears to be a publicly expressed feeling of a gap in judicial procedure. As to the role of the judiciary see De Gaay Fortman (2006a).

24 Zou and Zwart (2011) suggest to combine downstream human rights with a "receptor approach".

25 For a detailed history of the Huguenots in France see the magnum opus of Van Enk (2009).

26 In the context of public administration, the term "irony of equity" was introduced by Schaffer and Lamb (1981).

27 A similar and more modern reiteration of these basic guarantees for "minority protection" was contained within the (admittedly weak) International Protection of Minorities System that was active under the League of Nations (Dinstein 1976: 115).

28 The acid test of democracy, as Geoffrey Robertson once put it, "is a justice system where there is at least a chance, a possibility of beating the state at its own game" (1998).

29 In *Human Rights in a Pluralist World: Individuals and Collectivities* (Berting 1990), for example, this confusion pervades the argumentation.

30 See, for example, Donnelly (1990: 43).

31 It is true that class action suits or public interest litigation may well result in measures conducive to the protection of excluded collectivities, but the national jurisdictions in which these legal instruments pertain are generally not the most problematic in respect of minorities.

32 The most consistent method and the one most in line with the principle of self-determination is self-identification, but this method is rather unhelpful in the *legal* determination of a group's status.

33 Strikingly, a new international journal, published through Intersentia (Antwerp) presents itself as *Human Rights & International Legal Discourse*, as if it is here that the main vacuum in human rights studies must be located.

34 See, for example, De Gaay Fortman (2005).

35 For a brief account, see Noon (2009: 611).

36 Groups subject to this phenomenon have been called, confusingly, "minoritized majorities" (Kymlicka 2008: 26), which is evidence enough for removing this distinction between "majority" and "minority" from the vocabulary.

37 Article 153 § 1 provides that the government should act "in accordance with the provisions of this Article". The government has done this by implementing certain policies, particularly the New Economic Policy (NEP), that was recently changed into the New Economic Model (NEM). Meanwhile the Prime Minister has launched the One Malaysia Policy as an attempt to move towards a more inclusive society. Notably, the only major clash that Malaysia has witnessed is the 13 May 1969 bloodshed that followed election results, which the Malay majority regarded as unacceptable, leading to the stronger affirmative action policies of the NEP. Later "us–them" clashes have involved crackdowns on Muslim extremism.

38 Other notable examples of majority entrenchment arising out of an obvious historical context are Israel, which has been established as a Jewish state, and Sri Lanka, where Chapter II, Article 9 of its Constitution on Buddhism declares:

> The Republic of Sri Lanka shall give to Buddhism the foremost place and accordingly it shall be the duty of the State to protect and foster the Buddha Sasana, while assuring to all religions the rights granted by Articles 10 and 14(1)(e).

39 See the bibliography for the UPR reports.

40 Cf. "Self-Determination or Human Dignity: The Core Principle of Human Rights" by Matthijs de Blois (1998: 531). For a full discussion of human dignity as a core principle in human rights, see Chapter 5, on Human Dignity and Humiliation, of *Where Needs Meet Rights. Economic, Social and Cultural Rights in a New Perspective* (Klein Goldewijk and de Gaay Fortman 1999).

41 Given the "soft law" character of such a General Assembly declaration and the common law prerequisite of national incorporation, even for treaty law obligations, it is questionable whether that reservation had to be made explicitly. It may well have been meant to restrain the country's judiciary from using the declaration for interpretative purposes prior to the enactment of new legislation. For presumably internal reasons, New Zealand apparently wished to make clear that it *aspires* to protect its indigenous peoples in accordance with the Declaration.

42 Typically, as noted already, the Sub-Commission on the Prevention of Discrimination and the Protection of Minorities that used to fall under the Commission on Human Rights has not been a success. For the history of that set-up, see "The United Nations Sub-Commission on the Prevention of Discrimination and the Protection of Minorities" (Humphrey 1968).

Conclusion: the quest for realisation

1 "Il faut donc mettre ensemble la justice et la force; et pour cela faire que ce qui est juste soit fort, ou que ce qui est fort soit juste."

2 The list contains the following ten items:

A Human rights occupies the field of emancipatory possibility.
B Human rights views the problem and the solution too narrowly.
C Human rights generalises too much.
D Human rights particularises too much.
E Human rights expresses the ideology, ethics, aesthetic sensibility and political practice of a particular Western eighteenth-through twentieth-century liberalism.
F Human rights promises more than it can deliver.
G The legal regime of "Human Rights", taken as a whole, does more to produce and excuse violations than to prevent and remedy them.
H The human rights bureaucracy is itself part of the problem.
I The human rights movement strengthens bad international governance.
J Human rights promotion can be bad governance in particular contexts.

Bibliography

Abduh, Sheikh M. 1890, *An Egyptian in London*, London.

Acton, J.E.E.D. 1887, *Historical Essays and Studies*, Appendix, Letter to Bishop Mandell Creighton, London.

Adelman, I. 1979, "Redistribution before Growth – a Strategy for Developing Countries", *Development of Societies: The Next Twenty-Five Years. Proceedings of the Institute of Social Studies 25th Anniversary Conference*, The Hague: Martinus Nijhoff, 160–176.

African Development Bank Group. 2009, *Impact of the Crisis on African Economies: Sustaining Growth and Poverty Reduction*, Addis Ababa: African Development Bank.

African Learning Group on the Poverty Reduction Strategy Papers. 2001, Summary Report of the first meeting, 5–6 November, Addis Ababa, Ethiopia: Economic Commission for Africa, United Nations Conference Center.

AIV (Advisory Council on International Affairs). 2003, *Pro-Poor Growth in the Bilateral Partner Countries in Sub-Saharan Africa: an Analysis of Poverty Reduction Strategies*, The Hague: Ministry of Foreign Affairs.

AIV (Advisory Council on International Affairs). 2005, *The Influence of Culture and Religion on Development. Stimulus or Stagnation?* The Hague: The Ministry of Foreign Affairs (as in AIV above).

Ake, C. 1994, "A World of Political Ethnicity", in R. van den Berg and U. Bosma (eds), *Historical Dimension of Development, Change and Conflict in the South*, The Hague: Ministry of Foreign Affairs, 48–52.

Akuz, Y. 2000, *The Debate on the International Financial Architecture: Reforming the Reformers, United Nations Economic Commission for Europe*, UN/ECE Regional Conference, 5–7 December.

Al-Azm, S. 2004, *Islam, Terrorism and the West Today*, Amsterdam: Praemium Erasmianum Essay.

Albert, M. 1991, *Capitalisme contre capitalisme*, Paris: Editions de Seuil.

Ames, B., W. Brown, S. Devaran and A. Izquierdo. 2001, *Macroeconomic Policy and Poverty Reduction*, Washington, DC: International Monetary Fund and the World Bank (pamphlet, 20 August). Online. Available at: www.imf.org/external/pubs/ft/exrp/macropol/eng (accessed 4 February 2011).

Amnesty International UK. 2004, *Clouds of Injustice. Bhopal Disaster Twenty Years On*, Oxford: Alden Press.

Anouilh, J. 2001 [1944], *Antigone*, The Hague: Stichting Sitos.

An-Na'im, A. 1998, "Human Rights and the Culture of Relevance: The Case of Collective Rights", in M. Castermans-Holleman, F. van Hoof and J. Smith (eds), *The Role of the Nation-State in the 21st Century: Human Rights, International Organisations and Foreign Policy*, The Hague: Kluwer.

An-Na'im, A.A. 2004, "The Best of Times, and the Worst of Times: Human Agency and Human Rights in Islamic Societies", *Muslim World Journal of Human Rights*, 1(1).

Aporih Nkansah, L. 2010, *Transitional Justice. Perspectives on Truth, Justice and Reconciliation in Postconflict Sierra Leone*, Saarbrücken: VDM Verlag Dr. Müller.

Arendt, H. 1969, "Reflections on Violence. A Special Supplement", *New York Review of Books*, 12.

Arimah, B.C. 2004, "Poverty Reduction and Human Development in Africa", *Journal of Human Development*, 5(3), 399–415.

Arts, K. and P. Mihyo. 2003, *Responding to the Human Rights Deficit. Essays in Honour of Bas de Gaay Fortman*, The Hague, London and New York: Kluwer International.

Auby, J.B. 2003, *La globalisation, l'état et le droit*, Paris: Parution.

Austin, J. 2000, "Performative Utterances", in R. Stainton (ed.), *Perspectives in the Philosophy of Language*, Ontario: Broadview Press.

Baer, S. 2009, "Dignity, Liberty, Equality: a Fundamental Rights Triangle of Constitutionalism", *University of Toronto Law Journal*, 59, 417–468.

Bakker, J.W. 1998, *The Independence of the Judiciary. Summary of Four Case Studies*, Leiden: PIOOM.

Bassin, B. 1994, *What Role for the United Nations in World Economic and Social Development*, paper for UNDP Stockholm Roundtable on Global Change, 22–24 July.

Baxi, U. 2007, *Human Rights in a Posthuman World: Critical Essays*, Delhi: Oxford University Press.

Beckles, H. 1989, *Natural Rebels. A Social History of Enslaved Women in Barbados*, New Brunswick: Rutgers University Press.

Bedford, D. and T. Workman. 2001, "The Tragic Reading of the Thucydidean Tragedy", *Review of International Studies*, 27(1), 51–67.

Bello, A. 2010, *Are the Millennium Development Goals Proving Counter-Productive?* Policy Brief, Madrid: FRIDE August.

Bello, W. and S. Cunningham. 1994, "De l'adjustement structurel et ses implacables desseins", *Le Monde Diplomatique*, September, 8–9.

Bentham, J. 1975 [1690], *The Theory of Legislation*, Oxford: Oxford University Press.

Berkowitz, L. 1980, "The Frustration-Aggression Hypothesis", in R.A. Falk and S.S. Kim (eds), *The War System: An Interdisciplinary Approach*, Boulder: Westview Press.

Berlin, I. 1997, *The Sense of Reality: Studies in Ideas and their History*, New York: Farrar, Straus, and Giroux.

Berner, E. and B. Phillips. 2002, *Left to Their Own Devices? Community Self-Help Between Alternative Development and Neo-Liberalism*, paper presented to the ISS 50th Anniversary Conference Globalization, Conflict and Poverty, 7–9 October.

Berting, J., P.R. Baehr, J.H. Burgers, C. Flinterman, B. de Klerk, R. Kroes, C.A. van Minnen and K. van der Wal. 1990, *Human Rights in a Pluralist World. Individuals and Collectivities*, London: UNESCO/Roosevelt Study Center/Meckler.

Bhagwati, P.N. 1988, "Developing Human Rights Jurisprudence: the Domestic Application of International Human Rights Norms", Judicial colloquium in Bangalore, 24–26 February 1988, London: Commonwealth Secretariat.

Bhagwati, P.N. 1989, *Address to the Caribbean Human Rights Seminar*, Jamaica, September (unpublished).

Bhagwati, P.N. 1990, "Judicial Activism and Social Action in Asia", J. Ventura Aspiras, *Law as Weapon. Alternative Approaches to Distributive Justice*, Manila: Process.

Brownsword, R. 2003, "Bioethics Today, Bioethics Tomorrow: Stem Cell Research and the Dignatarian Alliance", *Notre Dame Journal of Law, Ethics & Public Policy*, 17(1), 15–51.

Bull, H. 1961, *The Control of the Arms Race: Disarmament and Arms Control in the Missile Age*, London: Weidenfeld and Nicholson for the Institute of Strategic Studies.

Bull, H. 1977, *The Anarchical Society*, New York: Columbia University Press.

Buruma, I. and A. Margalit. 2004, *Occidentalism: A Short History of Anti-Westernism*, London: Atlantic Books.

Buzan, B. 1991, *People, States and Fear*, London: Harvester Wheatsheaf.

Cairo Declaration on Human Rights in Islam. 1990, 5 August.

Campbell, A. 1993. *Men, Women, and Aggression*, New York: Basic Books.

Capotorti, F. 1979, *Study on the Rights of Persons Belonging to Ethnic, Religious and Linguistic Minorities, Report of the Special* Rapporteur *of the Sub-Commission on Prevention of Discrimination and the Protection of Minorities*, New York: United Nations E/CN.4/SUB.2/384/REV.1.

Carbonnier, J. 1961, "La Bible et le Droit", in *La Révélation Chrétienne et le Droit.* Annales de la Faculté de droit et des Sciences politiques et économiques de Strasbourg – IX, Colloque de philosophie du droit (24–25 November 1959): 115–129, Paris: Librairie Dalloz.

CELAM (Episcopal Conference of Latin America). 1993, *Nueva Evangelización, Promoción Humana, Cultura Cristiana, "Jesucristo Ayer, Hoy y Siempre*, IV conferencia General del Episcopado Latinoamericano, Santo Domingo, Republica Dominicana, 12–28 October 1992, Santo Domingo: Ediciones MSC.

Cernea, M.M. 1995, "Understanding and Preventing Impoverishment from Displacement", *Journal of Refugee Studies*, 8(3).

Chace, J. 2004, "Empire, Anyone?", *The New York Review of Books*, 51(15), 15–18.

Chambers, R. 2001, "The World Development Report: Concepts, Content and a Chapter 12", *Journal of International Development*, 13, 299–306.

Chan, S. 2007, *Grasping Africa: a Tale of Tragedy and Achievement*, London: I.B. Tauris.

Charlesworth, H. 2005, "Not Waving but Drowning: Gender Mainstreaming and Human Rights in the United Nations", *Harvard Human Rights Journal*, 18, spring, 1–18.

Chenery, H.B., M.S. Ahluwalia, C.L.G. Bell, J.H. Duloy and R. Jolly. 1974, *Redistribution with Growth*, Oxford: Oxford University Press.

Chittick, W. and A. Freyberg-Inan. 2001, "Chiefly for Fear, Next for Honour, and Lastly for Profit: An Analysis of Foreign Policy Motivation in the Peloponnesian War", *Review of International Studies*, 27(1), 69–90.

Chongwe, R.M.A. and N. Jägers. 2011, "Civil and Political Rights in Times of Political Oppression: Rights without Remedies? The Case of Zambia", in *Human Rights and Conflict: In Honour of Professor Bas de Gaay Fortman*, Antwerp: Intersentia, forthcoming.

Clark, G. and L.B. Sohn. 1958, *World Peace through World Law*, Cambridge, MA: Harvard University Press.

Clark, P. 2010, *The Gacaca Courts, Post-Genocide Justice and Reconciliation in Rwanda: Justice without Lawyers*, Cambridge: Cambridge University Press.

Clarke, K.M. 2009, *Fictions of Justice: The International Criminal Court and the Challenge of Legal Pluralism in Sub-Saharan Africa*, New York: Cambridge University Press.

Cole, D. 2006, "Why the Court Said No", *New York Review of Books*, 10 August.

Collier, P. 2007, *The Bottom Billion: Why the Poorest Countries Are Failing and What Can Be Done About It*, Oxford: Oxford University Press.

Contreras, M. 1996, "Tien jaar na Marcos", in E. De Boer (ed.), *Wij leerden mensenrechten niet uit boeken: De Filipijnen en mensenrechten in de periode 1986 tot 1996*, Dordrecht: FIDOC.

Costa, M. 2008, *Towards an Open Definition of Genocide: An Inquiry into the Construction of "Ethnic" Conflict in Darfur*, thesis written for the European Master's Degree in Human Rights and Democratisation, Utrecht University.

Crawford, J. 2006, *The Creation of States in International Law*, Oxford: Clarendon Press.

Dahl, R.A. 1989, *Democracy and Its Critics*, New Haven: Yale University Press.

David, C. 2006, "Why the Court Said No", *New York Review of Books*, 10 August.

De Blois, M. 1998, "Self-Determination or Human Dignity: The Core Principle of Human Rights", in A. Hendriks and J. Smith (eds), *To Baehr in Our Minds: Essays on Human Rights from the Heart of the Netherlands*, Utrecht: Netherlands Institute of Human Rights.

Deflem, M. 1996, *Habermas, Modernity and Law*, London: Sage.

De Gaay Fortman, B. 1966, *Theory of Economic Policy. A Confrontation of Economic, Political and Legal Principles*, Amsterdam: North Holland Publishing Company (Reed/Elsevier).

De Gaay Fortman, B. 1981, "Politiek en economische macht", in W.A.A.M. de Roos (ed.), *De pluriforme economische macht*, Alphen a/d Rijn: Samsom.

De Gaay Fortman, B. 1982a, "Parlement en hercodificatie", *Weekblad voor Privaatrecht, Notariaat en Registratie*, 5617, 474–478.

De Gaay Fortman, B. 1982b, "You Cannot Develop by Act of Parliament: Rethinking Development from the Legal Viewpoint", in B. de Gaay Fortman (ed.), *Rethinking Development*, The Hague: Institute of Social Studies.

De Gaay Fortman, B. 1990, "The Dialectics of Western Law in a Non-Western World", in J. Berting, P.R. Baehr, J.H. Burgers, C. Flinterman, B. de Klerk, R. Kroes, C.A. van Minnen and K. van der Wal (eds), *Human Rights in a Pluralist World: Individuals and Collectivities*, New York: RSC/Meckler, 237–251.

De Gaay Fortman, B. 1995, "Human Rights, Entitlement Systems and the Problem of Cultural Receptivity", in A. An-Na'im, J.D. Groot, H. Jansen and H.M. Vroom (eds), *Human Rights and Religious Values: an Uneasy Relationship*, Grand Rapids: Eerdmans.

De Gaay Fortman, B. 1999, "Beyond Income Distribution. An Entitlement Systems Approach to the Acquirement Problem", in J. van der Linden and A.J.C. Manders (eds), *The Economics of Income Distribution: Heterodox Approaches*, Brookfield/Cheltenham: Edward Elgar.

De Gaay Fortman, B. 2000a, "Rights-based Approaches: Any New Thing under the Sun?", *International Development Ethics Association Newsletter*, December.

De Gaay Fortman, B. 2000b, "Upholding Humanity. Challenges of Peace in the 21st Century", in B. De Gaay Fortman and J.P. Klein, *Peace in the 21st Century: Between the Supranational and the Grassroots*, Wageningen: Educatief Centrum Hotel De Wereld.

De Gaay Fortman, B. 2001, "Laborious Law", Inaugural Address on accepting the Chair in Political Economy of Human Rights, Utrecht: Utrecht University, 21 May.

De Gaay Fortman, B. 2002, "Racism and Poverty in a Human Rights Perspective", in E. Preckler (ed.), *Europe's New Racism*, New York and Oxford: Berghahn, 71–84.

De Gaay Fortman, B. 2003, "Persistent Poverty and Inequality in an Era of Globalisation: Implications of a Rights Approach", in P. van Seters, B. de Gaay Fortman and A. de Ruijter, *Globalization and Its New Divides: Malcontents, Recipes, and Reform*, Amsterdam: Dutch University Press; West Lafayette: Purdue University Press.

De Gaay Fortman, B. 2004a, "In Search of a New Paradigm. Development Interventionism in a Human Dignity Perspective", in Ananta Kumar Giri, A. van Harskamp and O. Salemink (eds), *The Development of Religion. The Religion of Development*, Delft: Eburon.

De Gaay Fortman, B. 2004b, "Quod Omnes Tangit", in R. Torfs (ed.), *Canonical Testament*, Louvain: Peeters.

De Gaay Fortman, B. 2004c, "The Golden Triangle of Human Dignity: Human Security, Human Development and Human Rights", in M. Muller and B. De Gaay Fortman, *From Warfare to Welfare: Human Security in a Southern African Context*, Assen: Royal Van Gorcum, 5–16.

De Gaay Fortman, B. 2005, "Violence Among Peoples in the Light of Human Frustrations and Aggression", *European Journal of Pharmacology*, 526, 2–8.

De Gaay Fortman, B. 2006a, "Adventurous Judgements. A Comparative Exploration into Human Rights as a Moral-Political Force in Judicial Law-Development", *Utrecht Law Review*, 2(2), 22–44.

De Gaay Fortman, B. 2006b, "Human Rights", in D. Clark (ed.), *Elgar Companion for Development Studies*, Brookfield/Cheltenham: Edward Elgar.

De Gaay Fortman, B. 2006c, "Safe Water: An Enquiry Into Water Entitlements and Human Rights", in J.W. de Visser and C. Mbazira, *Water Delivery: Public or Private?* Utrecht: Utrecht University (NILOS).

De Gaay Fortman, B. 2008, "Beating the State at its Own Game. An Inquiry into the Intricacies of Sovereignty and the Separation of Powers", in I. Boerefijn and J.E. Goldschmidt (eds), *Changing Perceptions of Sovereignty and Human Rights*, Antwerp: Intersentia, 41–57.

De Gaay Fortman, B. and B. Klein Goldewijk. 1998, *God and the Goods. Global Economy in a Civilizational Perspective*, Geneva: WCC Publications.

De Gaay Fortman, B. and C. Kortekaas. 1998, "Collective Violence within States from a Political Economy Perspective", in J. Rotblat (ed.), *Security, Cooperation and Disarmament: The Unfinished Agenda for the 1990s*, Singapore, New Jersey, London and Hong Kong: World Scientific, 362–385.

De Gaay Fortman, B. and P.B. Mihyo. 1993, "A False Start: Law and Development in the Context of a Colonial Legacy", *Verfassung und Recht in Übersee*, 26(2), 136–161.

De Gaay Fortman, B. and M.A. Mohamed Salih. 2003, "The Life and Times of Religion and Human Rights", in W.E.A. Beek, M. Fumerton and W. Pansters (eds), *Meeting Culture: Essays in Honour of Arie de Ruijter*, Maastricht: Shaker, 91–111.

De Gaay Fortman, B. and F. Tarifa. 1998, "Vulnerable Democracies: the Challenge of Legitimacy in Post-Communist Systems", *Journal of Social Sciences*, 2–3(I), 211–219.

De Gaay Fortman, B. and J. Tinbergen. 1990, "Een economische blauwdruk voor de vrede", *NRC/Handelsblad*, 25 May.

De Gaay Fortman, B., K. Martens and M.A. Mohamed Salih. 2010, *Between Text and Context: Hermeneutics, Scriptural Politics and Human Rights*, New York: Palgrave Macmillan.

De Gaay Fortman, W.F. 1966, "Recht en vrede", in B. de Gaay Fortman (ed.), *Christendom en oorlog*, Kampen: Kok, 1966, 142–155.

De Gaay Fortman, W.F. 1972, "Het geheim van het recht", Dies Natalis address at Free University, Amsterdam, 22 October 1962, W.F. de Gaay Fortman, *Recht doen*, Samson: Alphen aan den Rijn.

Denning, A.T. 1979, *The Discipline of Law*, London: Butterworth.

De Soto, H. 1999, *The Mystery of Capital. Why Capitalism Triumphs in the West and Fails Everywhere Else*, New York: Bantam Books.

De Soto, H. 2001, *The Mystery of Capital. Why Capitalism Triumphs in the West and Fails Everywhere Else*, London: Black Swan.

De Swaan, A. 1988, *In Care of the State: Health Care. Education and Welfare in Europe and the USA in the Modern Era*, Cambridge: Polity Press.

Dhanrajgir, N. and B. De Gaay Fortman. 2005, "From Dissociated Hegemony Towards Embedded Hegemony. Multilateralism as a By-product of American Security Concerns", *ISYP Journal on Science and World Affairs*, 1(2), 123–131.

Diamond, L. and F. Plattner. 2010, *Democratization in Africa: Progress and Retreat*, Baltimore: Johns Hopkins University Press.

Dinstein, Y. 1976, "Collective Human Rights of Peoples and Minorities", *The International and Comparative Law Quarterly*, 1(1), 102–120.

Dodgson, M. 1994, *Cultural Rights and Educational Responsibilities*, Aboriginal and Torres Strait Islander Social Justice Commissioner, University of New England.

Dollard, J., L.W. Doob, N.E. Miller, O.H. Mowrer and R.R. Sears. 1939, *Frustration and Aggression*, New Haven: Yale University Press.

Donders, Y. 2002, "Towards a Right to Cultural Identity?" *School of Human Rights Research Series No. 15*, Antwerp: Intersentia; Oxford and New York: Hart.

Donnelly, J. 1990, "Human Rights, Individual Rights and Collective Rights", in J. Berting, P.R. Baehr, J.H. Burgers, C. Flinterman, B. de Klerk, R. Kroes, C.A. van Minnen and K. van der Wal (eds), *Human Rights in a Pluralist World. Individuals and Collectivities*, London: Meckler/UNESCO/Roosevelt Study Center.

Dooyeweerd, H. 1957, *A New Critique of Theoretical Thought III*, Amsterdam: H.J. Paris.

Dow, S. 1990, "Post-Keynesianism as Political Economy: a Methodological Discussion", *Review of Political Economy*, 2(3), 345–358.

Dugan, M. 2003, "Aggression". Online. Available at: www.beyondintractability.org/m/aggression.jsp (accessed 7 June 2005).

Dupont, P. and S. Marijsse. 1994, "Het gruwelijke einde van de vredesverwachtingen voor Rwanda", *Internationale Spectator*, 48(7/8).

Dwivedi, R. 2001, *Resource Conflict and Collective Action. The Sardar Sarovar Project in India*, Maastricht: Shaker.

Dworkin, R. 1986, *Law's Empire*, London: Fontana.

Dworkin, R. 1993, *Life's Dominion: an Argument about Abortion, Euthanasia, and Individual Freedom*, New York: Knopf.

Dworkin, R. 2006, *Justice in Robes*, Cambridge, MA: Harvard University Press.

Easterly, W. 2010, "Foreign Aid for Scoundrels", *New York Review of Books*, 25 November, 37–38.

Easterly W. and R. Levine. 2002, "Tropics, Germs and Crops: How Endowments Influence Economic Development", *NBER Working Paper* 9106.

Economics Focus. 2002, *The Roots of Development*, London: The Economist, 5 October.

Ekins, R.E. 2002, *Secular Fundamentalism and Democracy*, Grand Rapids: Acton Institute Publications.

Elchardus, M. and I. Glorieux. 2002, *De Symbolische Samenleving: Een Exploratie van de Nieuwe Sociale en Culturele Ruimtes*, Tielt: Lannoo.

Falk Moore, S. 1978, *Law As Process: An Anthropological Approach*, London/Boston: Routledge & Kegan Paul.

Fesneaux, J. 1976, *Du passé faisons table rase?* Paris: Librairie François Maspero.

Filmer-Wilson, E. 2005, "The Human Rights-Based Approach to Development: The Right to Water", *Netherlands Quarterly of Human Rights*, 23(2), June, 213–242.

Flanders, A. 1970, "The Farley Productivity Agreements", in C.V. Brown (ed.), *Economic Principles Applied*, London: Martin Robertson, 85–88.

Flinterman, C. 2000, *Souvereiniteit en de rechten van de mens*, Utrecht: Netherlands Institute of Human Rights.

France, A. 1894, *Le Lys Rouge*, Paris: Editions du Houblon.

Franck, Th.M. 1990, *The Power of Legitimacy among Nations*, New York and Oxford: Oxford University Press.

Fromm, E. 1973, *The Anatomy of Human Destructiveness*, Greenwich: Fawcett Crest.

Fukuyama, F. 1992, *The End of History and the Last Man*, London and New York: Penguin Books.

Galbraith, J.K. 2002, "A Perfect Crime: Inequality in the Age of Globalization", *Daedalus*, winter.

Galtung, J. 1996, *Peace by Peaceful Means: Peace and Conflict Development and Civilization*, Oslo: International Peace Research Institute; London: Thousand Oaks; New Delhi: Sage.

Galtung, J. 1998, *Conflict Transformation by Peaceful Means (The Transcend Method)* [Manual prepared by The Disaster Management Training Program of the United Nations], New York: United Nations.

Garton Ash, T. 2003, "Are You With Us? Are We Against You?", *New York Times*, 30 May.

Gasper, D. 1994, "Culture and Three Levels in Development Ethics: From Advocacy to Analysis and from Analysis to Practice", in Arie de Ruijter and Lieteke van Vucht Tijssen (eds), *Cultural Dynamics in Development Processes*, The Hague: UNESCO.

Gerbrandy, P.S. 1935, "Het wetsontwerp: verbindende kracht van ondernemersovereenkomsten", *Antirevolutionaire Staatkunde*.

German Institute of Human Rights, Human Rights Budgeting – e-tool, Online. Available at: www.equalinrights.org/uploads/tx_wizzresources/GermanInstitute4HRs_2009_ETool_Budgeting_HRs.pdf (accessed 16 October 2010).

Ghai, Y. 1978, "Law and Another Development", *Development Dialogue*, 110–131.

Gilroy, P. 2009, *Race and the Right to be Human*. Inaugural address, delivered on accepting the Treaty of Utrecht Chair, Utrecht: Utrecht University, Faculty of Humanities, 3 December.

Glover, J. 1999, *Humanity. Moral History of the Twentieth Century*, Yale: Yale University Press.

Graver, H.P. 1988, "Norms and Decisions", *Scandinavian Studies in Law*, 4, 32–60.

Greenhouse, L. 2007, "Supreme Court Won't Hear Torture Appeal", *The New York Times*, 9 October. Online. Available at: www.nytimes.com/2007/10/09/washington/09cnd-cotus.html (accessed 3 March 2008).

Griffin, J. 2008, *On Human Rights*, Oxford: Oxford University Press.

Griffith-Jones, S. 2002, *Capital Flows to Developing Countries. Does the Emperor Have Clothes?*, paper for the ISS 50th Anniversary Conference "Globalization, Conflict and Poverty", The Hague, 7–9 October.

Grimké, A. 1838, Letter XII "Human Rights Not Founded On Sex", in *Letters to Catherine Beecher*, Boston: Isaac Knapp.

Grotius, H. 1625, *De Jure Belli ac Pacis Libri Tres*, trans. W. Kelsey (1925) *On the Law of War and Peace* in Three Volumes, Oxford: Clarendon Press.

Gunther, G. 1998, *Learned Hand: The Man and the Judge*, Cambridge, MA: Harvard University Press.

Gurr, T.R. 1968, "A Causal Model of Civil Strife: A Comparative Analysis Using New Indices", *American Political Science Review*, 62, December, 1104–1124.

Gurr, T.R. 1970, *Why Men Rebel*, Princeton: Princeton University Press.

Gurr, T.R. 1993, "Why Minorities Rebel: A Global Analysis of Communal Mobilisation and Conflict since 1945", *International Political Science Review*, 14(2), 161–201.

Habermas, J. 1988, "Law and Morality", in S.M. McMurrin (ed.), *The Tanner Lectures on Human Values*, Vol. 8, Salt Lake City: University of Utah Press.

Habermas, J. 1992, *Faktizität und Geltung*, Frankfurt am Main: Suhrkamp.

Habermas, J. 1997 [1973], *Legitimization Crisis*, Cambridge: Polity Press.

Hadiprayitno, I. 2010, *Hazard or Right? The Dialectics of Development Practice and the Internationally Declared Right to Development*, Antwerp: Intersentia.

Harrod, J. 1987, *Power, Production, and the Unprotected Worker*, New York: Columbia University Press.

Harrod, J. 1992, *Labour and Third World Debt*, Geneva: ICEF.

Haugen, G. and V. Boutros. 2010, "And Justice for All: Enforcing Human Rights for the World's Poor", *Foreign Affairs*, 89(3), 51–62, May/June.

Heemskerk, E., R. Mokken and M. Fennema. 2002, "De organisatie van het Nederlandse bedrijfsleven: graven naar macht 25 jaar later", *Tijdschrift voor Politieke Ekonomie*, 24(I), 109–134.

Hiebert, J.L. 2006, "Parliament and the Human Rights Act: Can the JCHR Help Facilitate a Culture of Rights?", *International Journal of Constitutional Law*, 4(1), 1–38.

Hirsch Ballin, E.M.H. 2003, *Gelijk in waardigheid. Over artikel 1 van de Grondwet*, Artikel 1 lezing. Online. Available at: http://soliscms.uu.nl/content/artikel1-lezing2003. PDF (accessed 29 September 2010).

Hoffmann, S. 1995, "Dreams of a Just World", *The New York Review of Books*, 2 November, 54–57.

Hoffmann, S. 2003, "World Governance: Beyond Utopia", *Daedalus*, winter.

Homer-Dixon, Th.F. 1999, *Environment, Scarcity and Violence*, Princeton: Princeton University Press.

Homer-Dixon, Th.F. 2000, *The Ingenuity Gap*, UK: Jonathan Cape.

Homer-Dixon, Th.F. 2002, *The Capitalist Trilemma*, paper presented at the 52nd Pugwash Annual Conference on Science and World Affairs, La Jolla, 9–14 August.

Human Rights Committee. 2000, General Comment No. 23 (50) (art. 27), adopted on 6 April 1994, CCPR/C/21/Rev.1/Add.5.

Human Rights Council. 2008a, "Universal Periodic Review. Report of the Working Group on the Universal Periodic Review. Czech Republic", A/HRC/8/33, 23 May 2008.

Human Rights Council. 2008b, "Universal Periodic Review. Report of the Working Group on the Universal Periodic Review. India", A/HRC/8/26, 23 May 2008.

Human Rights Council. 2008c, "Universal Periodic Review. Report of the Working Group on the Universal Periodic Review. Indonesia", A/HRC/8/23, 14 May 2008.

Human Rights Council. 2008d, "Universal Periodic Review. Report of the Working Group on the Universal Periodic Review. Pakistan", A/HRC/8/42, 4 June 2008.

Human Rights Council. 2008e, "Universal Periodic Review. Report of the Working Group on the Universal Periodic Review. The Philippines", A/HRC/8/28, 23 May 2008.

Human Rights Council. 2008f, "Universal Periodic Review. Report of the Working Group on the Universal Periodic Review. Poland", A/HRC/8/30, 23 May 2008.

Human Rights Council. 2008g, "Universal Periodic Review. Report of the Working Group on the Universal Periodic Review. Sri Lanka", A/HRC/8/46, 5 June 2008.

Human Rights Council. 2009a, "Universal Periodic Review. Report of the Working Group on the Universal Periodic Review. Burundi", A/HRC/10/71, 8 January 2009.

Human Rights Council. 2009b, "Universal Periodic Review. Report of the Working Group on the Universal Periodic Review. Malaysia", A/HRC/11/30, 5 October 2009.

Human Rights Council. 2009c, "Universal Periodic Review. Report of the Working Group on the Universal Periodic Review. Uzbekistan", A/HRC/10/83, 11 March 2009.

Human Rights Council. 2010, "Universal Periodic Review. Report of the Working Group on the Universal Periodic Review. Democratic Republic of the Congo", A/HRC/13/8, 4 January 2010.

Human Rights Watch. 2001, *World Report*, New York: HRW.

Humphrey, J. 1968, "The United Nations Sub-Commission on the Prevention of Discrimination and the Protection of Minorities", *The American Journal of International Law*, 62(4), 869–888.

Hunt, L. 2007, *Inventing Human Rights. A History*, New York and London: Norton.

Hunt, P. 1996, *Reclaiming Social Rights. International and Comparative Perspectives*, Aldershot: Dartmouth.

Hunt, P., M. Nowak and S. Osmani. 2002, *Draft Guidelines: A Human Rights Approach to Poverty Reduction Strategies*, Geneva: United Nations Office of the High Commissioner for Human Rights, 10 September.

Hunter, D. and L. Udall. 1994, The World Bank's New Inspection Panel: Will It Increase the Bank's Accountability?, CIEL Brief No. 1. Online. Available at: www.ciel.org/Publications/issue1.html (accessed 16 March 2011).

Huntington, S. 1993, "The Clash of Civilizations", *Foreign Affairs*, summer.

ICC. 2009a, "Facts and Figures from the Registry", 30 April. Online. Available at: www.icc-cpi.int/NR/rdonlyres/302CA5E0-E2B5–4663–96DE-93E55B1FD26C/280383/Facts_and_figures_30_April_2009_ENG.pdf (accessed 21 July 2009).

ICC. 2009b, "Situations and Cases". Online. Available at: www.icc-cpi.int/Menus/ICC/Situations+and+Cases/ (accessed 20 October 2010).

Idowu, A.A. 1999, "Human Rights, Environmental Degradation and Oil Multinational Companies in Nigeria: The Ogoniland Episode", *Netherlands Quarterly of Human Rights*, 17(2), 161–184.

Ignatieff, M. 1999, *Whose Universal Values? The Crisis in Human Rights*, Amsterdam: Praemium Erasmianum Essay.

International Commission on Intervention and State Sovereignty. 2001, *The Responsibility to Protect*, International Development Research Center: Ottawa.

International Development Research Centre. 2001, *The Responsibility to Protect.* Report of the International Commission on Intervention and State Sovereignty, Ottawa: International Development Research Centre.

International Monetary Fund. 2006, *United Republic of Tanzania: Poverty Reduction Strategy Paper*, IMF Country Report No. 06/142, Washington, DC: International Monetary Fund.

International Monetary Fund. 2009, *Impact of the Global Financial Crisis on Sub-Saharan Africa*, Washington, DC: International Monetary Fund.

Isaacman, A. 1996, *Cotton is the Mother of Poverty. Peasants, Work, and Rural Struggle in Colonial Mozambique, 1938–1961*, Portsmouth, NH: Heinemann.

Jägers, N. 2002, *Corporate Human Rights Obligations: In Search of Accountability*, Antwerp: Intersentia.

Janse, R. 2008, "Paardenmiddel of placebo? Over de export van de rechtsstaat", *De Academische Boekengids* 67, March.

Jhering, R. von and Husik, I. 1914, *Law as a Means to an End*, New York: Macmillan.

Kakwani, N. and Ernesto M. Pernia. 2000, "What is Pro-poor Growth?", *Asian Development Review*, 18(1).

Kanbur, R. 2001, "Economic Policy, Distribution and Poverty: The Nature of Disagreements", *Peace Economics, Peace Science and Public Policy*, 7.

Kaplan, B.J. 2007, *Divided by Faith. Religious Conflict and the Practice of Toleration in Early Modern Europe*, Cambridge, MA and London: The Belknap Press of Harvard University Press.

Karst, K.L. and K.S. Rosenn. 1975, *Law and Development in Latin America: A Case Book*, Berkeley: University of California Press.

Kazan-Allen, L. 2002, *British Asbestos Newsletter*, 47 (summer).

Kennedy, D. 2002, "The International Human Rights Movement: Part of the Problem?", *Harvard Human Rights Journal*, 15, 101–125, spring.

Kersley. R.H. (ed.) 1969, *A selection of Legal Maxims Classified and Illustrated by Herbert Broom*, London: Sweet and Maxwell.

Ketscher, K. 2007, "Cultural Rights and Religious Rights", in M.L.P. Loenen and J.E. Goldschmidt (eds), *Religious Pluralism and Human Rights in Europe: Where to Draw the Line?* Antwerp: Intersentia, 219–237.

Keynes, J.M. 1920, *The Economic Consequences of the Peace*, London: Penguin.

Khan, E. 2002, "Supreme Court Puts End to Anti-Green Fuel Crusade in Delhi", *Indo-Asian News*, New Delhi, 13 April.

Kim, M. 2009, "Too Late for Revenge", *New York Times*, 15 July, p. A27. Online. Available at: www.nytimes.com/2009/07/16/opinion/16kim.html?_r=2 (accessed 15 July 2009).

Kirby, M. 1999a, "Denning: Bold Spirit of the Law", *The Australian Financial Review*, 19 March.

Kirby, M. 1999b, "Lord Denning and Judicial Activism". Online. Available at: http://lawfoundation.net.au/ljf/app/&id=04FA7A2F1016634ACA2571A40022191D (accessed 31 July 2006).

Ki-Zerbo, J. 1999, *Apôtre Alfred Simon Diban Ki-Zerbo*, Colombelles: Corlet (Ressources Editions).

Klein Goldewijk, B. and B. De Gaay Fortman. 1999, *Where Needs Meet Rights. Economic, Social and Cultural Rights in a New Perspective*, Geneva: WCC Publications.

Kokaz, N. 2001, "Moderating Power: A Thucydidean Perspective", *Review of International Studies*, 27(1), 27–49.

Korzec, M. 1993, "Onzin op stelten. Mensenrechten als wereldreligie", *Intermediair*, 10 December.

Kumar-D'souza, C. 1986, "The Political Economy of Human Rights", *International Review of Education*, 29(3), 413–422.

Kurlantzick, J. 2010, "The Downfall of Human Rights", *Newsweek*, 1 March. Online. Available at: www.newsweek.com/2010/02/18/the-downfall-of-human-rights.html (accessed 12 June 2010).

Kymlicka, W. 2008, "The Internationalization of Minority Rights", *International Journal of Constitutional Law*, 6(1), 1–32.

Lambers, H.W. 1971, Ondernemingsmacht en concentratie, in *Macht. Voordrachten gehouden in 1970 voor Studium Generale te Groningen*, Haarlem.

Lambooy, T.E. 2010, *Corporate Social Responsibility. Legal and Semi-Legal Frameworks Supporting CSR. Developments 2000–2010 and Case Studies*, The Hague, London and New York: Kluwer.

Langemeijer, G. 1970, *De Gerechtigheid in ons burgerlijk vermogensrecht*, Deventer: Tjeenk Willink.

Lasch, C. 1994, *The Revolt of the Elites and the Betrayal of Democracy*, New York: W.W. Norton.

Leary, V.A. 1990, "The Effect of Western Perspectives on International Human Rights", in A.A. An-Na'im and F.M. Deng (eds), *Human Rights in Africa; Cross-Cultural Perspectives*, Washington, DC: The Brookings Institution.

Lederach, J.P. 1999, *Justpeace – The Challenge of the 21st Century, People Building Peace. 35 Inspiring Stories from Around the World*, Utrecht: European Centre for Conflict Prevention.

Leiserowitz, A.A. and L.O. Fernandez. 2008, *Toward a New Consciousness: Values to Sustain Human and Natural Communities*, New Haven: Yale School of Forestry & Environmental Studies.

Lekachman, R. 1979, "Foreword", in Warren J. Samuels (ed.), *The Economy as a System of Power, Vol. I: Corporate Systems*, New Brunswick: Transaction Books.

Liebenberg, S. 2002a, "The Courts and Socio-Economic Rights: Carving Out a Role", *Economic and Social Rights Review*, 3(1).

Liebenberg, S. 2002b, "South Africa's Evolving Jurisprudence on Socio-Economic Rights", *Law, Democracy and Development*, 6.

Loewenberg, G. 2007, "Paradoxes of Legislatures", *Daedalus*, summer, 58–59.

Lokin, J.H.A. 1994, *Tekst en uitleg. Opstellen over codificatie en interpretatie naar aanleiding van de invoering van het nieuwe Burgerlijk Wetboek*, Groningen: Chimaira.

Lokin, J.H.A. 2006, "Legal History and Comparative Law a Pair Bifocals", *European Journal of law Reforms*, 8(1), 13–27.

Lord Hailsham of St Marylebone. 1982, "Farewell to Lord Denning", speech reported in *The Times*, 31 July, 16.

Lorentz, K. 1966, *On Aggression*, New York: Harcourt, Brace, and World.

Lunney, M. and K. Oliphant. 2008, *Tort Law, Text and Materials*, Oxford: Oxford University Press.

Luxemburg, L. 1971 [1913], *The Accumulation of Capital*, London: Routledge.

Lyons, C. 2007, "The State Secrets Privilege: Expanding Its Scope through Government Misuse", *Lewis & Clark L. Rev.*, 11(1), 99–132.

McCorquodale R. and R. Fairbrother. 1999, "Globalization and Human Rights", *Human Rights Quarterly*, 21.

McCrudden, C. 2008, "Human Dignity and Judicial Interpretation of Human Rights", *The European Journal of International Law*, 19(4), 655–724.

McCullum, H. 1995, *The Angels Have Left Us: the Rwanda Tragedy and the Churches*, Geneva: WCC Publications.

"Macedonia Adopts a New Constitution". 2001, *BBC News. World Edition* 16 November. Online. Available at: http://news.bbc.co.uk/2/hi/europe/1659132.stm (accessed 12 June 2010).

Mahler, C. 2009, "Is Human Rights Education a Means of Supporting Minorities?", in C. Mahler, A. Mihr and R. Toivanen, *The United Nations Decade for Human Rights Education and the Inclusion of National Minorities*, Frankfurt am Main: Peter Lang.

Malkki, L. 1992 "National Geographic: The Rooting of Peoples and the Territorialization of National Identity among Scholars and Refugees", *Cultural Anthropology*, 7(1) (Space, Identity, and the Politics of Difference), February, 24–44.

Marx, K. 2009 [1875], *Critique of the Gotha Programme*, Goodridge: Dodo Press.

Meade, J.E. 1965, *The Stationary Economy*, London: Allen and Unwin.

Mibenge, C. 2010, *Show Me a Woman! Narratives of Gender and Violence in Human Rights Law and Processes of Transitional Justice*, Utrecht University: Doctoral Dissertation.

Milanovic, B. 2007, "Globalization and Inequality", in D. Held and A. Kaya (ed.), *Global Inequality*, Cambridge: Polity Press, 26–50.

Miller, Neal E. 1941, The Frustration-Aggression Hypothesis [1], *Psychol Rev*, 48, 337–342.

Mills, G. 2010, *Why Africa is Poor. And What Africans Can Do About It*, Johannesburg: Penguin S.A.

Mirmoosavi, A. 2010, "The Quran and Religious Freedom. The Issue of Apostasy", in B. de Gaay Fortman, K. Martens and M.A. Mohamed Salih (eds), *Between Text and Context: Hermeneutics, Scriptural Politics and Human Rights*, New York: Palgrave Macmillan, 125–141.

Morsink, J. 1999, *The Universal Declaration of Human Rights: Origins, Drafting, and Intent*, Philadelphia: University of Pennsylvania Press.

Moyo, D. 2009, *Dead Aid. Why Aid is Not Working and How There is a Better Way for Africa*, New York: Farrar, Straus, and Giroux.

Mshana, R. 2002, *Economic Globalization: A Critical View and an Alternative Vision*, Geneva: WCC Publications.

Mufazzar, C. 1994, *From Human Rights to Human Dignity*. Paper for the International Conference "Rethinking Human Rights". Kuala Lumpur, 6–7 December. Unpublished.

Murshed, S.M. 2001, *Notes on Poverty Reduction and Economic Development*, UNU/WIDER paper, 6 September.

Murshed, S.M. 2002, *Perspectives on Two Phases of Globalisation*, paper for the ISS 50th Anniversary Conference "Globalisation, Conflict and Poverty", The Hague, 7–9 October.

Murshed, S.M. 2010, *Explaining Civil War: A Rational Choice Approach*, Brookfield/Cheltenham: Edward Elgar.

Narayan, Deepa, R. Patel, K. Schafft, A. Rademacher and S. Koch-Schulte. 2000a, *Voices of the Poor. Can Anyone Hear Us?* Oxford: Oxford University Press (for the World Bank).

Narayan, Deepa, R. Chambers, M.K. Shah and P. Petesch. 2000b, *Voices of the Poor. Crying Out for Change*, Oxford: Oxford University Press (for the World Bank).

Ndahinda, M.F. 2009, *Indigenousness in Africa: A Contested Framework for Empowerment of "Marginalized" Ethno-Cultural Communities*, Tilburg: INTERVICT.

Neiman, S. 2005, *Before the Gallows: Heroes in the Face of Evil*, Amsterdam: Thomas More Annual Lecture.

Netherlands Ministry of Foreign Affairs. 1993, *Sustainable Energy Economy*, The Hague: Ministry of Foreign Affairs (Sectoral Document of Development Cooperation).

Noon, C. 2009, "The Use of Racial Preferences in Public Procurement for Social Stability", *Public Contract Law Journal*, 38(3), 618–622.

Normand, R. and S. Zaidi. 2008, *Human Rights at the UN. The Political History of Universal Justice*, Bloomington and Indianapolis: Indiana University Press.

Norris, P. and R. Inglehart. 2004, *Sacred and Secular: Religion and Politics Worldwide*, Cambridge: Cambridge University Press.

North, D.C. 1990, *Institutions, Institutional Change and Economic Performance*, Cambridge: Cambridge University Press.

North, D.C. 1994, "Economic Performance Through Time", *American Economic Review*, June, 359–368.

Nyanje, P. 2002, "Why So Many Studies on Poverty Eradication?", *Guardian*, 17 September.

OECD/DAC. 2001, *The DAC Guidelines on Poverty Reduction*, Paris: OECD.

Offe, C. 2002, *A Non-Productivist Design for Social Policies*, mimeograph.

Office of the High Commissioner for Human Rights. 2010, *Human Rights and MDGs in Practice: A Review of Country Strategies and Reporting*, Geneva: United Nations.

Olivier, P.J.J. 1973, *Legal Fictions: An Analysis and Evaluation*, Doct. Diss., Leiden: Beugelsdijk.

Olson, M. 2000, *Power and Prosperity. Outgrowing Communist and Capitalist Dictatorships*, New York: Basic Books.

Oorschot, W. van and P. Kolkhuis Tanke. 1989, *Niet gebruik van sociale zekerheid. Feiten, Theorieën. Onderzoeksmethoden*, Report for the Ministry of Social Affairs and Employment, Commission for Social Security, No.16A, The Hague, March.

Oran, B. 2007, "Minority Concept and Rights in Turkey. The Lausanne Peace Treaty and Current Issues", in Z.F.K. Arat (ed.), *Human Rights in Turkey*, Philadelphia: University of Pennsylvania Press, 35–56.

Pallares-Burke, M.L. 2006, "Raza, Mestizaje e Indentidad", *Arbor*, CLXXXII(722), 831–843.

Pascal, B. 1866, *Pensées*, Paris: Charpentier.

Peerenboom, R. 2005, "Human Rights and the Rule of Law: What's the Relationship?", *Georgetown Journal of International Law*, 36(3), 809–945.

Perraton, J., D. Goldblatt, D. Held and A. McGrew. 1997, "The Globalization of Economic Activity", *New Political Economy*, 2(2), July.

Perry, E. 2008, "Chinese Conceptions of 'Rights': From Mencius to Mao – and Now", *Perspectives on Politics*, 6(1), 37–50.

Perry, M.J. 1998, *The Idea of Human Rights: Four Enquiries*, Oxford and New York: Oxford University Press.

Pogge, Th. 2008, *World Poverty and Human Rights*, Cambridge: Polity Press.

Prieto, D.B. 2009, "War About Terror: Civil Liberties and National Security After 9/11", Council on Foreign Relations, Working Paper. Online. Available at: www.voltairenet.org/IMG/pdf/Civil_Liberties_and_National_Security_After_9_11.pdf (accessed 28 July 2009).

Pronk, J. 2003, "VS en VN", *Roodkoper*, 8(2), 16.

Prunier, G. 1995, *The Rwanda Crisis. History of a Genocide 1959–1994*, London: Hurst and Company.

Pyatt, G. 1999, *Poverty versus the Poor*, Dies Natalis Address, The Hague: Institute of Social Studies.

Pyatt, G. 2002, *Seeds of Conflict*, paper for the ISS 50th Anniversary Conference "Globalization, Conflict and Poverty", The Hague, 7–9 October.

Rabkin, J. 2003, "What We Can Learn About Human Dignity from International Law", *Harvard Journal of Law and Public Policy*, 27(1), 145–168.

Rajendra, C. 1987, *Voice of the Dispossessed, Dove on Fire. Poems on Peace, Justice and Ecology*, Geneva: WCC Publications.

Ramcharan, B.G. 2005, *Judicial Protection of Economic, Social and Cultural Rights*, Leiden and Boston: Martinus Nijhoff Publishers.

Rawls, A. 2003, "Conflict as a Foundation for Consensus: Contradictions of Industrial Capitalism in Book III of Durkheim's 'Division of Labor'", *Critical Sociology*, 29, 295–335.

Rawls, J. 1972, *A Theory of Justice*, Oxford: Oxford University Press.

Rawls, J. 1999, *The Law of Peoples. With 'The Idea of Public Reason' Revisited*, Cambridge, MA: Harvard University Press.

Rehman, J. 2000, *The Weaknesses in the International Protection of Minority Rights*, The Hague, London and Boston: Kluwer Law International.

Robertson, G. 1998, "Adventuring Advocates of the Adversarial System", Radio National

Transcripts: The Law Report, 31 March. Online. Available at: www.abc.net.au/rn/talks/8.30/lawrpt/lstories/lr980331.htm (accessed 8 July 2008).

Robertson, G. 2005, *The Tyrannicide Brief. The Story of the Man who sent Charles I to the Scaffold*, London: Chatto & Windus.

Robinson, M. 2006, "Human Rights: A Needed UN Reform", *International Herald Tribune*, 2 March.

Roosevelt, F.D. 1914, "The Four Freedoms", Address to the 77th US Congress, Washington, DC, 6 January. Online. Available at: www.dlhoffman.com/publiclibrary/AmericanHistory/roosevelt1.html (accessed 23 July 2009).

Rothschild, E. 1995, "What is Security?" *Daedalus*, summer, 53–98.

Rothuizen, G. 1962, *Primus Usus Legis. Studie over het burgerlijk gebruik der wet*, Kok: Kampen.

Ruggie, J. 2008, *Protect, Respect and Remedy: a Framework for Business and Human Rights*, Report of the Special Representative of the Secretary-General on the issue of human rights and transnational corporations and other business enterprises, Geneva: UNHRC.

Rummel, R.J. 1995, "Democracy, Power, Genocide, and Mass Murder", *Journal of Conflict Resolution*, 39(1).

Said, E.W. 1978, *Orientalism*, London: Routledge.

Salih, M.A. Mohamed. 2003, "Minorities and the Political in the Human Rights Deficit", in K. Arts and P. Mihyo (eds), *Responding to the Human Rights Deficit. Essays in Honour of Bas de Gaay Fortman*, The Hague, London and New York: Kluwer, 105–132.

Salih, M.A. 2011, "Climate Change, Conflict and the Protection of Vulnerable Collectivities", in *Human Rights and Conflict. In Honour of Professor Bas de Gaay Fortman*, Antwerp: Intersentia, forthcoming.

Samuels, W.J. 1974, "An Economic Perspective on the Compensation Problem", *Wayne Law Review*, 21, 113–134.

Samuels, W.J. and T.W. Kelsey. 1991, "Some Fundamental Considerations on the Positive Theory of Income Distribution", in W.L.M. Adriaansen and J.T.J.M. van der Linden (eds), *Post-Keynesian Thought In Perspective*, Groningen: Wolters Noordhoff, 119–138.

Samuels, W.J. and N. Mercuro. 1977, "The Role of the Compensation Principle in Society", *Research in Law and Economics*, I, 210–245.

Samuels, W.J. and N. Mercuro. 1980, "The Role and Resolution of the Compensation Principle in Society: Part Two – The Resolution", in *Research in Law and Economics*, 2, 103–128.

Santos, Th. dos. 1971, "The Structure of Dependence", in K.T. Fann and D.C. Hodges (eds), *Readings in U.S. Imperialism*, Boston: Porter Sargent Publisher.

Scarman, L.G. 1986, *Sunday Times*, 12 January.

Schaffer, B. and G. Lamb. 1981, *Can Equity be Organized? Equity, Development Analysis and Planning*, Aldershot: Gower.

Scholten, P. 1931, *Mr. C. Asser's Handleiding tot de beoefening van het Nederlandsch Burgerlijk Recht. Algemeen Deel*, Zwolle: Tjeenk Willink.

Schrijver, N. 1997, *Sovereignty over National Resources. Balancing Rights and Duties*, Cambridge: Cambridge University Press.

Schrijver, N. 2010, *Development without Destruction. The UN and Global Resource Management*, Bloomington: Indiana University Press.

Schumpeter, J.A. 1954, *History of Economic Analysis*, New York and Oxford: Oxford University Press.

Scully, G.W. 1988, "The Institutional Framework and Economic Development", *Journal of Political Economy*, 96(3), 652–662.

Sen, A. 1981, *Poverty and Famines. An Essay on Entitlement and Deprivation*, Oxford: Clarendon Press.

Sen, A. 1986, *Food, Economics and Entitlements*, Helsinki: World Institute for Development Economics Research of the United Nations University.

Sen, A. 1987, *Hunger and Entitlements*, Helsinki: World Institute for Development Economics Research of the United Nations University.

Sen, A. 1993, "Development: Which Way Now?", *Economic Journal*, 752–762.

Sen, A. 1999, *Development as Freedom*, Oxford: Oxford University Press.

Sen, A. 2004, "Operating in an Age of Uncertainty: New Challenges in Humanitarian and Development Work", Plenary Address to the Interaction Forum, Washington, DC, 19 May.

Sen, A. 2009, *The Idea of Justice*, Cambridge, MA: The Belknap Press of Harvard University Press.

Shani, Y. 2006, "Toward a General Margin of Appreciation Doctrine in International Law", *The European Journal of International Law*, 16(5), 907–940.

Sheth, D.L. 1990, "Limits and Possibilities of Using the Law for the Poor", in J. Ventura Aspiras (ed.), *Law as Weapon. Alternative Approaches to Distributive Justice*, Manila: Process.

Smith, A. 1900 [1776], *An Inquiry Into the Nature and Causes of the Wealth of Nations*, London: Routledge.

Stalpers, J.A. 1975, "Macht over de macht", in *Macht over macht. Veranderende opvattingen over gezag en macht*, Annalen van het Thijmgenootschap, Annum 63, No. 3, Bilthoven: Amboboeken.

Stein, P. 1966, *Regulae Iuris: From Juristic Rules to Legal Maxims*, Edinburgh: Edinburgh University Press.

Stüssi, M. 2008, "Banning of Minarets. Addressing the Validity of a Controversial Swiss Popular Initiative". *Religion and Human Rights*, 3, 135–153.

Sumner, A. 2010, "Global Poverty and the New Bottom Billion: What if Three-Quarters of the World's Poor Live in Middle-Income Countries?", Working Paper, Brighton: Institute of Development Studies.

Supreme Court of India. 2001, Writ Petition (Civil) No. 13 029/85, New Delhi, 26 March.

Sydenham, E. 2004, *The Governance Factor in Respect of Collectivities in Intra-state Collective Violence. An Emerging Right to Autonomy in International Law*, LLM final thesis, Utrecht School of Law.

Tambakaki, P. 2010, *Human Rights, or Citizenship*, London: Routledge.

Tawney, R.H. 1948 [1920], *The Acquisitive Society*, New York: Harvest Books.

Thomas, E.W. 2005, *The Judicial Process. Realism, Pragmatism, Practical Reasoning and Principles*, Cambridge: Cambridge University Press.

Thomassen, W. 2006, "The Margin of Appreciation in the Case Law of the European Court of Human Rights in Respect of the Manifestation of Religion", presented at *Religion and Human Rights Conference*, Utrecht University, 10 May.

Thucydides. 1972, *History of the Peloponnesian War*, translated by R. Warner, New York: Penguin.

Tilly, C. 1978, *From Mobilization to Revolution*, London: Longman.

Tinbergen, J. and D. Fischer. 1987, *Warfare and Welfare: Integrating Security Policy into Socio-Economic Policy*, New York: St. Martin's Press.

Tocqueville, A. 1945 [1835], *Democracy in America*, Bowen Translation, P. Bradley, New York: A.A. Knopf.

Toebes, B. 1999, *The Right to Health as a Human Right in International Law*, Antwerp: Intersentia.

Toenniessen, G., A. Adesina and J. De Vries. 2008, "Building an Alliance for a Green Revolution in Africa", *Annals of the New York Academy of Sciences*, 1136, 233–242.

Toivanen, R. 2004, "Contextualizing Struggles Over Culture and Equality. An Anthropological Perspective", in M. Scheinin and R. Toivanen, *Rethinking Non-Discrimination and Minority Rights*, Institute for Human Rights, Åbo: Åbo Akademi University Turku; Berlin: German Institute for Human Rights, 179–200.

Tolstoy, L. 1987 [1908], *A Confession and Other Religious Writings*, translated by Jane Kentish, Harmondsworth: Penguin.

Touray, I. 2010, "Locating Women's Sexuality and Women's Rights in the Context of Cultural Practices: The Case of Female Genital Mutilation", in B. de Gaay Fortman, K. Martens and M.A. Mohamed Salih (eds), *Between Text and Context: Hermeneutics, Scriptural Politics and Human Rights*, New York: Palgrave Macmillan, 237–251.

Trouwborst, A.A. 1994, "Ruanda en Burundi: historische achtergronden", *Internationale Spectator*, 48(7–8), July/August.

Tully, S. 2005, "A Human Right to Access Water", *Netherlands Quarterly of Human Rights*, 23(1), March.

United Nations. 1945, *Charter of the United Nations*, New York: United Nations.

United Nations. 1946, *Statute of the International Court of Justice*, New York: United Nations.

United Nations. 1948, *Universal Declaration of Human Rights*, entered into force 10 December, New York: United Nations.

United Nations. 1966a, *International Covenant on Civil and Political Rights*, entered into force 23 March. 1976, New York: United Nations.

United Nations. 1966b, *International Covenant on Economic, Social and Cultural Rights*, entered into force 3 January 1976, New York: United Nations.

United Nations. 1986, *General Assembly resolution 41/128*, 4 December.

United Nations. 2005, *Integrated and coordinated implementation of and follow-up to the outcomes of the major United Nations conferences and summits in the economic, social and related fields. Follow-up to the outcome of the Millennium Summit* A/60/L.1 General Assembly 15 September 2005 05–51130 Sixtieth session Items 48 and 121 of the provisional agenda.

United Nations Committee on Economic, Social and Cultural Rights. 2003, General Comment No 15, E/C.12/2002/11, 20 January.

United Nations Development Program. 1993, *Human Development Report 1993*, New York and Oxford: Oxford University Press.

United Nations Development Program. 1997, *Human Development Report 1997*, New York and Oxford: Oxford University Press.

United Nations Development Program. 1998, *Integrating Human Rights with Sustainable Development*, New York: United Nations.

United Nations Development Program. 1999, *Human Development Report 1999*, New York and Oxford: Oxford University Press.

United Nations Development Program. 2000, *Human Development Report (on "Human Development and Human Rights")*, United Nations: New York and Oxford: Oxford University Press.

United Nations Development Program. 2010, *Human Development Report 2010 (On*

"The Real Wealth of Nations: Pathways to Human Development"), New York and Oxford: Oxford University Press.

United Nations Economic Commission for Africa. 2009, *The Global Financial Crisis: Impact, Responses and Way Forward*, Addis Ababa: UNECA.

United States Senate. 2008, "State Secrets Protection Act" (Sec. 4051). Doc. S. 2533. 22 January. Online. Available at: www.fas.org/irp/congress/2008_cr/s 2533.html (accessed 3 March 2008).

UN Watch. 2009, *Mutual Praise Society. Country Scorecard and Evaluation of the Universal Periodic Review System of the U.N. Human Rights Council*, presented at the UN Human Rights Council on 6 February 2009. Online. Available at: www.unwatch.org/atf/cf/%7B6DEB65DA-BE5B-4CAE-8056–8BF0BEDF4D17%7D/Mutual%20 Praise%20Society.pdf (accessed 12 June 2010).

Usher, D. 1981, *The Economic Prerequisite to Democracy*, Oxford: Blackwell's.

Van Bommel, M. 2010, *Good Fences Don't Make Good Neighbours. Outlining the Complexities of Protecting Climate Displaces, with Special Reference to India and Bangla Desh*, MA final thesis, Utrecht University: Conflict Studies and Human Rights.

Van Creveld, M. 1991, *The Transformation of War*, New York: The Free Press.

Van Enk, P.L. 2009, *Frankrijk en de Hugenoten. Drie eeuwen onderdrukking en verzet*, Zoetermeer: Boekencentrum.

Van Gunsteren, H.R. and R. Andeweg. 1994, *Het grote ongenoegen. Over de kloof tussen burgers en politiek*, Haarlem: Aramith.

Van Ham, P. 2003, "Pax Americana als conservatieve revolutie: gevolgtrekkingen voor Europa", *Internationale Spectator*, 57(7/8), July/August.

Van der Kooy, T.P. 1954, *Over economie en humaniteit*, Wageningen: Zomer en Keuning.

Van der Kooy, T.P. 1956, *Tussen beginsel en belang*, Wageningen: Zomer en Keuning.

Van Krieken, P. 1993, *Apostasy & Asylum*, Lund: Raoul Wallenberg Institute of Human Rights and Humanitarian Law.

Van Putten, J. 1994, "Ze zijn gek geworden!" *Internationale Samenwerking*, June.

Verstegen, S. 2001, "Understanding and Preventing Poverty-related Conflict", presented at the workshop "Resources, Entitlement and Poverty-related Conflict", The Hague: Clingendael Institute, 5 March.

Walzer, M. 1983, *Spheres of Justice: A Defence of Pluralism and Equality*, Oxford: Blackwell's.

Weber, M. 1964 [1947], *The Theory of Social and Economic Organization*, translated by A.M. Henderson and Talcott Parsons, 1947, Glencoe, IL: The Free Press.

Weber, M. 1976 [1922], *Wirtschaft und Gesellschaft*, Tübingen: Mohr.

Wermiel, S.J. 1998, "Law and Human Dignity: The Judicial Soul of Justice Brennan", *William & Mary Bill of Rights Journal*, 7(1), 223–240.

Wiarda, G.J. 1999, *Drie typen van rechtsvinding* (new edition elaborated by T. Koopmans), The Hague: Tjeenk Willink.

World Bank 2000a, *Global Economic Prospects and the Developing Countries*, Washington, DC: World Bank.

World Bank. 2000b, *World Development Report 2000/2001: Attacking Poverty*, New York and Oxford: Oxford University Press.

World Bank. 2001, *Social Protection Sector Strategy. From Safety Net to Springboard*, Washington, DC: World Bank.

World Bank. 2003, *Accountability at the World Bank: The Inspection Panel 10 Years On*, Washington, DC: World Bank.

World Bank. 2009, *Accountability at the World Bank: The Inspection Panel at 15 Years*, Washington, DC: World Bank.

Wronka, J. 1998, *Human Rights and Social Policy in the 21st Century*, Lanham: University Press of America.

Wunsch, J.S. and D. Olowu. 1995, *The Failure of the Centralized State: Institutions and Self-Governing Africa*, Oakland: ICS Press.

Young, A. 2008, *Parliamentary Sovereignty and the Human Rights Act*, Oxford: Hart Publishing.

Young, O.R. 2008, "The Architecture of Global Environmental Governance: Bringing Science to Bear on Policy", *Global Environmental Politics*, 8(1), 14–32, February.

Zoller, A. 2002, "No One is Above the Law", *Human Rights Monitor*, 57–58.

Zou, M. and T. Zwart. 2011 (in press), "Rethinking Human Rights in China: Towards a Receptor Approach", in H. Nasu and B. Saul (eds), *Human Rights in the Asia-Pacific Region: Towards Institution Building*, London and New York: Routledge.

Cases

Associated Provincial Picture Houses v. *Wednesbury Corporation* (1948) Great Britain Court of Appeal, [1948] 1 KB 223.

Attorney General v. *Roy Clarke* (2008) Supreme Court of Zambia, Appeal No. 96-A/2004, Judgment of 24 January. Online. Available at: www.saflii.org/zm/cases/ZMSC/2008/4.html (accessed 6 May 2009).

Barcelona Traction, Light and Power Company, Limited (Belgium v. *Spain)* (1964) International Court of Justice, ICJ Rep. 6, 24 July.

Barker v. *Corus (UK) plc* (2006) UKHL 20.

Boehm v. *Superior Court* (1986) California Court of Appeals, 178 Cal. App. 3d 494.

Boumediene v. *Bush* (2008) United States Supreme Court, 128 S.Ct. 2229.

Bowers v. *Hardwick* (1986) 478 U.S. 186.

Council of Civil Service Unions v. *Minister for the Civil Service* (1985) Great Britain House of Lords, [1985] A.C. 374.

Cruisemissiles (1989) Supreme Court of the Netherlands: HR 10 November 1989, NJ 1991, 248.

El-Masri v. *Tenet* (2006) United States District Court, E.D. Virginia (Alexandria Division), 437 F. Supp. 2d 530.

Fairchild v. *Glenhaven Funeral Services Ltd and Others* (2002) Great Britain House of Lords, [2002] UKHL22;[2003] 1 AC 32.

F.K. Hussain v. *Union of India* (1990) Supreme Court of India, O.P. 2741/1988 (1990.02.26).

Gbemre and Others v. *Shell Petroleum Development Company Ltd and Others* (2005) Federal High Court of Nigeria, Benin City, Suit No: FHC/B/CS//53/05, 14 November. Online. Available at: www.climatelaw.org/cases/case-documents/nigeria/ni-shell-nov05-judgment.pdf (accessed 29 July 2009).

Grootboom v. *Oostenberg Municipality and others* (2000) Constitutional Court of South Africa, Case CCT 11/00, 4 October.

Hamdan v. *Rumsfeld* (2006) United States Supreme Court, 548 U.S. 557.

Hamdi v. *Rumsfeld* (2004) United States Supreme Court, 542 U.S. 507.

Lawrence v. *Texas* (2003) United States Supreme Court, 539 US 558.

Lindebaum v. *Cohen* (1919) Netherlands Supreme Court, HR, 31 January.

Sata v. *Post Newspapers Limited and Another* (1992) Supreme Court of Zambia, HP 1395 and 1804 and [1993] HP 821.

Shri D.K. Basu v. *State of West* Bengal (1996) Supreme Court of India, 1996(9), Scale 298.

Sørensen & Rasmussen v. *Denmark* (2006) European Court of Human Rights, Applications 52562/99 and 52620/99, 1 January.

South Africa v. *Grootboom* (2000) Constitutional Court of South Africa, (11) BCLR 1169.

The Prosecutor v. *Omar Hassan Ahmad Al Bashir* (2009) ICC-02/05-01/09.

Treatment Action Campaign and others v. *Minister of Health and Others* (2002) Constitutional Court of South Africa, Case No. 8/02 Judgment of 5 July.

Village of Bensenville et al. v. *Federal Aviation Administration*. U.S. App DC 05–1383 (2006)

Youngstown Sheet & Tube Co. v. *Sawyer* ("The Steel seizure case"), 343 US 579 (1952).

Index

Page numbers in *italics* denote tables, those in **bold** denote figures.